Lecture Notes
in Business Information Processing   **453**

Series Editors

Wil van der Aalst **ⓘ**
  RWTH Aachen University, Aachen, Germany

John Mylopoulos **ⓘ**
  University of Trento, Trento, Italy

Sudha Ram **ⓘ**
  University of Arizona, Tucson, AZ, USA

Michael Rosemann **ⓘ**
  Queensland University of Technology, Brisbane, QLD, Australia

Clemens Szyperski
  Microsoft Research, Redmond, WA, USA

More information about this series at https://link.springer.com/bookseries/7911

Boris Shishkov (Ed.)

Business Modeling and Software Design

12th International Symposium, BMSD 2022
Fribourg, Switzerland, June 27–29, 2022
Proceedings

 Springer

Editor
Boris Shishkov
Institute of Mathematics and Informatics
Bulgarian Academy of Sciences
Sofia, Bulgaria

Faculty of Information Sciences
University of Library Studies and Information
Technologies
Sofia, Bulgaria

IICREST
Sofia, Bulgaria

ISSN 1865-1348   ISSN 1865-1356 (electronic)
Lecture Notes in Business Information Processing
ISBN 978-3-031-11509-7   ISBN 978-3-031-11510-3 (eBook)
https://doi.org/10.1007/978-3-031-11510-3

This Springer imprint is published by the registered company Springer Nature Switzerland AG
The registered company address is: Gewerbestrasse 11, 6330 Cham, Switzerland

Preface

This book contains the *proceedings* of **BMSD 2022** (the 12th International Symposium on **B**usiness **M**odeling and **S**oftware **D**esign), held in *Fribourg, Switzerland*, on *27–29 June 2022* (https://www.is-bmsd.org). BMSD is an annual event that brings together researchers and practitioners interested in enterprise modeling and its relation to software specification.

Witnessing the *migrant crisis* in Europe from 2015–16, the *SARS-CoV-2 pandemic* starting in 2020, and the current *war in Ukraine*, one would ask "What's next?", and a key desire in such cases is MITIGATION. We should have known better what would come and we should have acted better at the beginning of all those crises. What is the meaning of "better"? In political terms this concerns governments (this goes beyond our current focus) and in terms of *ICT* (*Information and CommunicationTechnology*) this concerns RESILIENCE. *ICT* is especially mentioned because it enables very many current business processes regardless of the application domain. Hence, what we need today is *ICT*-driven *resilience against disruptive events*. This assumes *adaptive information systems* that in turn require CONTEXT-AWARENESS. We currently observe *context-aware applications* that are developed in various domains. Most of those applications are technology-driven (a "bottom-up" perspective), aiming to show new technology applications, without a thorough understanding of the effects produced by the corresponding *context-aware services* on the *user* and his/her environment and their contribution to context-dependent user goals (a "top-down" perspective). The latter is receiving increasing attention to date and it essentially concerns the **context-aware servicing of user needs** – they are changing during a *disruptive event*, for example: much of what a person needs would change during a lockdown. Further, system-internal processes are to be addressed as well in many cases – this concerns information systems supporting (critical) infrastructures, logistics, institutions, and so on; **system-internal optimizations** would be needed during a *disruptive event* when (many) process failures would inevitably occur, for example: during a lockdown, electricity outages and/or personnel unavailability may occur that in turn would affect corresponding information systems. Finally, **public values** (such as *privacy, transparency, accountability*, and so on) are to be taken into account as well, for example: during a lockdown, personal freedoms may be restricted, which means that many technical systems should start working differently. What is important with regard to all those challenges, is that they concern both ENTERPRISES and SOFTWARE since they both would be affected by such *disruptions*. Hence, **aligning enterprise modeling and software design** is important in this regard. What is also important is TRUST – if people would not trust the institutions and/or the key technical systems during a *disruptive event*, then the user cooperativeness would go down that would in turn decrease the effectiveness of provided ICT services.

It is inspiring for the *BMSD Community* to consider those challenges and it is not surprising that last year the BMSD Theme was: TOWARDS ENTERPRISES AND SOFTWARE THAT ARE RESILIENT AGAINST DISRUPTIVE EVENTS, and this year the BMSD Theme is: INFORMATION SYSTEMS ENGINEERING AND TRUST.

Since 2011, we have enjoyed **eleven successful BMSD editions**. The first BMSD edition (**2011**) took place in **Sofia, Bulgaria**, and the theme of BMSD 2011 was: "Business Models and Advanced Software Systems." The second BMSD edition (**2012**) took place in **Geneva, Switzerland**, with the theme: "From Business Modeling to Service-Oriented Solutions." The third BMSD edition (**2013**) took place in **Noordwijkerhout, The Netherlands**, and the theme was: "Enterprise Engineering and Software Generation." The fourth BMSD edition (**2014**) took place in **Luxembourg, Grand Duchy of Luxembourg**, and the theme was: "Generic Business Modeling Patterns and Software Re-Use." The fifth BMSD edition (**2015**) took place in **Milan, Italy**, with the theme: "Toward Adaptable Information Systems." The sixth BMSD edition (**2016**) took place in **Rhodes, Greece**, and had as theme: "Integrating Data Analytics in Enterprise Modeling and Software Development." The seventh BMSD edition (**2017**) took place in **Barcelona, Spain**, and the theme was: "Modeling Viewpoints and Overall Consistency." The eighth BMSD edition (**2018**) took place in **Vienna, Austria**, with the theme: "Enterprise Engineering and Software Engineering - Processes and Systems for the Future." The ninth BMSD edition (**2019**) took place in **Lisbon, Portugal**, and the theme of BMSD 2019 was: "Reflecting Human Authority and Responsibility in Enterprise Models and Software Specifications". The tenth BMSD edition (**2020**) took place in **Berlin, Germany**, and the theme of BMSD 2020 was: "Towards Knowledge-Driven Enterprise Information Systems". The eleventh BMSD edition (**2021**) took place in **Sofia, Bulgaria** (*We got back to where we once started!*), and as mentioned above, the theme of BMSD 2021 was: "Towards Enterprises and Software that are Resilient Against Disruptive Events". The current edition brings BMSD back to Switzerland (ten years after BMSD-Geneva-2012) – to Fribourg. BMSD-Fribourg-2022 marks the **12th EVENT**, with the theme: "**Information Systems Engineering and Trust**."

We are proud to have attracted distinguished guests as keynote lecturers, who are renowned experts in their fields: **Manfred Reichert**, *Ulm University*, Germany (2020), **Mathias Weske**, *HPI -University of Potsdam*, Germany (2020), **Jose Tribolet**, *IST - University of Lisbon*, Portugal (2019), **Jan Mendling**, *WU Vienna*, Austria (2018), **Roy Oberhauser**, *Aalen University*, Germany (2018), **Norbert Gronau**, *University of Potsdam*, Germany (2017 **and 2021**), **Oscar Pastor**, *Polytechnic University of Valencia*, Spain (2017), **Alexander Verbraeck**, *Delft University of Technology*, The Netherlands (2017 **and 2021**), **Paris Avgeriou**, *University of Groningen*, The Netherlands (2016), **Jan Juerjens**, *University of Koblenz-Landau*, Germany (2016), **Mathias Kirchmer**, *BPM-D*, USA (2016), **Marijn Janssen**, *Delft University of Technology*, The Netherlands (2015), **Barbara Pernici**, *Politecnico di Milano*, Italy (2015), **Henderik Proper**, *Public Research Centre Henri Tudor*, Grand Duchy of Luxembourg (2014), **Roel Wieringa**, *University of Twente*, The Netherlands (2014), **Kecheng Liu**, *University of Reading*, UK (2013), **Marco Aiello**, *University of Groningen*, The Netherlands (2013), **Leszek Maciaszek**, *Wroclaw University of Economics*, Poland (2013), **Jan L. G. Dietz**, *Delft University of Technology*, The Netherlands (2012), **Ivan Ivanov**, *SUNY Empire State College*, USA (2012), **Dimitri Konstantas**, *University of Geneva*, Switzerland (2012), **Marten van Sinderen**, *University of Twente*, The Netherlands (2012), **Mehmet Aksit**, *University of Twente*, The Netherlands (2011), **Dimitar Christozov**, *American*

University in Bulgaria – Blagoevgrad, Bulgaria (2011), **Bart Nieuwenhuis**, *University of Twente*, The Netherlands (2011), and **Hermann Maurer**, *Graz University of Technology*, Austria (2011).

The high quality of the BMSD 2022 technical program is enhanced by a keynote lecture delivered by an outstanding scientist: **Hans-Georg Fill**, *University of Fribourg*, Switzerland (the title of his lecture is: "Augmented Enterprise Modeling - Status and Future Directions"). Also, the presence (physically or distantly) of former BMSD keynote lecturers is much appreciated: *Norbert Gronau* (2017, 2021), *Roy Oberhauser* (2018), *Mathias Kirchmer* (2016), *Marijn Janssen* (2015), and *Marten van Sinderen* (2012). The technical program is further enriched by a panel discussion (featured by the participation of some of the abovementioned outstanding scientists) and also by other discussions, stimulating *community building* and facilitating possible *R&D project acquisition initiatives*. Those special activities are definitely contributing to maintaining the event's high quality and inspiring our steady and motivated Community.

The BMSD'22 Technical Program Committee consists of a Chair and 108 Members from 37 countries (*Australia, Austria, Brazil, Bulgaria, Canada, China, Colombia, Denmark, Egypt, Estonia, Finland, France, Germany, Greece, India, Indonesia, Italy, Latvia, Lithuania, Grand Duchy of Luxembourg, Malaysia, Mexico, New Zealand, Palestine, Poland, Portugal, Russia, Singapore, Slovak Republic, Slovenia, Spain, Sweden, Switzerland, Taiwan, The Netherlands, UK*, and *USA*, listed alphabetically) – all of them competent and enthusiastic representatives of prestigious organizations.

In organizing BMSD 2022, we have observed **highest ethical standards**: We guarantee *at least two reviews per submitted paper* (this assuming reviews of adequate quality), under the condition that the paper fulfills the BMSD'22 requirements. In assigning a paper for reviewing, it is our responsibility to *provide reviewers that have relevant expertise*. Sticking to a **double-blind review process**, we guarantee that a reviewer would not know who the authors of the reviewed paper are (we send anonymized versions of the papers to the reviewers) and an author would not know who has reviewed his/her paper. We require that a reviewer *respects the content of the reviewed paper* and would not disclose (parts of) its content to third parties before the symposium (and also after the symposium in case the manuscript gets rejected). We *guarantee against conflict of interests*, by not assigning papers for reviewing by reviewers who are immediate colleagues of any of the co-authors. In our decisions to accept/reject papers, we **guarantee against any discrimination based on age, gender, race, or religion**. As it concerns the EU data protection standards, **we stick to the GDPR requirements**.

We have demonstrated for a 12th consecutive year a high quality of papers. We are proud to have succeeded in establishing and maintaining (for many years already) a high scientific quality (as it concerns the symposium itself) and a stimulating collaborative atmosphere; also, our Community is inspired to share ideas and experiences.

As mentioned already, BMSD is essentially leaning toward **ENTERPRISE INFORMATION SYSTEMS (EIS)**, by considering the **MODELING OF ENTERPRISES AND BUSINESS PROCESSES** as a basis for **SPECIFYING SOFTWARE**. Further, in the broader EIS context, BMSD 2022 addresses a large number of research areas and topics, as follows:

› **BUSINESS PROCESSES AND ENTERPRISE ENGINEERING** - *enterprise systems; enterprise system environments and context; construction and function; actor roles; signs and affordances; transactions; business processes; business process coordination; business process optimization; business process management and strategy execution; production acts and coordination acts; regulations and business rules; enterprise (re-) engineering; enterprise interoperability; inter-enterprise coordination; enterprise engineering and architectural governance; enterprise engineering and software generation; enterprise innovation.*

› **BUSINESS MODELS AND REQUIREMENTS** - *essential business models; re-usable business models; business value models; business process models; business goal models; integrating data analytics in business modeling; semantics and business data modeling; pragmatics and business behavior modeling; business modeling viewpoints and overall consistency; business modeling landscapes; augmented and virtual-reality-based enterprise modeling; requirements elicitation; domain-imposed and user-defined requirements; requirements specification and modeling; requirements analysis and verification; requirements evolution; requirements traceability; usability and requirements elicitation.*

› **BUSINESS MODELS AND SERVICES** - *enterprise engineering and service science; service-oriented enterprises; from business modeling to service-oriented solutions; business modeling for software-based services; service engineering; business-goals-driven service discovery and modeling; technology-independent and platform-specific service modeling; re-usable service models; business-rules-driven service composition; web services; autonomic service behavior; context-aware service behavior; service interoperability; change impact analysis and service management; service monitoring and quality of service; services for IoT applications; service innovation.*

› **BUSINESS MODELS AND SOFTWARE** - *enterprise engineering and software development; model-driven engineering; co-design of business and IT systems; business-IT alignment and traceability; alignment between IT architecture and business strategy; business strategy and technical debt; business-modeling-driven software generation; normalized systems and combinatorial effects; software generation and dependency analysis; component-based business-software alignment; objects, components, and modeling patterns; generic business modeling patterns and software re-use; business rules and software specification; business goals and software integration; business innovation and software evolution; software technology maturity models; domain-specific models; crosscutting concerns - security, privacy, distribution, recoverability, logging, performance monitoring.*

› **INFORMATION SYSTEMS ARCHITECTURES AND PARADIGMS** - *enterprise architectures; service-oriented computing; software architectures; cloud computing; autonomic computing (and intelligent software behavior); context-aware computing (and adaptable software systems); affective computing (and user-aware software systems); aspect-oriented computing (and non-functional requirements); architectural styles; architectural viewpoints.*

› **DATA ASPECTS IN BUSINESS MODELING AND SOFTWARE DEVELOPMENT** - *data modeling in business processes; data flows and business* *modeling; databases, OLTP, and business processes; data warehouses, OLAP, and business analytics; data analysis, data semantics, redundancy, and quality-of-data; data mining, knowledge discovery, and knowledge management; information security and business process modeling; categorization, classification, regression, and clustering; cluster analysis and predictive analysis; ontologies and decision trees; decision tree induction and information gain; business processes and entropy; machine learning and deep learning - an enterprise perspective; uncertainty and context states; statistical data analysis and probabilistic business models.*

> **BLOCKCHAIN-BASED BUSINESS MODELS AND INFORMATION SYSTEMS** - *smart contracts; blockchains for business process management; blockchain schemes for decentralization; the blockchain architecture - implications for systems and business processes; blockchains and the future of enterprise information systems; blockchains and security/privacy/trust issues.*

> **IoT AND IMPLICATIONS FOR ENTERPRISE INFORMATION SYSTEMS** *- the IoT paradigm; IoT data collection and aggregation; business models and IoT; IoT-based software solutions; IoT and context-awareness; IoT and public values; IoT applications: smart cities, e-Health, smart manufacturing.*

BMSD 2022 received 56 paper submissions from which 21 papers were selected for publication in the symposium proceedings. Of these papers, 12 were selected for a 30-minute oral presentation (full papers), leading to a **full-paper acceptance ratio of 22%** (compared to 23% in 2021 and 2020, 22% in 2019 and 19% in 2018) - an indication for our intention to preserve a high-quality forum for the next editions of the symposium. The BMSD 2022 authors come from: Bulgaria, Cyprus, Finland, Germany, Indonesia, Norway, Portugal, Switzerland, The Netherlands, and USA (listed alphabetically); that makes a total of 10 countries (compared to 16 in 2021 and 2020, 10 in 2019, 15 in 2018, 20 in 2017, 16 in 2016, 21 in 2015, 21 in 2014, 14 in 2013, 11 in 2012, and 10 in 2011) to justify a strong international presence. Three countries have been represented at all twelve BMSD editions so far – **Bulgaria, Germany**, and **The Netherlands** – indicating a strong European influence.

Clustering BMSD papers is always inspiring because this gives different perspectives with regard to the challenge of **adequately specifying software based on enterprise modeling**. (a) As it concerns the BMSD'22 Full Papers: some of them are directed towards BUSINESS PROCESS MANAGEMENT AND MODEL VERIFICATION while others are touching upon KNOWLEDGE MANAGEMENT AND DECISION SUPPORT SYSTEMS; some papers address issues concerning ENTERPRISE MODELING AND REQUIREMENTS SPECIFICATION while others are leaning towards TRUST AND SECURITY. (b) As it concerns the BMSD'22 Short Papers: some of them are directed towards BUSINESS PROCESS MODELING while others are touching upon CONTEXT-AWARENESS AND PRIVACY-BY-DESIGN; some papers are directed towards OPEN DATA AND RISK ASSESSMENT while others address CCTV-AWARENESS AND RELATED PRIVACY ISSUES; finally, there is a paper touching upon INTERNET-OF-THINGS and particularly – on the assessment and visualization of device-usage-effects on human health.

BMSD 2022 was organized and sponsored by the *Interdisciplinary Institute for Collaboration and Research on Enterprise Systems and Technology* (*IICREST*), co-organized by the *University of Fribourg*, and technically co-sponsored by *BPM-D*. Cooperating organizations were *Aristotle University of Thessaloniki (AUTH)*, *Delft University of Technology (TU Delft)*, the UTwente *Digital Society Institute (DSI)*, the *Dutch Research School for Information and Knowledge Systems (SIKS)*, and *AMAKOTA Ltd*.

Organizing this interesting and successful symposium required the dedicated efforts of many people. First, we thank the *authors*, whose research and development achievements are recorded here. Next, the *Program Committee members* each deserve credit for the diligent and rigorous peer reviewing. Further, appreciating the hospitality of the *University of Fribourg*, we would like to mention the excellent organization provided by the *IICREST team* (supported by its *logistics partner, AMAKOTA Ltd.*) – the team (words of gratitude to *Aglika Bogomilova*!) did all the necessary work for delivering a stimulating and productive event, supported by the *Uni-Fribourg team* (words of gratitude to Fabian Muff!). We are grateful to *Springer* for their willingness to publish the current proceedings and we would like to especially mention *Ralf Gerstner, Christine Reiss*, and *Abier El-Saeidi*, appreciating their professionalism and patience (regarding the preparation of the symposium proceedings). We are certainly grateful to our *keynote lecturer, Prof. Hans-Georg Fill*, for his inspiring contribution and for his taking the time to synthesize and deliver his talk.

We wish you inspiring reading! We look forward to meeting you next year in *Utrecht, The Netherlands*, for the *13th International Symposium on Business Modeling and Software Design (BMSD 2023)*, details of which will be made available on: https://www.is-bmsd.org.

June 2022   Boris Shishkov

Organization

Chair

Boris Shishkov
Institute of Mathematics and Informatics - BAS, Bulgaria
University of Library Studies and Information Technologies, Bulgaria
IICREST, Bulgaria

Program Committee

Marco Aiello	University of Stuttgart, Germany
Mehmet Aksit	University of Twente, The Netherlands
Amr Ali-Eldin	Mansoura University, Egypt
Apostolos Ampatzoglou	University of Macedonia, Greece
Paulo Anita	Delft University of Technology, The Netherlands
Juan Carlos Augusto	Middlesex University, UK
Paris Avgeriou	University of Groningen, The Netherlands
Saimir Bala	Humboldt University of Berlin, Germany
Boyan Bontchev	Sofia University St. Kliment Ohridski, Bulgaria
Jose Borbinha	University of Lisbon, Portugal
Frances Brazier	Delft University of Technology, The Netherlands
Bert de Brock	University of Groningen, The Netherlands
Barrett Bryant	University of North Texas, USA
Cinzia Cappiello	Politecnico di Milano, Italy
Kuo-Ming Chao	Coventry University, UK
Michel Chaudron	Chalmers University of Technology, Sweden
Samuel Chong	Fullerton Systems, Singapore
Dimitar Christozov	American University in Bulgaria - Blagoevgrad, Bulgaria
Jose Cordeiro	Polytechnic Institute of Setubal, Portugal
Robertas Damasevicius	Kaunas University of Technology, Lithuania
Ralph Deters	University of Saskatchewan, Canada
Claudio Di Ciccio	Sapienza University, Italy
Jan L. G. Dietz	Delft University of Technology, The Netherlands
Aleksandar Dimov	Sofia University St. Kliment Ohridski, Bulgaria
Teduh Dirgahayu	Universitas Islam Indonesia, Indonesia
Dirk Draheim	Tallinn University of Technology, Estonia
John Edwards	Aston University, UK

Chiara Francalanci	Politecnico di Milano, Italy
Veska Georgieva	Technical University – Sofia, Bulgaria
J. Paul Gibson	T&MSP - Telecom and Management SudParis, France
Rafael Gonzalez	Javeriana University, Colombia
Paul Grefen	Eindhoven University of Technology, The Netherlands
Norbert Gronau	University of Potsdam, Germany
Clever Ricardo Guareis de Farias	University of Sao Paulo, Brazil
Jens Gulden	Utrecht University, The Netherlands
Ilian Ilkov	IBM, The Netherlands
Ivan Ivanov	SUNY Empire State College, USA
Marijn Janssen	Delft University of Technology, The Netherlands
Gabriel Juhas	Slovak University of Technology, Slovak Republic
Dmitry Kan	Silo AI, Finland
Marite Kirikova	Riga Technical University, Latvia
Stefan Koch	Johannes Kepler University Linz, Austria
Vinay Kulkarni	Tata Consultancy Services, India
John Bruntse Larsen	Technical University of Denmark, Denmark
Peng Liang	Wuhan University, China
Kecheng Liu	University of Reading, UK
Claudia Loebbecke	University of Cologne, Germany
Leszek Maciaszek	University of Economics, Poland
Somayeh Malakuti	ABB Corporate Research Center, Germany
Jelena Marincic	ASML, The Netherlands
Raimundas Matulevicius	University of Tartu, Estonia
Hermann Maurer	Graz University of Technology, Austria
Heinrich Mayr	Alpen-Adria-University Klagenfurt, Austria
Nikolay Mehandjiev	University of Manchester, UK
Jan Mendling	Humboldt University of Berlin, Germany
Michele Missikoff	Institute for Systems Analysis and Computer Science, Italy
Dimitris Mitrakos	Aristotle University of Thessaloniki, Greece
Ricardo Neisse	European Commission Joint Research Center, Italy
Bart Nieuwenhuis	University of Twente, The Netherlands
Roy Oberhauser	Aalen University, Germany
Olga Ormandjieva	Concordia University, Canada
Paul Oude Luttighuis	Le Blanc Advies, The Netherlands
Mike Papazoglou	Tilburg University, The Netherlands
Marcin Paprzycki	Polish Academy of Sciences, Poland
Jeffrey Parsons	Memorial University of Newfoundland, Canada

Oscar Pastor — Universidad Politecnica de Valencia, Spain
Krassie Petrova — Auckland University of Technology, New Zealand
Prantosh K. Paul — Raiganj University, India
Barbara Pernici — Politecnico di Milano, Italy
Doncho Petkov — Eastern Connecticut State University, USA
Gregor Polancic — University of Maribor, Slovenia
Hend*erik* Proper — LIST, Grand Duchy of Luxembourg
Mirja Pulkkinen — University of Jyvaskyla, Finland
Ricardo Queiros — Polytechnic of Porto, Portugal
Jolita Ralyte — University of Geneva, Switzerland
Julia Rauscher — University of Augsburg, Germany
Stefanie Rinderle-Ma — University of Vienna, Austria
Werner Retschitzegger — Johannes Kepler University Linz, Austria
Jose-Angel Rodriguez — Tecnologico de Monterrey, Mexico
Wenge Rong — Beihang University, China
Ella Roubtsova — Open University, The Netherlands
Irina Rychkova — University Paris 1 Pantheon Sorbonne, France
Shazia Sadiq — University of Queensland, Australia
Ronny Seiger — University of St. Gallen, Switzerland
Andreas Sinnhofer — Graz University of Technology, Austria
Valery Sokolov — Yaroslavl State University, Russia
Richard Starmans — Utrecht University, The Netherlands
Hans-Peter Steinbacher — FH Kufstein Tirol University of Applied Sciences, Austria
Janis Stirna — Stockholm University, Sweden
Coen Suurmond — Cesuur B.V., The Netherlands
Adel Taweel — Birzeit University, Palestine
Bedir Tekinerdogan — Wageningen University, The Netherlands
Ramayah Thurasamy — Universiti Sains Malaysia, Malaysia
Jose Tribolet — IST - University of Lisbon, Portugal
Roumiana Tsankova — Technical University - Sofia, Bulgaria
Martin van den Berg — Utrecht University of Applied Sciences, The Netherlands
Willem-Jan van den Heuvel — Tilburg University, The Netherlands
Han van der Aa — Humboldt University of Berlin, Germany
Marten van Sinderen — University of Twente, The Netherlands
Damjan Vavpotic — University of Ljubljana, Slovenia
Alexander Verbraeck — Delft University of Technology, The Netherlands
Hans Weigand — Tilburg University, The Netherlands
Roel Wieringa — University of Twente, The Netherlands
Dietmar Winkler — Vienna University of Technology, Austria
Shin-Jer Yang — Soochow University, Taiwan

| Benjamin Yen | University of Hong Kong, China |
| Fani Zlatarova | Elizabethtown College, USA |

Invited Speaker

| Hans-Georg Fill | University of Fribourg, Switzerland |

Augmented Enterprise Modeling - Status and Future Directions (Abstract of Keynote Lecture)

Hans-Georg Fill

University of Fribourg, Switzerland
`hans-georg.fill@unifr.ch`

Abstract. Enterprise modeling is today a standard practice for the holistic engineering of socio-technical information systems. Besides their traditional role as formal representations of requirements for system development and the support of human communication and understanding, enterprise models may be processed algorithmically by machines. This is well-known for domains such as business process modeling and the execution of workflows or the conduction of impact analyses in enterprise architecture management. In this talk we will explore how the machine-based processing of enterprise models can be generalized in the form of augmented enterprise models. Based on examples from business plan generation, data-driven business process improvement, risk simulation or blockchain-based attestation we will describe the current state and derive possible future.

Contents

Short Papers

Full Papers

Rapid Prototyping of Business Rule-Based Systems with Controlled Natural Language and Semantic Web Software

Lloyd Rutledge[(✉)], Jouke Corbijn, Boris Cuijpers, and Lieuwe Wondaal

Open University of the Netherlands, Heerlen, The Netherlands
Lloyd.Rutledge@ou.nl

Abstract. We present methods for applying controlled natural language (CNL) and Semantic Web user interfaces to make rapid prototypes of business rule-based systems. This helps system developers quickly demonstrate design choices to stakeholders. CNLs provide a balance between understandability for laypersons and unambiguous specificity for programmers. Executable CNLs generate rudimentary systems automatically and thus quickly, which suits rapid prototyping. The Semantic Web provides a wide range of free and open tools for standardized forms of data representation and logic, whose potential application includes business rules.

We identify several general categories of business rules that each map to a core form of Semantic Web logic that can implement it. This work then presents prototyping methods that apply these mappings. Different Semantic Web software interface components demonstrate different aspects of each form of logic. The Semantic Web ontology editor Protégé illustrates our methods, but any equivalent Semantic Web software can apply. Example rapid prototypes in Protégé from the frequently used fictional business rules case EU-Rent serve here as illustrative scenarios that evaluate our methods.

Keywords: Business rules · Rapid prototyping · Throwaway prototypes · Semantic Web

1   Introduction

Designing and implementing business information systems is a layered and complex process, with a variety of tools and approaches for different aspects of it. Business rules define agreements and requirements in a resilient and executable form, but often involve formal logic that not all development partners understand. Controlled Natural Languages (CNLs) for business rules define them in ways all parties can understand and which enforce clarity and unambiguity, but are not always directly executable well as software. The Semantic Web offers formats and software for formal logic and data processing, but in programmer-oriented code, with only limited support from CNLs. This work joins these

© Springer Nature Switzerland AG 2022
B. Shishkov (Ed.): BMSD 2022, LNBIP 453, pp. 3–20, 2022.
https://doi.org/10.1007/978-3-031-11510-3_1

aspects further as more quickly traversed layers in methods for making rapid prototypes of business information systems.

The lay client understands their own law, agreement or policy and would understand the results of its implementation, but is less capable of understanding formal computation logic and other program code that implements it. Development teams require thus methods for conveying to the client the influence that design choices for business rules would have on a resulting system's logical conclusions. In addition, a more quickly generated communication of a design's end-system influence would enable tighter iteration of development cycles.

This work proposes a standards-based method for making rapid prototypes of design choices with business rules. The use of standards supports the method's broad implementability and its use of widely recognized concepts. The method's technical focus applies automatically executable CNLs for business rules in order to generate prototypes quickly. We set this conversion in the context of business needs behind the CNL code going in, and on different aspects of design impact a prototype can demonstrate.

These methods account for three types of business rules: rules that automatically conclude new data, rules that block invalid data, and rules that request missing data from users. For these rule types, we apply, in order, the following Semantic Web forms of logic: inferencing, inconsistencies and constraints. Finally, three fundamental functionalities of Semantic Web software that apply to all three type of rules: showing where the reasoning occurred, why it occurred, and what impact it would have with a given data set.

The next section discusses other research related to business rules, CNLs and rapid prototyping. Then we describe our application of design science methodology to this research. Section 4 presents our proposed business rule rapid prototyping methods. The section after that presents several illustrative scenarios for different types of these methods. This paper then concludes with an overview and ideas for future work.

2   Related Work

Rapid prototyping is a component of rapid application development, as an approach for adaptive software development [2]. The agile business rule development (ABRD) methodology presents five circular phases for designing business rule-based systems [1]. The most important are the first three: *harvesting* rule specifications from sources, *prototyping*, and *building* test executions with realistic data. We address these three phases here.

In earlier work, we propose a reference architecture for traceability (RA4T), which Fig. 1 shows [15]. It is an architecture for information system development with a focus on providing traceability behind the execution of business rules in those systems. This traceability lets users, when presented conclusions by the system, access the origins of those conclusions, including which rules applied and what data triggered them. As such, the RA4T supports developing business systems that provide such traceability. The development phase in the RA4T involves writing and analyzing documents to design a CNL specification for the desired system. Our work here focuses on the next phase, automation, by making it rapid, and by applying it to making focused prototypes. The architecture's components in this phase apply to our methods for prototyping business systems. This work also proposes changes to this architecture, which Fig. 1 shows as underlined.

2.1 Controlled Natural Languages

Controlled Natural Languages (CNLs) help in system development by defining requirements in language the layperson client can understand [16]. In addition, they reduce the vagueness, ambiguity, and incompleteness that make system specifications hard for programmers to implement well. We treat such requirement elicitation as part of the harvesting phase, and explore the application of rule-based CNLs for business rules to define business system specifications.

The Dutch tax authority applies the CNL RegelSpraak to define tax law as not only readable by laypersons but also as executable by computers into running business rule systems [4]. As such, RegelSpraak code that is harvested from legal text can also directly generate prototypes. We apply a similar approach here, but apply instead standardized languages, such as SBVR instead of RegelSpraak for the harvested CNL, and Semantic Web formats and software for data and logic processing for implementing prototypes.

Semantics of Business Vocabulary and Business Rules (SBVR) is a CNL for concept models and business rules from the standardization community Object Management Group (OMG) [11]. The original RA4T focuses on

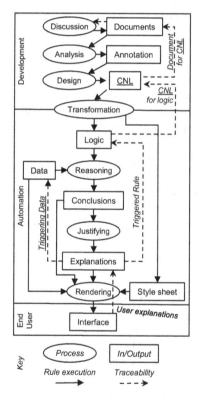

Fig. 1. The reference architecture for traceability (RA4T) in business rule-based systems [15]. Changes this work proposes to the RA4T are underlined.

SBVR and mentions no other CNL [15]. Because other CNLs for business rules such as RegelSpraak text, we propose changing the RA4T to generalize from SBVR to any rule-based CNL.

2.2 SBVR and OWL

The Semantic Web's Web Ontology Language (OWL) defines constructs for logical reasoning, which we apply here to implement our method's prototypes. Applying the Semantic Web also supports the building phase because OWL reasoning applies directly to data stored in the Resource Description Format (RDF), which defines an enormous amount of information available online, which can be used here for testing with prototypes. This subsection presents literature that proposes mappings from SBVR to its implementation in OWL.

Reynares proposes general mappings from SBVR to OWL [14]. He illustrates this using the same example case that we do: EU-Rent. Karpovič structures extensive mappings from SBVR constructs to OWL functional equivalents in a comprehensive table [9]. This table includes his own newly proposed mappings, combined with those from others, including Reynares. He then implements a selection of these mappings in the software s2o (SBVR to OWL) [8]. We apply s2o here as a functioning example of a tool for converting executable SBVR code to OWL.

Later, in Sect. 4, we apply and extend the table's structure from Karpovič [9]. There, Table 1 offers a selection of the SBVR-to-Semantic Web mappings that we apply in this work. Those mappings all happen to originate with Reynares [14]. S2o implements the mappings as well unless stated otherwise in Table 1.

OWL reasoners process minimal cardinality as inferred data. We apply this in prototyping how business systems automatically draw conclusions from given information. SBVR's "exactly" maps to OWL's qualified cardinality [9], whose implementation in s2o this work also uses. Exceeding qualified cardinality triggers inconsistencies in OWL reasoners. This work proposes applying such inconsistencies to demonstrate preventing entry of invalid data in business system prototypes.

3 Methodology

Peffers describes illustrative scenarios as an evaluation method in design science research (DSR) [13], which we apply here. In additional DSR terminology, our proposed prototyping methods and proposed changes to the RA4T are artifacts. That is, they are the objects that the experiment evaluates. The artifact types of this paper's contribution and RA4T are, respectively, method and framework, according to Peffers's definitions. We follow DSR methodology to develop the methods and RA4T modifications, which we evaluate with illustrative scenarios. The specification document for SBVR includes an extensive example of SBVR code that describes a fictional car rental business called EU-Rent [12]. EU-Rent serves here as an example case from which to extract illustrative scenarios that evaluate our proposed methods.

The next section presents the structure of document text, CNL and OWL code in our general method for rapid prototyping of business rules. This method includes demonstrating this OWL reasoning with Semantic Web software. We illustrate this here with the Semantic Web ontology editor Protégé [10].

Then subsections of Sect. 5 specify this general method further for specific types of business logic and Semantic Web software interface components. Each subsection evaluates its method with an illustrative scenario from EU-Rent. User interface displays from Protégé for each scenario further illustrate the methods presented.

4   General Method

This section presents the general method this paper proposes for rapid prototyping of business rules. The general method applies to different types of rules and different types of impact they can have. The next section's subsections then each fine-tune this method to a specific type of rule and end-system impact.

First, we present here three components of this general method. The upcoming subsection extends the related works' mapping between SBVR and OWL constructs to include general business systems needs and corresponding broad categories of logic. Then we present our phases for writing and generating the various layers of specification code and test data needed for making and running prototype demonstrations. Finally, Subsect. 4.3 shows the specific Semantic Web software user interface components we apply to demonstrating different aspects of the broad categories of business rule logic. Applying these together, system designers can start with general business requirements, specify their logic, and then quickly demonstrate them with well-suited software interface components.

4.1   Logic Mapping

The first phase in our method is defining the logic that business system rule engines run. We show this in Table 1, which structures various types of business rule situations and maps each to a means of implementing it with Semantic Web logic. We base the core of this table on the larger mapping table from Karpovič [9]. This core is the middle two columns and top two rows of Table 1: the mapping from SBVR to OWL.

We add a column to the left for different ways in which a business system can handle data, each described as understandable to a layperson seeing the prototype demonstration of it. These are variations of how a business rule system reacts to data in the system, including data entered by the user. On the other side of the table, we add the "rule type" column on the right. These are general forms of Semantic Web logic, which correspond to the left-most column. That existing data can trigger automatic conclusions from the rule system that adds information is directly equivalent to inferencing, including how the Semantic Web processes it. Semantic Web inconsistencies are more complex than inferencing, and are not always applied to implementing desired end-system behavior. We present here ways that software interfaces for inconsistency can prototype a system's reaction to blocking the user that is invalid.

Table 1. Rapid Prototyping Logic Mapping

Data is ...	SBVR	Semantic Web		Rule Type
automatic	at least $\begin{smallmatrix}1\\n\end{smallmatrix}$	*owl:someValuesFrom*		inference
			minimal*	
forbidden	exactly	OWL cardinality	qualified	inconsistency
	at most		*maximum*	
needed	*at least*	SHACL* cardinality	*minimal*	constraint
	exactly		qualified	

* = *not implemented in s2o*
italics = not applied in this work

4.2   Coding Phases

Our method involves three main phases: CNL, OWL code, and the OWL software user interface. Table 2 shows the components of the first two of these phases: the making code for both CNL and the Semantic Web. The tables in the coming subsections each apply CNL and OWL code phases to an EU-Rent scenario.

Table 2. Text-to-code sequence in the general method

Code		Ontology?	Data?
Source document			No
CNL	Source	Yes	Yes
	Executable		
Semantic Web	Converted		
	Tailored		

The CNL phase ends with *executable CNL* that software can directly convert into OWL. This phase may begin with text in a *document source* for the business rule, such as legal text. This corresponds with the "Documents" box in the RA4T. Such documentation may already exist, or designers may write it as part of the whole development process. In some cases, *source CNL* mainly for human-to-human communication may already exist, but that still needs to be adapted into executable CNL.

Executable CNL is typically a subset of source CNL, with a necessarily stricter syntax that laypersons understand as easily. Our method accounts for automated conversion of this executable CNL into *converted OWL* code for the Semantic Web. If the converted code is not enough, designers can add *tailored Semantic Web* code to complete the Semantic Web implementation of the rule. This automatic conversion, with possible human editing of OWL code, fits in the "Transformation" activity of the RA4T.

All these types of code can define parts of the general ontology, consisting of the conceptual model, and the rules that apply to it. While the ontology defines the general system, prototype demonstrations require test data that defines scenarios. Various types of code can define this test data. While source documentation usually only defines the ontology, CNL and Semantic Web code can also define test data for the ontology to populate the demonstration. Executable CNL can define this test data and be processed just like the CNL for the model and rules into Semantic Web code. This Semantic Web code for the scenario can then be processed together with the code for the model and rules to allow a prototype to run. Furthermore, appropriate test data for the prototype may already exist on the Semantic Web. This can be handy for testing, as it may be real-world data, and in large amounts.

The converter we use here is s2o [8], which has an executable CNL syntax. The s2o web form has separate fields for vocabulary and rules, so our tables for the scenarios in Sect. 5 list their executable CNL in these two categories for both implementation and test data. The cited work regarding these mappings focuses on the mapping from SBVR to the OWL itself, while we focus here on applying these as input to Semantic Web software for prototype demonstrations.

4.3 Interface Mapping

While Table 1 maps general data-oriented business rules situations to Semantic Web logic, Table 3 maps the situations and their corresponding logic to their demonstration as prototypes using particular Semantic Web software interface components. Here, we identify three aspects of business rule design to demonstrate with prototypes: instance-level occurrences, traceability of rule execution, and large-scale impact of design choices on the logical conclusions made for a given data set.

Table 3. Rapid Prototyping Interface Mapping

Rule Type	Prototype Interface		
	Instance level	Traceability	Large scale
inference	Protégé highlights (5.1)	Protégé	Protégé (5.5) & SPARQL
inconsistency	Protégé input error (5.3)	explanations (5.2)	n/a
constraints	Protégé SHACL view (5.4)	Validatrr	Currently none

The subsection presenting the scenario for each cell is shown in parentheses

5 Illustrative Scenarios

This section applies the general method from the previous section to several scenarios, each presented in one of the subsections here. Subsection 5.1 shows how to demonstrate the primary form of Semantic Web logic, inferencing, and how it applies to automated conclusions in business systems. We then describe the implementation of traceability for executed business rules with explanation functionality. How another important form of Semantic Web logic, inconsistencies, can prototype the blocking of invalid information is the topic of Subsect. 5.3.

The newest form of Semantic Web logic, SHACL constraints, then applies to having business rules instruct the user to provide new information. This section then concludes with a method for having prototypes analyze test data to help assess the impact of rule design choices. In addition, Table 1 indicates which subsection here presents a scenario for each given rule type and corresponding interface component.

5.1   Inferencing for Automatic Conclusions

This section's scenario derives from EU-Rent's "driver is barred" rule [12]. Here, an employee should consider any driver responsible for at least three bad experiences for being barred from further rentals. Table 4 shows the code in various languages that generates this scenario. We implement this rule in OWL by automatically concluding that any driver with at least three bad experiences is in the class of candidates for barred drivers. An employee can then review each member of this class to determine whether to bar that driver.

The EU-Rent specification provides source document text for this rule. Not every rule has source text in the specification. This rule, however, has no source SBVR code in the EU-Rent document. This is probably because an employee checks the validity of the drastic decision of barring a driver, instead of the system doing so automatically. However, we make an executable rule that presents potential barred drives for an employee to check. We write this rule directly in executable SBVR. As a model restriction, this "rule" is SBVR vocabulary. No s2o rule code is necessary for the ontology behind this system prototype.

This SBVR defines the concepts driver and bad experience and the "is authorized by" relation between them. It also defines a class "candidate barred" as a driver who was the authorized driver for at least three bad experiences. The converter s2o shows a shortcoming in the OWL code it generates for this, which necessitates some tailored Semantic Web code to make the prototype run as intended. S2o implements any "at least" SBVR rule as an owl:someValuesFrom, which functions as an "at least 1" regardless of the number entered. We replace this triple in the OWL restriction with an OWL minimal qualified cardinality of three, as Table 4 shows.

The SBVR vocabulary code for this test data defines one driver and three bad experiences, and authorizes the driver for all three. The Semantic Web operates without a unique name assumption, which means different resources with different names, here URIs, could actually represent the same thing. That means our three bad experiences could have duplicates, making the actual number potentially less than three. To address this, we add SBVR rule test data code explicitly stating that each bad experience is different from the others by using the "it is impossible that" construct with "is". S2o converts these into owl:differentFrom triples so Semantic Web software recognizes them as truly distinct from each other. This is required for any prototype using Semantic Web logic requiring recognition of multiple different individuals.

Figure 2 shows a Protégé display for this scenario. It presents the class "candidate barred", which shows the driver to be inferred as a member, demonstrating

Table 4. Inferred barred driver candidate scenario code

Document source: *EU-Rent specification [12]*
"A barred driver is a person known to EU-Rent as a driver (either a renter or an additional driver), who has at least 3 bad experiences."
"Each bad experience that occurs during a rental is the fault of a driver who is authorized for the rental that includes the bad experience"

Executable CNL: *SBVR in s2o vocabulary text box*

```
driver
bad_experience
driver is_authorized_for bad_experience
candidate_barred
 Definition: driver that is_authorized_for at_least 3 bad_experience
 Concept_type: verb_concept_role
 General_concept: driver
```

Test data: *SBVR in s2o vocabulary text box*

```
John
  General_concept: driver
Late_return
  General_concept: bad_experience
Car_damage
  General_concept: bad_experience
Speeding_ticket
  General_concept: bad_experience
John is_authorized_for Late_return
John is_authorized_for Car_damage
John is_authorized_for Speeding_ticket
```

Test data: *SBVR in s2o rules text box*

```
It is impossible that Late_return is Car_damage;
It is impossible that Late_return is Speeding_ticket;
It is impossible that Car_damage is Speeding_ticket;
```

Tailored Semantic Web

```
<ns:s2o#candidate_barred>
  owl:equivalentClass [ rdf:type owl:Restriction ;
    owl:onProperty <ns:s2o#is_authorized_for__bad_experience> ;
    owl:minQualifiedCardinality "3"^^xsd:nonNegativeInteger ;
    owl:onClass <ns:s2o#bad_experience> ] ;
```

that the intended inference indeed occurs. Protégé shows inferred data with a yellow background, which helps these rapid prototypes demonstrate that target inferencing has occurred. In terms of the RA4T, these highlighted inferred triples fall in the "Conclusions" box. These pass through the "Rendering" activity, which gives them yellow backgrounds in the interface.

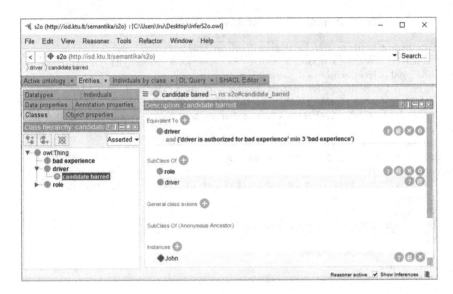

Fig. 2. Prototype inference display for the barred driver scenario.

5.2 Explanations for Traceability

The previous method demonstrates that an assertion was inferred automatically. In this case, it is that a driver is a candidate for being barred. An end user of such a system presenting such a conclusion about his or herself may also want to know why the banning occurred. Another type of potential end user in this scenario is an employee assessing this driver as a candidate for being barred. Developers may want to trace logical conclusions to their origins as part of debugging. They may also want to demonstrate traceability to the client as an intended end-system feature.

This section proposes a method for prototyping traceability of executed rules in business systems. Our demonstration of this method here exploits Protégé explanation pop-up displays. These explanations displays show all the triples, or data units, involved in a Semantic Web reasoned conclusion, be it an inference or inconsistency. These triples include both the OWL specifications for the rule and that data that triggers it. The user can then click on the individual resources in these triples. These navigate in the Protégé interface to more information on those resources, which triggered the conclusion. This click-based navigation provides the fundamental mechanism for traceability of business rule logic in our method.

In Fig. 2, clicking on the question mark button next to the driver brings a Protégé pop-up explanation window, shown in Fig. 3. Figure 3 shows a Protégé explanation box for the barred driver scenario from the code in Table 4. This explanation window displays all the triples that were involved in inferring that this driver is a candidate for being barred. It demonstrates the system's ability to access the reasoning behind such automated decisions. Here, we see the rule regarding at least three bad experiences, along with the specific bad experiences that trigger it here. The display here of the OWL logic defining the rule corresponds with the "triggered rule" arrow of the RA4T in Fig. 1.

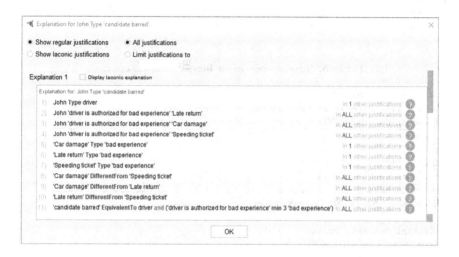

Fig. 3. Prototype explanation display for the barred driver scenario.

One result of this illustrative scenario is the proposed addition of the "triggering data" traceability arrow to the architecture, again shown in. A motivation for this addition to the barred driver candidate scenario is the end user's need to see the bad experiences triggering being barred. Here, either the employee needs to assess the severity of the bad experiences, or the driver want a full explanation if indeed barred from renting cars.

5.3 Inconsistencies from Invalid Input

Here, we base our scenario on the rule from EU-Rent that a driver license can only apply to one driver. Therefore, it must never be the case that one license has multiple drivers. If it ever happens, the system should show it clearly as a data error, preferably when an employee attempts to enter the second driver, so it can stop the user from entering it. In this scenario for this constraint, the designer shows the client how the system reacts to entering a second driver for one license, and how the logic behind that reaction works.

Table 5 shows the code for the scenario here. While the previous scenario had some document text but no SBVR from the EU-Rent specification, this scenario has SBVR without document text, which is more typical of EU-Rent.

This SBVR from EU-Rent is then translated into s2o's SBVR "dialect", with the data model as vocabulary, and the constraint in s2o's rule field. S2o converts the SBVR constructs "it is necessary that" and "exactly 1" here into a subclass of an OWL cardinality restriction. Identification numbers are implemented more typically in OWL with inverse functional properties. However, the goal here is a rapid prototype, not ideal ontology code. This implementation as a restriction is sufficient for a design session demonstration. Furthermore, while the OWL code converted is not ideal, no human-tailored Semantic Web code is necessary.

Table 5. Inconsistent driver license scenario code

Source CNL: *SBVR from EU-Rent specification [12]*
Each driver license is for exactly one driver
Executable CNL: *SBVR in s2o vocabulary text box*
driver
driver_license
driver_license is_attached_to driver
Executable CNL: *SBVR in s2o rules text box*
It is necessary that driver_license is_attached_to exactly 1 driver;
Test data: *SBVR in s2o vocabulary text box*
John General_concept: driver Mary General_concept: driver DV_247612 General_concept: driver_license DV_247612 is_attached_to John
Test data: *SBVR in s2o rules text box*
It is impossible that John is Mary;

Executable SBVR also defines the test data as two distinct drivers, and one license assigned to one of them. As with the banned driver scenario's test data, the individuals and their property assignments are s2o vocabulary, and a rule establishes the individuals as distinct. There is not yet any inconsistency in the scenario this code defines, but the stage is set for a user to attempt entering one.

Figure 4 shows a Protégé explanation box for this inconsistency in our scenario for this rule. In the demonstration of this scenario with the generated rapid prototype, the user attempts to add Mary as a driver for a license in addition to John. This generates an inconsistency, whose explanation appears in this display. This emulates the application of Semantic Web inconsistency to stop the user from entering invalid data when they try to do so.

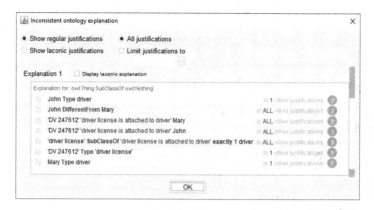

Fig. 4. Explanation box for the scenario presenting the reason for the inconsistency to the product owner.

5.4 SHACL Constraints for Data Requiring Input

The Shapes Constraint Language (SHACL) is a relative newcomer to the Semantic Web. Officially published in 2017, it arrived later than much core research applying Semantic Web technologies. Most, if not all, research on converting SBVR to the Semantic Web does not account for SHACL as output. We propose here a mapping from SBVR to SHACL to exploit new possibilities for prototyping business rules that SHACL brings to Semantic Web software.

One type of business rule that SHACL implements better than the rest of the Semantic Web is the system requesting specific missing information from the user. Minimum cardinality in OWL infers rather than constrains. We see this in the barred driver scenario in Sect. 5.1, where a driver having at least three bad experiences triggers the inference that they are a candidate for being barred. SHACL, however, treats minimal cardinality as a constraint. If a resource does not match a SHACL minimal cardinality constraint, then the system displays the corresponding SHACL message, which describes the unmet constraint for the user.

We extend the driver license scenario from Sect. 5.3 to apply SHACL minimal cardinality. There, the "exactly one" SBVR constraint maps to OWL as a qualified cardinality of one, which is both a maximum and a minimum cardinality. Section 5.3's scenario triggered the maximum cardinality as an inconsistency, preventing multiple drivers for one license. Here, we map the same SBVR to a minimal cardinality in SHACL to display a message stating that a driver has no license in the system. This then instructs the user to enter one for the driver.

Table 6 shows the code for the scenario here. Figure 5 shows a Protégé display for this scenario applying SHACL. Here, we repeat the executable CNL code from the previous driver license scenario for the general concept model and rule. However, as said, existing converters from SBVR to the Semantic Web, such as s2o, only convert to OWL, and not to SHACL. Thus, we enter our own tailored Semantic Web code as the SHACL constraint giving the has_driver_license property a minimal cardinality of one. This SHACL code along with the generated Semantic Web code for the concept model leads to the Protégé display that Fig. 5 shows.

Table 6. Missing driver license scenario code

Source CNL: *SBVR from EU-Rent specification [12]*
driver has driver license
Necessity: Each driver has at least one driver license.
Executable CNL: *SBVR in s2o vocabulary text box*
driver
driver_license
driver has driver_license
Executable CNL: *SBVR in s2o rules text box*
It is necessary that driver has at_least 1 driver_license
Test data: *SBVR in s2o vocabulary text box*
Jack
General_concept: driver
Tailored Semantic Web
ex:PersonShape
a sh:NodeShape ;
sh:targetClass <ns:s2o#driver> ;
sh:property [
sh:path <ns:s2o#has__driver_license> ;
sh:minCount 1] .

While Protégé offers explanation pop-windows for inferences and inconsistencies, it currently offers none for triggered SHACL constraints. This, of course, makes current versions of Protégé insufficient for applying traceability in demonstrations of SHACL logic; Protégé shows only that instances of applied SHACL logic have occurred. Validatrr, on the other hand, does provide the equivalent of Protégé explanations for SHACL constraint violations [6]. It does so by treating each SHACL violation as an inference, and then providing a list of all triples involved in forming it. A rapid prototyping method could put SHACL code generated from CNL into Validatrr for quickly demonstrating traceability behind SHACL constraint violations.

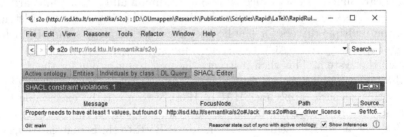

Fig. 5. A Protégé SHACL display instructing entry of missing driver license.

5.5   Effect of Ontology Changes on Inferred Data

The previous methods each demonstrate that specific reasoning has occurred, and how and why. The scenarios presented with them each required some test data for defining the scenario illustrating and evaluating that method. Here, we present a method for demonstrating the effect that a change to the ontology has on the data that it infers.

Figure 6 shows the developer's client the impact that a change to the ontology has on automated assignments of barred drivers. This scenario uses the ontology and data from the driver license scenario presented earlier. Previously, the rule was that three bad experiences make a driver a candidate for being barred. The test data for the scenario was driver John with three bad experiences. Here, we add driver Jane with two bad experiences to the test data. We then show the effect changing the number of bad experiences to two has on which drivers the altered rule now infers as candidates. This change make Jane also become a candidate.

Such demonstrations of the effects of ontology adjustments typically require more test data than the methods previously shown. The methods simply demonstrating a single rule for inferencing or inconsistency only need to create a simple moment in a fictional user session. Ontology adjustment effects, on the on the other hand, usually apply over a larger amount of data. Another aspect of data here is that it can stay the same, while the ontology changes. Both this amount and this context of data for demonstrating ontology choices means it more often starts as Semantic Web data, rather than being converted from SBVR. This also facilitates the use of real-world data already on the Semantic Web, which means we demonstrate the impact of ontology design choices on the situation as it is.

Italiaander evaluates the impact of ontology design choices on the efficiency of inferencing [7]. As with this work, he applies EU-Rent as an example case and Protégé to process the inferencing. He also created a large amount of synthetic EU-Rent raw data as Semantic Web triples to perform this inferencing from. SPARQL queries then count the amount of inferred data different design options make in order to compare them. Such SPARQL-generated analyses can augment our prototyping methods by showing large-scale impact of design choices given large amount of realistic or real-world data.

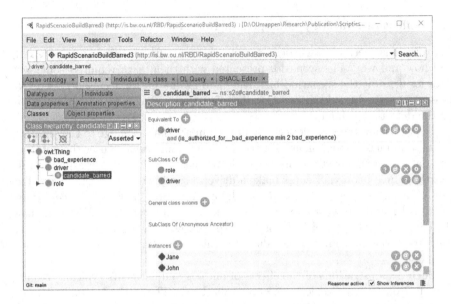

Fig. 6. Prototype display for effect on class assignment from a change inference rule, compared with the equivalent display before the change in Fig. 2. The minimum cardinality is now 2, making Jane a candidate for being barred along with John.

6   Conclusion

This paper presents methods for making rapid prototypes of design choices for business rule by using CNLs and their automated conversion to the Semantic Web. We illustrate these methods with the CNL SBVR, the converter s2o and the Semantic Web user interface tool Protégé, but any rule-based CNL and software conforming to it and the Semantic Web can apply as well. Executable CNL is the core of this method's first step, which converters then process into Semantic Web code. These methods deliver rapid prototypes, meaning they make neither robust end systems nor well-crafted ontology code. Instead, the prototypes help design the system and underlying ontology better, so system programmers and ontologies can make better code from the design.

These methods enable further hand editing of the converted Semantic Web code to have the prototype run as intended. Cases requiring this can sometimes motivate further improvements to the conversion software. In other cases, they can simply exemplify the required flexibility for adapting converted OWL code for unique situations. We describe inputting not only CNL for data models and rules but also test data to define complete scenarios for running in a prototype demonstrations. The Semantic Web's lack of a unique name assumption requires SBVR's "is impossible that" to distinguish individuals that must be handled as distinct. Addition future work could include implementation of SBVR-to-OWL conversion features whose absent in s2o this work demonstrates, such as cardinalities greater than one, numeric necessities and simple equalities.

Acknowledgments. This work comes from the Master's Theses in the Rapid Rules Thesis Circle in the BPMIT (Business Process Management and Information Technology) Master's program at the Open University of the Netherlands, completed in February of 2022. This work's authors are the writers of these thesis documents and their supervisor [3,5,17]. Ella Roubtsova was the co-supervisor for the group, and provided insightful and useful feedback on the thesis document, which has helped this work as well.

References

1. Boyer, J., Mili, H.: Agile Business Rule Development - Process, Architecture, and JRules Examples. Springer, Heidelberg (2011). https://doi.org/10.1007/978-3-642-19041-4

2. Camburn, B., et al.: Design prototyping methods: state of the art in strategies, techniques, and guidelines. Des. Sci. **3** (2017)

3. Corbijn, J.: Rapid prototyping for explaining business rules with Semantic Web technology. Master's thesis, Open University of the Netherlands, Heerlen, The Netherlands (2022)

4. Corsius, M., Hoppenbrouwers, S., Lokin, M., Baars, E., Sangers-Van Cappellen, G., Wilmont, I.: RegelSpraak: a CNL for executable tax rules specification. In: Proceedings of the Seventh International Workshop on Controlled Natural Language (CNL 2020/21). Special Interest Group on Controlled Natural Language, Amsterdam, Netherlands, September 2021. https://aclanthology.org/2021.cnl-1.6

5. Cuijpers, B.: Flexible subsumption-based throwaway prototypes: demonstrating increased flexibility with design choices in class hierarchies through Semantic Web throwaway prototypes. Master's thesis, Open University of the Netherlands, Heerlen, The Netherlands (2022)

6. De Meester, B., Heyvaert, P., Arndt, D., Dimou, A., Verborgh, R.: RDF graph validation using rule-based reasoning. Semant. Web J. **12**, 117–142 (2020)

7. Italiaander, R.H.J.: AgentRole, TimeInstant and InverseOf Ontology Design Patterns for more efficient inferencing from asserted data. Master's thesis, Open University of the Netherlands, Heerlen, The Netherlands (2019)

8. Karpovič, J., Kriščiūnienė, G., Ablonskis, L., Nemuraitė, L.: The comprehensive mapping of semantics of business vocabulary and business rules (SBVR) to OWL 2 ontologies. Inf. Technol. Control **43**(4), 289–302 (2014)

9. Karpoviič, J., Nemuraitė, L.: Transforming SBVR business semantics into web ontology language OWL2: main concepts. Inf. Technol. Control (2011)

10. Musen, M.A., Protégé, T.: The Protégé project: a look back and a look forward. AI Matters **1**(4), 4–12 (2015)

11. Object Management Group: Semantics of Business Vocabulary and Business Rules (SBVR) (2016)

12. Object Management Group: Semantics of Business Vocabulary and Business Rules (SBVR) Appendix G - EU-Rent Example (2016)

13. Peffers, K., Rothenberger, M., Tuunanen, T., Vaezi, R.: Design science research evaluation. In: Peffers, K., Rothenberger, M., Kuechler, B. (eds.) DESRIST 2012. LNCS, vol. 7286, pp. 398–410. Springer, Heidelberg (2012). https://doi.org/10.1007/978-3-642-29863-9_29

14. Reynares, E., Caliusco, M., Galli, M.: SBVR to OWL 2 mappings: an automatable and structural-rooted approach. CLEI Electron. J. **17** (2014)

15. Rutledge, L., Italiaander, R.: Toward a reference architecture for traceability in SBVR-based systems. In: Proceedings of the Seventh International Workshop on Controlled Natural Language (CNL 2020/21). Special Interest Group on Controlled Natural Language, Amsterdam, Netherlands, September 2021. https:// aclanthology.org/2021.cnl-1.13
16. Veizaga, A., Alferez, M., Torre, D., Sabetzadeh, M., Briand, L.: On systematically building a controlled natural language for functional requirements. Empir. Softw. Eng. **26**(4), 1–53 (2021). https://doi.org/10.1007/s10664-021-09956-6
17. Wondaal, L.: Rapid prototyping of business rules to demonstrate inconsistencies using Semantic Web software. Master's thesis, Open University of the Netherlands, Heerlen, The Netherlands (2022)

Agile Innovation Through Business Process Management: Realizing the Potential of Digital Transformation

Mathias Kirchmer[✉]

Affiliated Faculty, BPM-D and Organizational Dynamics at the University of Pennsylvania, PA
Philadelphia, USA
Mathias.Kirchmer@bpm-d.com

Abstract. Companies must apply their innovation capabilities in an agile way to achieve an immediate impact while preparing for disruptive improvements. This is especially important for digital transformations which deliver their value through the resulting business processes. Business process management (BPM) as a management discipline helps to address these needs. Correctly set up, the BPM-Discipline delivers more than just efficiencies, quality, or compliance. It establishes an agile and focused innovation capability within an organization. Process management delivers process innovation in the form of new or enhanced business processes, organizes the way organizations address innovation, and helps manage the innovation process. This paper examines the relationship between process management and innovation. It shows how the discipline of BPM becomes a major enabler of agile innovation that delivers the full potential of digital transformation initiatives.

Keywords: BPM · Business process management · Design thinking · Digitalization · Digital transformation · Innovation · Innovation process · Process design · Process innovation · Process of process management

1 The Significance of Process Management for Innovation

The volatile business environment and the all-present digitalization continuously provide opportunities and threats for organizations. Permanently changing market conditions force organizations to make innovation a part of their day-to-day business [1]. This requires the realization of the business potential of digital technologies to achieve the innovation goals. Companies must apply their innovation capabilities in an agile way to achieve an immediate impact while preparing for disruptive improvements. This article shows how business process management (BPM) as a management discipline supports these needs for ongoing innovation and related digitalization [2, 3].

In practice, process management is often limited to achieving tactical operational improvements. However, correctly set up, the BPM-Discipline delivers more than just efficiencies, quality, or compliance. It helps establishing an agile and focused innovation capability within an organization. Process management delivers innovation in the form

© Springer Nature Switzerland AG 2022
B. Shishkov (Ed.): BMSD 2022, LNBIP 453, pp. 21–34, 2022.
https://doi.org/10.1007/978-3-031-11510-3_2

of new or enhanced business processes and organizes the way organizations address innovation.

This paper examines this relation between process management and innovation. This shows a different, little examined dimension of process management by explaining how the discipline of BPM becomes a major enabler of agile innovation that realizing the full potential of digital transformation initiatives as a component of this process-led innovation.

1.1 Impact of Business Process Management on Innovation

Widely used definitions of innovation include the following [4]:

- the introduction of something new
- a new idea, method, or device
- the successful exploitation of new ideas
- change that creates a new dimension of performance

Hence, innovation is about creating a business impact through something new. It is not just about inventing, for example, in a new technology. But it is about using this invention to create business value. Here an example: A German research institute, the *Frauenhofer Institut*, invented the MP3 format to digitize music. Hence, they are the inventor. However, they sold the invention to Apple which created a business around this new way of delivering music as realized through their iTunes Store, iPods, and many other components. Apple is the innovator. They create a business impact through the invention.

Agility in a business context means the ability to react in a quick and nimble way to changes in the business environment [5]. Consequently, agile innovation is being able to come up with innovations within short time frames, correcting them quickly when necessary, and to adjust the way the organization innovates to changing requirements.

Business process management (BPM) is defined as the discipline that moves strategy into people and technology-based execution, at pace with certainty [6]. This definition shows that it can impact the innovation capability of an organization in two ways [3, 7]. On one hand, BPM can deliver, through appropriate design and implementation, new or significantly enhanced business processes; hence, providing "process innovation". On the other hand, process management helps to organize the way a company innovates in different areas. It supports the management of the "innovation process." The innovation process can even deliver process innovation as a specific innovation result. Figure 1 illustrates this relation between process management and innovation.

The transparency of process management enables the required agility in process innovation. Supporting process management tools, such as modelling and repository applications, allows for the rapid evaluation of different process scenarios and for the nimble adjustment of the innovative processes. The discipline of process management also supports an agile organization of the innovation process to react to new business situations. Hence, process management does not only support innovation in general, but is the foundation for agile innovation. This agile innovation is especially important for digital transformations.

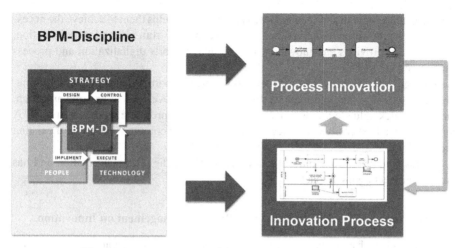

Fig. 1. Impact of Business Process Management on Innovation

1.2 Importance of Innovation Through Process Management for Digitalization

Digital transformation (used synonymously to digitalization) is about integration products and services with people, leveraging digital technologies, in most cases based on the internet. The value from these technologies is delivered through appropriately designed new or improved business processes. This definition of digital transformation is visualized in Fig. 2.

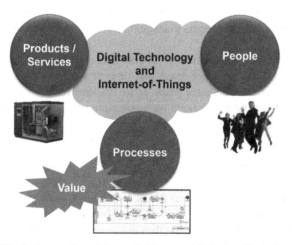

Fig. 2. Illustration of the Definition of Digital Transformation

Organizations often struggle to address this process dimension of digitalization. Only 1% of companies master their business processes sufficiently to realize the full potential of digital technologies [10]. All those successful organizations have a formalized process management discipline in place. This discipline helps them to achieve the necessary process innovation to deliver the full value expected from a digital transformation. In addition, it provides an innovation process that supports digitalization and process innovation [11, 12].

The agility that process management produces is important for digitalization initiatives. It makes sure that intermediate digital solutions, developed in an agile approach, can bring quick value to the organization by realizing appropriate process scenarios. A company can adjust easily to new technologies or a more comprehensive use of existing ones.

Process innovation has played a significant role in digital transformation and has shown major economic impact.

1.3   The Need to Examine the Impact of Process Management on Innovation

Most of the research about business process management has been centered around its use to achieve tactical improvements of the business operations. Process-led improvement and optimization approaches focus mostly on delivering value in form of higher cost and time efficiency, better execution quality or compliance with legal and company-specific requirements. However, in the digital time, the role of process management to create innovation has become increasingly more important. This is not yet reflected appropriately in research initiatives.

This article aims to contribute to filling this gap. It examines the role of process management as enabler of innovation, leveraging digital technologies and providing the necessary agility for the innovation capability. This analysis is done in two steps:

- Examination of the role of process management for process innovation
- Examination of the role of process management for the innovation process

This structure reflects the relation of process management and innovation outlined previously. However, this does not mean that process management is the only factor important for innovation. There are many other relevant research fields, such as the use of creative techniques or collaboration innovation with partners. These will not be examined in this article.

2   Process Innovation

More and more inventions are not about things, but about business processes [2, 3]. People invent new processes and build a business based on this process innovation. Amazon, for example, did not invent the book. But they did invent a new process to sell books and established their company based on this process innovation. In a further innovative step, they became a broader online retailer, leveraging their process innovation with its infrastructure. eBay did not invent the auction. But its online, easy-to-use processes increased the popularity of auctions and the opportunity to make money with them. LinkedIn and Facebook invented new processes to manage relationships and personal networks. When Dell was founded, the enterprise did not invent the PC. But it did invent new business processes to bring PCs to market, eliminating unnecessary steps in the supply chain, while offering more flexibility and control to the customer. These processes had become Dell's main differentiator in the competitive marketplace. Process innovation was the basis for starting and growing the company. A supermajority of e-businesses, such as Uber, Expedia, Grubhub and many more, are founded on process innovation – as part of the digital transformation of the economy.

Traditional companies are also focusing more of their attention on process innovation. For example, enterprises in the machinery industries offer more convenient and reliable service processes based on internet connections to their clients or directly to the delivered equipment. Airlines have simplified the ticketing process to reduce costs and increase service levels through online ticketing. Banks reduce costs and improve their service levels through online banking. Mortgages are offered through convenient internet-based processes. Hence, process innovation, mostly combined with digitalization, has also made a significant impact for traditional companies.

2.1 Delivering Process Innovation through Process Management

The discipline of process management supports process innovation in two ways: it enables a more efficient and flexible design of new processes and supports their reliable implementation [3]. It speeds up process innovation and makes changes easy to execute. Hence, it makes innovation more agile. The influence of business process management (BPM) on process innovation is shown in Fig. 3.

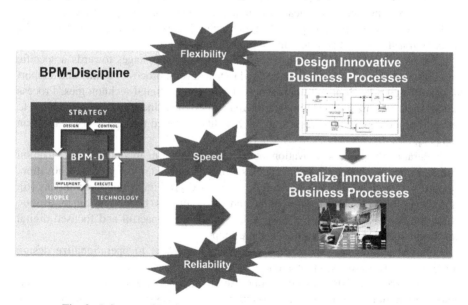

Fig. 3. Influence of Business Process Management on Process Innovation

Process management supports the design of innovation processes by operationalizing creative techniques like design thinking in a process context [13]. Design thinking is about [14]:

- Empathy: understanding the issues stakeholders have to come up with an appropriate solution
- Transfer: delivering innovative solutions by transferring successful practices from one business area into another
- Agility: testing solutions quickly to be able to correct and to adjust as required
- Story Telling: supporting the roll out of successful solutions through the right context and related narratives

The discipline of BPM provides methods to apply all these aspects of design thinking. Through integrated stakeholder journey planning, one gets an outside-in view on processes from the perspective of a specific group of stakeholders [15]. This methodology is done by identifying the touchpoints a stakeholder has with the organization and linking those touchpoints to the underlying processes. Desired changes in stakeholder experience can thus be transformed into operational process improvements. Customer journey maps are widely used to address customer experience, but the approach can also be applied to other stakeholder groups, such as supplier journey maps or employee journey maps. In digital transformations, the use of journey maps is critical to achieve the new enhanced experience, especially customer experience, that often represents a key value of the digitalization.

The use of process reference models allows for the pragmatic transfer of good practices from one area (e.g., one industry) to another [3]. So, a biologics company, for example, can benefit from the product configuration know-how of machinery companies to produce patient specific medications. In digital transformations, the use of reference models makes the business impact of digital technologies transparent and enables the effective transfer of best practices in using a technology [16].

Process scenarios are defined to represent intermediate stages towards a specific target process. Those scenarios can be used to test several process variants and support the use of agile development approaches of underlying digital technologies. Process management organizes the incrementation realization of business processes and helps to set appropriate expectations regarding the benefits delivered through every realization step [17].

Integrating the process innovation into an overall operating model of an organization with its hierarchical decomposition enables a smooth roll-out of the process innovation, supported through appropriate storytelling about its overall impact on the company [6]. This also ensures the consideration of the end-to-end process context for the innovation which may only cover a sub-process. The result is an impactful and focused digital transformation initiative with a manageable scope.

Figure 4 summarizes the use of process management to operationalize design thinking to deliver process innovation.

The transparency BPM creates can be used to support informed outsourcing decisions. Important core processes stay in-house. This makes sure that process innovation initiatives and digital transformation focus on the core capabilities of the organization [6, 18, 19]. Establishing the related partnerships can lead to innovative inter-enterprise processes, hence collaboration innovation [3].

The discipline of BPM, realized through the process of process management, covers the entire lifecycle of the business process from design through implementation, and

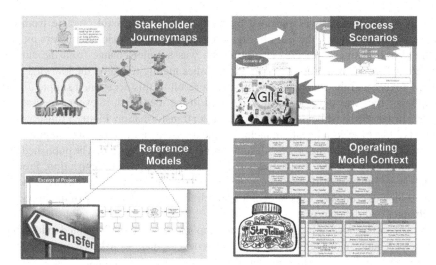

Fig. 4. Process Management to Operationalize Design Thinking for Process Innovation

the ongoing execution and control of the process [20]. Hence, it identifies the required realization actions for the process innovation and organizational governance to ensure an ongoing adjustment of the resulting business process as required. The use of appropriate process management tools, such as modelling, mining, analytics, or prioritization tools, makes process governance and the entire process of process management even more efficient and reliable [21].

2.2 Process Innovation in Practice

Now, we can examine a simple example of process innovation in practice. A leading biologics company had the challenge that an increasing number of its products could not be shipped because of compliance issues. Of those issues, 99% were not related to the products themselves but to the required documentations which were either incomplete or inconsistent. These problems resulted in a significant impact on cash flow and revenue. The continuous process improvement, including regular Kaizen events, had not let to the desired result. A more significant process innovation was required.

The relevant business processes were identified by looking at the company through the lens of the Quality Assurance (QA) organization. The identification of the touch points with QA where issues with the compliance documentation were found, allowed the identification of the underlying processes, a small subset of the overall supply chain process.

The initial idea to address those issues was to move those processes to the next level through a broad, digital transformation, which would leverage an automation platform in combination with a document management system. The resulting process innovation would essentially eliminate the identified issues. However, the realization of this new process would take at least 8–12 months. Faster results were required. Hence, an intermediate process scenario was required to address the issues at pace.

This agile approach was executed by transferring a successful practice from the production environment: the use of "digital check lists" and tablet computers as part of the overall business process. This approach was a major change from the current situation where the resolution of compliance issues mainly relied on the knowledge of the employees and their manual activities. As a result of this decision, a simple digital compliance tool was developed and integrated in the identified, relevant processes to achieve faster results while preparing for the larger transformation. Figure 5 illustrates an excerpt of this process innovation, including the use of the new compliance application. It shows the structure of the process design, details of the content cannot be published due to confidentiality reasons. It illustrates the focused use of process innovation. Process models were integrated in the process hierarchy in the context of the operating model of the biologics company. This integration simplified the understanding of the impact of the changes and the enterprise-wide roll-out.

The processes leveraging the compliance application were implemented in less than six weeks. Change management and application development were based on the process models. After eight weeks the number of document-related compliance issues was cut in half. After 12 weeks, these issues were reduced by 80%. This improvement resulted in a significant increase of cash flow and revenue.

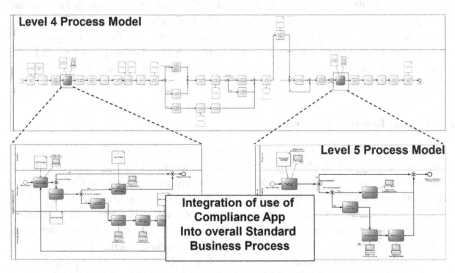

Fig. 5. Process Innovation Leveraging the Digital Compliance Application

3   Innovation Process

All forms of innovation are influenced through the business process that creates and manages them: the innovation process. To come up with innovations systematically, an organization must establish a process that delivers the desired innovation as a result [3]. This process must be defined, implemented, executed, and controlled just like any other business process. It goes through the same process life cycle, managed through the discipline of business process management.

3.1 Delivering an Effective Innovation Process through Process Management

The generic structure of an innovation process is shown in Fig. 6 [7]. This structure can also be sued to examine other aspects of innovation, not addressed in this article. The process evolves from the preparation of an innovation initiative, to the "idea finding" activities, and finally to the execution of the innovation idea. The innovation manager identifies relevant mega-trends. This identification is the basis to detect the relevant innovation areas. These innovation areas guide the definition of the company-specific innovation focus. This focus directs the idea finding, using internal and external resources. The innovation ideas are evaluated, and the ones considered most promising are transferred into innovation projects. These projects develop prototypes and business cases. Then, the innovation team decides which innovation ideas will be brought to market, hence, which of those ideas become actual innovations.

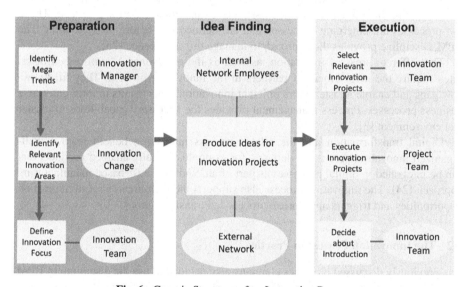

Fig. 6. Generic Structure of an Innovation Process

Agility is a key criterium for the optimization of the innovation process, combined with quality and efficiency. It addresses different innovation areas and minimizes the time-to-market of innovations as well as the related development cost.

The discipline of BPM manages the innovation processes toward those goals by addressing four, key characteristics of a high-performance innovation process:

- Process variants due to the different innovation areas
- Different degrees of freedom for people involved in the innovation
- Emerging processes due to unknown intermediate innovation results

- Inter-enterprise processes to include innovation partners

Since an innovation process delivers new products or services in many different areas, different variants of that process must be defined and managed. A manufacturing company, for example, may develop new physical products, new services around those products, which create new processes, and innovative software components that enable the physical products for a digital environment. This development is supported through appropriate process management capabilities [22].

Within the innovation process, people require different degrees of freedom. There are sub-processes where people have to work very creatively. Hence, processes are only loosely defined to support creativity. Other areas of the innovation process are transactional and are normally optimized towards efficiency and compliance; hence, they are clearly defined. The organization of clinical trials, for example, requires the combination of efficiency in handling all the required documentation with initial creativity of coming up with the new treatment solutions. Process management provides the transparency to manage the innovation process in this differentiated way [3, 20].

The result of one activity in the innovation process may trigger different steps to follow. Hence, in some areas the process cannot immediately be fully defined. Those sub-processes are emerging processes that are defined just before the execution. The BPM-Discipline provides the approach to manage this emergence [23].

The different areas of innovation, as well as the emergence of unforeseen tasks, often require the involvement of partners in the innovation process. They fill know-how gaps and enable a faster, more efficient innovation. This results in inter-enterprise business processes. Process management provides the necessary capabilities to master that environment [3].

Digital transformation and the related process innovation benefit from a well-organized innovation process. It delivers, for example, digitally enabled products that can be integrated in digital processes as part of an "Industry 4.0" based manufacturing approach [24]. The innovation process also supports the identification of digitalization opportunities and triggers appropriate process-led transformations.

3.2 The Innovation Process in Practice

The previously discussed biologics company also decided to use the discipline of BPM to address the way they develop and commercialize new products and related services. The main goals of this transformation of the innovation process were the following:

- Improve planning accuracy
- Increase predictability
- Reduce cycle time and shorten the time to take products to market
- Increase of the number of successful innovation projects
- Provide transparency over the process to accommodate different innovation areas
- Commit to adherence to compliance standards
- Deliver greater flexibility

Most important was the predictability of the launch date of new products and services to set and meet appropriate expectations in the market. This objective was difficult to achieve due to a number of reasons, including the need for early information about new equipment required for the production of a product, or the big variety of products and related services.

The analysis of the as-is process was challenging due to the many process variants and t the different views of different people on the process. The use of a top-down approach and identification of a 4-level process hierarchy helped to capture and analyze the different sub-processes. The analysis delivered 19 improvement opportunities. Here are four of the most critical ones:

- Eliminate bottlenecks for identifying promising ideas to work on
- Conduct early equipment feasibility assessment
- Ensure full characterization of products before design freeze
- Formalize needs for adjustments of the manufacturing process

A top-be process hierarchy was developed in a way that the different sub-processes simplified a systematic realization of the improvement opportunities. Different sub-processes were improved in different ways to address those opportunities and target the defined goals. The design of the processes on the "task level," the lowest level of detail, allowed an efficient definition of "value packages," or small manageable realization projects. Figure 7 shows an excerpt of the hierarchy of the transformed innovation process.

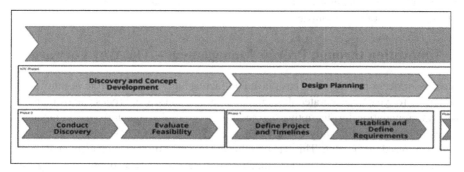

Fig. 7. Hierarchy of the to-be Innovation Process (Excerpt)

The excerpt of a to-be process model on the task level can be seen in Fig. 8. Some related, key changes are noted. The to-be process includes a higher degree of digitalization of the innovation process, such as managing the collection and selection of ideas.

While the realization projects were executed, a process governance approach was defined to enable the necessary ability while meeting the efficiency, quality, and compliance requirements. This approach was achieved through ongoing use of the process models to maintain transparency over the process as well as to provide the definition of

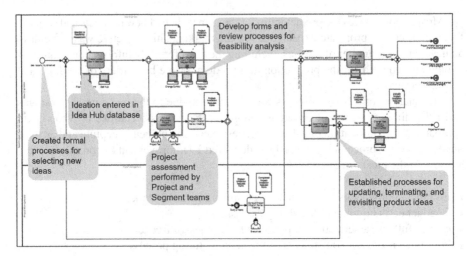

Fig. 8. Process Model of the Innovation Process on Task Level (Excerpt)

clear responsibilities and accountabilities. The development of key performance indicators allowed the value-driven management of the process and the realization of the defined goals.

After six months of realization activities, the first improvements regarding predictability and cycle times were measured. The process owner now adjusts the developed process models continuously to address new findings and to implement the required changes. The innovation process has become agile. It addresses the continuously changing needs of the organization.

4 Innovation through Process Management – The Way Forward

Business process management has played an increasingly important role in innovation initiatives for years, accelerated through the digitalization wave. Process innovation has been the foundation for disruptive business models and the launch of new companies. It has delivered significantly new or enhanced processes that have changed the way organizations deliver value. This can be achieved by using process management to operationalize design thinking. The described research has shown that supports an empathic approach, for example through stakeholder journey maps, the transfer of knowledge between different areas, using e.g. process reference models, agility through realization of process scenarios and it helps to develop and overall story line by embedding the process into an operating model and its process structure.

BPM is also crucial for organizing the innovation process of a company, or the way it comes up with innovative solutions, including new products, services, or processes. It addresses the specific characteristics of an innovation process, such as the handling of process variants due to the different innovation areas, allows the definition of different degrees of freedom for people involved in the innovation, helps to manage emerging processes due to unknown intermediate innovation results, and enables the organization of inter-enterprise processes to include innovation partners.

Process management makes innovation agile, which enables quick adaptation to the changing requirements of the business environment. This happens through agile process innovation and an appropriate management of the innovation process.

Since digital transformation delivers its value though business processes Therefore process innovation through appropriate BPM plays a key role to deliver the desired business benefits through digitalization. A well-organized innovation process provides components for digitalization initiatives, such as new digital products. As a result, innovation through process management has become a foundation of successful digital transformation. It helps to realize the appropriate business potential of digital technologies and adjusts their use in an agile way to the needs to the organization.

The increasing need of innovation through process management suggests further research and development in this area. Here some examples for areas to be further examined:

- Systematic approach for process innovation
- Reference model for the innovation process
- Governance for the innovation process
- Integrated stakeholder planning from different perspectives

While this article outlines key techniques to be used for process innovation, this approach can be further defined and operationalized. A reference model for the innovation process would provide an important starting point and accelerator for the transformation of this important business process. The innovation process requires specific governance to ensure the high degree of agility required. Process innovation is often triggered through external views on a process. This can be operationalized through stakeholder journey maps. Traditionally, one journey map which looks at the process from one point of view is used. However, in many areas, the combination of multiple views, such as provided through customer and employee journey maps, are required. The integrated use of journey maps and their link to underlying processes is another interesting topic for further investigation.

Agile innovation through process management plays an increasingly important role in the digital world. Every organization must address this topic. The discipline of process management has become a key enabler for systematic and effective innovation.

References

1. Fingar, P.: Extreme Competition – Innovation and the Great 21st Century Business Reformation. Meghan-Kiffer, Tampa (2006)
2. Kirchmer, M.: Process innovation through open BPM. In: Pantaleo, D., Pal, N. (eds.) From Strategy to Execution – Turning Accelerated Global Change into Opportunity, pp. 87–105. Springer, Berlin (2008)
3. Kirchmer, M.: High Performance through Business Process Management – Strategy Execution in a Digital World, 3rd edn. New York, e.a, Berlin (2017)
4. Wikipedia (ed.): Innovation. https://en.wikipedia.org/wiki/Innovation (2022)
5. Wikipedia (ed.): Agility. https://en.wikipedia.org/wiki/Agility_(disambiguation) (2022)

6. Franz, P., Kirchmer, M.: Value-driven Business Process Management – The Value-Switch for Lasting Competitive Advantage. New York (2012)
7. Davila, T., Epstein, M.J., Shelton, R.: Making Innovation Work. Wharton School Publishing, Upper Saddle River (2006)
8. McDonald, B.: Digital Strategy does not equal IT Strategy. Harvard Business Review (19 Nov 2012)
9. Scheer, A.-W.: Industry 4.0: From Vision to Implementation. Whitepaper Number 5, August-Wilhelm Scheer Institute for Digital Products and Processes. Scheer GMBH, Saarbruecken, Germany (2015)
10. Cantara, M.: Start up your Business Process Competency Center. In: Documentation of The Gartner Business Process Management Summit. National Harbor (2015)
11. Antonucci, Y., Fortune, A., Kirchmer, M.: An examination of associations between business process management capabilities and the benefits of digitalization: all capabilities are not equal. In: Business Process Management Journal, vol. ahead-of print. (2021). https://doi.org/10.1108/BPMJ-02-2020-0079
12. Kirchmer, M.: Value-driven digital transformation: performance through process. In: IM+io, Best & Next Practices aus Digitalisierung | Management | Wissenschaft, Heft 2, Juni (2019)
13. Levrick, M., Link, P., Leifer, L.: The Design Thinking Toolbox: A Guide to Mastering the Most Popular and Valuable Innovation Methods. Hoboken (2020)
14. Nixon, N.: Viewing ascension health from a design thinking perspective. Journal of organization design (2013)
15. Kalbach, J.: Mapping Experiences: A Complete Guide To Customer Alignment Through Journeys, Blueprints and Diagrams, 2nd edition. Boston, e.a., Beijing (2021)
16. Kirchmer, M., Franz, P.: Process Reference Models: Accelerator for Digital Transformation. In: Shishkov, B. (ed.) BMSD 2020. LNBIP, vol. 391, pp. 20–37. Springer, Cham (2020). https://doi.org/10.1007/978-3-030-52306-0_2
17. Kirchmer, M., Franz, P.: Value-driven robotic process automation (RPA) – a process-led approach for fast results at minimal risk. In: Proceedings of the 9th International Symposium on Business Modelling and Software Design. Lisbon (1–3 July 2019)
18. Christensen, C., Johnson, M.: Business model innovation. Report to the US Council of Innovation. The Conference Board (2007)
19. Christensen, C.M., Raymour, M.: The Innovator's Solution: Using Good Theory to Solve the Dilemmas of Growth. Harvard Business School Press, Boston (2003)
20. Kirchmer, M.: The process of process management – mastering the new normal in a digital world. In: Proceedings of the 5th International Symposium on Business Modelling and Software Design. Milan (6–8 July 2015)
21. Kirchmer, M.: Digital Transformation of Business Process Governance. In: Shishkov, B. (ed.) BMSD 2021. LNBIP, vol. 422, pp. 243–261. Springer, Cham (2021). https://doi.org/10.1007/978-3-030-79976-2_14
22. Franz, P., Kirchmer, M.: Standardization and Harmonization of Business Processes – Enabling Agile Customer Service in a Digital World. BPM-D Publications, London, Philadelphia (2016)
23. Majchrzak, A., Logan, D., McCurdy, R., Kirchmer, M.: Four keys to managing emergence. In: MIT Sloan Management Review **47**(2). Winter (2006)
24. Scheer, A.-W.: Enterprise 4.0 – From Disruptive Business Model to the Automation of Business Processes, 1st edition. AWSi Publishing, Saarbrucken, Germany (2019)

Requirements for Dynamic Jumps
at the Execution of Business Processes

Thomas Bauer[(✉)] [iD]

Neu-Ulm University of Applied Sciences, Wileystr. 1, 89231 Neu-Ulm, Germany
thomas.bauer@hnu.de

Abstract. At process-aware information systems, it is sometimes necessary to deviate from the modelled business process. For instance, in exceptional cases or to correct mistakes, users shall be able to jump dynamically forward and backward in the process. Until now, this topic was hardly respected in scientific literature and it is insufficiently realized in commercial process engines. In this paper, very comprehensive requirements and the expected behavior of a process engine are presented for such dynamic jumps during run-time of a business process. The approach does not only respect forward and backward jumps within sequences of activities but also jumps into and out of parallel branches, conditional branches, and within loops. In addition, configuration options allow to define the desired behavior: For instance, activities bypassed by a forward jump may be caught up later on. As well, it is configurable whether activities that were already executed earlier, shall be repeated after a backward jump or whether their results (output data) shall be reused. Furthermore, it is discussed when and by whom such configuration options may be defined.

Keywords: Business process management · Workflow management · Run-time · Process engine · Flexibility · Jump · Process graph

1 Motivation

An advantage of process-aware information systems [1], compared to purely data- or function-oriented IT-systems, is that the process management system (PMS) ensures that the business process (BP) that was defined at build-time is really respected at run-time (process safety). Additionally, end users are unburdened from unnecessary tasks as searching for the required functions of the software (e.g. in a menu) or the data necessary for the current process instance. The PMS automatically starts the right function (e.g. a form) of the right application and uses the right input data. The restriction of the possible execution orders of process activities, however, also comes with disadvantages: In exceptional cases, it may not be allowed at run-time to execute the activities in a specific execution order despite it is necessary from the business perspective. This may result in disadvantages for the enterprise. In order to avoid such disadvantages, it must be possible to deviate from the modelled BP at run-time [1]. In the project CoPMoF (Controllable Pre-Modelled Flexibility) it is examined which types of deviations can

© Springer Nature Switzerland AG 2022
B. Shishkov (Ed.): BMSD 2022, LNBIP 453, pp. 35–53, 2022.
https://doi.org/10.1007/978-3-031-11510-3_3

be pre-modelled already at build-time in order to use them at run-time of the process instances. For the control-flow perspective of BP, several such topics were identified [2, 3]. This includes pre-modelling of optional activities (which may be not required in exceptional cases), alternative activities (which may be used in such cases), and process-graph-independent activities (which are necessary sometimes but not located at a specific position within the process graph). Pre-modelled flexibility is also necessary for other process perspectives. For instance, pre-modelling the possibility to modify a specific process variable dynamically (e.g. with a form) concerns the data perspective and alternative actor assignments the organizational perspective. A further topic, that belongs to the control-flow perspective, is pre-modelling of allowed dynamic jumps and configuring their intended behavior. We define a (dynamic) jump as follows: A user detects an exceptional situation, he decides (dynamically) that a jump becomes necessary, and he selects the target activity of the jump. Then, the process instance is continued at this activity. That means, an operation similar to a dynamic change [4] is performed, but only the execution states of the activity instances are changed but not the structure of the process instance. Completely arbitrary jumps, however, are not the goal of our approach in order to avoid errors and to guarantee process safety. Therefore, the process area where the jump may start from, its possible target activities, who is allowed to trigger the jump (e.g. the actor of the activity, an administrator), and the desired behavior of this jump (configuration options) are pre-modelled at build-time. Despite this pre-modelled information, the jump is a dynamic operation since the user has a high degree of freedom, e.g. he may select one of the possible target activities or change the configuration options. [2, 3, 5] introduce pre-modelled flexibility for many aspects of BP. Dynamic jumps were mentioned as well, but the requirements are described only at a very abstract and imprecise level. In the following, they are explained in detail, inclusive different types of run-time behavior (the configuration options), the interaction of multiple configuration options, and their behavior at several control flow structures as, for instance, parallelism (i.e. after an AND-Split).

Jumps within BP are very relevant in practice: Fig. 1 shows a simplified[1] change management process for vehicle parts. An arbitrary employee is allowed to request the change of a vehicle part (Act. A). This request is detailed (Act. B) and rated (Act. C) by a development engineer. Afterwards, ratings by other business domains are performed in parallel (Act. D): After-Sales (Act. D1), Production (Act. D2), Marketing (Act. D3), and Prototyping (Act. D4). Then the project leader decides (Act. E) whether this change shall be realized in Act. F. Assume the exceptional situation that a specific change is enforced by a new law. Then, the cost ratings in Act. C and D are irrelevant. After detailing the change in Act. B, the BP has to jump forward directly to the decision in Act. E. As another exceptional situation, assume that an actor detects during Act. D4 that errors were made at the detailing in Act. B. Then a backward jump becomes necessary in order to correct these errors. Despite forward and backward jumps are very relevant in practice, this topic is hardly respected in scientific publications and commercial PMS offer only very limited functions (cf. Sect. 2).

---

[1] In reality, this process is more complex and not only Act. D is composed of several single activities. For details see [3].

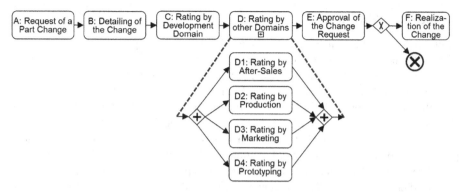

Fig. 1. Change Management Process (CMP) for Parts at Vehicle Development

One reason for this situation may be that the intended semantics of such a jump is not always obvious: At the example depicted in Fig. 2, a dynamic backward jump to Act. A shall be performed, before Act. E is started. Thereby, for the already finished Act. B of the parallel branch, it is not clear whether it has to be executed again (at the "forward execution" after completion of Act. A) or whether its originally created result data shall be used further on. The same applies to Act. D that is located in the same branch as the source activity (E) of the jump. Furthermore, it is not clear whether the execution of Act. C shall be continued or whether it shall be aborted when the jump is triggered. In principle, each kind of behavior may be desirable. Therefore, this paper presents many requirements, including possibilities to define the desired behavior of activities at and after a jump with so-called configuration options.

Fig. 2. Example for a Backward Jump Out of a Parallel Region

In Sect. 2, the current state of the art and the resulting research question are presented. Section 3 describes requirements concerning jumps, especially the different configuration options. These options are an important part of the presented requirements, since they determine the behavior of the process engine at runtime. Therefore, Sect. 4 discusses possibilities, when and by whom these configuration options may be defined. The paper closes with a summary and an outlook to future work.

2 State of the Art and Research Question

This section presents scientific work that concerns dynamic jumps in BP. In addition, at the example of products of the company IBM, respective functions of commercial PMS are explained. This builds the foundation to explain the research gap and to present the research question of this paper.

2.1 Scientific Literature

In principle, flexibility in BP is a well-elaborated research topic [1]. Dynamic jumps within BP, however, were hardly respected, but main research areas are variability within process templates, exception handling, dynamic structural changes, and rule-based approaches: [6] categorizes approaches for process variability. They have in common that different process variants of a process family are defined at build-time. The PMS automatically selects the required variant at run-time; i.e. dynamic interventions of an end user (e.g. trigger a jump to another activity) are not covered by such approaches. [7] presents patterns for exception handling in BP. At the corresponding approaches, an error is detected automatically by the PMS and a predefined recovery action (exception handler) is executed. Such actions include a rollback to a previous activity what is similar to a backward jump. However, there remains a main difference to jumps: the rollback is not triggered by a user and he cannot select the target activity when the jump is triggered; i.e. this is not an interactive user action at run-time as at dynamic jumps. [1, 4] present patterns for dynamic changes. However, these do not include jumps to other activities; i.e. the modification of the execution states of activity instances. Instead, structural changes of a process instance are performed; e.g. insertion of an additional activity. Approaches for dynamic (run-time) planning (e.g. [8]) allow to modify rules and data (the process context) what may result in a different execution order of the activities. This is a possibility to realize dynamic jumps. For users who know the process graph (e.g. because of a training for this BP), however, it may be more difficult (or even impossible) to perform a change in such a manner than to simply select the target activity for the desired jump. Therefore, rule- und constraint-based approaches are not considered in our work.

In the following, some work is discussed that is related to dynamic jumps. However, some of these papers only mention this topic or may only serve as a work-around to realize jumps. Literature that is more appropriate was not found[2] since, as already explained, dynamic jumps were hardly covered by the research concerning BP flexibility. This assumption is confirmed by the fact that such jumps were not mentioned at all in [9], a book that gives an overview on the whole topic of BP management.

[10] describes control-flow patterns, but does not explicitly mention dynamic jumps triggered by end users. However, this work describes the pattern "Arbitrary Cycles" that allows to model arbitrary forward and backward edges. They can be used as a basis to pre-model edges for jumps at build-time. The pattern, however, only describes the necessity of this construct but [10] does not describe variants for its desired behavior as the configuration options already mentioned in Sect. 1 (e.g. repeating an activity of a parallel branch that was completed already before the jump).

In [11], expectable jumps are pre-modelled at build-time. These jumps are mapped to regular building blocks of the ADEPT meta model to enable their execution at run-time. For this purpose, the process model of ADEPT is extended by priorities for activities and edges. Mapping jumps to building blocks of the ADEPT meta model requires graph transformations and results in a complex process graph. Configuration options for the

---

[2] A literature search was performed with the following words, each in combination with "jump": "business process", "workflow", and "process engine". Furthermore, a search was performed for "forward jump" and "backward jump" in combination with the word "process".

behavior of activities at jumps are not mentioned. Therefore, it is not possible to define, for instance, whether an activity shall be repeated after a backward jump. An advantage of this approach is that the correctness of the resulting process graph can be validated formally, i.e. its structural correctness can be ensured.

In [12], dynamic jumps are mentioned, but it presents no detailed requirements. An exception is the requirement that activities, that were skipped due to a forward jump, shall be caught up later on. Furthermore, this work allows to define whether this shall happen at any time or before a specific (succeeding) activity is started.

To summarize, research concerning BP flexibility typically does not consider dynamic jumps (but other relevant topics). Only a few and rather old publications explicitly handle jumps within a BP. None of them, however, discusses the configuration options and advanced requirements presented in the following.

2.2 Commercial PMS Products

Because of this lack of literature, we decided to analyze a commercial PMS. As explained, jumps are very relevant in practice. Therefore, jumps are offered by several commercial process engines. The available functionality is explained at the example of several generations of IBM PMS products. This product analysis demonstrates that this topic is not only hardly respected in scientific literature, but not solved in commercial products as well. For this purpose, products of the company IBM were analyzed, since IBM works in this area for decades and has developed several generations of process engines over time. Due to the continuous advances of these products, it is reasonable that the functionality of the current IBM product is at least similarly powerful than other products for BP execution.

At the product IBM FlowMark [13], it was not possible at all to jump to a different activity of the current process instance at run-time.

IBM WebSphere Process Server (WPS) [14] enables dynamic jumps since Version 6.1.2 (earlier versions do not support jumps). These jumps may be triggered by calling functions of the API or by using the tool BPC-Explorer. Forward and backward jumps are possible, but only within such process regions where only one single activity can be executed at the same time. The simplest possibility would be to allow jumps only within pure sequences. At WPS 6.1.2, however, IBM additionally enables jumps into and out of regions with XOR-Branches: To model such regions, the building block "Cyclic Flow" was introduced. Within a Cyclic Flow, it is possible to model arbitrary XOR-Splits with forward and backward edges, but no AND-Splits are allowed (i.e. no parallelism). This enables arbitrary dynamic jumps (forward and backward) to other activities of the same Cyclic Flow.

With the WPS Version 6.2, IBM introduced the building block "Generalized Flow". A Generalized Flow may contain exclusive splits as well as parallelism (realized with "Fork-Gateways"). Nevertheless, there still exists the restriction for dynamic jumps that jumps into or out of a parallel region are prohibited [14]. At run-time, the WPS automatically determines which activities are currently allowed as target for the jump. If the source activity of the jump is executed currently (state Running) it has to be aborted or completed before the jump, e.g. with the API functions skipAndJump() or forceCompleteAndJump() [14].

All versions of the succeeding product IBM Business Process Manager [15] as well as the newest product IBM Business Automation Workflow Version 21.0.2 [16] do not support jumps into or out of a region with parallel branches as well. This restriction is comprehensible since the intended behavior of such a jump is ambiguous (cf. the example of Fig. 2). To solve this problem, this paper proposes a step towards the development of the necessary foundations.

2.3 Research Question

As mentioned, there exist only a few publications that handle dynamic jumps. Commercial PMS offer only limited functions, probably because the expected behavior of some types of jumps is not clear, e.g. jumps into and out of parallel branches. Therefore, it is a risk to allow such jumps, since they may result in a behavior that was not expected by the users or even erroneous execution states (e.g. deadlocks). In order to reduce the described research gap, this paper handles the following research question: Which requirements (scenarios, use cases, variants) exist with respect to dynamic jumps in BP and which behavior shall be realized by a process engine in such cases? In order to define the behavior of an activity at a jump, configuration options for activities are introduced. These configuration options are explained in detail (incl. the resulting behavior at a jump) and it is discussed, when and by whom they may be defined.

3   Requirements for Jumps in Business Processes

This section presents requirements that concern dynamic jumps. Partially, the necessity of these requirements is explained at examples from practice. An ID is assigned to each requirement that indicates its category: Gx = General requirement, Fx = Forward jump, Bx = Backward jump, Ox = jump between branches of a (X)OR split, Px = jump into or out of a Parallelism, and Lx = jump within a Loop. To increase readability, at the end of this section, Table 1 summarizes all requirements and the corresponding configuration options.

3.1   Forward Jumps

Figure 3a shows a travel application process. The approval of the travel request happens in Act G. Journeys without prior approval are prohibited and the ratings and cost estimations (Act. B to Act. F) may take a long time. A travel application for a near-term appointment is an exceptional case, where a faster process execution is required. Then, a dynamic jump, starting at one of the activities B to F, directly to Act. G (approval) is triggered by a user. Otherwise, the very important appointment would be missed what may result in an economic loss.

In this example, a jump may start at many different source activities. In theory, as depicted in Fig. 3b, all possible jumps can be modelled as "normal edges" in the process graph. But this results in a very confusing process model. Therefore, for allowed dynamic jumps, a special edge type shall be offered (*Requirement G1*) that can be visualized differently, e.g. as gray arrow as in Fig. 3a. As depicted in this example as gray blocks, a

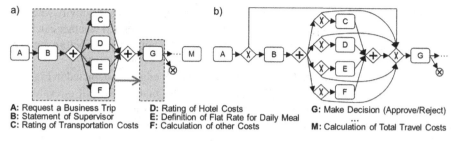

A: Request a Business Trip
B: Statement of Supervisor
C: Rating of Transportation Costs

D: Rating of Hotel Costs
E: Definition of Flat Rate for Daily Meal
F: Calculation of other Costs

G: Make Decision (Approve/Reject)
...
M: Calculation of Total Travel Costs

Fig. 3. Travel Application Process as Example for a Forward Jump

jump may have more than one potential source and/or target activity (*Requirement G2*), i.e. a whole process region. This is necessary to avoid the large number of "single" jump edges depicted in Fig. 3b. At a jump with several target activities, the user is allowed to select the intended one (*G3*). If the activities belong to parallel branches, the user shall be able to select one target activity at each branch, e.g. the activities E (or F), H (or I), and K in Fig. 5a (see Sect. 3.4). In order to reduce the effort for the end users, it shall be possible to pre-model default target activities for jumps (*G4*). Finally, the process designer shall be able to define who is allowed to trigger a specific jump (*G5*), e.g. the current actor of the source activity or the owner (administrator) of the process instance resp. process template.

The simplest case is that a forward jump happens before its source activity (i.e. the starting point of the jump) is started. With the configuration option CatchUpMode, it can be defined whether this source activity S shall be caught up later on (*Requirement F1*: CatchUpMode(S) = true) or whether it shall be omitted (CatchUpMode(S) = false). A dynamic jump shall be enabled as well, if the source activity was already started: For the case that catching up is desired (i.e. CatchUpMode(S) = true), the execution of this source activity continues (despite the jump). Otherwise (i.e. CatchUpMode(S) = false) the source activity S is aborted. Assume for the process of Fig. 3a that the supervisor has already started the execution of Act. B. Then he or she[3] detects that this trip is very urgent and triggers the depicted jump. With CatchUpMode(B) = false Act. B is aborted immediately and the process continues with Act. G. That means, the CatchUpMode is used to define whether the source activity of the jump shall be continued or omitted (and therefore aborted, if it is already running).

Also for the bypassed activities (between the source and the target activity of a forward jump) it can be defined whether they shall be caught up (*F2a*). Often these activities have to be omitted (CatchUpMode(X) = false) because this is the "normal intention" of a user when triggering a jump. It may be necessary, however, to execute missed activities later on (CatchUpMode(X) = true). At the example of Fig. 3a, for each activity that can be bypassed by the jump (Act. B to F) it has to be analyzed whether its output data is required in the further process execution. If this is the case, it must be caught up later on. For instance, it is necessary to catch up Act. E since its output data (the flat rate for the daily meal) is required by Act. M to calculate the total amount that

---

[3] In order to increase readability, in the following, only the male form will be used.

has to be paid to the employee.[4] At build-time it can be defined for each activity whether it shall be caught up after a jump (*F2a*). Furthermore, it can be defined whether catching up is allowed at an arbitrary point in time, or whether this must happen before a given activity (here: Act. M) resp. several given activities can be started (*F2b*).

To model jumps with XOR-Split gateways and normal edges, as depicted in Fig. 3b, is not a meaningful work-around: The condition of the first XOR-Split is evaluated directly after Act. A has completed. That means, jumping is no longer possible when Act. B is offered to the supervisor (i.e. is in his worklist) or even after he started this Act. B. Therefore, at run-time, this work-around results in a different behavior as intended for dynamic jumps. Furthermore, as already mentioned, it results in a confusing process diagram since it contains several additional gateways and edges. If the target region contains more than one activity, this situation becomes even worse since edges from each source to each target activity are required. But also the single additional arrow and the two blocks of Fig. 3a make the diagram more complicated. Therefore, a modelling tool shall be able to hide jump edges (*G6a*) and visualize such edges different from regular control-flow edges (*G6b*), e.g. as depicted in Fig. 3a as a thick gray arrow with multiple source resp. target activities marked as a region.

3.2 Backward Jumps

Assume for the process depicted in Fig. 4a that a user detects during the execution of Act. G that erroneous data were captured in Act. C. Therefore, he triggers a jump back to Act. C in order to repeat it. After the jump, the process is executed again (now with correct data) starting with Act. C. That means, the backward jump is followed by a "second forward execution". At build-time, it shall be possible to define how the original results (output data) of each activity are treated at this forward execution (*Requirement B1*). There exist the three variants described below. Again, it depends on the "meaning" (semantics) of an activity, which value for this configuration option RepeatMode is suited best:

1. RepeatMode(X) = Discard: The original results (created before the jump) are discarded and Act. X is executed again (normally) as at its original execution (*B1a*).
2. RepeatMode(X) = Control: Act. X is executed again, but the original data are preserved. At the later forward execution, for instance a form pre-filled with these original data is presented to the end user who performs this activity. He has to control these data and can correct it, if necessary (*B1b*).
3. RepeatMode(X) = Keep: The Act. X is not executed again, i.e. all output data of this activity stay unchanged (*B1c*).

At a backward jump starting at the source activity S, it may be meaningful to abort this Act. S or to continue its execution. The same applies to activities that succeed Act. S in the process graph. Such activities may be activated even later on, i.e. a user

---

[4] For all other types of costs, the amount that arose in fact, is paid to the employee. The ratings (Act. C, D, F) are only used to calculate the expected costs as basis for the decision in Act. G.

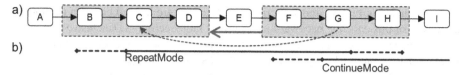

Fig. 4. a) Process Example with a Pre-Modelled Backward Jump b) Relevance of the Configuration Options for Activities at a Backward Jump from Act. G to Act. C

can start such an activity when its predecessor has completed. For instance, at the jump depicted in Fig. 4a, it may be meaningful to complete Act. G (the source activity of the jump) if its output data will not change because of the backward jump and the following forward execution. After completion of Act. G, the Act. H may be started despite this jump if it only depends on the (already correct and in future unchanged) output data of Act. G. Whether this applies, again, depends on the "meaning" of the concerned activities. The favored variant for an Act. X can be selected with the configuration option ContinueMode(X) at build-time (*B2*):

1. ContinueMode(X) = Abort (i.e. no Start and no Completion): Act. X shall be aborted (automatically) if it is currently executed, i.e. if it is in the state Running (*B2a*). For instance, it is meaningful to abort an Act. X if its results will be discarded anyway at the later forward execution because of the RepeatMode(X) = Discard (cf. *B1a*). It is wasted effort to complete (or even start) the execution of such an activity. Therefore, in this process branch no further activities will be started anymore.
2. ContinueMode(X) = Complete (i.e. no Start): An already started Act. X can be completed, but it must not be started if it is not running yet (*B2b*). Assume that the already started Act. G of Fig. 4a has the RepeatMode(G) = Control (cf. *B1b*). This activity can be completed in order to avoid the loss of already performed work, that perhaps can be kept at the forward execution due to its RepeatMode. If ContinueMode(H) = Complete is specified for the successive Act. H as well, it cannot be started after the completion of Act. G. This may be meaningful since, until now, Act. H was not started, i.e. no work is lost.
3. ContinueMode(X) = Start&Complete: With this ContinueMode, an Act. X can be even started after completion of its preceding activity (*B2c*). Now assume that this mode was assigned to Act. G and H of Fig. 4a. Then, after completion of Act. G (the source activity of the jump), Act. H can be executed as well. This is meaningful if the output data of Act. H are used later on, e.g. because of RepeatMode(H) = Keep (cf. *B1c*). Then, much time is available for the execution of these both activities, till the forward execution (after the backward jump) reaches this point in the process graph. This reduces the risk that this process instance causes a delay, that results from waiting for the completion of Act. H (due to its unnecessarily delayed start). The execution of this branch may continue until an Act. X with ContinueMode(X) = Abort or Complete is reached. This means for the example of Fig. 4a, that with ContinueMode(I) = Start&Complete the early execution of Act. I is allowed as well, despite it is located behind the source area of the jump.

As depicted in Fig. 4b, for the activities C to F that are located between the source activity G of this concrete backward jump and its target activity C (inclusive), only the RepeatMode is relevant.[5] For the source activity G and its successors, the ContinueMode is relevant additionally: First, the ContinueMode(X) of such an Act. X defines whether it may be completed or can even be started despite the jump. This "early execution" of the activity has the goal to save time. When, after the backward jump, the forward execution of the process has reached this Act. X, the RepeatMode(X) defines whether the created results shall be discarded, controlled, or kept (with the goal to save effort). In combination with RepeatMode(X) = Control all variants of ContinueMode(X) may be meaningful: The process designer can choose between a fast process execution (no delays caused by waiting at Start&Complete) and the safety that no further work will be performed that may be discarded later on (at Abort). Thereby, ContinueMode(X) = Complete is a compromise: Effort already spent to perform the activity may be saved, but no additional effort will be spent for activities that were not started yet (what would be a risk since it is possible that their output data will be discarded later on). At RepeatMode(X) = Keep the output data of Act. X are never discarded. In this case, ContinueMode(X) = Start&Complete can be selected without any risk of losing result data (but it may be not desirable for other reasons). The same applies to ContinueMode(X) = Complete, however, with a higher risk that this process instance will cause a delay. As already mentioned, in combination with RepeatMode(X) = Discard only ContinueMode(X) = Abort makes sense since the output data of this Act. X are always discarded later on.

At a backward jump, it is sometimes necessary to compensate (undo) an Act. X that was executed before the jump. This is defined with RepeatMode(X) = Compensate (*B3*). Assume an ordering process where a backward jump is performed to a target activity that is located in front of the Act. X "Send Order to Supplier". Then, Act. X has to be revoked resp. the supplier shall be informed that this order has to be adjourned. For this purpose, a "compensation activity" is modelled. In principle, it is a normal activity, with the difference that it is modelled especially for backward jumps. That means, it does not belong to the normal control-flow but is assigned to the original activity as compensation action. Except for this compensation, RepeatMode(X) = Compensate has the same behavior as RepeatMode(X) = Discard, i.e. the output data of the original execution of Act. X are not valid after the jump anymore.

3.3 Jumps into Another Conditional Branch

One of several modelled branches, that are located after an XOR-Split node, is executed. Normally, a predefined condition is used to select this branch. During process execution, it shall be possible to jump to a target activity that belongs to another XOR-Branch. For the pre-modelling of jumps at build-time, this case is already respected since *Requirement G2* does not restrict the source and target regions of a jump.

The resulting behavior of the process engine is the same as at forward and backward jumps described in the Sects. 3.1 and 3.2. The reason is that a jump from a source

---

[5] The RepeatMode may be relevant for Act. G, as well, if (intermediate) results were already saved before the jump. The dotted lines in Fig. 4b mark activities where the configuration options are relevant at other possible jumps concerning this source and target regions; e.g. RepeatMode is relevant for Act. H at a jump that starts at this (source) Act. H.

activity S to a target activity T, that belongs to a different XOR-Branch, can be mapped to a backward and a forward jump: A jump to another XOR-Branch is the same as a backward jump from Act. S to the XOR-Split node, followed by a forward jump to Act. T. The process engine may realize such jumps this way (*O1*). For an end user, however, it is not recognizable how that jump was realized by the process engine internally.

No further configuration options (in addition to CatchUpMode, RepeatMode, and ContinueMode) are required for such jumps. That means, no additional cases must be implemented by a process engine. When defining the configuration options for such a jump, typically the ContinueMode(S) = Abort will be used for the source activity S of the jump and all its succeeding activities. The reason is that process execution switches to a different XOR-Branch, with the result that the activities of the original branch will not be executed later on (at the forward execution). For the case that a second jump occurs, however, it is possible that these activities will be executed despite. Therefore, it shall not be prohibited to use ContinueMode(A) = Complete or even Start&Complete for these activities.

All this holds for jumps into an originally not selected branch of a (not exclusive) OR-Split as well. The difference is that there may exist further branches (in addition to the branches containing the source and the target activities of this jump) that are currently executed. Since these branches are not involved in this jump, they do not influence its behavior.

3.4 Jumps into and Out of Parallel Regions

At jumps into a parallel region and jumps out of such a region, several additional aspects have to be considered. Again, the source and the target regions of such jumps are pre-modelled at build-time (cf. Fig. 5). As described in Sect. 3.1, rights for users to trigger the jump etc. are defined additionally. That means, as for all types of jumps, the *Requirements G1 to G7* are relevant in combination with parallel regions as well.

At the process of Fig. 5a, for instance, Act. E and F for the upper, Act. H and I for the middle, and Act. K for the lower branch are possible target activities of the jump. The user who triggers this jump has to select one activity of each parallel branch as jump target (cf. *Requirement G3* in Sect. 3.1). As an alternative, a default jump target activity may be pre-modelled for each branch (*Requirement G4*).

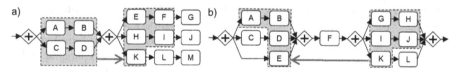

Fig. 5. a) Forward Jump and b) Backward Jump into and out of Parallel Branches

Forward Jumps and Parallel Branches: At the forward jump depicted in Fig. 5a, target activities are required for 3 branches. Assume that the user selects the activities E, I, and K for this purpose. The selection for the lower branch may be omitted since in this branch, Act K is the only possible target activity for the jump. Therefore, it is meaningful to define it as default target activity (G4), perhaps automatically by the process modelling tool.

To define whether an Act. X, that was bypassed by a forward jump, shall be caught up, the configuration option CatchUpMode(X) = true resp. false exists (F2, cf. Table 1). Additionally, CatchUpMode is relevant for activities of branches that are located in parallel to the source activity of the jump (Requirement P1). Assume for the process of Fig. 5a that the actor of Act. A triggers the jump (as described above to Act. E, I, and K). Also assume that the execution of Act. C was not started yet. Then, CatchUpMode defines for Act. C and Act. D, whether they shall be caught up, since they are located in a parallel branch of the source activity A of this jump. Also dependent on their CatchUpMode, the activities A and B (located in the branch of the source activity A) and Act. H (located before the target activity I) may be caught up. To catch up all these activities is necessary since the output data of an activity of a parallel branch (e.g. Act. D) or an activity in front of a jump target (e.g. Act. H) may be required as input for an activity that is executed after the jump (e.g. Act. I).

Backward Jumps and Parallel Branches: For a backward jump, again, one activity of each branch may be pre-modelled at build-time as default target activity. The user who triggers the jump may keep these defaults or may select different target activities. For a jump into a parallel region (this also applies to forward jumps), it can be pre-modelled, that it is allowed to select the end of a specific branch as jump target: The target activities of the jump depicted in Fig. 5b may be Act. B and D. Furthermore, for the lower branch, the jump target shall be located after Act. E; i.e. no activity of the branch shall be executed after the jump at all, but process execution directly continues in front of the AND-Join gateway. It shall be possible to define such an "end of the branch" as default jump target as well.

As described in Sect. 3.2, at a backward jump there exist several variants concerning the repeated execution of activities at forward execution (RepeatMode, *Requirement B1*). Now, RepeatMode is relevant for all activities of all parallel branches between the source and target activities of the backward jump (*Requirement P2* = Discard, Control, or Keep). Assume for the process of Fig. 5b that the actor of Act. G triggers the backward jump, Act. J and K are currently in execution, and the target activities are as described above (Act. A, Act. D, and after Act. E). Then, RepeatMode is relevant for the activities A, B, and D (of the jump target region), Act. F (located between the source and the target region), and Act. I (of the source region of the jump but in front of the currently executed Act. J). Depending on the value of the ContinueMode (see next paragraph) the RepeatMode may also be relevant for the activities G, H, J, K, and L if they are executed before the regular forward execution (that follows the jump) reaches these activities.

For the activities that succeed the source activities of the jump in the process graph, there exist three variants concerning their early execution after the jump (Continue-Mode, B2). Now, with parallel branches, these configuration options are also relevant for activities of parallel branches (P2). Assume, as described above for Fig. 5b, that the jump is triggered by the actor of Act. G while the activities J and K are currently executed as well. Then, with the ContinueMode(J) = Complete and ContinueMode(K) = Complete, it is possible to finish these already running activities despite the jump. With ContinueMode(L) = Start&Complete, it is even allowed to start the Act. L that is located in a branch parallel to the source activity G of the jump. This is meaningful, for instance, if the lower branch is not affected by the error that was the reason for the backward jump.

The CMP depicted in Fig. 1 is used to explain why all presented values for the configuration options RepeatMode and ContinueMode are meaningful in practice. This especially applies to jumps starting at a parallel branch since the other branches may be or may be not influenced by the reason that caused this jump. Assume that an error was made in Act B and it is detected during the execution of Act. D4. Therefore, a backward jump to Act. B is triggered with the source activity D4.

1. RepeatMode(D1) = Discard (*B1a*) is used for Act. D1 (Rating by After-Sales): The original output data of this activity are irrelevant (therefore discarded) because a changed part causes different purchase and installation costs at repair. Since it does not make sense to continue an activity and discard its results later on, ContinueMode(D1) = Abort (*B2a*) is used.
2. RepeatMode(D2) = Control (*B1b*) was selected for Act. D2 (Rating by Production): The results of Act. D2 are influenced only seldom by changed development data since the installation effort for a part stays unchanged if a better material (e.g. harder steel) is used. Therefore, the output data of Act. D2 have to be controlled and modified only seldom. Such a modification becomes necessary, for instance, if the changed part data results in a more difficult assembly procedure, for instance, because its size or shape was changed. Since the results of Act. D2 are retained often, the production clerk shall have the possibility to finish his already started work. Therefore, ContinueMode(D2) = Complete (*B2b*) is selected. Start&Complete (*B2c*) is not used since, as mentioned. there also exists the possibility that the results must be discarded later on.
3. RepeatMode(D3) = Keep (*B1c*) was specified for Act. D3 (Rating by Marketing): It is not necessary to execute this activity again (after the backward jump) since changed development details are not relevant for marketing. Therefore, it even makes sense to start the Act. D3 after the jump (early execution to save time) what results in the ContinueMode(D3) = Start&Complete (*B2c*).

The Variants 2. and 3. have the advantage that effort and time may be saved at the repeated execution of these activities.

3.5 Jumps Between Iterations of Loops

The requirements presented above already cover jumps within the same iteration of a loop since a "loop body" is composed of sequences, conditional branches, and parallel branches. Additionally, it may be necessary to jump forward into a future iteration or backwards into a previous iteration of a loop.

Forward Jumps: At a forward jump into the next iteration of a loop, it is possible that the remaining activities of the current iteration shall be skipped (CatchUpMode =

Table 1. Requirements for Pre-Modelled Jumps (Overview)

ID	Description of the Requirement and Values of the Configuration Options
General:	
G1	Special edge type offered for jump edges
G2	Multiple source and multiple target activities can be pre-modelled for a jump
G3	The target activities of a jump can be selected at run-time
G4	One default target activity can be pre-modelled for each parallel branch
G5	It can be defined which users are allowed to trigger a specific jump
G6	G6a The modelling tool is able to hide jump edges G6b Different visualizations are supported for control-flow edges and jump edges
G7	Different methods are offered to define values for configuration options G7a For each type of configuration option a default value is defined by the PMS tool G7b The value can be defined at build-time for each activity, different values are allowed for different pre-modelled jumps concerning the same activity G7c The value of a configuration option of an activity can be modified at run-time
Forward Jumps:	
F1	It can be defined whether the source activity S of a jump shall be caught up later on CatchUpMode(S) = true: yes CatchUpMode(S) = false: no (the Act. S is aborted if it is currently executed)
F2	F2a Shall the activities between the source and the target activity be caught up later on CatchUpMode(X) = true: yes CatchUpMode(X) = false: no F2b Catching up must occur before another given activity can be started
Backward Jumps:	
B1	Handling of the original results of an Act. X located between the source activity and the target activity of a backward jump B1a RepeatMode(X) = Discard: the output data of Act. X are discarded B1b RepeatMode(X) = Control: the output data are kept, but must be controlled during the forward execution later on B1c RepeatMode(X) = Keep: the output data are kept (Act. X is not executed again)
B2	Early execution of an Act. X located after the source activity of a backward jump B2a ContinueMode(X) = Abort: Act. X is aborted (completion or start are not possible) B2b ContinueMode(X) = Complete: a running Act. X can be completed but it is not possible to start it B2c ContinueMode(X) = Start&Complete: starting and completion of Act. X are allowed

(continued)

Table 1. (*continued*)

ID	Description of the Requirement and Values of the Configuration Options
B3	RepeatMode(X) = Compensate: compensation of an Act. X located between the source and the target activity of the backward jump (later on: completely new execution)
Jumps to other Conditional Branches (XOR resp. OR):	
O1	It shall be possible to pre-model jumps to other conditional branches
Jumps into and out of Parallel Regions:	
P1	Forward jumps: the CatchUpMode (catching up skipped activities, cf. F2) can be defined for activities located in branches parallel to the source activity of the jump as well
P2	Backward jumps: RepeatMode (keeping results, cf. B1 and B3) and ContinueMode (early execution, cf. B2) can be defined for activities located in parallel branches as well
Jumps between Iterations of Loops:	
L1	A forward jump to an arbitrary activity of the next iteration of a loop is possible
L2	A backward jump to an arbitrary activity of an arbitrary earlier loop iteration is possible

false): For instance, at a treatment cycle of a patient the current course of a chemotherapy shall be aborted since unexpected complications occurred. Instead, the treatment shall be continued with the next course later on. This requires a forward jump to the first activity of the next loop iteration.

It is also possible that activities shall be caught up after a forward jump (CatchUp-Mode = true): At a development process, several iterations of a loop are executed in order to improve vehicle parts. For each iteration, a specific quality level is defined as a goal that shall be reached. The loop consists of one parallel branch for each part. Each branch contains a development activity that is finished when the part reaches the quality level assigned to this iteration. Assume that, at the current iteration, only some parts have reached the given quality level (i.e. development is completed). Due to lack of time, the project leader decides to jump to the next iteration of the loop. This allows to continue development of the already completed parts (of the last iteration). For the other parts, however, the quality level assigned to the last iteration is not reached yet. In order to reach this level, the activities of the last iteration must be caught up (i.e. they are not aborted, but continued).That means, also catching up bypassed activities can be necessary at forward jumps to the next iteration, i.e. the CatchUpMode (cf. Table 1) is relevant for loops as well.

We have found no good examples for jumping forward two or more iterations (i.e. to the iteration after the next one). Therefore, we assume that this is hardly relevant in practice. If such a forward jump is required despite, it may be realized with several forward jumps, each to the next iteration. Therefore, *Requirement L1* only demands that a forward jump must be possible to an arbitrary activity of the next iteration of a loop.

Backward Jumps: Jumps to a previous iteration of a loop are necessary as well, for instance when an error was made at an activity execution of this iteration. Normally, a history (log) of the process instance is used to store all its activity instances. Therefore, the user has the possibility to select the concerned activity instance from this list and to trigger a backward jump to this target. Since it is possible that the error occurred at any time in the past, a backward jump to an arbitrary iteration of a loop must be allowed (Requirement L2). Thereby, as always at backward jumps, RepeatMode(X) defines whether an Act. X is repeated at the subsequent forward execution. ContinueMode(X) defines whether an early execution of an Act. X (of the current and future loop iterations) is allowed in order to save time.

4   Alternatives for the Definition of Configuration Options

We have developed several configuration options that used to influence the process behavior at jumps. At run-time, it is necessary that the process engine knows the corresponding values to realize the desired behavior. That means, these values have to be defined at least when a dynamic jump is triggered resp. the concerned activities shall be executed. Of course, it is possible to define these values earlier. The following alternatives describe when and by whom the configuration options may be defined:

- For each type of configuration option, a standard value shall be defined by the manufacturer of the PMS (*Requirement G7a*). Since these values define the "normal behavior" at jumps, these values shall result in the same behavior as at a "classic PMS" without advanced jumps (i.e. without configuration options, cf. the IBM products presented in Sect. 2). That means, for all activities X of a process template, skipped activities will not be caught up at forward jumps (CatchUpMode(X) = false). At backward jumps, the old results are discarded (RepeatMode(X) = Discard) and currently running activities are aborted (ContinueMode(X) = Abort).
- During BP development, the process designer shall have the possibility to overwrite the default values of the configuration options (*G7b*). The process designer typically has a deep understanding of the meaning of the BP and the intended behavior of the pre-modelled jumps. Furthermore, such persons have comprehensive BP skills and are able to understand the consequences of the configuration options. Therefore, they are capable to configure the behavior of a pre-modelled jump.
- As an extension of this requirement, it shall be possible to define different values for a configuration option of the same Act. X, which are valid for different pre-modelled jumps. This is necessary if multiple jumps (e.g. with different target regions) are pre-modelled that concern Act. X. Assume for a backward jump, that ContinueMode(X) = Start&Complete is used because this jump does not influence the results of Act. X (early execution does make sense since the output data will always be reused). However, for another pre-modelled jump to an other XOR-Branch, ContinueMode(X) = Abort is used because the original XOR-Branch and its Act. X will not be executed

in future once again (early execution of Act. X does not make sense since its output data will be discarded).

- It shall be possible to modify the value of configuration options at run-time (*G7c*). Assume a source activity S that belongs to an XOR-Branch and a backward jump to a target activity located in front of the XOR-Split. If the user knows that a different branch will be used at forward execution for this special process instance, he can change the predefined ContinueMode(S) = Start&Complete to ContinueMode(S) = Abort. This value was not chosen already at build-time, since only when triggering the jump, the user may know that the originally used XOR-Branch will not be selected again and that the output data of Act. X will be discarded. Often "normal end users" do not have such detailed knowledge of the BP. Thus, modifications of a configuration option at run-time normally will be performed by a BP administrator or an especially knowledged user.

  The configuration options RepeatMode(X) and ContinueMode(X) may be modified at run-time as well. It may not be meaningful to do this (already) when the backward jump is triggered, but only when the forward execution reaches this Act. X. At this later point in time, more information is available to the user, e.g. he may know that the repeated activities extensively changed the process data. Therefore, it is also allowed to change a configuration option at any time after a jump, if the user has sufficient rights to do this.

Normally, the presented possibilities will be used in combination: The PMS product defines default values for all configuration options (*G7a*). The process designer may overwrite these defaults with values that match better to the requirements of the specific BP and activity for this pre-modelled jump (*G7b*). These predefined values for the configuration options are used normally. Only in exceptional cases, they may not be appropriate and an especially skilled user can modify these values at run-time (*G7c*), perhaps only for some of the activities concerned by the jump.

5   Summary and Outlook

Dynamic jumps, triggered by users at run-time, are important to react appropriately to exceptional cases in BP. For instance, it is necessary to jump forward within a BP in order to save time by skipping activities. Backward jumps are required to correct errors that were made in previous process steps. To keep process safety, arbitrary jumps shall be prevented. Instead, the presented approach allows to pre-model expectable jumps at build-time, i.e. its potential source and target activities, user rights for triggering this jump, etc. Additionally, it becomes possible to define what shall happen with the activities that are concerned by this jump. Therefore, configuration options for pre-modelled jumps were presented. They allow to specify, for instance, whether activities that are bypassed by a forward jump shall be caught up later on, e.g. since their output data are required by succeeding activities. At backward jumps, configuration options determine whether the results of an already executed activity shall be kept and reused at the subsequent forward execution. Similarly, it is possible to define whether an early execution of activities is allowed, in order to reduce the total execution time of the BP instance.

This paper presents comprehensive requirements for pre-modelling jumps and explains their necessity with examples from practice. This includes jumps that concern conditional branches, parallel branches, and loops. For all of these types of jumps and additionally in combination with the configuration options, the intended behavior of the process instance was explained (informally). As a next step, a formal execution semantics for such jumps will be developed. Compared to the execution rules described for instance in BPMN 2.0 [17] or [12] additional rules are required, e.g. to catch up skipped activities. These extensions will build the foundation for a prototypical implementation of a PMS that supports advanced jumps at run-time. The long-term goal, however, is that commercial PMS will enable such jumps as well.

As further future work, usability of the presented approach for process designers and end users has to be evaluated. This may be realized based on the (prototypical) PMS implementation mentioned above. One goal will be to evaluate whether the presented concepts and configuration options can be handled by the users, are really useful, and powerful enough. In addition, the usability of different user interaction concepts for pre-modelling and for triggering jumps shall be compared. For instance, jump target(s) may be simply selected within a list of activities, or they may be marked in a graphical visualization of the process instance. As described in [18], such a process visualization can be generated automatically in a manner that the resulting process graph fits to this specific jump, i.e. only that part of the process is depicted that is relevant to trigger this jump.

References

1. Reichert, M., Weber, B.: Enabling Flexibility in Process-Aware Information Systems. Challenges, Methods, Technologies. Springer (2012)
2. Bauer, T.: Business processes with pre-designed flexibility for the control-flow. In: Proc. 22nd Int. Conf. on Enterprise Information Systems, pp. 631–642 (2020)
3. Bauer, T.: Pre-modelled Flexibility for the Control-Flow of Business Processes: Requirements and Interaction with Users. In: Filipe, J., Śmiałek, M., Brodsky, A., Hammoudi, S. (eds.) ICEIS 2020. LNBIP, vol. 417, pp. 833–857. Springer, Cham (2021). https://doi.org/10.1007/978-3-030-75418-1_38
4. Weber, B., Reichert, M., Rinderle-Ma, S.: Change patterns and change support features - enhancing flexibility in process-aware information systems. Data and Knowledge Engineering 66, 438–466 (2008)
5. Bauer, T.: Pre-modelled flexibility for business processes. In: Proc. 21th Int. Conf. on Enterprise Information Systems, pp. 547–555 (2019)
6. La Rosa, M., van der Aalst, W., Dumas, M., Milani, F.P.: Business process variability modeling: a survey. ACM Comput. Surv. 50, 1–45 (2018)
7. Russell, N., Aalst, W. van der, Hofstede, A. ter.: Exception handling patterns in process-aware information systems. In: Proc. Int. Conf. on Advanced Information Systems Engineering, pp. 288–302 (2006)
8. Vasilecas, O., Kalibatiene, D., Lavbič, D.: Rule- and context-based dynamic business process modelling and simulation. J. Syst. Softw. 122, 1–15 (2016)
9. Weske, M.: Business Process Management - Concepts, Languages. Springer, Architectures (2007)
10. Russell, N., Hofstede, A. ter: Workflow Control-Flow Patterns. A Revised View. BPM Center Report BPM-06-22 (2006)

11. Reichert, M., Dadam, P., Bauer, T.: Dealing with forward and backward jumps in workflow management systems. Softw. Syst. Model. **2**, 37–58 (2003)
12. Reichert, M., Dadam, P.: ADEPTflex - supporting dynamic changes of workflows without losing control. J. Intell. Info. Sys. Speci. Issue Workf. Manage. Sys. **10**, 93–129 (1998)
13. IBM: FlowMark - Programming Guide, Version 2 Release 2, Document Number. SH19–8240–01 (1996)
14. IBM: WebSphere Process Server Knowledge Center. https://www.ibm.com/support/knowle dgecenter/SSQH9M_7.0.0. Last accessed 15 July 2018
15. IBM: Business Process Manager V8.6.0 Documentation. https://www.ibm.com/support/kno wledgecenter/en/SSFPJS_8.6.0. Last accessed 16 Feb 2022
16. IBM: IBM Business Automation Workflow 20.x and 21.x. https://www.ibm.com/docs/en/ baw/20.x. Last accessed 16 Feb 2022
17. Object Management Group: Business Process Model and Notation (BPMN) 2.0. http://www. omg.org/spec/BPMN/2.0 (2011)
18. Reichert, M., Kolb, J., Bobrik, R., Bauer, T.: Enabling personalized visualization of large business processes through parameterizable views. In: Proc. 27th Symposium On Applied Computing, pp. 1653–1660 (2012)

Results from the Verification of Models of Spectrum Auctions

Elaheh Ordoni[✉], Jutta Mülle, and Klemens Böhm

Institute for Program Structures and Data Organization,
Karlsruhe Institute of Technology (KIT), 76131 Karlsruhe, Germany
{elaheh.ordoni,jutta.muelle,klemens.boehm}@kit.edu

Abstract. The revenue gained by spectrum auctions has been an essential source of governmental income. Even though numerous studies have been conducted in auction literature, many catastrophic results occurred in the real world. In this paper, we demonstrate how one can use verification techniques to improve the design of spectrum auctions, i.e., to prevent the unexpected outcomes to happen. To do so, we model the spectrum auction in BPMN and verify certain properties of the auction model. To do so, we assign different *capacity points* to the bidders and check how it affects the revenue. A capacity point defines the maximum number of products that a bidder can win. Our study reveals which assignment of capacity points to the bidders leads to the worst auctioneer's revenue.

1 Introduction

Spectrum auction revenue is a significant source of governmental income. Germany and the U.K., for example, have earned respectively 50.8 and 37.5 billion Euros in 2000 [7]. Although auctions should be designed so that undesirable outcomes do not occur, catastrophic results have happened in several cases. In the Netherlands, a political fiasco occurred in 2000 because of the low revenue of the Dutch UMTS auction [27]. In another example in the U.S., an auction policy that raised bid prices caused a loss of 30 MHz for a decade. This flaw cost around 70 billion dollars [13]. In yet another case [2], about half of the products were left out.

Literature offers two possible ways of studying auctions: (a) experimental analyses performed in laboratories with human subjects [14], and (b) theoretical analyses. Finding undesirable outcomes with either technique continues to be challenging: When it comes to (a), laboratories perform relatively few experiments. To illustrate, to investigate all experimental designs in [4], over 13 million experiments would be necessary. No institution would be able to accommodate such a setup. In (b), researchers use auction theory to predict equilibria, relying on assumptions regarding bidding behavior [26]. In general, rational behavior of bidders is part of the assumptions [17]. But this assumption is not always

© Springer Nature Switzerland AG 2022
B. Shishkov (Ed.): BMSD 2022, LNBIP 453, pp. 54–68, 2022.
https://doi.org/10.1007/978-3-031-11510-3_4

valid [15]. In spite of developing frameworks for truthful bidding under interference constraints [8], bidders can still be irrational. In consequence, design errors that go unnoticed can lead to catastrophic auction results.

To detect such cases, verification techniques can be applied before executing the auctions, i.e., one can detect unexpected outcomes before they actually happen. Authors in [24], for example, have proposed a Petri-Net-based approach to verify data-value-aware process models. In such processes, values of data objects such as the price of products play an important role, and process elements can modify these values while the process is executed. Our approach allows verifying certain properties of spectrum auctions. For example, one can derive the value of the lowest *auctioneer's revenue*, i.e., the sum of the final prices of the products. The evaluation in [24] only covers one setting, i.e., selling two products to three bidders with fixed auction parameters. So this study alone does not provide much information to auction designers.

In this paper, we report on the results of a systematic analysis of a real-world application, the German 4G spectrum auction, to sell one of the most valuable bandwidths, the 800 MHz band [5]. This auction has had four bidders and has sold six products. More specifically, we study the effect of so-called *capacity points* in this auction. A capacity point is the maximum number of licenses that a bidder can win. This parameter prevents bidders from winning too many items. With this feature, an auction designer can guarantee a certain number of bidders being awarded a good and prevent bidders from forming a monopoly. Our study focuses on capacity points for two reasons: (1) The capacity points assigned to each bidder influence the revenue of the auctioneer. (2) In contrast to other parameters like the budgets of the bidders, the auctioneer controls the value of capacity points. In other words, he or she can change their number. We study the impact of capacity points by systematically distributing different capacities among the bidders and assigning a random budget according to [4]. Studying all such distributions in combination with all different budgets that are possible is future work. In particular, we consider the following research questions:

1. Which assignments of capacity points lead to the lowest and the highest revenue of the auctioneer?
2. With a certain allocation of the capacity points, how often the lowest revenue can happen for the auctioneer?
3. Does increasing capacity points always increase the revenue?
4. What is the best assignment of capacity points to the bidders, i.e., making the worst revenue possible not too low?
5. Does changing the capacity point of a single bidder always change the auction's outcome?

To verify properties of the process model of a spectrum auction, we make use of a Petri-Net based verification technique developed in [24]. We come up with a rigorous formulation of the above questions, referred to as properties in what follows, as CTL formulas [6]. To do so, we have verified more than 2 million properties. Our findings are interesting: Varying the capacity points does not always affect the revenue. More specifically, varying the capacity points of some bidders does not have any impact on the lowest revenue, whereas varying the points of other bidders dramatically changes the results. Our method allows identifying bidders whose capacity points have a significant impact on the lowest revenue, as well as the corresponding allocation of capacity points that leads to this outcome. Next, we have observed a trade-off between the 'extent of monopolism' vs. the 'expected revenue' which the allocation of capacity points may influence. This might help the auctioneer to assign capacities in line with his/her objectives.

Paper Outline: Section 2 explains SMR spectrum auctions. Section 3 features our approach. Section 4 discusses the evaluation. Section 5 covers related work and Sect. 6 concludes.

2   Simultaneous Multi-round (SMR) Auctions

For more than two decades, simultaneous multi-round (SMR) auctions have been the standard format for allocating spectrum licenses to bidders [22]. This auction type allows the sale of several products, i.e., spectrum licenses. A respective auction typically consists of several rounds of bidding. Before the auction starts, the auctioneer specifies the lowest acceptable price for each product, referred to as a *reserve price*. Bidders may bid simultaneously on zero, one, or multiple products in each round. In the type of auction we analyze here, each bidder has a separate budget for each product. This budget is a reasonable reflection of the bidder's valuation of the individual product. Thus, bidders are not able to use any leftover budget for a different product. Next, bidders do not issue combined bids on different products, unlike combinatorial auctions, in which they can bid on bundles of products. Additionally, there is a so-called *capacity rule* [18]: Each bidder has a *capacity*, the maximum number of products he or she may win. In the round following the previous one, the highest bid for each product will become the reserve price. This bid is made known to all bidders, but not the other bids. Bidders also do not know the bids their competitors are issuing in the current round. Bidding for a particular product ends when no new bids are submitted in a round. The winner of a product is the bidder with the highest standing bid.

3   Our Approach

We collect a dataset describing the different outcomes of a spectrum auction in order to answer the research questions. We obtain this dataset by verifying the respective model of the spectrum auction. In the following, we describe the verification approach used. We do so because the specifics of what we can verify (both on a functional and on a non-functional level) rely on it. Figure 1 serves as an overview. (1) We model the SMR auction in BPMN notation [23]. BPMN is a suitable language for the description of spectrum auction models in a visual way and allows the subsequent analysis using the existing verification techniques.

(2) We transform the SMR process model into Petri Nets. We use plain Petri Nets as a target for the mapping because of the availability of efficient analysis techniques [1]. (3) Given the resulting Petri Nets, one must specify properties of SMR auction in a formal language such as Computation Tree Logic (CTL) for verification. (4) In the final step, Activity *model checking* verifies the properties against the resulting Petri Nets and outputs the verification results.

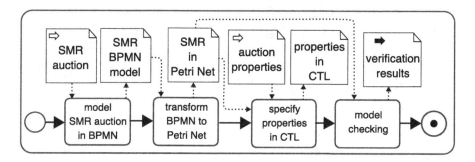

Fig. 1. Overview of verification procedure

3.1 SMR Auction in BPMN Model

In Fig. 2, we show a simplified version of an SMR auction in BPMN notation. The complete BPMN model is also available[1]. Observe that the model does not specify a certain bidding behavior. To do so, we issue a random bid that falls between the current price of a product and the budget of the qualified bidders. Doing without such an assumption is in some contrast to auction theory, which tends to focus on rational bidders, even though this kind of behavior is not guaranteed. We consider all possible valid bids to derive extreme outcomes of an auction, including the lowest prices that are possible. The BPMN model has three subprocesses. (1) The first subprocess examines whether a bidder can afford further products he or she has not won yet (*availability of bidders*). The auction continues with Subprocess *bidding of each bidder*. (2) Activity *place bid* issues a random bid. If a bidder has both budget and capacity left to acquire the product, he or she will always submit a bid. Activity *decrease capacity* reduces the bidder's capacity right after having won a product. Activity *remove bid* removes bids from bidders who have no capacity left. (3) Subprocess *winner determination* determines the new reserve prices and the winners. Until no more bids are submitted, these three subprocesses are repeated. Note that changing the parameter values (e.g., capacity points), but leaving the BPMN structure unchanged, gives us a different auction process model in our terminology.

---

[1] https://doi.org/10.5445/IR/1000143697.

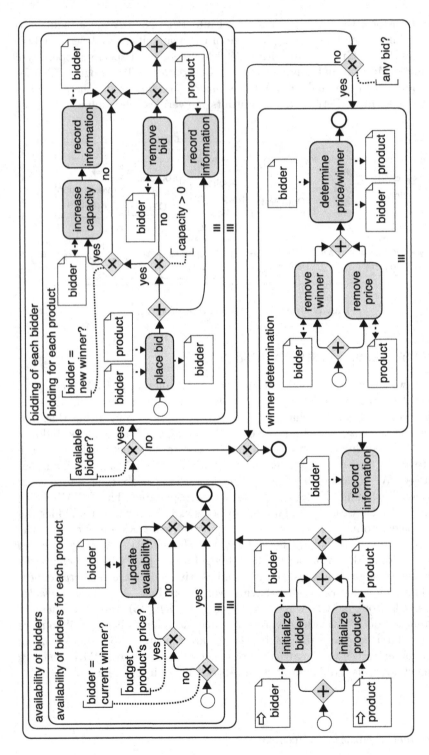

Fig. 2. Simplified process model of an SMR auction in BPMN notation.

3.2   SMR Process Model to Petri Nets

We use an existing verification framework [24], to verify properties of the SMR auction. It transforms the BPMN model of the auction into a Petri net. We use plain Petri Nets, in contrast to, say, colored Petri Nets, as the target of the mapping. This is because efficient analysis techniques are available [19]. Another reason is that plain Petri nets provide counterexamples when they verify a property. This makes it relatively easy for the designer of the model to detect where the unintended behavior of the process occurs and to fix it as necessary. To illustrate, think of spectrum auctions. When the model checker finds a path leading to the lowest revenue, this helps the auction designer with that chore.

3.3   Specification of Properties

The result of the transformation just described is a Petri Net representing the semantics of the use of data values in the process. To verify a spectrum auction, one must specify properties in a formal language such as Computation Tree Logic (CTL) [6]. In the following, we show how such properties referring to data values can be defined in CTL.

Definition 1 *(Data Property [24]).* *A Data Property ϕ is a CTL formula in which an atomic formula refers to either an activity/event, or a data value in a process model.*

Example 1. The data property for the question: "Can *product*.2 have a *price* of 2 at the end of the auction?" is:

$$EF(product.1.price.2 \wedge e.end).$$

In this formula, "*product*.2.*price*.2" is the "price" of 2 for "product.2". The atomic formula "*e.end*" is an end event, i.e., represents the end of the process.

To detect the lowest revenue of the auctioneer, we first find the lowest final *price* of *products*, starting with the reserve prices, using the property in Example 1. In case this property is not satisfied, we now verify a new property with an increased price. We continue increasing prices until there is a state that fulfills the property. Next, we detect the winner who won a product at a certain price. To do so, for each bidder who has a budget equal to or higher than the final price of the product, we check whether they can be the winner.

Example 2. Suppose that the lowest price for *product*.1 is 4, and the budget of *bidder*.1 is higher than 4. Then the property to check is:

$$EF(p.product.1.price.4 \wedge product.1.bidder.1 \wedge e.end).$$

In this property, "p.product.1.price.4" fixes the price for *product*.1 to 4, and "product.1.bidder.1" expresses that *product*.1 belongs to *bidder*.1, i.e., *bidder*.1 wins this product.

If the model checker can find a state, i.e., an execution path fulfilling the property, we record the bidder whose budget is sufficient as the winner of the product and continue to check whether other bidders can be the winner as well. In case two bidders (e.g., *bidder*.1 and *bidder*.2) are the potential winners for a certain product, we continue with both cases. The first case is to fix *bidder*.1 as the winner, decrease his/her capacity points and verify the price of other products, i.e., to check whether the other products can be sold for a certain price. The second case is to identify *bidder*.2 as the winner, decrease her/his capacity point, and continue verifying the other products.

4   Evaluation

In the following, we describe the auction parameters used in the process models to be verified, Sect. 4.1. In Sect. 4.2, we first report on characteristics of the verification procedure itself and then describe the dataset obtained that we will then use to answer those research questions. Using the obtained dataset results, we address the research questions listed in Sect. 1; see Sect. 4.3.

4.1   Evaluation Setting

The SMR auction model evaluated here consists of 4 bidders and 6 products. This is exactly in line with the German 4G spectrum auction to allocate licenses belonging to the 800 MHz band. Having four different bidders in the auction results in $3^4 = 81$ different assignments of capacity points. Each assignment results in a different process model. However, assignments where the sum of capacity points is less than 6 cannot happen. This is because the number of products to be auctioned off is 6, so the sum of capacity points must be at least 6 to sell all of them. After reducing such assignments, we get 76 pairwise different process models, i.e., bidders have different capacity points. Table 1 lists the capacity points of the bidders in each process model. At first, we keep the capacity points of *Bidder*.1 at 1 and vary the capacity points of the other bidders (Processes 1 to 22). In order to do this, we keep the capacity points of *bidder*.2 at 1, and we vary the capacities of *bidder*.3 and *bidder*.4 (Processes 1 to 6). Therefore, we keep the 's capacity points of *bidder*.3 at 1 and change the ones of bidder.4 from 1 to 3. The capacity points of 2 and 3 are distributed the same among the bidders. To each bidder we have assigned a random budget for a certain product in the range of [2..10], similarly to [4].

4.2   Verification of Properties

The number of properties to be verified in each process model varies between 24,844 and 29,880. Namely, verifying the price of a certain product might be fast, i.e., without having to verify many properties. For example, when the lowest final price is 2, the higher prices do not need to be verified. However, when the bidders have higher budgets and enough capacity points left, the competition is harder

Table 1. The distribution of capacity points in each process model

process model	capacities	process model	capacities	process model	capacities
Process 1	$[1, 1, 1, 3]$	Process 27	$[2, 1, 2, 2]$	Process 53	$[3, 1, 2, 1]$
Process 2	$[1, 1, 2, 2]$	Process 28	$[2, 1, 2, 3]$	Process 54	$[3, 1, 2, 2]$
Process 3	$[1, 1, 2, 3]$	Process 29	$[2, 1, 3, 1]$	Process 55	$[3, 1, 2, 3]$
Process 4	$[1, 1, 3, 1]$	Process 30	$[2, 1, 3, 2]$	Process 56	$[3, 1, 3, 1]$
Process 5	$[1, 1, 3, 2]$	Process 31	$[2, 1, 3, 3]$	Process 57	$[3, 1, 3, 2]$
Process 6	$[1, 1, 3, 3]$	Process 32	$[2, 2, 1, 1]$	Process 58	$[3, 1, 3, 3]$
Process 7	$[1, 2, 1, 2]$	Process 33	$[2, 2, 1, 2]$	Process 59	$[3, 2, 1, 1]$
Process 8	$[1, 2, 1, 3]$	Process 34	$[2, 2, 1, 3]$	Process 60	$[3, 2, 1, 2]$
Process 9	$[1, 2, 2, 1]$	Process 35	$[2, 2, 2, 1]$	Process 61	$[3, 2, 1, 3]$
Process 10	$[1, 2, 2, 2]$	Process 36	$[2, 2, 2, 2]$	Process 62	$[3, 2, 2, 1]$
Process 11	$[1, 2, 2, 3]$	Process 37	$[2, 2, 2, 3]$	Process 63	$[3, 2, 2, 2]$
Process 12	$[1, 2, 3, 1]$	Process 38	$[2, 2, 3, 1]$	Process 64	$[3, 2, 2, 3]$
Process 13	$[1, 2, 3, 2]$	Process 39	$[2, 2, 3, 2]$	Process 65	$[3, 2, 3, 1]$
Process 14	$[1, 2, 3, 3]$	Process 40	$[2, 2, 3, 3]$	Process 66	$[3, 2, 3, 2]$
Process 15	$[1, 3, 1, 1]$	Process 41	$[2, 3, 1, 1]$	Process 67	$[3, 2, 3, 3]$
Process 16	$[1, 3, 2, 1]$	Process 42	$[2, 3, 1, 2]$	Process 68	$[3, 3, 1, 1]$
Process 17	$[1, 3, 1, 3]$	Process 43	$[2, 3, 1, 3]$	Process 69	$[3, 3, 1, 2]$
Process 18	$[1, 3, 2, 1]$	Process 44	$[2, 3, 2, 1]$	Process 70	$[3, 3, 1, 3]$
Process 19	$[1, 3, 2, 2]$	Process 45	$[2, 3, 2, 2]$	Process 71	$[3, 3, 2, 1]$
Process 20	$[1, 3, 2, 3]$	Process 46	$[2, 3, 2, 3]$	Process 72	$[3, 3, 2, 2]$
Process 21	$[1, 3, 3, 1]$	Process 47	$[2, 3, 3, 1]$	Process 73	$[3, 3, 2, 3]$
Process 22	$[1, 3, 3, 2]$	Process 48	$[2, 3, 3, 2]$	Process 74	$[3, 3, 3, 1]$
Process 23	$[2, 1, 1, 2]$	Process 49	$[2, 3, 3, 3]$	Process 75	$[3, 3, 3, 2]$
Process 24	$[2, 1, 2, 1]$	Process 50	$[3, 1, 1, 1]$	Process 76	$[3, 3, 3, 3]$
Process 25	$[2, 1, 2, 2]$	Process 51	$[3, 1, 1, 2]$		
Process 26	$[2, 1, 2, 3]$	Process 52	$[3, 1, 1, 3]$		

between bidders, i.e., the product is not sold for a low price, and one must verify more properties to identify the final lowest prices. Figure 3 graphs the number of properties verified in each process model. In Process 76, for example, we have verified 29,880 properties.

In the process models on the right side of the figure, the sum of capacity points tends to be higher than on the left side. This means that more properties on process models in which the sum of capacity points is higher need to be verified, See Fig. 4. Observe that the distribution of capacity points among bidders matters as well. In Process 50, for example, Bidder 1 has a capacity of 3, and the other bidders each have a capacity of 1. Since the first bidder has a high budget for the products and the other bidders have few capacity points left, this

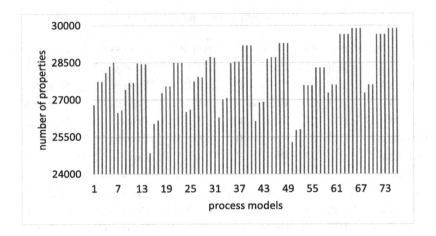

Fig. 3. Number of properties verified in each process model

process model requires fewer properties to be verified. In total, we have verified 2,129,637 properties. The longest verification time required to verify properties in each process model varies between 6 to 14 s. In particular, it makes a big difference for verification time if a bidder still has capacity left or not. In the second case, verification turns out to be false very quickly. The average time to verify properties is about 1 s in all process models. The maximum time to do so is 14 s and occurs with Process Models 39, 40, and 49. Each model has a standard deviation of one to two seconds for verification times. Figure 5 represents the time required to verify all properties in each process model. This number tends to grow with the total number of capacity points, as does the total verification time. Verifying each process model has required almost 6 h and 41 min on average to verify all properties, i.e., 487 h in total to finish the experiment. Across all process models, the standard deviation of verification time has been around 2 h.

4.3   Research Questions

In this section, we answer the research questions described in Sect. 1.

1. Which assignments of the capacity points lead to the lowest and highest revenue? Figure 6 shows the lowest possible revenue when assigning different capacity points to the bidders. In general, the lowest revenue for higher total numbers of capacity points is relatively high. The lowest revenue is 19 and happens in Process 1, when capacity points are $[1, 1, 1, 3]$. Some of the lowest revenues, i.e., 22, 28, 33, and 34 never occur in any of the process models. The revenue of 26 only occurs once, when the capacity points are $[2, 3, 1, 1]$. The lowest revenue in Process Models 62 to 67 is higher than that of the other process models. Here it is 35. In Process Models 68 to 70, the revenue is 29, probably in line with Bidder 3 having only one capacity point. In Process Models 71 to 76 where this

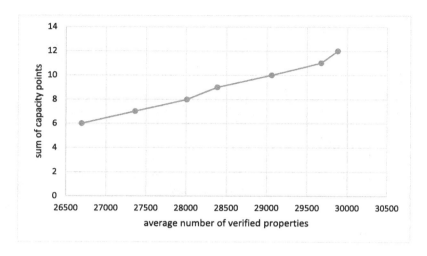

Fig. 4. The average number of properties per total number of capacity points

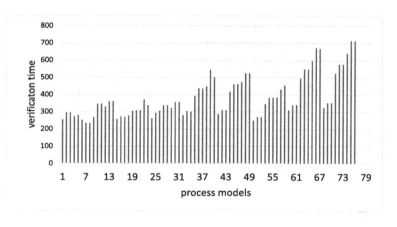

Fig. 5. Time required to verify all properties in each process model

number is again 3, the lowest revenue becomes higher again. In the process models with the maximum lowest revenue, the capacity point of Bidder 1 is always 3, the ones of Bidder 2 and Bidder 3 vary between 2 and 3, and the one of Bidder 4 varies from 1 to 3. We see that the lowest revenue is maximal when Bidder 1 has 3 capacity points. This might be because the budget of Bidder 1 for certain products is higher than that of the other bidders, and assigning a higher capacity point to this bidder increases the revenue.

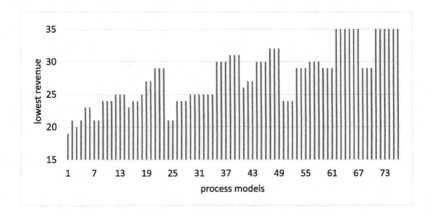

Fig. 6. The lowest possible revenue of each process model

2. With a certain allocation of the capacity points, how often can the lowest revenue occur? It is important for the auctioneer to know the lowest possible revenue before the auction. However, how often the lowest revenue can happen matters as well. Figure 7 represents the number of scenarios which lead to the lowest possible revenue. In general, when the lowest revenue increases, the number of scenarios yielding the lowest revenue increases as well. The lowest revenue in process 76 is higher than the lowest revenue of the other process models. In other words, the worst possible scenario is not too bad, as the revenue is 35. However, the number of scenarios which lead to the lowest revenue is relatively high. In total, 180 scenarios out of 720 lead to the lowest revenue. In contrast, Process 7, to give an example, has the minimal revenue of 21, but this only happens six times out of 720 scenarios.

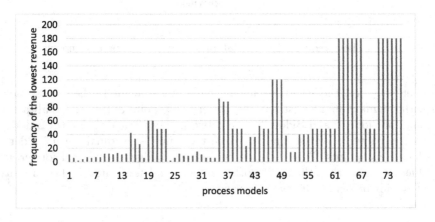

Fig. 7. The frequency of happening the lowest revenue in each process model

3. Does increasing capacity points always increase the revenue? As shown in Fig. 6, the lowest revenue increases with the capacity points of bidders. This is because, when bidders have lower capacities, they cannot win a product, even though they can afford it, and a bidder with a lower budget gets the chance to win the product. But when the auctioneer increases the capacities, this becomes less frequent because the bidder with a higher budget has capacity left to win the product. However, increasing the number of capacities may lead to a monopoly. So, when the capacity points increases, the chance of earning a higher revenue is higher; at the same time, the chance of monopoly gets also higher. At this point, an auctioneer can trade off 'extent of monopolism' vs. 'expected revenue' and assign capacities accordingly.

4. What is the best assignment of capacity points to the bidders, i.e., making the worst possible revenue not too low? As explained, the lowest revenue is maximum in Processes 62 to 67 and 71 to 76. On one side, one can take an allocation of capacity points from there to avoid bad outcomes. However, the process model where bidders have fewer capacity points (Process 69) might be a better choice, since it prevents from any monopoly to some extent. On the other side, the process models in which the lowest revenue is maximal lead to this lowest revenue more often. Put differently, the number of scenarios that lead to the lowest revenue is relatively high.

5. Does changing the capacity point of a single bidder change the outcome of the auction? Another interesting observation is that increasing capacity points does not always change the revenue of the auctioneer. For example, the lowest revenue of the auction is 24 by assigning capacity points of $[3, 1, 1, 1]$. It is the same when we increase the capacity points of Bidder 4. So, when the auctioneer increases the capacity points to avoid the lowest revenues, it also matters which bidder obtains more points. Another example is that changing the capacity of only Bidder 1 by 1 point changes the lowest revenue of the auction from 23 to 25. This shows that the capacity of this bidder has a significant effect on the final prices.

5   Related Work

We first review verification techniques, to give an indication why the verification technique used here is appropriate for the use case studied. Second, we summarize studies on spectrum auctions that bear a relationship with this article.

Verification of Process Models. Many approaches exist for the verification of process models. In the following, we only mention work that is relevant for this article. [24] studies the verification of data-aware process models that allow for modification of data values. That approach only allows verifying spectrum auctions with three bidding parties and products at most. [9] uses colored Petri Nets to verify data-aware process models. The entire domain of data objects is modeled: To represent a data object with n distinct colors, they generate n new states. In consequence, there are too many states, and the verification procedure becomes computationally expensive.

Various abstraction techniques have been developed with the aim of reducing the size of the processes models and, thus, the state space [10,16]. An abstract value is constructed by combining all the unnecessary values into one and then determining the values of the data objects necessary for verification. There is a risk that such techniques produce incorrect results. This effect may occur when elements of the process, like activities, modify the values of data objects. For example, when activities increase the price of a product during the process execution. As a result, the new value of price which might have been unnecessary before, now is relevant for verification and changes the execution of the process model. Another approach [20] abstracts from a process model and evaluates all data objects in each abstracted process fragment for three sets of rules. Each rule maintains or deletes a data object in the process model. The rules provided in [20] might change data values, and this may falsify verification results. A symbolic abstraction approach is used in [12] to support data modifications based on decision tables. The approach consists of a list of conditions and expressions for inputs and outputs. When an activity modifies the value of a large domain object, the abstraction technique featured in [12] is ineffective. In addition, they cannot provide counterexamples in case of an undesirable outcome.

Spectrum Auctions. Regarding spectrum auctions, many studies have been conducted. An auction-theoretic analysis of simultaneous ascending auctions is in [21]. A study by [11] demonstrates the limitations of theoretical analyses of simultaneous multi-round (SMR) auctions. [25] compares the design of the 3G auction in the UK and in Germany. In [3], the 3G auction is analyzed using auction theory. [5] analyses the 4G auction from a theoretical perspective. Despite the auction ending efficiently, the authors concluded that implicit collusion to achieve low prices is possible. Having said this, rationality remains to be an assumption behind all these mechanisms and frameworks.

6   Conclusions

The revenue of spectrum auctions has been an important source of income for governments. In this paper, we have identified extreme outcomes and the factors leading to them in a systematic manner. We have done this by means of existing verification techniques. In particular, we have focused on the lowest possible revenue of a spectrum auction, with different *capacity points*. We have compared the outcomes of process models with different capacity points and explained how an auction designer can take our analysis as a starting point to improve existing designs. In future work, we plan to analyze the impact of other auction parameters, such as the budget of bidders, on the revenue.

References

1. Van der Aalst, W.M.: The application of petri nets to workflow management. J. Circ. Syst. Comput. **8**(01), 21–66 (1998)
2. Ausubel, L.M., Cramton, P., Milgrom, P.: The clock-proxy auction: a practical combinatorial auction design. In: Handbook of Spectrum Auction Design, pp. 120–140 (2006)
3. Bichler, M., Gretschko, V., Janssen, M.: Bargaining in spectrum auctions: a review of the German auction in 2015. Telecomm. Policy **41**(5–6), 325–340 (2017). https://doi.org/10.1016/j.telpol.2017.01.005
4. Brunner, C., Goeree, J.K., Holt, C.A., Ledyard, J.O.: An experimental test of flexible combinatorial spectrum auction formats. Am. Econ. J.: Microecon. **2**(1), 39–57 (2010)
5. Cramton, P., Ockenfels, A.: The German 4G spectrum auction: design and behaviour (2017)
6. Emerson, E.A.: Temporal and modal logic. In: Formal Models and Semantics, pp. 995–1072. Elsevier (1990)
7. Engelmann, D., Grimm, V.: Bidding behaviour in multi-unit auctions-an experimental investigation. Econ. J. **119**(537), 855–882 (2009)
8. Gandhi, S., Buragohain, C., Cao, L., Zheng, H., Suri, S.: A general framework for wireless spectrum auctions. In: Proceedings of DySPAN, pp. 22–33 (2007). https://doi.org/10.1109/DYSPAN.2007.12
9. Ghilardi, S., Gianola, A., Montali, M., Rivkin, A.: Petri nets with parameterised data: modelling and verification. arXiv preprint arXiv:2006.06630 (2020)
10. Groefsema, H., van Beest, N., A-Cervantes, A.: Efficient conditional compliance checking of business process models. Comput. Ind. **115**, 103181 (2020)
11. Gul, F., Stacchetti, E.: Walrasian equilibrium with gross substitutes. J. Econ. Theory **87**(1), 95–124 (1999). https://doi.org/10.1006/jeth.1999.2531
12. Haarmann, S., Batoulis, K., Weske, M.: Compliance checking for decision-aware process models. In: Daniel, F., Sheng, Q.Z., Motahari, H. (eds.) BPM 2018. LNBIP, vol. 342, pp. 494–506. Springer, Cham (2019). https://doi.org/10.1007/978-3-030-11641-5_39
13. Hazlett, T.W., Muñoz, R.E., Avanzini, D.B.: What really matters in spectrum allocation design. Nw. J. Tech. Intell. Prop. **10**, viii (2011)
14. Kagel, J.H., Levin, D.: Behavior in multi-unit demand auctions: experiments with uniform price and dynamic Vickrey auctions. Econometrica **69**(2), 413–454 (2001). https://doi.org/10.1111/1468-0262.00197
15. Kirchkamp, O., Reiss, J.P.: Heterogeneous bids in auctions with rational and markdown bidderstheory and experiment. Technical report (2008)
16. Knuplesch, D., Ly, L.T., Rinderle-Ma, S., Pfeifer, H., Dadam, P.: On enabling data-aware compliance checking of business process models. In: Parsons, J., Saeki, M., Shoval, P., Woo, C., Wand, Y. (eds.) ER 2010. LNCS, vol. 6412, pp. 332–346. Springer, Heidelberg (2010). https://doi.org/10.1007/978-3-642-16373-9_24
17. Krishna, V.: Auction Theory. Academic Press (2009)
18. Kwasnica, A.M., Sherstyuk, K.: Multiunit auctions. J. Econ. Surv. **27**(3), 461–490 (2013)
19. Lohmann, N., Verbeek, E., Dijkman, R.: Petri net transformations for business processes – a survey. In: Jensen, K., van der Aalst, W.M.P. (eds.) Transactions on Petri Nets and Other Models of Concurrency II. LNCS, vol. 5460, pp. 46–63. Springer, Heidelberg (2009). https://doi.org/10.1007/978-3-642-00899-3_3

20. Meyer, A., Weske, M.: Data support in process model abstraction. In: Atzeni, P., Cheung, D., Ram, S. (eds.) ER 2012. LNCS, vol. 7532, pp. 292–306. Springer, Heidelberg (2012). https://doi.org/10.1007/978-3-642-34002-4_23
21. Milgrom, P.: Putting auction theory to work: the simultaneous ascending auction. J. Polit. Econ. **108**(2), 245–272 (2000). https://doi.org/10.1086/262118
22. Milgrom, P., Milgrom, P.R.: Putting Auction Theory to Work. Cambridge University Press, Cambridge (2004)
23. OMG: Business Process Model and Notation (BPMN), Version 2.0, January 2011. http://www.omg.org/spec/BPMN/2.0
24. Ordoni, E., Mülle, J., Böhm, K.: Veryfying workflow models with data values - a case study of SMR spectrum auctions. In: IEEE Conference on Business Informatics, pp. 181–190. IEEE (2020)
25. Seifert, S., Ehrhart, K.M.: Design of the 3G spectrum auctions in the UK and Germany: an experimental investigation. Ger. Econ. Rev. **6**(2), 229–248 (2005). https://doi.org/10.1111/j.1465-6485.2005.00128.x
26. Vickrey, W.: Counterspeculation, auctions, and competitive sealed tenders. J. Financ. **16**(1), 8–37 (1961). https://doi.org/10.2307/2977633
27. Wolfstetter, E.: The swiss UMTS spectrum auction flop: bad luck or bad design? (2001). SSRN 279683

Context-Aware, Intelligent Musical Instruments for Improving Knowledge-Intensive Business Processes

Marcus Grum[✉]

Postdam, Germany
marcus.grum@wi.uni-potsdam.de

Abstract. With shorter song publication cycles in music industries and a reduced number of physical contact opportunities because of disruptions that may be an obstacle for musicians to cooperate, collaborative time consumption is a highly relevant target factor providing a chance for feedback in contemporary music production processes. This work aims to extend prior research on knowledge transfer velocity by augmenting traditional designs of musical instruments with (I) Digital Twins, (II) Internet of Things and (III) Cyber-Physical System capabilities and consider a new type of musical instrument as a tool to improve knowledge transfers at knowledge-intensive forms of business processes. In a design-science-oriented way, a prototype of a sensitive guitar is constructed as information and cyber-physical system. Findings show that this intelligent SensGuitar increases feedback opportunities. This study establishes the importance of conversion-specific music production processes and novel forms of interactions at guitar playing as drivers of high knowledge transfer velocities in teams and among individuals.

Keywords: Business process · Knowledge transfer · CPS · Prototype

1 Introduction

Traditionally, musical instruments are considered as tangible tools, which are used to create sound and express the creativity of musicians. Aside electric guitars, which generate analogous signals on the basis of electricity, stringed instruments generate sound on the basis of string vibration. These vibrations are either amplified by resonance, by microphones or by electric amplifiers. Although recently more and more kinds of computer components enhance stringed instruments, these kinds of instruments are neither digital, autonomous, nor Artificial Intelligence (AI)-based. Further more, feedback that focuses on the musician's activities is neither provided nor supported by the instrument. Hence, knowledge transfers at the creative business process of making music and making sound activities are inefficient [1].

Supplementary Information The online version contains supplementary material available at https://doi.org/10.1007/978-3-031-11510-3_5.

© Springer Nature Switzerland AG 2022
B. Shishkov (Ed.): BMSD 2022, LNBIP 453, pp. 69–88, 2022.
https://doi.org/10.1007/978-3-031-11510-3_5

The only chance for a valuable feedback about making music and sound is a team session in which for instance a teacher, a band member or production team member perceives the musician's activities on-site and communicates about it. Regrettably, physical contact situations might be reduced because of disruptions that may be an obstacle for musicians to cooperate, so that the chances for valuable feedback opportunities decrease drastically. If it was possible to make stringed instruments intelligent so that feedback opportunities are expanded, one can expect learning curves and song publication cycles to be shortened because of (a) more efficient knowledge transfers as instruments can adapt to the specific conversion, (b) earlier feedback as instruments can adapt to the guitarist's current activities and (c) more qualitative collaboration settings because trivial feedback already has been considered in advance.

This article works out the prototype of a concept about sensitive instruments and clarifies the improvement of knowledge transfers in the case of electric guitars being used at three example scenarios at making music (e.g. teaching to play an instrument or to play a song) and making sound (e.g. creating effect chain combinations). Thus, the following research will address the improvement of knowledge transfers and focuses on the following research question: *"How can stringed musical instruments, such as guitars, be made intelligent to enhance knowledge transfer?"*

The research does not intend to provide a sophisticated empirical proof of improved knowledge transfers because of sensitive instruments. It rather intends to clarify the basis of such an instrument that shall show quantified knowledge transfer improvement in on-building empirical research.

The research approach is intended to be design-oriented in accordance with the Design-Science-Research Methodology (DSRM) [2]. Thus, the second section provides the foundation of guitar construction, knowledge transfers and digital sound engineering from which requirements are derived that need to be reflected by the prototype. The third section justifies the concrete requirements for the sensitive instrument. The design artifact is then presented in the fourth section. Its usefulness will be demonstrated with the aid of three example scenarios in section five. It issues how to examine quantitative effects on knowledge transfers and clarifies how to use sensitive instruments to improve knowledge transfers. In section six, it will be evaluated inhowfar the prototype design is suitable to enhance knowledge transfers. The insights are concluded in the last section.

2   Theoretical Foundation

Since this research exemplifies the concept of sensitive instruments by guitars, after all, stringed instruments, such as violins, contrabasses, electric basses, banjos, can also be used as an example, the following shows underlying concepts, such as the characterization of traditional guitar construction and the sound engineering of electric guitars (first sub-section). Knowledge that is required at making music and guitar playing is specified in sub-section two. Basing on this, in sub-section three, typical knowledge transfer situations are characterized.

2.1   Traditional Guitar Building and Sound Design

Traditionally, stringed instruments consist of numerous, solid-wood components [3]: The instrument's *body* holds control components and the instrument's *neck* extends the body, so that *strings* can be lead from the body's bottom to the neck's top. The string tension can be controlled manually by *tuning keys* at the neck's head. A *tone* is generated by hitting one of six string. It can be varied by shortening the string by tapping the string with a finger on the neck's flat surface known as *fret board*. In the case of non-electric guitars, the string vibrations are amplified by *physical resonance* because the guitar body is hollow. In the case of electric guitars, the string vibration leads to changes in the pickup's *magnetic fields* that cause an amplifiable electric signal.

More modern and visionary guitars start to consider an update of individual components. For instance, *pressable LEDs* are mounted on the guitar's fret board [4–6], the simple fret boards are made *touchable* [7,8], or acoustic pickup kits generating *midi signals* from electric signals [9].

However, traditionally, electric signals are either routed through external effect chain devices (sometimes these are integrated in amplifiers) or they are effected by software via effect chain simulation applications. These realize effects, such as stereo delay, tremolo, or reverb [10]. While external devices can be accessed easily at live sessions, they are expensive, very space-consuming, unhandy, not updatable and inflexible in ad-hoc rerouting. On the other side, simulated effect chain devices are made for studio settings. Hence, they are impracticable at live sessions because a computer is needed for handling them.

Interim-Conclusion. Faced with the traditional way of stringed musical instrument or guitar construction, one can identify not any feedback or interaction being initiated by the instrument. These guitars are further not accompanied with Digital Twins because they are fully analogous. Hence, they are not integrated within IoT structures at all. While traditional instruments mostly are made from wood only, displays are not part of the instrument. Further, they do not provide Cyber-Physical System (CPS) capabilities, such as components of *sensors* perceiving the devices environment, *actuators* manipulating its environments, *processors* realizing data processing and intelligence and *communicators* supporting a dialog among any kind of entities [11]. Thus, signals are non-digitally processed only. Here, a gap in research becomes apparent.

Although being transformed to electricity sooner or later in the signal processing chain (either via pickups or microphones generating electric signals), electric sound of a guitar is mostly non-digital and effect chain devices come into play when signals have crossed the guitar's body (e.g. when the signal is routed to effect device hardware or to computers providing simulated effect devices). Neither were effects chains integrated into guitars, nor could these devices be modified remotely and in collaboration with other sound engineers or music producers. Hence, traditional guitar building and sound design have a research gap, here.

2.2   Knowledge in Guitar Context

Quite a lot of knowledge is required for mastering a stringed instrument. The following focuses on a selection of the most relevant knowledge objects for this research.

Guitars. Either the musician or the guitar need do know the *instrument mechanics*. In the case of guitars, it needs to be known that there are six strings that have a certain tuning. Traditionally, this refers to *E*, *A*, *d*, *g*, *h* and *e'* according to the Helmholtz pitch notation (a system for naming musical notes of the Western chromatic scale) or

E_2, A_2, D_3, G_3, H_3 and E_4 according to the Scientific pitch notation [12]. Due to this mechanics, theoretically, the same note can be tapped on six different strings. Of course, the standard tuning of a guitar can be changed, so that one needs to consider knowledge about the instrument's *current tuning*.

Playing the Guitar. The way of playing the guitar is influenced by the knowledge of the *biological autonomy* of the human guitar player. To play a note, in principle, the hand has five fingers to shorten a string by tapping it on the fingerboard. However, some people have only four fingers, for example.

Music. From a music theoretic side, the set of attractive notes is limited by knowledge about the *formation rule* of a certain scale. Just some examples from the category of chromatic or dodecatonic scales: for each of the twelve notes per octave, there do exist variants of major scales, natural minor, harmonic minor, melodic minor scales [13]. Since a song mostly refers to a certain scale and the scale-oriented, chord-specific context changes several times within the song, knowledge of the *time-dynamic understanding* of the song in terms of scale choice and harmonic chord focus is required.

Interim-Conclusion. By now, stringed musical instruments do not reflect their current musical context, such as the selected scale or temporal position in a song. Further, the instrument mechanics are not reflected by the instrument at all, Since the same note is accessible at multiple positions of the fret board, a decision is required to tap a note. So far, the instruments do not reflect the biological mechanics of musicians who tap mainly with four fingers. For example, the instruments do not provide feedback on which finger is comfortable to pick a note on the fret board. Not to mention that temporal feedback that takes into account the current time step in a song has not been generated by the instruments autonomously. Hence, a research gap becomes apparent, here.

2.3   Knowledge Transfer Situations in Guitar Context

Knowledge transfer can be interpreted as conversion of different types of knowledge being bound to various kinds of knowledge carriers [1]. While the first form of knowledge refers to well documentable *explicit knowledge* [14], that can be handed among any kind of process participant easily (e.g. a book), the second form of knowledge is hard to document as it is knowledge-bearer-bound (e.g. experience). It is referred to as *tacit knowledge* [14]. The third form of knowledge refers to the physical manifestation of explicit and tacit knowledge (e.g. produced guitar bodies supporting the comfortable string attack) and is referred to as *embodied knowledge* [15]. However, Table 1 clarifies the corresponding nine knowledge transfer types (KTT) [16], which are based on the conversions among explicit, tacit and embodied forms of knowledge.

Generalization and Abstraction of a Process. Although the moment of creativity in which a new song is born mostly is lived through alone, making music is a collaborative process and one needs to focus on the individual musician and its interconnection with a team, such as (a) the guitar learner being taught to play an instrument by a teacher (education scenario), (b) the guitarist and band members working on how to play a song (band scenario), or (c) the guitarist and a producer or rather a production team working on how to create a certain guitar sound (production scenario). Hence, Fig. 1 presents a synthesis of these collaborative processes on the basis of interviews about the three

Table 1. Knowledge transfers.

ID	Knowledge transfer description
1	**KTT** *(Internalization)*: An explicit knowledge carrier (origin) is perceived by a knowledge carrier (target), so that the target integrates perceived knowledge with its individual knowledge base [14]. An example refers to a person studying a sheet of music about a famous song. As knowledge about harmonics is enriched e.g. by mental models and personal experiences, new knowledge is constructed at the target carrier
2	**KTT** *(Extraction)*: Embodied knowledge (origin) is perceived by a knowledge carrier (target), so that the target recognizes knowledge by interpretation and integrates it with its individual knowledge base [15]. For instance, the formation rule is recognized by studying scale examples. If a person recognizes the formation rule set, person-bound tacit knowledge is created
3	**KTT** *(Socialization)*: Knowledge carrier-bound tacit knowledge is transferred among knowledge carriers through interactive data and information exchange [14]. For example, two persons are speaking about how to modify an instrument's sound. Here, each person functions as both origin and target. Because of their interaction, knowledge is integrated with their individual knowledge bases
4	**KTT** *(Externalization)*: Knowledge carrier-bound tacit knowledge (origin) is explicated so that the knowledge carrier-unbound explicit form of knowledge is created (target) that can be transmitted easily [14]. When a person writes a book, its tacit knowledge is made explicit so that the book can be easily passed among people
5	**KTT** *(Engineering)*: Knowledge carrier-bound tacit knowledge is applied in a task to embody knowledge at a physical object [15]. For instance a person composes a musical piece. Here, tacit knowledge about the act of making music and and being creative are applied to the sheet of music
6	**KTT** *(Codification)*: Embodied knowledge (origin) is perceived by a knowledge carrier and transferred to an explicit form of knowledge (target) [17]. If a person recognizes the formation rule set on the basis of a song's scale (extraction) and the rule set is written down to a book (externalization), the description holds the codified knowledge about the formation rule set
7	**KTT** *(Combination)*: Explicit knowledge (origin) is perceived by a knowledge carrier and conversed to new explicit knowledge (target) [14]. For instance, an evaluation of a guitarist's composing shall be realized on the basis of a scale. Here, explicit knowledge forms of the sheet of music about the composing and formation rule set are combined into the explicit form of a failure report
8	**KTT** *(Decodification)*: Explicit knowledge (origin) is perceived by a knowledge carrier and transferred by engineering activities into an object embodying knowledge (target) [17]. If a person studies the composing of a musician (internalization) and comes up with a modification idea because of attractive notes of a scale (engineering), the note change constructed holds the decodified knowledge about the formation rule set
9	**KTT** *(Transformation)*: Embodied knowledge (origin) is modified by a knowledge carrier so that a new object manifests embodying knowledge (target) [11]. For instance, a sheet of music is transformed from one scale to another. If both sheet of music satisfy the same formation rule set, both of its sheet examples would lead to the same rule set description (codification result)

scenarios mentioned. In the following, its abstracted meaning is clarified first. Then, it will be clarified in the context of the individual scenario thereafter. The process model has been based on the Neuronal-Modeling-And-Description-Language (NMDL) [18], because of the intention to consider sensitive instruments as intelligent CPS and the NMDL has proven to be the superior modeling language for contemporary AI-based, neuronal systems [19].

In Fig. 1, one can see the process of giving feedback with non-sensitive instruments. Hence, it is called *traditional feedback process*. It consists of the following three

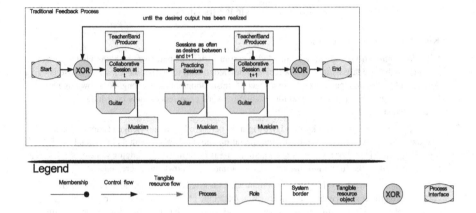

Fig. 1. The traditional collaborative process design for guitars.

sequential, non-cyclic and non-parallel process steps. Please remark, the *Guitar* is taken by the *musician* as wooden tangible resource object throughout all process steps.

A first collaborative session at time step *t* is realized with the corresponding team member. Here one can find either the *teacher* in the education scenario, the *band* members (band scenario) or the *producer* (production scenario). In this process step, a first feedback can be obtained by team members. Thus, the first process step is called *Collaborative Session at t*.

A second process step refers to a private or rather non-collaborative kind of session, that is only carried out by the *musician* dealing with its *guitar*. It is carried out as often as the guitarist desires. Feedback is not obtained by further process participants here, because team members are not available at all. Thus, it is referred to as individual *Practicing Sessions* realizing a sticky, self-imposed kind of feedback: The musician needs to perceive environmental conditions because of its own actions, extract knowledge from this perception, and build upon it.

The third process step refers to the next collaborative session, that is realized in the original team configuration of the first collaboration session. Here, the team builds on the outcomes of the *Practicing Sessions* and feedback is provided by team members. Thus, the third process step is called *Collaborative Session at t + 1*.

This sequence is repeated until the desired output has been realized (see loop between XOR operators). In the next feedback iteration, the time counter *t* is incremented, so that the *Collaborative Session at t + 1* refers to the *Collaborative Session at t* for the next iteration. Hence, feedback is provided by collaborative sessions as long as the desired outcome is realized. Let's clarify the abstracted and synthesized process design at the three scenarios introduced.

(a) Education Scenario. Having interviewed 18 teachers at music schools and 33 musicians learning how to play an instrument, feedback is provided mostly once a week in collaborative sessions with the teacher. Activities of a lesson refer to the following: First, the teacher reviews homework from the current week's exercise and provides feedback. This corresponds to a *socialization* (see KTT 3 of Sect. 2.3). Second, the teacher presents new educative material, such as new exercises, songs, scales, etc. The material is viewed in cooperation, challenges are identified and a first feedback is generated, which shall support the practicing in home sessions. In home sessions, the musician tries to master the homework. Here, the only kind of feedback is self-imposed and builds on knowledge *extracted* by the musicians perception of its environment (KTT 2). Questions coming up are not answered until the next collaborative session (KTT 3). If failures and inefficient patterns solidify during the week, there is no chance for the teacher to provide corrective actions until the next collaborative session.

(b) Band Scenario. Having interviewed 15 bands and 32 musicians making music and working on songs in weekly band meetings, a collaborative feedback about being in harmony with the band is provided only at the band sessions. For example, if a new song is worked out and the musician is composing a passage for the refrain, or the musician (as a tribute band member) intends to reproduce exactly as the original, feedback about the musician's creative ideas is discussed in the collaborative band sessions only (KTT 3). Although the musician makes experiments and modifications of the current composing or playing in individual sessions, feedback is not provided by the band members until the next collaborative session. However, self-imposed feedback by individual sessions builds on sticky knowledge *extracted* by the musician's perception of its environment (KTT 2).

(c) Production Scenario. Having interviewed 7 music producing teams and 12 musicians recording a song in music studios, a collaborative feedback is provided only at expensive studio sessions. For example, if the musician is in the search for a great sound design fitting to a certain recording, feedback about the musician's effect chain combination and its current configuration is discussed in the collaborative session, first (KTT 3). Then, the musician makes experiments on modifications of the current sound design in individual sessions. The only kind of feedback acquired here is self-imposed. It builds on sticky knowledge *extracted* by the musicians perception of its environment (KTT 2), such as sound produced and its individual gusto in terms of harmonic fitting to the current song. A collaborative feedback is not provided by the team until the next collaborative session.

Interim-Conclusion. Interpreting making music as a creative process of individuals collaborating as team with band members, teachers and producers for instance, the synthesized process model of traditional collaboration is inefficient in terms of knowledge transfers. It further does not provide numerous feedback options, which is a limitation because of a limited cooperation for example. Hence, a research gap becomes apparent with respect to the current process design and inefficient knowledge transfers.

3 Objectives of a Solution

Following the DSRM [2], requirements of a prototype are defined before the design of artifacts is carried out. The requirements of Table 2 have served as the design maxims for the sensitive guitar design. Further, they have functioned as quality gates for artifacts presented here and they can stand as quality gates for subsequent research.

Table 2. Requirement collection.

ID	Requirement description
1	**Req.** *(Enhancement)*: Traditional stringed musical instrument designs need to be enhanced. It is not intended to construct a completely new product. A new potential shall be realized, such as increased feedback opportunities, because of the integration of technical components. However, the traditional handling of stringed musical instruments may not be limited because musicians are used to it
2	**Req.** *(Digitization)*: The mechanics of a stringed musical instrument need to be digitized so that a Digital Twins is created. Analog electric signals need to be transformed to digital signals, so that these can be processed by computers embedded at the instrument before analogizing them again and routing them through standard output sockets
3	**Req.** *(IoT-Integration)*: The stringed musical instrument as technical device needs to be integrated in the IoT structure, so that a communication by the stringed musical instrument and further dialog partners can be realized. These partners can refer to further sensitive instruments, alternative devices and human process participants
4	**Req.** *(CPS-Capabilities)*: The stringed musical instrument needs to provide components of sensors, actuators, processors and communicators, so that CPS capabilities can be realized
5	**Req.** *(Knowledge Transfer Improvement)*: As the instrument design has not a purpose in itself, the artifact needs to improve knowledge transfers. In accordance with the validated knowledge transfer models [1], here, for instance, task complexity or knowledge stickiness needs to be reduced, or competence needs to be raised in order to raise knowledge transfer speed

4   Design

In regard with the DSRM [2], the design presents research problem solution in form of artifacts, which will demonstrate their usefulness in the demonstration section. As was identified in section two, these artifacts refer to (a) the physical design of the guitar, (b) its architectural integration within IoT environments, as well as (c) novel forms of interactions and corresponding (d) process designs that can be realized because of the new guitar design. Each will be presented in an individual sub-section.

4.1   Design of Intelligent Instruments

The new instrument design presented in the following enhances the traditional guitar design of Les Paul guitars. It exemplary clarifies the intelligent design of stringed musical instruments, such as violins, basses and guitars having fret boards. Because of their ability to be sensitive, these shall be called *SensInstruments* and the concrete design of the *SensGuitar* can be found in Fig. 2.

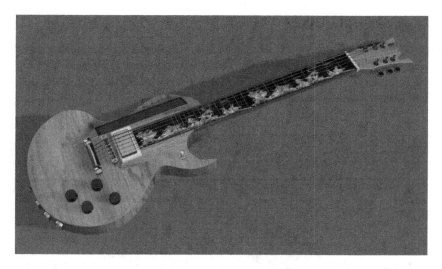

Fig. 2. The SensInstrument design for guitars called SensGuitar (animation). (See Supplementary Material)

Please note: If you see only a rigid image here, you should use a different PDF reader, such as Adobe DC, so that the animations are displayed correctly. However, in the figure, one can recognize an electric guitar having two different types of displays. The *first display* provides full color visualization capabilities at the instrument's fret board. Instrument strings are lead right above it so that it replaces the traditional wooden fret board. The *second display* provides full color visualization capabilities, so that the musician easily can have a look on it while making music. So, for instance, the song's note sheet and chords can be displayed on it. Further, application control flow can be managed easily via this display, which is comparable to smartphone control because of its state-of-the-art capacitive touch.

Within the wooden body of the instrument, processing units, WiFi and Ethernet components are installed, so that the individual SensInstrument realizes capabilities of CPS as follows: Via all the instrument's sensors, the activities of musician can be perceived by the sensitive device. Via its actuators, such as its displays, rumble-packs and speakers, the instrument can manipulate its environment. Its communicators, such as WLAN antenna and Bluetooth, enable the dialog with other instruments.

Sensors of the musical instrument refer to its pickups and piezoelectric microphones perceiving each string individually. Further sensors refer to capacitive touch fields of displays, in the case of guitars, its four buttons and signal switch (traditionally managing volume and tone of two pickup signals) as well as the audio signals being inserted via one of the three XML and Jack socket options. So, for example external sound devices, such as computers, mp3-players, smartphones, and further microphones can be connected as required. However, the environmental perception of the SensGuitar is processed by system-on-module computers, such as the apalis IMX8, and field-programmable-gate-array computers, such as the Xilinx Artix-7, for efficient audio processing.

4.2 Architectural Layout

Going beyond the context of an individual instrument as CPS conceptualized in the previous sub-section, its integration with the IoT environment can be realized as Fig. 3 shows. It therefore issues the creation of a cyber-physical music production system containing numerous interacting CPS.

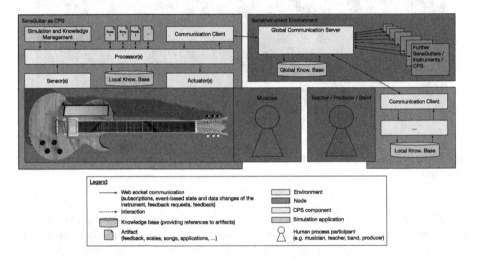

Fig. 3. The architectural design for SensInstruments.

In the left of the figure, one can recognize the SensGuitar being conceptualized as CPS. Applying the conceptual model of CPS [11] and following the design described in Sect. 4.1, the individual instrument provides sensors, actuators, processors, and communicators that are integrated with and IoT-infrastructure as follows.

Any kind of event-based state and data changes of an individual CPS, such as triggered by a finger press or string attack, are sent to a *global communication server* via a web-socket-based dialog. Since further CPS are subscribed to the very same communication server, activities on the individual instrument can be displayed on devices at different physical environments (see separate gray boxes within the figure). So, for instance a teacher, band colleagues or a production team can perceive the activity of a remote musician playing the SensGuitar.

Having interpreted the musicians activities remotely, feedback can optionally be sent back in real-time. For example, the feedback is visualized right at the fret board, so that the musician being feedbacked can perceive remote activities on its own device. By this, it can be visualized if a false string was attacked. As a further example, feedback can be sent back by the production team, which refers to an update of the guitars current sound configuration. By this, recording can be improved in real-time. Of course, these are just a view examples of many.

Since a web-socket-based communication is coordinated by a global communication server, to which all the CPS are connected, a real-time event-based state update can be used in order to synchronize numerous instruments. Thus, band members being at different physical locations can make music in sync. As they are jamming as a remote band, each member can derive an individual feedback about its own playing and the harmony with its band colleagues.

Throughout the nodes, one can find *knowledge bases* providing songs and scale material. As the guitar has an individual simulation component (e.g. providing the songs current time step and caring about the songs current tempo, etc.), the guitar is enabled to provide feedback by automatic replies.

4.3 Novel Forms of Interactions

Being equipped with these two displays and having added numerous sensors to the instrument, because of the CPS capabilities, novel forms of interactions (NFI) can be derived (see Table 3). These enable the inclusion of Human-Machine-Interfaces (HMI) in the context of stringed instruments. Please remark, the following does not claim to present a sophisticated, complete set of forms. It rather shows the most valuable and intuitive new forms from the view point of the author.

Focusing on these forms of interactions only, the way of making music and collaborating is ready to be modernized: By design, one still has the opportunity to handle the instrument as usual. However, the novel forms of interactions hold a potential for improving knowledge transfers. For this, interactions need to be brought in harmony with novel forms of feedback processes. These will be presented next.

4.4 Novel Forms of Feedback Processes

Because of being faced with Req. 1 (see Sect. 3), novel forms of interactions shall be treated as an opportunity. Thus, these are optional and will be considered in addition to the traditional collaborative process design (see Fig. 1), such as in education, production and band scenarios. Hence, Fig. 4 presents the collaboration process for SensInstruments clarifying how to realize new forms of interactions by design. The process models are described by the Neuronal-Modeling-And-Description-Language (NMDL) [19], because of preparing the SensGuitar for being enhanced by Artificial Intelligence with the aid of the Concept of Neuronal Modeling, which is an ongoing research and not considered, here.

In the figure, one can identify the same three kinds of activities, that already have been explained in Sect. 2.3. They have been characterized as relevant process steps of collaboration and feedbacking in a *traditional feedback process*. In comparison with Fig. 1, please remark the breaking up of the task called *Practicing Sessions* into *Practicing Session Parts* and their combination by the inner XOR operators. Because of this breaking up, changes can be implemented as Table 4 summarizes.

Interim-Conclusion. In comparison with the *traditional feedback process* of Fig. 1, the *optimized feedback process* allows the provision of valuable feedback because of sensitive instruments, which is in all *Practicing Sessions*. These additional feedback opportunities are valuable because e.g. (1) failures and inefficient patterns do not solidify, (2) the period between t and $t + 1$ is useful because of interim feedback, and (3)

Table 3. The SensInstrument-induced new forms of interactions for SensGuitars.

ID	Novel Form of Interaction (NFI) description
1	**NFI** *(Next Notes)*: Visualizing *next notes* on the guitar fret board that are required by a certain song. Aside highlighting the precise finger tip position, this includes highlighting the corresponding string attack position, so that a note is characterized
2	**NFI** *(Finger Tip Type)*: Visualizing the intended *type of finger tip* on the guitar fret board, so that it becomes clear which finger should take a note
3	**NFI** *(Finger Tip Movement)*: Visualizing the *finger tip movement* on the guitar fret board, so that is becomes clear how a vibrato or sliding effect is caused by each finger
4	**NFI** *(Attractive Note)*: Visualizing *attractive notes* on the guitar fret board that are legitimate in regard with a certain scale. Aside the precise finger tip position on the fret board, this includes the corresponding string attack, so that a note is characterized
5	**NFI** *(Tip Correctness)*: Visualizing *correct finger tips* on the guitar fret board. Here, for instance, green plus symbols appearing next to the correct finger tapping could visualize a positive feedback
6	**NFI** *(Tip Incorrectness)*: Visualizing *false finger tips* on the guitar fret board. Here, for instance, red minus symbols appearing next to the incorrect finger tapping could visualize a negative feedback
7	**NFI** *(Attack Correctness)*: Visualizing *correct string attacks* below the corresponding guitar strings. Here, for instance, green string surroundings appearing next to the correct string attack could visualize a positive feedback
8	**NFI** *(Attack Incorrectness)*: Visualizing *false string attacks* below the corresponding guitar strings. Here, for instance, red string surroundings appearing next to the incorrect string attack could visualize a negative feedback
9	**NFI** *(Sound Configuration)*: Modification of a *sound configuration* that changes the digital sound design. Here, for instance, shadowing an effect device could visualize the switching on or switching off of a device
10	**NFI** *(Audio Signal)*: Audio-based interactions are realized from *acoustic signals* that can be inserted via microphone and made audible via speakers

expensive and valuable collaborative sessions with *teachers, band members* or *producers* (mostly in place) can focus on more important topics. Thus, it can be assumed that collaborative sessions will operate on higher quality levels.

Please remark: It is neither intended nor realistic to expect that technology, such as the SensGuitar, can replace a human in creatively making and teaching music and sound creation. The SensInstruments rather shall support collaborative activities in that context and to improve corresponding knowledge transfers, which will be clarified in the demonstration section.

5 Demonstration

In accordance with design-oriented research [2], the application of designed artifacts demonstrates their use, so that one is able to evaluate if the original research problem

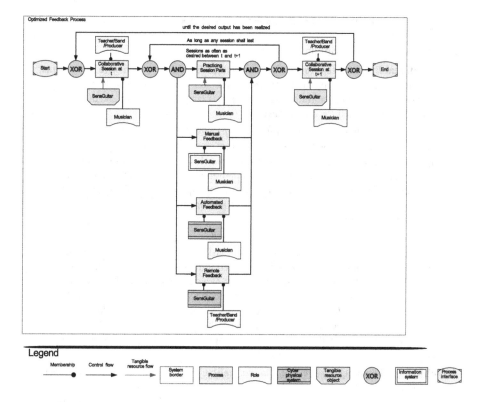

Fig. 4. The SensInstrument-based collaborative process design for SensGuitars.

can be overcome. In this research context, the novel kind of musical instrument called SensInstrument (constructed in Sect. 4.1) will be used as tool to carry out novel forms of interactions (designed in Sect. 4.3). It will be applied to the well known scenarios in guitar context (Sect. 2.3). Hence, in the demonstration case presented, the SensInstrument manifests as guitar and refers to the SensGuitar. The scenarios follow the architectural layout (put up in Sect. 4.2) in order to carry novel forms of feedback processes (Sect. 4.4). Since all these sub-artifacts are brought together by one new type of device, Fig. 5 draws attention to the interplay of the musician with the sensitive musical instrument and focuses on HMI.

As different forms of interactions are considered scenario-wise, the following sub-sections clarify the animated Fig. 5(a)–Fig. 5(d) in the context of each scenario. However, some SensGuitar-based process steps are not varied so far. Hence, the following sub-sections focus on the varied process steps of Fig. 4.

Please remark: It is not intended to demonstrate all the three scenarios at the following sub-sections. The *education scenario* will be considered at all sub-sections because of focusing on the demonstration of context-aware intelligent musical instruments. The *production scenario* and the *band scenario* will extend the third sub-section demonstration only because the focus is on the demonstration of the instrument and its

Table 4. The SensInstrument-induced process changes.

ID	Process change description
1	**Additional Process Steps** *(see AND operators)*: With the aid of sensitive instruments, three further process steps can be realized in parallel, which becomes clear by the AND operators. Thus, the following steps a) - c) occur in addition to and during the traditional task called *Practicing Sessions*
2	**a) Manual Feedback** *(see first additional step)*: Considering the sensitive instrument as information system, on the basis of visual information (e.g. showing next finger tips on the fret board), feedback can be *extracted* (KTT 2) by the musician at any time. In difference to the traditional, self-imposed feedback of practicing sessions, knowledge stickiness can be decreased because of supportive visualizations e.g. So, knowledge extracted because of the sensitive instrument's support, can be transferred to the musician faster [1]
3	**b) Automated Feedback** *(see second additional step)*: Considering the sensitive instrument as CPS, feedback can be autonomously provided and visualized by the SensGuitar: sensing the string attacks and interpreting finger tips at a certain time step and in regard with the current musical context of a song, its scale and the guitar's tuning, etc., for instance, the visualization of a correct or false finger tip on the fret board can be *internalized* (KTT 1) by the musician at any time. Hence, knowledge transfers are optimized because of a reduced complexity of knowledge [1]. So, knowledge provided by the sensitive instrument can be transferred to the musician faster [1]
4	**c) Remote Feedback** *(see third additional step)*: Considering the sensitive instrument as CPS, feedback can be autonomously given by remote teachers, band members or producers: sending the musician's current string attacks and finger tips via the IoT to remote team members of the current scenario, feedback can be sent back from remote team members to the musician. For instance, team members can talk about video camera interfaces and speak about their feedback (*socialization*, see KTT 3). In addition, their feedback can be supported by the visualization of their remote finger tip on the musician's fret board (used for *internalization*, see KTT 1). So, remote knowledge provided via the local sensitive instrument can be transferred to the musician faster. Going beyond this, the CPS can identify if individual or cooperative sessions are more efficient and trigger socialization-specific knowledge transfers when optimal (see knowledge-transfer optimization of [1])
5	**Continual Feedback** *(see XOR operator)*: Faced with the new process of Fig. 4, feedback can be acquired when required: instead of realizing one *Practicing Session* and waiting from one *Collaborative Session at t* until the next *Collaborative Session at t + 1*, feedback can by collected as often as desired by the musician - several times a week and even several times during one session. This becomes clear by the XOR operator and the closed control flow circle. By intention, this iterative proceeding is repeated until the musician decides to finish each practicing session

architectural IoT embedding enabling knowledge transfers. Here, the integration with alternative scenario-specific devices, such as further SensGuitars, alternative instruments or workstations, will be issued.

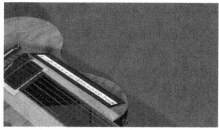

(a) Visualizing finger tips, finger types and finger movements of next time steps (animation).

(b) Visualization based on correct (green) and incorrect (red) string attacks (animation).

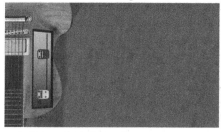

(c) Individual and collaborative effect chain creation (animation).

(d) Microphone input and speaker output via one of three audio sockets (static figure).

Fig. 5. Selected CPS capabilities of SensInstruments enabling different forms of HMI. (See Supplementary Material)

5.1 Optimized Manual Feedback

Aside the traditional practicing session using the instrument as tangible resource object, a manual feedback is optimized. The education scenario shall clarify this.

Education Scenario. The SensGuitar visualizes notes of a next time step on the guitar fret board, which becomes clear by the animated Fig. 5(a). This means that the guitar knows the current song, the selected scale, the current tuning, etc., so that the position to be tipped by a finger next is highlighted. This corresponds to NFI 1 of Sect. 4.3. Since colors of a highlighting are associated with a finger number, the musician can recognize the intended type of finger (see NFI 2). If a song requires a certain vibrato or sliding effect caused by a finger tip moved over the fret board, arrows next to the highlighted note show direction, strength and timing of the movement required (see NFI 3). Alternative finger tips are visualized in addition to the next note to be played (see NFI 4). These can either refer to notes from the same scale so that one can improvise easily, or these can refer to finger tips on the very same note at different positions, so that one can select an alternative easily. Based on these four kinds of visual forms of feedback, the musician can *extract* knowledge more easily (KTT 2) because knowledge stickiness is reduced [1]. Further, these forms of feedback are enabled because of the SensGuitar designed. They have not been available at the traditional process of Fig. 1.

5.2 Optimized Automated Feedback

In addition to the previous form of manual feedback, an automated feedback is generated by the device. So, feedback is optimized as the education scenario shall clarify.

Education Scenario. Assuming the musician to have pressed a certain finger tip on the guitar fret board and attacked the corresponding string, the SensGuitar perceives this activity and generates feedback about its correctness. For this, the feedback is visualized right next to the intended note tip or string attack on the displayed fret board: As is animated in Fig. 5(b) (this corresponds to NFI 7 and NFI 8), a red color highlights incorrect string attacks and a green color highlights correct string attacks. Similarly, at a certain time step, correct and incorrect finger tips are visualized by red and green finger tip surroundings (see NFI 5 and NFI 6). Aside the visual feedback described, an audio-based feedback can indicate incorrect finger tips and string attacks (see NFI 10). It is made audible by speakers that have been connected to one of three audio sockets, that can be seen in Fig. 5(d).

Based on these four kinds of visual forms of feedback, the musician does not need to *extract* (KTT 2) knowledge any more: As the feedback is generated automated by the SensGuitar, the musician can *internalize* knowledge about the correct and incorrect activity more easily (KTT 1). Since this reduces complexity, knowledge transfers are improved [1]. These forms of feedback are enabled because of the SensGuitar designed. They have not been available at the traditional process of Fig. 1.

5.3 Optimized Remote Feedback

If a manual feedback and an automated feedback does not satisfy the musician's feedback needs, remote parties can become part of the feedback process as the following scenarios shall clarify.

Education Scenario. The *teacher* becomes part at individual *Practicing Session Parts*. While holding a second SensGuitar in hands, the teacher sees the activities of the musician on the first SensGuitar remotely. According to the animated Fig. 5(a), the teacher sees the musician's current finger tips and string attacks (see NFI 2), finger tip movements (see NFI 3), and attractive alternative notes (see NFI 4) on its remote guitar. In addition, a dialog can be realized because the musician and the teacher have plugged in a microphone and a speaker in the audio sockets (see NFI 10), that can be seen in Fig. 5(d). Since the two SensGuitars are connected bidirectionally, an oral dialog about the musician's current playing and singing can be supported visually (internalization and externalization): The teacher's feedback is supported because the teacher's activities at the remote SensGuitar are visualized at the musician's SensGuitar. Because of the visualization of the other's activities on the one's SensGuitar, a *socialization* (KTT 3) of the teacher and musician about the correct and false finger tips and string attacks, finger movements and attractive alternative notes can be carried out efficiently in educative settings. So, remote socializations can improve knowledge transfers. These have not been available at the traditional process of Fig. 1 at all.

Production Scenario. The *producer* becomes part at individual *Practicing Session Parts*, too. While the musician holds a SensGuitar in hands, the producer sees the effect chain combination of the musician's device remotely on a workstation (see NFI 9). According to the animated Fig. 5(c), the musician and the producer combine effect chain combinations in cooperation. The musician's guitar playing then is made audible via the speakers plugged into one of three audio sockets. (see NFI 10).

Please remark: There is no doubt that dialogues of producers and musicians will focus on how the music sounds. The producer probably will ask for some variation in the musical result, but it will not tell the guitarist how to do his job. However, the focus of the SensGuitar is on supporting knowledge transfers, so that an additional visualization might make dialogues about the act of making music and sound more efficient, e.g. Because of the remote feedback of the producer, a knowledge *combination* can be realized in creative and interactive settings (KTT 7). So, knowledge can be transferred faster and more efficiently. These kinds of knowledge transfers have not been available at the traditional process of Fig. 1 at all.

Band Scenario. Similar to teachers and producers, *band members* become part at individual *Practicing Session Parts*. Independent from the question if band members hold an own SensGuitar in hands or they hold different forms of devices (e.g. basses, pianos or laptops) visualizing the same information because of adequate *transformation* of knowledge (KTT 9), band members can get to know the activities of the musician remotely.

Since the musician's current playing is streamed via WiFi, band members can hear the remote musician activities (guitar playing and singing): the musician and the members have plugged in individual microphones and speakers in the audio sockets (see NFI 10) at one of three input and output sockets shown in Fig. 5(d). Thus, on the basis of a live, remote jamming of the entire band, feedback can be generated and communicated via microphone by any band member. For example, this feedback can be about the musician's current composing at making music, such as a passage for the refrain, or about the current guitar playing and inhowfar the musician (as a tribute band member) reproduces exactly as the original. The feedback will be made audible at any device, so that a dialog can evolve.

Please remark: There is no doubt that hearing seems to be the primary organ in making music. However, the focus of the SensGuitar is on supporting knowledge transfers, so that an additional visualization might make dialogues about the act of making music and sound more efficient, e.g. Hence, any kinds of visualizations (NFI 1-NFI 8) issued before, can be activated by band members remotely and visualized at the musician's SensGuitar.

As band members further can see and work on a musician's current effect chain combination (this is similar to the producer scenario), the band members can decide on the basis of a live, remote jamming session if a sound configuration fits to the current song. Via microphones and speakers, band members can exchange feedback about the tone (NFI 10) and they can modify the current effect chain of a musician remotely (NFI 9) as can be seen at the animated Fig. 5(c). So, remote *socializations* (KTT 3) on jamming sessions have the potential to improve knowledge transfers: the remote feedback (socialization with band members) can address the correct and false string attacks, finger tipping, harmonic playing and guitar sound. By a *combination* (KTT 7) of local visualization on the one device and remote information coming from band colleague devices, the musicians can work cooperatively on finger tipping, string attacks and sound configurations. These process steps have not been available at the traditional process of Fig. 1 at all.

6 Evaluation

In order to satisfy design-science-oriented research approaches [2], it has been evaluated inhowfar requirements of Sect. 3 have been fulfilled and knowledge transfers have been improved in the three knowledge transfers scenarios demonstrated. Table 5 summarizes the requirement fulfillment.

7 Conclusion

This paper has presented a design for sensitive musical instruments that provides a (I) Digital Twin, (II) an IoT embedding as well as (III) CPS capabilities. It so extends the state-of-the-art of guitar building and provides a new example for CPS, IoT and Digital Twins. The demonstration has clarified the usefulness of the SensGuitar prototype [20] in the 1) education, 2) production and 3) band scenario by optimizing knowledge transfers. It so contributes with further examples and optimization methods for knowledge transfer improvement. Further, the demonstration has confirmed that requirements specified in advance have been satisfied.

Critical Appraisal. The research question (*"How can stringed musical instruments, such as guitars, be made intelligent to enhance knowledge transfer?"*) can be answered with regard to the design of sensitive instruments: stringed instruments are setup as CPS, which is clarified by the prototype of SensGuitars. They have a Digital Twin and they are based on the traditional tangible resource of guitars. Intelligence is carried out with the aid of novel forms of interactions. This contributes with further examples for the domain of HMI. These potential interfaces are enabled because of the CPS capabilities, so that sensitive instruments can adapt to the current musical context of a song and reflect on the musician's activities. By generating and providing different forms of feedback, knowledge transfers are improved efficiently. This contributes to business process standards, since this leads to a novel form of process models (see Fig. 4). Further, education and collaboration standards are improved, because the number of feedback opportunities can be increased easily. Being embedded in the new architectural infrastructure design of Fig. 3, the creation of new business models is supported and new roles come into play. Thus, the knowledge base of Enterprise Architecture Management is extended.

Limitations and Outlook. The results and insights presented need to be limited in regard with the validation level. The technical functionality has been proven by a demonstrator and the knowledge transfer improvement has been clarified by argumentation. Validated knowledge transfer models have been applied for this. Future research will therefore examine the empirical examination of improvements identified and stress the artifacts created by real-world conditions. This will be realized the aid of

Table 5. Evaluation of requirement fulfillment.

ID	Requirement fulfillment description
1	**Enhancement** *(Req. 1)*: This requirement has been satisfied because the SensGuitar can be handled as traditional guitars only: Comparing the traditional process design of Fig. 1 and the novel process design of Fig. 4, the same usage of *Guitars* and *SensGuitars* can be recognized. The novel process design enhances the traditional design by additional process steps. Further, the SensGuitar prototype of Fig. 2 provides the very same components than traditional guitars: one can also find a guitar body, a neck, strings being lead from the guitar body bottom to the guitar neck's head, tuners, etc. Thus, the traditional guitarist will be used to the SensGuitar's handling
2	**Digitization** *(Req. 2)*: This requirement has been satisfied because the SensGuitar is setup as CPS, that knows the availability of six strings having a certain tuning. Further, it has a digital representation of all the note positions on the fret board. Also, a Digital Twin is created from scales, biologic mechanics of guitarists and the temporal dynamics of a song, so that the entire musical context is characterized
3	**IoT-Integration** *(Req. 3)*: This requirement has been satisfied because the SensGuitar is embedded by design into IoT structure. Figure 3 clarifies the architectural design with which a communication of stringed instruments are realized by an arbitrary high number of dialog partners via a web socket communication and interactive architecture components
4	**CPS-Capabilities** *(Req. 4)*: This requirement has been satisfied because the SensGuitar implements the conceptual model of CPS: Numerous sensors have been implemented, such as capacitive touch display, digitized and analog pickup and piezoelectric signals, actuators refer to visualizations at two displays and sound signals being amplified via speakers. Different processors analyze signals and derive decisions and feedback, which are distributed via communicators over Ethernet or WiFi. As these components can be modified and further components can be integrated easily, CPS-capabilities can be extended efficiently
5	**Knowledge Transfer Improvement** *(Req. 5)*: This requirement has been satisfied because the SensGuitar as improved knowledge transfers. As was clarified scenario-wise in Sect. 5, this has reduced complexity and stickiness of knowledge transfers. Further, competence of the SensGuitar was raised (e.g. by visualizing scales or next notes). In addition, the SensGuitar has provided additional feedback opportunities (compare process models of Fig. 1 and Fig. 4), so that the total number of feedback can be raised in the three scenarios examined: Using the SensGuitar, feedback even can be taken at individual practice sessions, so that valuable knowledge transfers occur additionally

experiments offering the artifacts conceptualized at this contribution. By measuring the time taken, feedback opportunities realized and failures made by test persons of the three scenarios conceptualized here, the validation can be improved.

References

1. Gronau, N., Grum, M.: Knowledge Transfer Speed Optimizations in Product Development Contexts. GITO mbH Verlag, Berlin (2019)
2. Peffers, K., et al.: The design science research process: a model for producing and presenting information systems research. In: 1st International Conference on Design Science in Information Systems and Technology (DESRIST), vol. 24, pp. 83–106, August 2006
3. Koch, M.: Building Electric Guitars. Martin Koch, Gleisdorf (2001)
4. Williams, A.J.: RS components, September 2014. https://www.youtube.com/watch?v=N4AjuhZexk4. See Video at 1:30–1:50
5. Incident: gTar: The first guitar that anybody can play, February 2014. https://www.kickstarter.com/projects/incident/gtar-the-first-guitar-that-anybody-can-play
6. Artiphon: The artiphon instrument 1, November 2019. https://www.kickstarter.com/projects/artiphon/introducing-the-artiphon-instrument-1
7. Zivix: Jamstik+ smart guitar, November 2015. https://www.kickstarter.com/projects/zivix/jamstik-the-smartguitar?ref=category
8. O'Reilly, R.: Expressiv MIDI guitar: Real MIDI. Real guitar. Real control, March 2016. https://www.kickstarter.com/projects/733246303/expressiv-midi-guitar-real-midi-real-guitar-real-c
9. Graph Tech Guitar Labs Ltd.: Ghost guitar acousti-phonic and hexpander preamp, December 2021. https://graphtech.com/collections/ghost-pickup-systems-kits/products/ghost-acousti-phonic-hexpander-preamp
10. Boulanger, R.: The Csound Book: Perspectives in Software Synthesis, Sound Design, Signal Processing, and Programming. MIT Press, Cambridge (2000)
11. Gronau, N., Grum, M., Bender, B.: Determining the optimal level of autonomy in cyber-physical production systems. In: 2016 IEEE 14th International Conference on Industrial Informatics (INDIN), pp. 1293–1299, July 2016
12. Weissmann, D.: Guitar Tunings - A Comprehensive Guide. Routledge (2006)
13. Tymoczko, D.: Scale networks and Debussy. J. Music Theory **48**, 219–294 (2004)
14. Nonaka, I., Takeuchi, H.: The Knowledge-Creating Company: How Japanese Companies Create the Dynamics of Innovation. Oxford University Press, Oxford (1995)
15. Gronau, N.: Knowledge Modeling and Description Language 3.0 - Eine Einführung. Empirical Studies of Business Informatics. GITO (2020)
16. Grum, M., Gronau, N.: Quantification of knowledge transfers. In: Shishkov, B. (ed.) BMSD 2021. LNBIP, vol. 422, pp. 224–242. Springer, Cham (2021). https://doi.org/10.1007/978-3-030-79976-2_13
17. Kruse, R., Borgelt, C., Braune, C., Klawonn, F., Moewes, C., Steinbrecher, M.: Computational Intelligence, 2 edn. Springer Fachmedien Wiesbaden, Wiesbaden (2015)
18. Grum, M.: NMDL repository, November 2020. https://github.com/MarcusGrum/CoNM/tree/main/meta-models/nmdl. Version 1.0.0
19. Grum, M.: Construction of a Concept of Neuronal Modeling. Potsdam University (2021)
20. SensGit UG: SensGuitar, December 2021. https://www.sensguitar.com

Detecting Data Incompatibilities in Process-Driven Decision Support Systems

Jonas Kirchhoff[(✉)], Sebastian Gottschalk, and Gregor Engels

Department of Computer Science, Paderborn University, Paderborn, Germany
{jonas.kirchhoff,sebastian.gottschalk,engels}@upb.de

Abstract. Decision makers in complex business environments have different goals and constraints and therefore require tailored decision support systems (DSS). Following a low-code approach, a tailored DSS can be created by a decision maker as a process-based composition of existing, interoperable decision support services. Data incompatibilities may be introduced during the design or execution of such a process-driven DSS, e.g., when a service always generates or a decision maker selects data which violates a data constraint of a subsequent service. These incompatibilities cause interrupted or erroneous decision processes. In this paper, we contribute an approach which enables the detection of data incompatibilities in process-driven DSS during process design and execution. Our approach utilizes the *JSON Schema* specification to define service interfaces and associated type constraints which data produced by services or decision makers can be validated against. We demonstrate our approach in the context of decision support for energy network planning using a prototypical open-source implementation.

Keywords: Decision support systems · Process-driven applications · Low-code · Service composition · Business process dataflow

1 Introduction

Individual decision makers have different goals and constraints during decision making, e.g., they want to optimize different metrics with their decision or they are limited in the data available for decision making [9]. Decision makers therefore require tailored decision support systems (DSS) which assist them in the identification of optimal decisions considering their individual goals and constraints [9,11,20]. One approach for generating such tailored DSS are *process-driven DSS* which resemble the individual decision making process of a decision

Partially supported by the North Rhine Westphalian Ministry of Economic Affairs, Innovation, Digitalisation and Energy (MWIDE) through grant 005-2011-0022, the European Regional Development Fund (ERDF) through grant EFRE-0801186, and the German Research Foundation (DFG) through grant 160364472SFB901.

B. Shishkov (Ed.): BMSD 2022, LNBIP 453, pp. 89–103, 2022.
https://doi.org/10.1007/978-3-031-11510-3_6

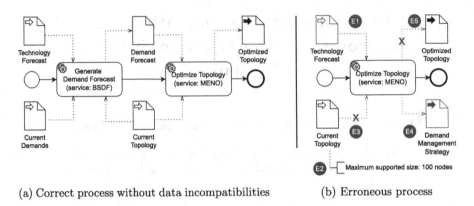

(a) Correct process without data incompatibilities   (b) Erroneous process

Fig. 1. Example BPMN process models for a process-driven DSS

maker [14]. Process-driven DSS utilize a process model to capture the necessary decision support activities and the interoperable software services with decision support functionality used to implement these activities. Based on an individualized process model, a tailored DSS can be generated which prompts the decision maker for input data, forwards the data to and between decision support services in the background, and returns output data to the decision maker. An example for a simplified process driving a DSS for regional electricity distribution network planning [8] is shown in Fig. 1a. Here, an electricity demand forecast is generated which is subsequently used to plan cost-minimizing network topology reinforcements to meet the demand. The decision maker can use the generated DSS to plan network reinforcements for different cities following the same decision process with different input data.

Based on a low-code approach [19], a tailored DSS can even be generated by a decision maker without software development knowledge by specifying a structurally well-formed process model [9]. However, due to working with potentially unfamiliar third-party services, errors are easily introduced in the *dataflow* of the process model which describes how data is provided to services implementing the decision support activities [26]. Although aiming for the process model shown in Fig. 1a, a decision maker may accidentally introduce some or all of the dataflow errors E^* shown in Fig. 1b: The wrong type of data may be provided to a service (E1: *Technology Forecast* instead of *Demand Forecast*), a provided input may not meet certain constraints (E2: the network topology selected by the decision maker at runtime or produced by another service may exceed the maximum size of 100 nodes supported by the service), a required data input is not provided (E3), an output is assumed which is not actually produced by a task (E4), or no output of a task is utilized, i.e., consumed by another service or returned to the decision maker (E5). The latter missing utilization of an output can be considered as an error in the context of decision making as decision support services are free of side effects, i.e., they compute decision recommendations in form of data outputs (e.g., a network reinforcement plan), but they do not actually make decisions and act on them (e.g., they do not instruct engineers to implement the reinforcement plan – this is up to the decision maker).

The previously described dataflow errors must be avoided for process-driven DSS as they prevent the proper execution of the DSS. This reduces user satisfaction [5], either by introducing a delay in the decision making process, or worse, by recommending suboptimal or erroneous decisions. Especially challenging are errors of type E1 and E2 as they can be attributed to data incompatibilities which can be introduced both during process design (because decision makers mistakenly expect the data produced by one service to be compatible with a subsequent service) *and* during process execution (because decision makers select data which is not compatible with the constraints of a consuming service). As we explain in Sect. 2, existing work has primarily focused on detecting errors of type E3–E5 during process design. In this paper, we therefore focus on detecting the equally significant errors of type E1 and E2 during process design and execution. Our contribution consists of a solution concept and prototypical implementation which uses the existing *JSON Schema*[1] specification to model data requirements of services and algorithmically detects data incompatibilities with respect to these requirements during design and execution of a process-driven DSS. We applied the design science research approach by Peffers et al. [16] to ensure that our solution concept can support the design of tools and environments for the generation of process-driven DSS. Following the design science research approach, we first present research objectives for detecting data incompatibilities in process-driven DSS (Sect. 3). Subsequently, we explain and demonstrate the domain-agnostic concepts behind our solution approach in the example application domain of energy distribution network planning (Sect. 4). We discuss our approach based on the insights from its prototypical implementation which is publicly available as an open-source command-line application (Sect. 5). Lastly, we conclude the paper with a summary accompanied by an outlook on future work (Sect. 6).

2   Research Background

In this section, we present additional background information on process-driven DSS to support the explanations throughout the paper. Furthermore, we discuss existing and related work for detecting dataflow errors in process models.

2.1   Process-Driven DSS

Decision makers regularly depend on computerized decision support systems for decision making in increasingly volatile, uncertain and complex business environments [4,20]. These DSS assist decision makers in identifying optimal decisions by combining algorithms and tools for data mining, simulation, optimization, data visualization and general knowledge management [20]. The suitability of

---

[1] https://json-schema.org/.

algorithms and tools depends on the individual requirements of decision makers, e.g., the metrics they want to optimize or data and time they have available to identify an optimal decision [9]. Considering that the decision process largely influences the effectiveness of strategic decisions [6], decision makers consequently need tailored DSS which are customized to their individual requirements for decision support, i.e., goals and constraints.

Recent work on the creation of tailored DSS such as [9,11] describes a DSS as a composition of interoperable software services. In the context of service-oriented architectures, service compositions have previously been captured in the form of process models, thereby giving rise to *process-driven applications* (PDAs) [25]. An analogous approach seems suitable for DSS given the fact that decision making is a process spanning potentially multiple activities for the preparation, analysis and interpretation of data [14,28]. An additional benefit of this process-driven approach is expressiveness: Process models are not only able to capture the functional perspective of process-driven DSS (i.e., the execution of decision support activities to identify a decision recommendation), but also the informational perspective (= *dataflow*, i.e., the data required for and generated during decision support activities) and the operational perspective (i.e., the software services used to execute decision support activities) [26]. We designed our approach to work with all process modeling languages that support these perspectives. Nevertheless, BPMN [13] has emerged as a "de-facto standard" [2] for process modeling which is popular with many stakeholders [10]. This essentially allows decision makers without an extensive software engineering background to create tailored (process-driven) DSS themselves by specifying its functionality using a process-model. This can be compared to the *low-code* approach for software development where non-developers utilize abstractions to specify application functionality from which application code is generated and deployed [19]. In case of process-driven DSS, this low-code approach results in a tailored DSS that prompts the decision maker for input data, forwards the data to and between decision support services in the background, and returns output data to the decision maker (cf. explanation of Fig. 1a in the previous section).

A low-code approach for the creation of tailored DSS offers the benefit that decision makers are provided with individualized decision support in a shorter amount of time compared to relying on DSS developers to perform customizations for them [9]. However, as elaborated in the previous Sect. 1, working with unfamiliar third-party services also introduces a risk of dataflow errors which renders the generated DSS unusable. These dataflow errors may be introduced during design or execution of a process-driven DSS. In the upcoming subsection, we therefore review existing work that focuses on detection of dataflow errors in process-driven applications and process models in general.

2.2   Dataflow Validation in Process Models

Fundamental dataflow errors documented in early work are *missing data* (E3 in Sect. 1), *redundant data* (E5 or an unneeded data input which is not consumed), *lost data* (a data object produced by one activity is overwritten by another activity) or *inconsistent data* (a data object is simultaneously read by one activity and written by another or modified by an external source) [18,27]. The fundamental dataflow errors have been translated to specific process model notations such as BPMN with algorithms for error detection [17,24].

Some work also mentions *mismatched data* where the structure/format of data object produced by a activity does not align with the structure required by a consuming activity, or *insufficient data* which does not include enough information to perform an activity [18]. Although related, the latter two errors do not immediately align with error types E1 and E2 of Sect. 1, as data may be well-formed and complete but still incompatible with a service implementing an activity (e.g., a correct network topology which is too large to be processed by a service). We found work specifically targeting errors of type E1 and E2 (which are the focus of this paper) to be limited: Awad et al. [2] present an approach which detects dataflow errors by associating each data object with a state value from a predefined enumeration. The approach of Borrego et al. [5] supports the definition of constraints on quantitative variables used throughout a process model. Both approaches do not support constraints on complex data types which can be expected in complex business environments, e.g., to express "the size of the network topology must be below 100 nodes". The UML- and OCL-based approach by Estañol et al. [7] is more expressive in this regard, but only supports dataflow validation throughout process design.

The sole focus on process design can also be observed for all other approaches discussed so far and extends to existing work in the context of process-driven applications. Those approaches either focus on detecting anomalies in the process model from the implementing source code of process activities [21,23] or generating tests for the validation of the PDA after design and before usage in production [22]. Approaches such as [29] are inspired by service matching based on side effects of services which is not applicable for decision support as services can be assumed to be free of side effects and only operate on input data. Existing work utilizing constraints in process models do so for purposes other than ensuring data compatibility, e.g., resource allocation [3].

3   Research Objectives

In this section, we present five research objectives *R1–R5* for an approach to detect data incompatibilities in process-driven DSS (E1 and E2 in Sect. 1). The objectives are derived based on our experience in decision support for energy distribution network planning [8] and the discussion of existing work for error detection in process models in the previous section. The objectives are demonstrated with examples referring to the process model shown in Fig. 1a. Data exchanged between services in that process model can be characterized by the types and attributes shown in Fig. 2.

The objectives can be categorized into objectives for modeling data constraints of services (R1 and R2), for validating that these constraints are not violated during design and execution of a process-driven DSS (R3 and R4), and for providing validation feedback (R5).

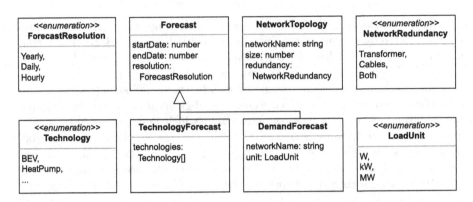

Fig. 2. UML class diagram representing data types and characteristic attributes

R1 – Type Constraints. Validation should detect incompatible types for data exchanged between services. This is important to distinguish data which is structurally equivalent, but needs to be interpreted differently. For example, the topology optimization service may only be able to support electricity networks and not gas networks which potentially use the same topology format.

R2 – Attribute Constraints. Validation should detect that data produced by a service or a decision maker exhibits characteristics that render it incompatible with a service which is supposed to consume the data. For instance, the service for topology optimization may specify that *"The provided demand forecast must be of yearly resolution"* or *"The size of the consumed network topology must be below 100 nodes"*. There may also be references within these constraints to data inputs, e.g., *"The provided demand forecast and network topology must be for the same electricity network"*.

R3 – Design Compatibility. Validation should guarantee the absence of data incompatibilities during process design. This ensures that the process can be enacted when a decision maker uses the resulting DSS during a later point in time. For example, validation could detect that the demand forecast generation service will always produce a forecast with daily resolution, which is incompatible with the yearly resolution expected by topology optimization service.

R4 – Execution Compatibility. Validation should ensure data compatibility during process execution in the context of the process-driven DSS. This ensures that a decision maker cannot select input data which cannot be consumed by the intended service(s). For example, validation could detect that a selected network topology consists of 250 nodes which exceeds the maximum of 100 nodes supported by the topology optimization service.

R5 – Feedback. Validation should provide traceable feedback containing information where and why data incompatibilities occur so that they can be resolved by decision makers. Feedback should furthermore be provided within one second (ideally 100 ms) to avoid interruptions in the flow of thought [12].

4 Solution and Demonstration

In this section, we present our solution approach for detecting data incompatibilities in process-driven DSS. After an overview of our solution in Sect. 4.1, we explain how to describe data constraints in Sect. 4.2 and validate them during design and execution of a process-driven DSS in Sects. 4.3 and 4.4 respectively.

4.1 Solution Overview

Our approach is based on capturing key characteristics of data objects exchanged throughout a process model as *metadata*, e.g., the temporal resolution of a forecast. We then use *metadata schemas* to express constraints on metadata attributes which may be interpreted as *data guarantees* (e.g., a produced forecast always *will* have a certain resolution) or *data requirements* (e.g., a consumed forecast always *must* have a certain resolution). By associating these data constraints with *service interfaces* documenting the data produced and consumed by each service, we can validate data compatibility during process design and execution. During process design, we validate *interface compatibility* by checking if the metadata schema of the data produced by a service is compatible to the schema of a subsequent service in the dataflow consuming the data. During process execution, we validate *instance compatibility* by checking if metadata associated with a data instance validates against the metadata schema of the service which is supposed to consume it.

We built our approach on the existing *JSON Schema* specification, "a JSON-based format for describing the structure of JSON data" [30]. An example for a JSON instance describing a person is shown in Listing 1 conformant to the JSON Schema shown in Listing 2.

Listing 1. Person JSON	**Listing 2.** Person Schema
```{ /* "$schema": ---> */ "name": "John Doe", "age": 43 } ```	```{ "type": "object", "properties": { "name": { "type": "string" }, "age": { "type": "int", "minimum": 0 } }} ```

We decided in favor of JSON Schema for multiple reasons: First, we can use the key-value structure of JSON to specify metadata. Second, we can implement instance validation by validating a JSON document with metadata against the corresponding metadata JSON Schema. Third, we can implement interface validation by programmatically checking if one metadata schema is a subset of another metadata schema. Fourth, JSON Schema is widespread among developers and therefore comes with tool support as part of its (third-party) ecosystem.

4.2 Data Constraint Modeling

In this section, we present a meta-model which allows the definition of service interfaces and associated data constraints as metadata schemas based on JSON

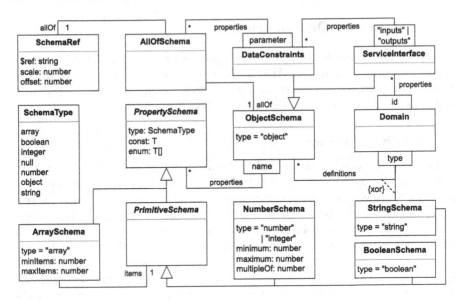

Fig. 3. Meta-model for data constraints as a UML class diagram

Schema (cf. *R1 – Type Constraints* and *R2 – Attribute Constraints*). The meta-model is shown in Fig. 3 as a UML class diagram which is subsequently explained in more detail. The `Schema`-classes are provided by JSON Schema which heavily relies on representing collections as maps instead of lists. We use qualified associations to represent this in the class diagram. All attributes are optional.

The `Domain` class captures all metadata types and service interfaces in the application domain. Metadata types are captured with the `definitions` attribute of `Domain` indexed by their name. Each metadata type is either a `StringSchema` defining an enumeration, or an `ObjectSchema` describing a type's metadata `properties` indexed by their `name`. Metadata properties (represented by the `PropertySchema` class) can be a primitive attribute (i.e., a number, string or boolean represented by the analogously named subclasses of `PrimitiveSchema`) or an array of primitive types (represented by `ArraySchema`). The `items` property of the `ArraySchema` denotes the schema of all items in the array. Annotated examples for metadata schemas are given in Listing 3.

Service interfaces are represented by the `ServiceInterface` class documenting the `DataConstraints` for *input* and *output* `parameter`s of a service. Constraints, which we also refer to as *metadata schema*, are represented as an `AllOfSchema`[2]. This schema is defined as the combination of two other schemas: The first schema is a `SchemaReference` which references the data objects' metadata schema (specified in the `Domain`'s `definitions`). The reference is provided as a JSON Pointer [1] in the `$ref`-attribute. The second schema is an

---

[2] Data object collections can be represented as `ArraySchema` with `AllOfSchema` as `items`. (Not shown in Fig. 3 to reduce complexity.).

Listing 3. Examples of modeling metadata types (cont. in Listing 4)

```
1   {
2     "$schema": "http://json-schema.org/draft-07/schema",
3     "definitions": { /* data types & metadata attributes */
4       "Resolution": { "enum": ["Yearly", "Daily", "Hourly"] },
5       "TechnologyForecast": { "properties": {
6         /* A Technology Forecast specifies a resolution... */
7         "resolution": { "$ref": "#/definitions/Resolution"},
8         /* ... and a list of included technologies */
9         "technologies": {
10          "items": { "$ref": "#/definitions/Technology"}
11        }}},
12      "NetworkTopology": { "properties": {
13        "size": { "type": "number" }
14      }} /* other types of Fig. 2 abbreviated */
15    },
```

ObjectSchema describing constraints on metadata properties. Constraints can ensure value equality (const of PropertySchema) or membership in an enumeration (enum of PropertySchema). The T as datatype of the const and enum attributes denotes a generic type which is set based on the schema's type. Inequality for numbers is supported based on the minimum and maximum properties of NumberSchema. Although not shown in Fig. 3, a SchemaReference may be used as an alternative to PropertySchema to reference assertions on a data input with number manipulation (scale and offset). Annotated examples for service interfaces with inputs and outputs are shown in Listing 4.

4.3   Interface Compatibility Validation

Metadata schemas can be used to validate *interface compatibility* during design of a process-driven DSS to ensure that data produced by a service can be consumed by a subsequent service in the dataflow (cf. *R3 – Design Compatibility*). In the following, we first focus on validating interface compatibility for a single data object exchanged between services in the process model.

Metadata, which for instance documents that a demand forecast has a daily resolution, can only be associated with concrete data instances available during process execution. When validating interface compatibility during process design, only metadata *schemas* are available which are defined for service input and output parameters. These metadata schemas document *data guarantees* for data produced by a service output parameter, i.e., specify that all produced forecasts will have a yearly resolution. For input parameters of a service, metadata schemas document *data requirements*, i.e., that all forecasts to be consumed by this parameter must have a yearly or daily resolution (cf. line 24 of Listing 4). To ensure interface compatibility, we must check that all metadata which validates against the metadata schema of the producing service parameter will also validate against the schema of the consuming service parameter. For this

Listing 4. Examples of modeling service interfaces (cont. from Listing 3)

```
16    "properties": { /* = service interfaces */
17     "TopologyOptimization": { "properties": {
18      "inputs": { "properties": { /* = data constraints */
19       "demandForecast": { "allOf": [
20        /* The input is of type "DemandForecast" ... */
21        { "$ref": "#/definitions/DemandForecast" },
22        { "properties": {
23         /* ... with a yearly or daily resolution. */
24         "resolution": { "enum": ["Yearly", "Daily"] }
25        }}
26       ]},
27       "currentTopology": { "allOf": [
28        { "$ref": "#/definitions/NetworkTopology"},
29        /* Network size must be below 100 */
30        { "properties": { "size": { "maximum": 100} }}
31       ]}
32      }},
33      "outputs": { "properties": {
34       "optimizedTopology": { "allOf": [
35        {"$ref": "#/definitions/NetworkTopology"},
36        { "properties": {
37         /* Optimized size is 50% of current size */
38         "size": { "$ref": "...", "scale": 0.5 },
39         /* Network is redundant in transformers */
40         "redundancy": { "const": "Transformers"}
41        }}]}}}}
42    }}} /* other services abbreviated */
43    }
```

purpose, it is not necessary to enumerate and compare all metadata instances which validate against the producing and consuming metadata schema. Instead, the compatibility can be computed on schema-level by checking if the metadata schema of the producing parameter is a subset of the metadata schema of the consuming parameter. For instance, if the *DemandForecast* service were to specify the resolution of its produced forecast as {"enum": ["Yearly"]}, it would be a sublist of the {"enum": ["Yearly","Daily"]} of the *TopologyOptimization* service (cf. line 24 in Listing 4). Consequently, the demand forecast produced by *DemandForecast* can be used with the *TopologyOptimization* service. If the resolution guarantee/requirement were reversed between services (i.e., *Demand-Forecast* producing a yearly or daily forecast and TopologyOptimization only supporting yearly resolution), the data could no longer be exchanged as the potentially daily resolution of the demand forecast would not be supported by the *TopologyOptimization* service.

In addition to checking if the producing metadata schema is a subset of the consuming metadata schema, we also have to ensure equality of the (meta)data type. Otherwise we risk errors due to "duck typing", i.e., two schemas being structurally equal with respect to metadata attributes and constraints but being interpreted differently (e.g., a topology for an electricity network and a gas network). For checking the metadata type, we just have to compare the `$ref`-string in the `SchemaReference` of the `AllOfSchema` (cf. line 21 of Listing 4).

The previously described steps only validate the interface compatibility for a single data object exchanged between services. For validation of a complete process model, they can be repeated for each exchanged data object. However, instead of validating the whole process model at once, we recommend an incremental validation for each newly defined data exchange during design to provide continuous feedback to decision makers (cf. *R5 – Feedback*). The feedback can also contain the reason of incompatibility, i.e., why two metadata schemas are incompatible (cf. *yearly* vs. *yearly/daily* example explained before). During validation, the conditional execution sequence of services is irrelevant. Consider for instance a data object which is produced by a service which is selected based on the condition of an exclusive gateway. Then, interface conformity must hold for each path through the process, regardless which service is executed based on the evaluation of the exclusive gateway's condition. Otherwise, if one path fails, the absence of errors during DSS execution can no longer be guaranteed.

4.4 Instance Compatibility Validation

The goal of *instance compatibility validation* is to ensure that data provided by a decision maker during DSS execution is compatible with the service parameter which is supposed to consume it (cf. *R4 – Execution Compatibility*).

Since instance validation is performed during execution, concrete metadata describing the selected data instance is available. For example, the metadata for a selected topology may document the topology size to be 250 nodes. This makes instance validation inherently easier than interface validation because a JSON document containing the metadata can be validated against the metadata schema of the service parameter it should be used for. For example, the topology metadata can be validated against the metadata schema of the *TopologyOptimization*'s `currentTopology` parameter which specifies a maximum topology size of 100 nodes (lines 27 to 31 of Listing 4).

Similar to validation of interface compatibility, the validation of instance compatibility also requires an additional validation of the metadata type to avoid accidental duck typing. As indicated by Listing 1, the metadata type can be annotated by the `$schema`-attribute which provides a reference to the metadata type. This can then be compared against the value of `$ref` in the `SchemaReference` of the `AllOfSchema` in the metadata schema.

When selecting a data instance, the reason for incompatibility with respect to metadata values can be returned to the decision maker for quick feedback (cf. *R5 – Feedback*). Since the selected data instance can be consumed by multiple services (cf. *Current Topology* in Fig. 1a), the metadata must validate against all of their relevant parameter's metadata schemas.

For increased usability, the JSON document containing metadata could be derived from the data instance. Alternatively, a form for manual metadata documentation could be generated from the metadata schema[3].

---

[3] Forms can for instance be generated using https://jsonforms.io/.

5   Implementation and Discussion

We prototypically implemented our approach to demonstrate its technical feasibility. The open-source implementation is publicly available[4]. Our implementation contains a command-line application which supports incremental interface and instance validation as described in Sects. 4.3 and 4.4. For most of the functionality related to JSON Schema, we could leverage existing libraries, e.g., for computing that a schema is a subset of another schema[5] and that a JSON document validates against a schema[6]. We extended the functionality provided by libraries with support for type checking, the format of service interfaces described in Sect. 4.2 and unified reporting of validation errors for traceability. Our implementation furthermore includes a test suite and demonstration based on the running example used throughout this paper. When applying our implementation in this context, we were able to complete each validation in less than 100ms with commodity hardware. Based on these insights and the conceptual explanation of our approach in the previous section, we can conclude that our approach is fundamentally able to address type validation (*R1 – Type Constraints*) and data attribute validation (*R2 – Attribute Constraints*) during design (*R3 – Design Compatibility*) and execution (*R4 – Execution Compatibility*) of a process-driven DSS with traceable feedback being provided in a reasonable amount of time (*R5 – Feedback*) – thereby addressing all research objectives of Sect. 3.

In addition to insights regarding the technical feasibility, the implementation and demonstration also revealed some insights regarding the expressiveness of our approach with respect to constraints on data attributes. *R2 – Attribute Constraints* essentially defines two types of constraints, namely *value-based constraints* (which assert that a data attribute has a static value) and *reference-based constraints* (where the asserted value is obtained by reference to another data input). Although we discovered no difficulties with value-based constraints, the expressiveness of reference-based constraints is limited. While references between schemas are technically possible and presented in our prototypical implementation, the example "The provided demand forecast and network topology must be for the same electricity network" given in *R2 – Attribute Constraints* cannot be expressed. This is due to the design of JSON Schema which only allows the definition of schema constraints with respect to static values known during schema authoring and not with respect to values that are obtained from attributes in the JSON document validated against the schema. We believe this lack of expressiveness can be addressed with a custom domain specific language (DSL) specifically designed for expressing (meta)data attribute constraints. This observation also indicates that requirements regarding the expressiveness of the constraints may vary between different application domains. It therefore seems useful to apply our solution approach to more application domains in order to transform the research objectives in Sect. 3 into more detailed solution requirements.

---

[4] https://github.com/krchf/schema-based-dataflow-validation.
[5] https://www.npmjs.com/package/is-json-schema-subset.
[6] https://ajv.js.org/.

In addition to expressiveness, another argument in favor of a custom DSL is developer experience (although not explicitly captured in Sect. 3). Developers are primarily service providers which write schemas to document data constraints of their services. Despite IDE support being helpful while writing schemas, we found the resulting schemas to be quite verbose. For instance, a constraint of the form `currentTopology.size < 100` is expressed using lines 27 to 31 of Listing 4. A sufficient familiarization with JSON Schema is required to write (and understand) such a constraint. Additionally, the JSON Schema specification is constantly evolving[7]. Developers must therefore pay attention to use the same version of specification and that their IDE and other tools support this version.

6   Summary and Future Work

Decision makers can create tailored DSS by specifying the recombination of interoperable decision support services via a process model. Such tailored, process-driven DSS need to execute properly in order to enable uninterrupted and error-free decision processes. For this purpose, it is important to ensure interface compatibility during process design (i.e., data produced by one service is compatible with the data requirements of a subsequent service) and instance compatibility during execution of the process-driven DSS (i.e., data selected by decision makers during execution can be consumed by a service). In this paper, we first derived research objectives for an approach to detect such data incompatibilities from the domain of energy distribution network planning. Based on the research objectives, we presented a meta-model based on the existing JSON Schema specification to model the data guarantees and requirements of services with respect to metadata specific to a given application domain. Subsequently, we explained how the modeled data guarantees and requirements can be used to validate interface and instance compatibility. We demonstrated our approach for decision support in energy distribution network planning using an open-source prototypical implementation. Our discussion revealed that the initially derived research objectives can be addressed using this approach, but future work independent of JSON Schema could further increase expressiveness and developer experience. Additional future work may extend our approach to also support error types E3–E5 currently covered by related work, or integrate it into BPMN editors to visually depict (violations of) data constraints. We also want to further study the benefits of our approach in establishing a decision support ecosystem [9] where decision makers, domain experts and DSS developers collaborate on best practices for creating tailored DSS using a shared platform. In this context, it seems valuable to not only validate dataflow correctness, but also consider semantic correctness. For instance, a decision maker may utilize a topology reduction service to simplify a network topology in order to meet size constraints imposed by the topology optimization service. However, if the decision maker forgets to undo the topology reduction after optimization, the optimization results are only applicable to the reduced topology and cannot be interpreted with respect to

---

[7] Versions are listed at https://json-schema.org/specification-links.html.

the original network topology. Such mistakes involving multiple activities of the process model also negate the usefulness of the generated DSS. This idea can be further extended to check if the requirements for decision support of a decision maker are actually addressed by a process-based service composition, e.g., similar to [15].

References

1. JavaScript Object Notation (JSON) Pointer. Standard, Internet Engineering Task Force (2013)
2. Awad, A., Decker, G., Lohmann, N.: Diagnosing and repairing data anomalies in process models. In: Rinderle-Ma, S., Sadiq, S., Leymann, F. (eds.) BPM 2009. LNBIP, vol. 43, pp. 5–16. Springer, Heidelberg (2010). https://doi.org/10.1007/978-3-642-12186-9_2
3. Awad, A., Grosskopf, A., Meyer, A., Weske, M.: Enabling resource assignment constraints in BPMN. Technical report, Hasso Plattner Institute (2009)
4. Bennett, N., Lemoine, G.J.: What a difference a word makes: understanding threats to performance in a VUCA world. Bus. Horiz. **57**(3), 311–317 (2014)
5. Borrego, D., Eshuis, R., Gómez-López, M.T., Gasca, R.M.: Diagnosing correctness of semantic workflow models. Data Knowl. Eng. **87**, 167–184 (2013)
6. Dean, J.W., Sharfman, M.P.: Does decision process matter? A study of strategic decision-making effectiveness. Acad. Manag. J. **39**(2), 368–392 (1996)
7. Estañol, M., Sancho, M.-R., Teniente, E.: Verification and validation of UML artifact-centric business process models. In: Zdravkovic, J., Kirikova, M., Johannesson, P. (eds.) CAiSE 2015. LNCS, vol. 9097, pp. 434–449. Springer, Cham (2015). https://doi.org/10.1007/978-3-319-19069-3_27
8. Kirchhoff, J., Burmeister, S.C., Weskamp, C., Engels, G.: Towards a decision support system for cross-sectoral energy distribution network planning. In: Energy Informatics and Electro Mobility ICT (2021)
9. Kirchhoff, J., Weskamp, C., Engels, G.: Decision support ecosystems: definition and platform architecture. In: Cabral Seixas Costa, A.P., Papathanasiou, J., Jayawickrama, U., Kamissoko, D. (eds.) Decision Support Systems XII: Decision Support Addressing Modern Industry, Business, and Societal Needs. ICDSST 2022, vol. 447. Springer, Cham (2022). https://doi.org/10.1007/978-3-031-06530-9_8
10. Lohmann, N., Nyolt, M.: Artifact-centric modeling using BPMN. In: Pallis, G., et al. (eds.) ICSOC 2011. LNCS, vol. 7221, pp. 54–65. Springer, Heidelberg (2012). https://doi.org/10.1007/978-3-642-31875-7_7
11. Mustafin, N., Kopylov, P., Ponomarev, A.: Knowledge-based automated service composition for decision support systems configuration. In: Silhavy, R., Silhavy, P., Prokopova, Z. (eds.) CoMeSySo 2021. LNNS, vol. 231, pp. 780–788. Springer, Cham (2021). https://doi.org/10.1007/978-3-030-90321-3_63
12. Nielsen, J.: Usability Engineering. Morgan Kaufmann Publishers Inc., San Francisco (1993)
13. Object Management Group: Business process model and notation (2014). https://www.omg.org/spec/BPMN/. Accessed 21 Mar 2022
14. Ou, L., Peng, H.: Knowledge and process based decision support in business intelligence system. In: First International Multi-symposiums on Computer and Computational Sciences (IMSCCS 2006), vol. 2, pp. 780–786 (2006)

15. Parsa, S., Ebrahimifard, A., Amiri, M.J., Arani, M.K.: Towards a goal-driven method for web service choreography validation. In: 2016 Second International Conference on Web Research (ICWR), pp. 66–71 (2016)
16. Peffers, K., Tuunanen, T., Rothenberger, M.A., Chatterjee, S.: A design science research methodology for information systems research. J. Manag. Inf. Syst. **24**(3), 45–77 (2007)
17. Rachdi, A., En-Nouaary, A., Dahchour, M.: Dataflow analysis in BPMN models. In: Proceedings of the 19th International Conference on Enterprise Information Systems (ICEIS 2017), vol. 2, pp. 229–237. Scitepress (2017)
18. Sadiq, S., Orlowska, M., Sadiq, W., Foulger, C.: Data flow and validation in workflow modelling. In: Proceedings of the 15th Australasian Database Conference, ADC 2004, vol. 27, pp. 207–214. Australian Computer Society Inc, Sydney (2004)
19. Sahay, A., Indamutsa, A., Di Ruscio, D., Pierantonio, A.: Supporting the understanding and comparison of low-code development platforms. In: 2020 46th Euromicro Conference on Software Engineering and Advanced Applications (SEAA), pp. 171–178 (2020)
20. Savić, D.A., Bicik, J., Morley, M.S.: A DSS generator for multiobjective optimisation of spreadsheet-based models. Environ. Model. Softw. **26**(5), 551–561 (2011)
21. Schneid, K., Kuchen, H., Thöne, S., Di Bernardo, S.: Uncovering data-flow anomalies in BPMN-based process-driven applications, pp. 1504–1512. Association for Computing Machinery, New York (2021)
22. Schneid, K., Stapper, L., Thöne, S., Kuchen, H.: Automated regression tests: a nocode approach for BPMN-based process-driven applications. In: 2021 IEEE 25th International Enterprise Distributed Object Computing Conference (EDOC), pp. 31–40 (2021)
23. Schneid, K., Usener, C.A., Thöne, S., Kuchen, H., Tophinke, C.: Static analysis of BPMN-based process-driven applications. In: Proceedings of the 34th ACM/SIGAPP Symposium on Applied Computing, SAC 2019, pp. 66–74. Association for Computing Machinery, New York (2019)
24. von Stackelberg, S., Putze, S., Mülle, J., Böhm, K.: Detecting data-flow errors in BPMN 2.0. Open J. Inf. Syst. (OJIS) **1**(2), 1–19 (2014)
25. Stiehl, V.: Definition of process-driven applications. In: Process-Driven Applications with BPMN, pp. 13–41. Springer, Cham (2014). https://doi.org/10.1007/978-3-319-07218-0_2
26. Sun, S.X., Zhao, J.L., Nunamaker, J.F., Sheng, O.R.L.: Formulating the data-flow perspective for business process management. Inf. Syst. Res. **17**(4), 374–391 (2006)
27. Trčka, N., van der Aalst, W.M.P., Sidorova, N.: Data-flow anti-patterns: discovering data-flow errors in workflows. In: van Eck, P., Gordijn, J., Wieringa, R. (eds.) CAiSE 2009. LNCS, vol. 5565, pp. 425–439. Springer, Heidelberg (2009). https://doi.org/10.1007/978-3-642-02144-2_34
28. Wang, Y., Ruhe, G.: The cognitive process of decision making. Int. J. Cogn. Inform. Nat. Intell. **1**(2), 73–85 (2007)
29. Weber, I., Hoffmann, J., Mendling, J.: Beyond soundness: on the verification of semantic business process models. Distrib. Parallel Databases **27**(3), 271–343 (2010)
30. Wright, A., Andrews, H., Hutton, B., Dennis, G.: JSON schema: a media type for describing JSON documents. Internet-draft, IETF (2020). https://json-schema.org/draft/2020-12/json-schema-core.html. Accessed 21 Mar 2022

Semantic Relations of Sub-models in an Enterprise Model

Ella Roubtsova(✉) and Sefanja Severin

Open University, Valkenburgerweg 177, 6419 AT Heerlen, The Netherlands
ella.roubtsova@ou.nl

Abstract. Enterprise modeling is a set of tools, methods and practices for an aligned development of business, functional, organizational and technical aspects of an enterprise. Therefore, an enterprise model is always a set of sub-models of different semantics. In order to form a consistent enterprise model, its sub-models should be aligned to each other. The practice of modeling shows the difficulties in design of an aligned set of sub-models of an enterprise model. In this paper we present a review of enterprise modeling approaches aiming to find the reasons of difficulties. Our review shows that enterprise modeling approaches not sufficiently use the semantic relations of sub-models for building an enterprise model. This paper identifies and formalizes the semantic relations of sub-models and suggests to use them as constraints directing the design of aligned sub-models. The constraints imposed by sub-models of the enterprise model to each other are illustrated with a case study in ArchiMate.

Keywords: Enterprise modeling · Sub-models · Goal sub-model · Concept sub-model · Process sub-model · Semantic relations of sub-models · Model consistency · Sub-models alignment · ArchiMate

1 Introduction

Enterprise modeling is a set of tools, methods and practices "for an aligned development of all parts of an enterprise, e.g. business, functional, organizational and technical aspects" [23].

Enterprise modeling (EM) approaches present these different parts of an enterprise as sub-models. There are sub-models that use the same semantics and notation of concepts and relations (boxes and arrows). Such sub-models separate sub-domains of the modeled enterprise (resources, technical components, actors, business concepts). There are sub-models that present dynamics with a process semantics. They use processes and flow relations, states, events and triggering relations. Other sub-models present the motivation of the modeled enterprise and use goals and requirements as elements and their refinement relations.

The sub-models in a consistent enterprise model should be related or aligned to each other [8]. The practice shows how difficult it is to align sub-models into a consistent enterprise model. Many authors, for example, [12,17], emphasize

© Springer Nature Switzerland AG 2022
B. Shishkov (Ed.): BMSD 2022, LNBIP 453, pp. 104–121, 2022.
https://doi.org/10.1007/978-3-031-11510-3_7

the critical alignment of enterprise sub-models to the goal sub-model. Kaisler at al. [8] identify the critical problems of alignment, such as using in sub-models the non-matching levels of abstraction, limited tool support for business process alignment with other sub-models and for managing the integrated enterprise life cycle. All these problems cannot be solved without methodological support for designing aligned sub-models.

Section 2 of this paper presents the result of our review of enterprise modeling approaches that shows some history of accumulating and aligning a set of sub-models in an enterprise model. By evaluating enterprise modeling approaches, we have recognized that the relations of sub-models can be defined only at some level of detail and these relations may direct the modeling to a consistent enterprise model. We define an aligned or consistent[1] enterprise model as follows:

An aligned or consistent enterprise model is a set of sub-models of different semantics, where sub-models restrict or constrain each other and the restrictions and constraints are defined in terms of semantics of sub-models.

Section 3 of this paper shows a case study of enterprise modeling, directed with semantic relations of sub-models.

Section 4 generalizes the semantic relations of sub-models in an enterprise model.

Section 5 concludes the paper and presents ideas for future work.

2   Related Work. Attempts to Address Consistency of an Enterprise Model

The notion of consistency of an enterprise model, meaning aligning of all its sub-models to each other, faces difficulties caused by the need to include a sub-model representing requirements for the model and by the different semantics of sub-models. Let us show how it was recognized and handled historically.

The 4+1 approach has been designed "for describing the architecture of software-intensive systems" [10]. The *+1* in the *4+1* approach is an attempt to include a sub-model of requirements, into a *4+1* enterprise model and make all sub-models aligned with this sub-model and with each other.

The *+1* sub-model is a set of scenarios presented in the UML Use Case Diagram. "Scenarios are used to identify architectural elements and to illustrate and validate the architecture design. They also serve as a starting point for tests of an architecture prototype" [10]. Each scenario corresponds to a set of requirements, often combined as a set of milestones or presenting separation of domains. Speaking about the order of designing of sub-models, we see that the *+1* sub-model should be the first, however, the *+1* is never seen as a complete presentation of requirements. The architectural elements identified in the *+1* are depicted in other sub-models presented using *4* semantics: (1) Class Diagrams, (2) State Machines or Protocol State Machines, (3) Sequence or Communication or Activity Diagrams, (4) Component and Package Diagrams [5,9,16]. The relations of sub-models are defined as rules on *4* semantics. The *+1* sub-model is

---

[1] Both terms are used, even by the same group of authors, for example [8].

excluded. Egyed [3] reports that there is "a division between those who compare design models directly and those who transform design models into some intermediate, usually formal, representation to compare there". The comparison of sub-models directly requires consistency rules, for example, "Name of a message must match an operation in receiver's class"; "Calling direction of a message must match an association". There is an analyzer for "instant error feedback that profiles consistency rules" [3]. The analyzer needs an external information to collect semantic rules for consistency checks of sub-models.

The need of a sub-model representing requirements in an enterprise model has initiated the attempts to combine goal models with UML models. *The KAOS approach* [19] has introduced a practical goal modeling with refinement of goals and its application for system modeling. However, Letier et al. [11] have identified a semantic difference between the goal models and the UML behavior semantics (State Machines, Sequence or Communication or Activity Diagrams). The goal models define quiescent states that should be achieved by the system. A quiescent state means that the system cannot change this state by itself; the system preserves this state indefinitely long time until an external event. In a UML behavior semantics, the changes of the system state may be caused by events taken from the bags or queues of earlier arrived events [21].

In parallel, the enterprise modeling approaches have tried to include the goal sub-model into an enterprise model and choose the behavior semantics that can be aligned with the semantics of goal models.

The 4EM approach has defined an Enterprise Model as a tuple of six sub-models.

- Goal sub-model uses the semantics of [19]. An element (box) is a goal, business rule or requirement. A relation (arrow) is a refinement relation of a goal to a sub-goal or a requirement, a business rule to requirement.
- Concept Model, Actors and Resource Model and Technical Components Model types use the semantics of object models. An element (box) presents a business object or a physical resource. A relation (arrow) can be a binary, an operation or a specialization or an aggregation relation [23, p. 112].
- Business Process Model uses a process semantics. There are two types of elements (boxes): information sets and processes. A relation(arrow) between a process and an information set or between an information (material) set and a process presents a control flow. *AND* and *OR* join and split connectors are used to present alternatives and cycles [23, p. 121].

The relations of sub-models in an enterprise model are abstractly described in [23, p. 78] with a diagram. For example, a Goal Model "uses" and "is related" to the Concept Model, "motivates" and "requires" Business Process Model and Technical Components Model [23, p. 78]. The restrictions that sub-models impose on each other in an enterprise model are expressed as "a number of consistency rules" [23, p. 211]. For example, the rule: *"Every information set or material set in a Business Process Model must be expressed using concepts of the Concept Model,"* relates concepts in the Concept Model and information sets in the Business Process Model.

To design a consistent enterprise model, the 4EM approach suggests the modeler to (1) integrate the sub-models, so that "the inter-model links should establish a clear line of reasoning" [23, p. 211]; (2) visually check the consistency rules; (3) identify inconsistencies and make iterations to improve the model. The practice of application of the 4EM shows that the integration can be applied in small cases and usually results in a model having boxes and arrows with different meaning, what makes the model difficult to observe and understand. The examples can be seen in [23, p. 213, 214]. The visual checks of consistency rules are very useful for small models, however, the consistency rules just partially define the semantic relations of sub-models and do not direct the design of sub-models.

The ExtREME approach [20,22] presents an enterprise model as a set of a Goal, a Concept, and an executable Protocol sub-models. ExtREME exploits the similarity of semantics of a goal, being a quiescent state of the modeled system, in a Goal sub-model and a quiescent state in an executable Protocol sub-model [13].

The relations of sub-models are used to direct the design of the enterprise model from a Goal sub-model to a Protocol sub-model. The refinement patterns of the Goal sub-model identify the states of life cycles of concepts.

A Protocol sub-model is a set of *protocol machines*. Each protocol machine presents a life cycle of a concept. The elements of a protocol machine are the following: a local structure (to present states of the life cycle of a concept) and a set of transition relations. A transition from state "a" to another state "b" is labeled with an event "e", that can happen in state "a".

An event "e" is a happening in environment. An event is presented with a data structure. The data of an event and the local structure of the protocol machine are used to check if the event can happen and to update the local structure of the protocol machine after the transition.

The instances of life cycles of concepts (instances of protocol machines) are synchronized using the CSP-parallel composition [13,14]: if an event is recognized by several instances protocol machines, it can happen only if all these instances are in the state where this event can happen. A business process is a set of sequences of synchronized executions of instances of protocol machines. The consistency of sub-models in ExTREME is achieved by executing the protocol sub-model and testing all requirements presented in the goal sub-model.

The ArchiMate approach [24] has been designed as a foundation for a consistent enterprise model. ArchiMate provides a "structure or a storage for an internal model of an enterprise", that includes sets of elements and relations. If an internal model of an enterprise model has been filled in with unique (non-duplicating) elements and relations, then this model can be used as a source for designing views being consistent with the internal model.

The practice of enterprise modeling shows that it is difficult to fill the internal model in with the unique (not duplicating) elements and relations. The reasons of the difficulties are caused by the team modeling and human factors: (1) modelers draw different sub-models and even their parts (views) as teams and the internal model is filled in from these drawings; (2) the sub-models and the order of their building, and the naming of elements and relations are chosen by modelers (often different team members). Modelers can make typos, duplicate names, miss elements or relations.

The structure of an internal ArchiMate model of an enterprise model is the following:

- 'Two main types of elements: "structure elements" and "behavior elements", " inspired by natural language, where a sentence has a subject (active structure), a verb (behavior), and an object (passive structure) [24, sec. 4].
- The element "event" in ArchiMate is defined differently than in many other notations [4,6,14]. An event in ArchiMate is actually a state: "*A business event represents an organizational state change*" [24, sec. 8.3.4].
- There are motivation elements. "A motivation element represents the context of or a reason behind the architecture of an enterprise" [24, sec. 4]. Elements "Goal" and "Requirement" are among motivation elements.
- There is a set of relations: access, composition, flow, aggregation, assignment, influence, association, realization, specialization, triggering, serving [24, sec. 5.6]. There is a table [24, B.5] that specifies what kinds of relations are allowed for what kinds of elements. The semantics of most relations corresponds to the Concept sub-model semantics. Some relations are applicable in Process sub-models.
- The refinement relation used in Goal sub-models does not exist in ArchiMate.

Providing an internal model structure for an enterprise model, the ArchiMate does not provide any systematic way or method for collecting elements and relations for the internal model. The internal model is often filled in with elements and relations from sub-models or their partial views drawn by modelers on the spur of the moment. As a result, the internal model may contain double copies of elements, not-related elements, elements that are not related to goals and all typos and mistakes that a modeler can make, trying to capture a case description. Although there is a tool support to mark suspicious model elements [1], but the decision about any model correction is delegated to the modeler and the correction is often postponed and forgotten.

Our review of enterprise modeling approaches shows that the semantic relations of sub-models of an enterprise model are recognized in all approaches, but they are not used to direct the design of sub-models. The semantic relations of sub-models, expressed in 4EM, KAOS and ExtREME, need generalization to direct the design of sub-models aligned to each other in a consistent enterprise model.

3   Semantic Analysis of Sub-models

In order to identify the semantic relations of sub-models, we use a combination of research methods, namely, a case study and a semantic analysis of sub-models within the case study.

Our case study is an executable enterprise model of an insurance business taken from [22]. This enterprise model includes sub-models that represent all three semantics: goals, concepts and behaviors. The sub-models have been already made consistent in ExREME by executing and testing techniques.

By redrawing of sub-models of this enterprise model in ArchiMate, we use the internal ArchiMate model, i.e. elements and relations (Sect. 2). The initial elements are (1) goals and requirements. The initial relations of goals and requirements are the goal refinement patterns. We also use the ArchiMate elements of two categories: (2) objects (concepts) and (3) events.

In majority of enterprise modeling notations, the terms "concept" is used to present enterprise objects at different levels of abstraction.[2] Therefore, we use the term "concept" instead of "object".

Concepts (objects) can be identified by the lexical and semantic analysis of goals and requirements. A concept can be a business object, a role, an technical component named as a noun in a sentence presenting a goal. A relation of concepts is a named pair of concepts. A name of relation is identified as a verb or a preposition in a sentence presenting a goal.

An event (a behavior element) in ArchiMate is defined differently from other notations. "*A business event represents an organizational state change*" [24, sec. 8.3.4]. Because there is no any data structure associated with an event in ArchiMate, a name of an event is a goal-sentence representing a state in a life cycle of a concept. Two events can be related with a triggering relation. "The triggering relationship is used to model the temporal or causal precedence of behavior elements in a process." [24, sec. 5.3.1].

A sequence of events is identified using a milestone refinement pattern of a goal. An alternative refinement pattern of a goal corresponds to an alternative ArchiMate events. A cycle of events can be identified by lexical analysis of a goal, when it expresses that the life cycle of a concept needs a set of instances of other concepts.

In terms of these elements and relations of the ArchiMate internal model, we define the sub-models and the semantic relations of sub-models.

3.1   Relations of Concepts and Relations of Process States Identified in the Goal Sub-model

In goal-oriented approaches, the refinement relation is used between goals, sub-goals, requirements and constraints. The ArchiMate does not specify the refinement relation. The same way as [18], we use the realization relation to present refinement. The interpretation of a realization relationship is that the whole or part of the source element realizes the whole of the target element [24, sec. 5.1.5.]. The realization relation can express the sufficient condition of refinement relation. We have modified the Archi-tool and made realization relation allowed for all pairs of motivation elements.

---

[2] In ArchiMate, both elements and relations are concepts [24, sec. 2.8].

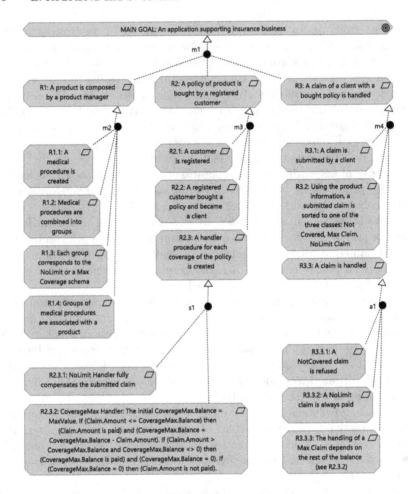

Fig. 1. Goal sub-model

The Goal sub-model of the case is presented in Fig. 1. Figures 2, 3, 4, 5 present the Relations of Concepts and Relations of Process States (ArchiMate events) identified in the Goal sub-model.

In Fig. 2, the reader can see that *"MAIN GOAL: Application supporting insurance business."* is refined to a tuple R1, R2 and R3. The refinement uses the mile-stone pattern, which means that R1, R2, R3 is a sequence of states of the concepts from the Main Goal: "Application" and "Insurance business". Each of these concepts represents the entire model. We have chosen the "Application" point of view, i.e. we focus on the data structure and relations and do not model actors.

R1, R2 and R3 are formulated as sentences in natural language. For example, *"R1. A product is composed by a product manager."* Using lexical analysis of this sentence, we can find a *is-composed(Product)* applied to any object of type

Requirements, Refinement	Nouns	Verbs, prepositions	Relations of Concepts	Relations of Process States (ArchiMate Events)
MAIN GOAL: An application supporting insurance business". **Refinement milestones-of** (MAIN GOAL, (R1,R2,R3))	Insurance business, Application			***state-sequence-of*** "An application supporting insurance business". *named in requirements R1,R2,R3*
R1: A product is composed by a product manager	Product Product Manager (role)	is-composed-by	***is-composed-by***(Product, Product Manager)	**state-of**(Product,(Product is composed)) **added by the modeler is-created** (Product)
R2: A policy of product is bought by a registered customer	Policy Product Customer	of is-bought-by	*of*(Policy, Product) ***is-bought-by***(Policy, Registered Customer)	***state-of*** *(Policy, (Policy is bought by a Registered Customer))*
R3: A claim of a client with a bought policy is handled	Claim	is-handled		***state-of*** *(Claim, (Claim is handled))*

Fig. 2. Relations from the refinement of the Main Goal

Requirements Refinement	Nouns	Verbs	Relations of Concepts	Relations of Process States
Refinement R1 **milestones-of**(R1, (R1.1, R1.2. R1.3, R1.4))				State sequences defined by synchronized business objects named in requirements.
R1.1: A medical procedure is created	Medical Procedure	is-created		***state-of***(Medical Procedure, (A Medical Procedure is created))
R1.2: Medical procedures are combined into groups	Group of Medical Procedures	is-combined	*Is-combined*(Medical Procedure, Group of Medical Procedures)	***state-sequence-of***(Medical Procedure, (A Medical Procedure is created; A Medical Procedure is combined with a Group of Medical procedures)).
R1.3: Each group corresponds to the NoLimit or a Max Coverage schema	NoLimit Schema MaxCoverage Schema Group with NoLimit Coverage Group with Max Coverage	corresponds-to	*correspond-to*(Group of Medical Procedures, NoLimit Schema) corresponds -to (Group of Medical Procedures, MaxCoverage Schema) corresponds-to(Group with NoLimit Coverage, NoLimit Schema) corresponds-to(Group with Max Coverage, MaxCoverage Schema)	***state-sequence-of*** (Group of Medical Procedures, (A Group of medical procedures is created; ***state-alternative***(Group of Medical Procedures, (A group corresponds to the NoLimit Schema; A group corresponds to the Max Coverage Schema); A Medical Procedure is combined with a Group of Medical procedures)). ***state-of***(NoLimit Schema, (NoLimit Schema is created)); ***state-of***(MaxCoverage Schema, (MaxCoverage Schema is created)); States "is created" for the Schemas and the Group are added by a modeler to enable specified events.
R1.4: Groups of medical procedures are associated with a product		are-associated	*is-associated-with*(Group of Medical Procedures, Product)	***state-sequence-of***(Product, (A Product is created; A Group of medical procedures is associated with a Product; A product is composed)); ***state-of***(Group of Medical Procedures, (A Group of medical procedures is associated with a Product)); State "A Product is created" is added by a modeler to enable specified events.

Fig. 3. Relations identified in the Goal sub-model by refinement of R1.

Requirements, Refinement	Nouns	Verbs, prepositions	Relations of Concepts	Relations of Process States
Refinement R2 milestones-of (R2, (R2.1, R2.2, R2.3))				State sequences defined by synchronized business objects named in requirements
R2.1: A customer is registered	Customer	is-registered		*state-of*(Customer, (A Customer is registered))
R2.2: A registered customer bought a policy and became a client		of is-bought	of(Policy, Product) is-bought-by(Product, Customer)	*state-of*(Policy,(A policy of a product is bought by a customer))
R2.3: A handler procedure for each coverage of the policy is created	Handler Claim NoLimit Handler CoverageMax Handler	is-created is-created	is-created-for(NoLimit Handler, NoLimit Coverage Schema) is-created-for (CoverageMax Handler, Max Coverage Schema)	*state-of* ((Policy, (NoLimit Handler is created; AND CoverageMax Handler is created))
R2.3.1 Figure 1	NoLimit Handler	is-created	is-created	
R2.3.2 Figure 1	*added by the modeler* *CoverageMax Balance* *Max Value* *Claim Amount*	*is-composed-of*	*added by the modeler:is-composed-of(CoverageMax Handler,CoverageMax Balance);* *is-composed-of(MaxCoverage Schema,Max Value);* *is-composed-of(Claim,Claim Amount)*	

Fig. 4. Relations from the refinement of R2

Requirements, refinement	Nouns	Verbs	Relations of Concepts	Relations of Process States
Refinement R3: milestones-of(R3, (R3.1,R3.2, R3.3))				State sequences defined by synchronized business objects named in requirements
R3.1: A claim is submitted by a client	A Customer is a Client	is-submitted	is-submitted-by(Claim, Customer)	*state-of* (Claim, (A Claim is submitted by a customer)).
R3.2: Using the product information, a submitted claim is sorted to one of the three classes: Not Covered, Max Claim, NoLimit Claim	NotCovered Claim Max Claim NoLimit Claim	is-sorted	*specializes(NotCovered Claim, Claim)* *specializes(Max Claim, Claim)* *specializes(NoLimit Claim, Claim)* *one-of(Claim, Medical Procedure)* – added	*state-alternative-of*(Claim, (Is sorted to NotCovered Claim OR Is sorted to NoLimit Claim OR Is sorted to MaxClaim))
R3.3: A claim is handled		is-handled		*state-of*(Claim, (A Claim of a Customer with the bought policy is handled)) *state-sequence-of*(Claim, (A Claim is submitted by a Customer; (Is sorted to NotCovered Claim OR Is sorted to NoLimit Claim OR Is sorted to MaxClaim)), A Claim of the registered customer with the bought policy is handled)
Refinement R3.3 Alternative-of(R3.3, (R3.3.1, R3.3.2, R3.3.3))				State alternatives defined by R3.3.1, R3.3.2, R3.3.3.
R3.3.1: A NotCovered claim is refused	NoCoverage Handler – added for symmetry	is-refused-by	is-refused-by(No Coverage Handler)	*state-alternative-of*(Claim, (is-refused))
R3.3.2: A NoLimit claim is always paid		is-paid-by	is-paid-by(NoLimit Handler)	*state-alternative-of*(Claim, (is-paid))
R3.3.3: The handling of a Max Claim depends on the rest of the balance		is-calculated-by	is-calculated-by(CoverageMax Handler)	*state-alternative-of*(Claim, (is-calculated-using-MaxClaim-and-Balance))

Fig. 5. Relations from the refinement of R3

Product, so it defines a life cycle of a *Product*. Only one state of this life cycle is seen in R1: *state-of(Product,(Product is composed)*. The modeler adds the state *is-created(Product)*, because a product should exist to be composed. Analogically, R2 defines the life cycle of an object *Policy* and R3 defines the life cycle of an object *Claim* (Fig. 2).

Figure 3 shows the concepts identified by lexical analysis of R1.1, R1.2, R1.3, R1.4. Requirement *"R1.3. Each group corresponds to the NoLimit or MaxCoverage Schema"* defines a specialization relation of the object *Group of medical procedures* to *Group with Nolimit Coverage* and *Group with Max Coverage* and objects *NoLimit Schema* and *MaxCoverage Schema*. R1.3 also defines a state-alternative of a *Group of Medical Procedures*.

Figure 4 presents Relations of Concepts and Relations of Process States used for a *Policy* life cycle are shown in Fig. 4. A *Policy* object is created when it is bought.

Relations of Concepts and Relations of Process States used for a *Claim* life cycle are shown in Fig. 5. The alternative states of the business object *Claim* are caused by sorting each instance of object *Claim*. A Claim state *is-handled* may be one of the following states: *is-refused, is-paid* or *is-calculated-using-MaxClaim-and-Balance*.

Internal model of ArchiMate. "Elements" is an existing structure of the internal model presenting an enterprise model in ArchiMate. It can be filled in with "Nouns"(Objects). "Relations of Concepts" is an existing structure of the internal model, presenting an enterprise model, in ArchiMate. The elements of this structure are the results of lexical analysis of the Goal sub-model (Figs. 2, 3, 4, 5).

Because a goal represents a state of the modeled system and the ArchiMate defines an event as a state change, we use the names of goals to fill in events in the internal ArchiMate model. "Relations of Process States" (Figures 2, 3, 4, 5) are now filled in the "Relations of Concepts" in ArchiMate, but we visually check that each relation of process states is a triggering relation between a pair of ArchiMate events.

3.2   A Concept Sub-model Using Relations of Concepts

Using the "Relations of Concepts" identified in the Goal sub-model we build the Concept sub-model. Building of Concept sub-models is well guided by Archi-Mate [24, sec. 4], so we have depicted the Concept sub-model aligned with the Goal sub-model in Fig. 6.

The constraints imposed by sub-models on each other is the basis of our method. Ideally, the set of "Relations of Concepts" of the Concept sub-model is equal to the set of "Relations of Concepts" identified from the Goal sub-model. The first version of the Concept model can be generated from the internal ArchiMate model.

In practice of enterprise modeling, there are two possible deviations from this constraint.

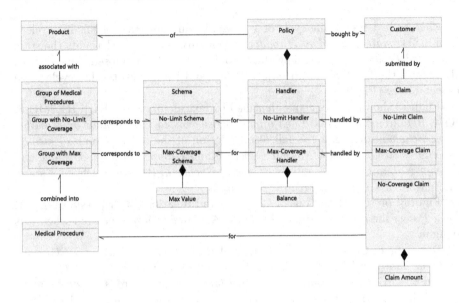

Fig. 6. Concept sub-model

1. A Concept sub-model may present a subset of "Relations of Concepts" identified from the Goal sub-model. It is a partial Concept sub-model called a view. Views are often used in enterprise modeling. A set of views may eventually cover all "Relations of Concepts" found in the Goal sub-model. Views can be generated from "Relations of Concepts" identified from the Goal sub-model.
2. A concept sub-model may contain extra relations added by designers. These extra relations have not been presented in the Goal sub-model.

Our case study illustrates the second deviation. Our Concept sub-model contains extra relations a *Policy* is composed by *handlers*. Also a *Claim* has an extra relation with a Medical Procedure.

So, in general, the set of "Relations of Concepts" identified from the Goal sub-model is a subset or an equal set of "Relations of Concepts" used in a Concept sub-model (or in a set of partial Concept sub-models).

3.3   A Process Sub-model Using Relations of Process States

Figure 7 depicts a Process sub-model built on "Relations of Process States" identified the Goal sub-model. We have already mentioned, that an ArchiMate event is a state change, so we present states using ArchiMate events. Each sentence presenting goals (requirements) is transformed to an ArchiMate event.

Most concepts *Medical Procedure, Group of Medical Procedures, Product* are business objects and have their life cycles shown in Fig. 7.

We use only one of possible semantics for the Process Model, namely Protocol Modeling. Events with the same name in different life cycles of this model mean

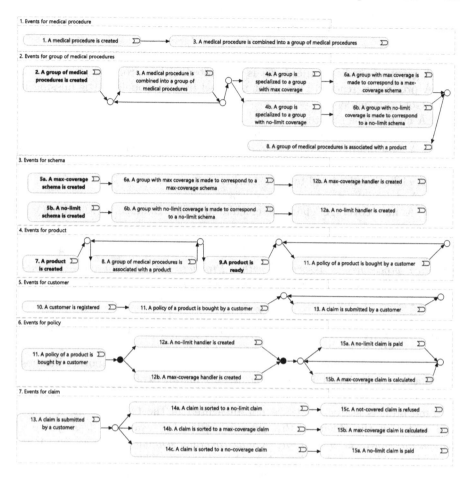

Fig. 7. Business Process sub-model

the CSP-parallel composition [14]. The CSP-parallel composition restricts the events allowed in each system state as it is explained in Sect. 2: if an event is recognized by several instances of protocol machines, it can happen only if all these instances are in the state where this event can happen.

A business process is a set of sequences of synchronized execution of instances of protocol machines. We have numbered the events in Fig. 7 to work the reader through one of the possible sequences of the process presented in Fig. 7.

- 1. A medical procedure is created.
- 2. A group of medical procedures is created.
- 3. A medical procedure is combined with a group of medical procedures.
- 4a. A group is specialized to a group with max coverage.
- 5a. A max-coverage schema is created. (This event is added by the modeler. It is missing in the Goal sub-model.)

- 6a. A group with max coverage is made to correspond to a max-coverage schema.
- 7. A product is created.
- 8. A group of medical procedures is associated with a product.
- 9. A product is ready. (This event is added by the modeler. It is missing in the Goal sub-model.)
- 10. A customer is registered.
- 11. A policy of a product is bought by a customer.
- 12a. A no-limit handler is created. AND 12b. A max-coverage handler is created.
- 13. A claim is submitted by a customer.
- 14b. A claim is sorted to a max-coverage claim.
- 15b. A max-coverage claim is calculated (The Balance of the Policy is updated).

Figure 7 shows that there are synchronous events. For example, *"A Group of medical procedures is associated with a Product"* for a *Group* and a *Product*; *"A Medical Procedure is combined with a Group of Medical procedures"* for a *Medical Procedure* and a *Group*.

The life cycle of a *Group of Medical Procedures* has alternative states *4a. A group is specialized to a group with max coverage.* and *4b. A group is specialized to a group with no-limit coverage.*

If a life cycle of an business object needs a set of instances of another business object, a cycle is designed. For example, a set of instances of "Medical Procedure" can be added to each "Group of Medical procedures".

Some process states, that are not presented in the Goal sub-model, have been added in the Business Process sub-model. For example, *2. A group of medical procedures is created, 5a. A max-coverage schema is created, 5b. A no-limit schema is created* and *9. A product is ready.* This means that the set "Relations of Process States" identified in the Goal sub-model is a subset of "Relations of Process States" used in the Business Process sub-model.

4   Generalization of Semantic Relations Between Sub-models of an Enterprise Model

In the presented case study, we used the semantic relations of sub-models of an enterprise model to organize a modeling process that results in aligned set of sub-models. In this section, we formalize the semantic relations of sub-models in one enterprise model.

4.1   Analysis of a Goal Sub-model

A $Goal\ sub - model = (G, R_m, R_s, R_a)$.

The elements $g \in G$ in Fig. 1 are indexed to show how they are refined into sub-goals or how they refine a parent goal. To show how a parent goal is refined, we use the following notation. Let g_{tn} be a goal under refinement tn:

$$\{g_{tn} | t \in \{m, s, a\} \wedge n \in \mathbf{N}\}.$$

where $t \in \{m, s, a\}$ denote the type of refinement, being milestone (m), sub-domain(s) and alternative(a) refinement respectively. And where n is used to distinguish refinements of the same type (such as refinements $m1, m2, m3$ and $m4$ in the goal sub-model in Fig. 1).

To show how a sub-goal refines its parent goal, we use the following notation:

$$G_{tn} = \{g_{tn_k} \in G \,|\, t \in \{m, s, a\} \wedge n \in \mathbf{N} \wedge k \in \mathbf{N}\}.$$

The set of sub-goals $G_{tn} = \{g_{tn_1}, ...g_{tn_k}\}$ refines the parent goal g_{tn}.

- G is a finite set of goals, sub-goals and requirements. Each element $g \in G$ is a sentence in the natural language presenting a state or a partial state of the modeled system.
- R_m is a set of milestone-type refinement relations.
  An element $r_{mn} \in R_m$ refines a goal g_{mn} to a finite set of goals, that are ordered, namely, form a sequence to complete the goal g_{mn}:

$$r_{mn} = (g_{mn}, (G_{mn}, O_{mn})),$$

$$G_{mn} = \{g_{mn_k}\}, \; n, k \in \mathbf{N},$$

$$O_{r_{mn}} = \{(g_{mn_1}, g_{mn_2}), ..., (g_{mn_{k-1}}, g_{m_k})\} \models g_{mn}.$$

- R_s is a set of sub-domain AND refinement relations. An element $r_{sn} \in R_s$ refines a goal g_{sn} to a set of goals, union of which means the completion of g_{sn}:

$$r_{sn} = (g_{sn}, (G_{sn}, U_{sn})),$$

$$G_{sn} = \{g_{sn_1}, ..., g_{sn_k}\}, \; n, k \in \mathbf{N}, \; (g_{sn_1} \cap ..., \cap g_{sn_k}) = \emptyset.$$

$$U_{sn} = (g_{sn_1} \cup ... \cup g_{sn_k}) \models g_{sn}.$$

- R_a is a set of alternatives, i.e. OR refinement relations. An element $r_{an} \in R_a$ refines a goal g_{an} to a set of goals, appearance of one of which means the completion of g_{an}:

$$r_{an} = (g_{an}, (G_{an}, A_{an})),$$

$$G_{an} = \{g_{an_k}, ..., g_{an_k}\}, \; n, k \in \mathbf{N}, \; (g_{an_1} \cap ..., \cap g_{an_k}) = \emptyset.$$

$$A_{an} = \forall \, i = 1, ...k : (g_{an_i} \models g_{an}).$$

4.2 Goal Sub-model and Concept Sub-model

A *Concept sub − model* $= (C, R)$ is a tuple

- C a finite set of concepts; $c_i \in C$, $i = 1, ..., n$, $n \in N$.
- R is finite set of relations; $r \in R$, $r = (c_i, c_j)$, $c_i, c_j \in C$.

The lexical analysis of goals G expressed in natural language in a goal model is aimed to identify the constraints imposed by the Goal sub-model on the Concept sub-model in one enterprise model:

- $Nouns(G)$ is a finite set of nouns (noun phrases), $n \in Nouns(G)$, forming the sentences presenting goals, sub-goals and requirements.
- $Verbs(G)$ is a finite set of verbs (verb phrases, prepositions), $v \in Verbs(G)$, used in the sentences presenting goals, sub-goals and requirements.
- $Relations\ of\ Concepts(G) = \{(v, n_i, n_j) \mid v \in Verbs(G),\ n_i, n_j \in Nouns(G)\}$, is a finite set of triples (v, n_i, n_j) found in the sentences presenting goals, sub-goals and requirements; where v is a verb, n_i, n_j are nouns.

The $Nouns(G)$ and $Relations\ of\ Concepts(G)$ are subsets of concepts and relations of the Concept sub-model. It is because the designers of the Concept sub-model often add some new concepts-attributes and their relations with other concepts.

Figure 6 shows a Concept sub-model that respects the constraints imposed by the Goal sub-model in Fig. 1.

4.3   Process, Goal and Concept Sub-models

A $Process\ sub-model$ is a set of behaviors.
$Process\ sub-model = \{Behaviour_k \mid k = 1, ..., K,\ K \in N\}$.
A behavior is a tuple $Behaviour = (S, T)$, where

- S is a finite set of states, $s_i, s_j \in S$; $i, j \in N$.
- T is a finite set of transitions between states: $t_h \in T$ $h \in N$, $t_h = (s_i, s_j) \in T$. Transitions are relations of process states.

The constraints imposed by the Goal and Concept sub-models on the Process sub-model in one enterprise model are the following.

- Each noun $n \in Nouns(G)$, being a concept $c \in C$ of the Concept sub-model, has a corresponding $Behavior$, except if the concept composes or specializes another concept.
- Each goal $g \in G$ of a Goal sub-model has a corresponding state $s \in S$ in the Process sub-model.
- The transitions (being Relations of Process States) are identified by analysis of each milestone refinement of the Goal sub-model. Each pair of goals of an milestone refinement r_{mn} in the Goal sub-model:

$$O_{r_{mn}} = \{(g_{mn_1}, g_{mn_2}), ...(g_{mn_{k-1}}, g_{m_k})\} \models g_{mn},$$

corresponds to a transition of states in the Process sub-model. The states are named after the goals in the set G_{mn}.
- Each alternative refinement r_{an} in the Goal sub-model:

$$A_{an} = \forall i = 1, ...k : (g_{an_i} \models g_{an}),$$

corresponds to an OR-split of states in the Process sub-model. The states are named after the goals in the set G_{an}.

– Each sub-domain refinement r_{sn} in the Goal sub-model:

$$U_{sn} = (g_{sn_1} \cup ... \cup g_{sn_k}) \models g_{sn},$$

corresponds to an AND-split of states in the Process sub-model. The states are named after the goals in the set G_{sn}.

Figure 7 presents a Process sub-model that respects constraints imposed by the Goal and Concept sub-models (Figs. 1, 6).

In this work, we have defined the semantic relations or constraints that are imposed by sub-models in an enterprise model. The semantic relations cover three modeling semantics used for sub-models. The goal modeling semantics is the leading semantics. The concept modeling and the process modeling semantics are applied within constraints imposed by the goal sub-model. The Concept and Process sub-models are complete if they present the elements (*concepts*, *states*) and relations (*relations-of-concepts*, *relations-of-process-states*) identified in the Goal sub-model.

If a sub-model is depicted as a set of partial sub-models (views), then the semantic relations, defined in this paper, can be applied to the union of elements and relations of views of the sub-model. For the partial sub-models, that do not form a complete sub-model, the partial constraints can be derived from the semantic relations of sub-models, however, this needs more investigation.

5   Conclusion and Future Work

Enterprise modeling approaches have difficulties in producing enterprise models with aligned sub-models. Even the ArchiMate [24] approach, which has been designed for consistent enterprise modeling, experiences these difficulties. The ArchiMate provides a storage for an internal model of each enterprise model. This internal model is to be used for generating sub-models. However, the filling the internal model in with elements and relations is done by drawing sub-models of different semantics. The drawing and naming of elements and relations is made by a team of enterprise architects. Team members are humans and may duplicate elements of models using different names, forget the details of the semantics of sub-models and the semantic relations of sub-models. This results in unaligned sub-models of an enterprise model.

We have reviewed several enterprise modeling approaches and found out that the semantic relations of sub-models are recognized, but not used to direct the design of aligned sub-models.

In order to analyze and formalize the semantic relations of sub-models in an enterprise model, we have analyzed a case study depicted in ArchiMate. We have identified the structures and formulated semantic constraints imposed by sub-models to each other. All these structures can be identified in the Goal sub-model of an enterprise model and can be used for design of a Concept and a Process sub-models. The identified structures and constraints can be used in any enterprise modeling approach.

Currently, we apply the found structures for the design of aligned sub-models directed by the semantic relations via the integration of sub-models. We are experimenting in one of the ArchiMate tools, namely, Archi [2]. In the future work, building on our former results [7,15], we plan to define constraints imposed by sub-models for tool extensions to enable automated checks and directed design of aligned sub-models.

References

1. Beauvoir, P., Sarrodie, J.: Archi-the free archimate modelling tool. User Guide, The Open Group (2018)
2. Beauvoir, P., Sarrodie, J.B.: Archi-Open Source Archimate Modelling (2019)
3. Egyed, A.: Instant consistency checking for the UML. In: Proceedings of the 28th International Conference on Software Engineering, pp. 381–390 (2006)
4. Hoare, C.A.R.: Communicating sequential processes. Commun. ACM **21**(8), 666–677 (1978)
5. Hui, L.M., Leung, C.W., Fan, C.K., Wong, T.N.: Modelling agent-based systems with UML. In: Proceedings of the Fifth Asia-Pacific Industrial Engineering and Management Systems Conference (2004)
6. Jackson, M.: System Development. Prentice-Hall, Englewood Cliffs (1983)
7. Joosten, S., Roubtsova, E., Haddouchi, E.M.: Constraint formalization for automated assessment of enterprise models. In: International Conference on Enterprise Information Systems (ICEIS), vol. 2, pp. 430–441 (2022)
8. Kaisler, S., Armour, F., Valivullah, M.: Enterprise architecting: critical problems. In: Proceedings of the 38th Annual Hawaii International Conference on System Sciences, p. 224b (2005)
9. Kontio, M.: Architectural Manifesto: Designing Software Architectures. Part 5. Introducing the 4+ 1 View Model. IBM developerWorks (2005)
10. Kruchten, P.B.: The 4+ 1 view model of architecture. IEEE Softw. **12**(6), 42–50 (1995)
11. Letier, E., Kramer, J., Magee, J., Uchitel, S.: Deriving event-based transition systems from goal-oriented requirements models. Autom. Softw. Eng. **15**(2), 175–206 (2008)
12. Marosin, D., van Zee, M., Ghanavati, S.: Formalizing and modeling Enterprise Architecture (EA) principles with Goal-Oriented Requirements Language (GRL). In: Nurcan, S., Soffer, P., Bajec, M., Eder, J. (eds.) CAiSE 2016. LNCS, vol. 9694, pp. 205–220. Springer, Cham (2016). https://doi.org/10.1007/978-3-319-39696-5_13
13. McNeile, A., Roubtsova, E.: CSP parallel composition of aspect models. In: Proceedings of the 2008 AOSD Workshop on Aspect-Oriented Modeling, pp. 13–18 (2008)
14. McNeile, A., Simons, N.: Protocol modelling: a modelling approach that supports reusable behavioural abstractions. Softw. Syst. Model. **5**(1), 91–107 (2006)
15. Michels, G., Joosten, S., van der Woude, J., Joosten, S.: Ampersand. In: de Swart, H. (ed.) RAMICS 2011. LNCS, vol. 6663, pp. 280–293. Springer, Heidelberg (2011). https://doi.org/10.1007/978-3-642-21070-9_21
16. OMG: Unified Modeling Language (UML, formal) 01 March 2015. https://www.omg.org/spec/UML/2.5/

17. Pereira, C.M., Sousa, P.: Enterprise architecture: business and IT alignment. In: Proceedings of the 2005 ACM Symposium on Applied Computing, pp. 1344–1345 (2005)
18. Quartel, D., Engelsman, W., Jonkers, H., Van Sinderen, M.: A goal-oriented requirements modelling language for enterprise architecture. In: 2009 IEEE International Enterprise Distributed Object Computing Conference, pp. 3–13. IEEE (2009)
19. Respect-IT: A KAOS Tutorial, V1.0 (2007)
20. Roubtsova, E.: EXTREME: EXecuTable requirements engineering, management, and evolution. In: Progressions and Innovations in Model-Driven Software Engineering, pp. 65–89. IGI Global (2013)
21. Roubtsova, E.: Advances in behavior modeling. In: Advances in Computers, vol. 97, pp. 49–109. Elsevier (2015)
22. Roubtsova, E.: Interactive Modeling and Simulation in Business System Design. Springer, Heidelberg (2016). https://doi.org/10.1007/978-3-319-15102-1
23. Sandkuhl, K., Stirna, J., Persson, A., Wißotzki, M.: Enterprise Modeling. Springer, Heidelberg (2014). https://doi.org/10.1007/978-3-662-43725-4
24. The Open Group: ArchiMate 3.1 Specification (2012–2021). https://pubs.opengroup.org/architecture/archimate3-doc/

VR-EA+TCK: Visualizing Enterprise Architecture, Content, and Knowledge in Virtual Reality

Roy Oberhauser[1]($\boxtimes$) (iD), Marie Baehre[1], and Pedro Sousa[2]

[1] Computer Science Department, Aalen University, Aalen, Germany
{roy.oberhauser,marie.baehre}@hs-aalen.de
[2] Instituto Superior Técnico, University of Lisbon, Lisbon, Portugal Link Consulting, Lisbon, Portugal
pedro.manuel.sousa@tecnico.ulisboa.pt

Abstract. A complex and dynamic IT landscape with evermore digital elements, relations, and content presents a challenge for Enterprise Architecture (EA). Disparate digital repositories, including Knowledge Management Systems (KMS), Enterprise Content Management Systems (ECMS), and Enterprise Architecture Tools (EAT), often remain disjointed. And even if integrated, insights remain hindered by current visualization limitations, making it increasingly difficult to analyze, manage, and gain insights into the digital enterprise reality. This paper contributes our nexus-based Virtual Reality (VR) solution concept VR-EA+TCK that enhances and amalgamates EAT with KMS and ECMS capabilities. By enabling visualization, navigation, and interaction in VR with dynamically-generated EA diagrams, knowledge/value chains, and KMS/ECMS digital entities, it sets the groundwork for stakeholder-accessible grassroots enterprise modeling/analysis and future collaboration in a metaverse. An implementation shows its feasibility, while a case study demonstrates its potential using enterprise analysis scenarios: ECMS/KMS coverage in the EA, business processes, knowledge chains, Wardley Maps, and risk analysis.

Keywords: Virtual reality · Enterprise architecture · Enterprise modeling · Knowledge management · Enterprise content management · Visualization

1 Introduction

Enterprise Architecture (EA) comprises the structural and behavioral aspects needed for an enterprise to function and adapt in alignment with some vision. EA provides a comprehensive set of cohesive models to describe the enterprise structure and functions, logically arranging individual models to provide further detail about an enterprise [1]. The digital reality that EA attempts to depict has grown in complexity, spanning disparate silos (repositories) of information and content across organization and system types. As enterprises evolve, explicit knowledge of and insight into the EA becomes indispensable, be it for enterprise governance, engineering, compliance, maintenance, etc. And

© Springer Nature Switzerland AG 2022
B. Shishkov (Ed.): BMSD 2022, LNBIP 453, pp. 122–140, 2022.
https://doi.org/10.1007/978-3-031-11510-3_8

although architectural representations are an enterprise asset that must be governed [2], the effort expended to keep architectural views updated is known to be very high in current organizations [3]. This is mainly due to the organization's structure being the result of an asynchronous, distributed, and heterogeneous process, producing representations in different languages/notations, with different levels of detail, in different tools at different times. [4] presents an enterprise modeling vision and associated research challenges to exploit "grassroots modeling" and embed modeling in everyday work while including more stakeholder groups. Towards this vision, our contribution addresses the challenge of making enterprise models more accessible to additional stakeholders, while providing a low-effort method for supporting updated architectural views regardless of the desired timepoint via the Enterprise Architecture Tool (EAT) Atlas[1] [3], described in Sect. 3.

With increasing digitalization, collecting, managing, and depicting data, information, knowledge, knowledge work, knowledge workers, their associated processes (business and knowledge), and other enterprise elements and the relations between them becomes increasingly critical [5]. While there are many possible perspectives for viewing and interpreting enterprise information and knowledge, here we apply the DIKAR (Data, Information, Knowledge, Action, and Result) model [6] in an enterprise context. For digital organizations, actions taken in activities and processes are often dependent on knowledge, which presupposes information and may involve data. To support Knowledge Management (KM), Enterprise Content Management Systems (ECMS) involve the collection, management, and publishing of enterprise information in various forms or mediums via supporting technologies and processes. Since it is often a matter of a user's competency, context, perspective, or intention as to if and how digital entities are viewed, processed, or aggregated, be they DIK (*content* being a form of DIK). Thus, for this paper we view digitized enterprise *knowledge* or enterprise *content* to mean potentially any of these DIK possibilities, intentionally abstracted or generalized and serving the purpose or intention of the stakeholder involved in their enterprise context. As the digital enterprise and respectively EA Management (EAM) grows in size and complexity, integrating, modeling, visualizing, and supporting Enterprise Information Management (EIM) and KM and explicitly associating relevant DIK elements with EA elements across disparate repositories is a further challenge we seek to address.

Virtual Reality (VR) is a "real or simulated environment in which the perceiver experiences telepresence" [7], a mediated visual environment created and then experienced. By leveraging VR for the enterprise digital reality, an immersive experience in a digital context of surrounding enterprise elements can be provided to various stakeholders, while avoiding non-immersive visual distractions inherent with 2D displays (analogous to being outside an aquarium versus scuba diving). As support, [8] investigated VR vs. 2D for a software analysis task. The study found that VR did not significantly decrease comprehension and analysis time nor significantly improve correctness (although fewer errors were made). And although interaction time was less efficient, VR improved the UX (user experience), being more motivating, less demanding, more inventive/innovative, and more clearly structured. In our view, EAM could thus reap similar VR benefits without incurring significant liabilities.

---

[1] https://atlas.linkconsulting.com.

Our prior work includes various VR solution concepts, including VR-EAT [9] for dynamically-generated Atlas EA diagrams, VR-EA [10] for ArchiMate® EA models, and VR-BPMN [11] for Business Process Model and Notation (BPMN™) models. This paper contributes our nexus-based VR solution concept VR-EA+TCK (EA enhanced with Tools, Content, and Knowledge), extending our VR-EAT by amalgamating KM and ECMS capabilities. It enables visualizing, navigating, and interacting with dynamically-generated EA diagrams enhanced with DIK elements from Knowledge Management Systems (KMS) and ECMS, including value and knowledge chains. By visualizing enterprise models and associated knowledge and content in VR, EA-related collaboration for additional stakeholder types in a future metaverse becomes feasible and accessible. This paper is structured as follows: Sect. 2 discusses related work while Sect. 3 provides background on Atlas. Our solution concept is described in Sect. 4. Section 5 details our prototype implementation. The evaluation is described in Sect. 6, followed by a conclusion.

2 Related Work

EA visualization work includes Rehring et al. [12] that investigated possible EAM actions in Mixed Reality (MR) and VR, finding VR/MR offers affordances that can positively influence EAM decision-making quality and effectiveness. VR is not mentioned in the Roth et al. [13] survey of EA visualization tools. [14] describe PRIMate based on PRIM-ROSe, a visual graph-based enterprise analysis framework, and show a 2D tool PRIMate containing a graph, treemap, and 3D visualization of an the ArchiSurance ArchiMate model. Beyond our prior work, we are unaware work applying VR to the EA area with integrated EAT heterogenous metamodel, multidiagram, and EA-related standard (ArchiMate, BPMN, UML) and custom model support.

With regard to KM, Yan [15] utilizes a knowledge and an agent mesh as a representation method for complicated-knowledge, dealing with multiples sets, mapping relations, union, intersection and other operations. While graph-based and using an inference engine, it is focused on self-reconfiguration of systems and does not address EA. KOMDEVRS [16] presents an approach and methodology for open knowledge formalization and management in VR, focusing on industrial domain. It attempts to address and externalize the closed nature of the knowledge and metadata often contained in VR applications. It does not address the EA or ECMS context. Zenkert et al. [17] creates a dynamic graphical layout structure for knowledge maps based on dimensional information, using distance to arrange associated information based on word association strength. Although VR is mentioned, their solution is not applied to VR. We found no direct work applying VR visualization to enterprise KM.

As to Content Management (CM) or Enterprise Content (EC), [18] provides a comprehensive review of ECM research, while [19] evaluates ECM tools, giving insight into the various tool types and interfaces. Utilizing an asset definition language, [20] describes a means for abstractly defining content visualizations for concept-oriented CM (which can support subjective views regarding represented entities). [21] applies graph theory to enhance search results of an ECM in an innovation process to support new knowledge creation. We found no direct work applying VR visualization to enterprise CMS.

3 Background on the EA Tool Atlas

To keep architectural views up-to-date in fast-changing organizations, Atlas was developed based on an Enterprise Cartography paradigm [22, 23]. Atlas consists of a repository with a fully configurable metamodel that dynamically generates fully configurable views. It contains all the information required to represent views at any timepoint and can represent each artifact in its lifecycle state [3]. Hence, the evolution of an architecture over time can be viewed. The view's contents regarding the future are computed, processing the plans of transformation initiatives pipeline (both ongoing and planned) to produce a consolidated enterprise model state in any point in time. Therefore, one can foresee the contents of an architecture view in some desired future date by consolidating the current view's content with the expected changes of ongoing and planned transformation initiatives whose completion date precedes the desired date [22, 24]. For business processes, Atlas can generate and support time navigation in BPMN models [25]. This is a unique feature of Atlas and, in our experience, fundamental to reducing the effort of maintaining architectural views in large organizations. The configuration of the view types is based on the metamodel defined by the user. Figure 1 shows some of the supported view types.

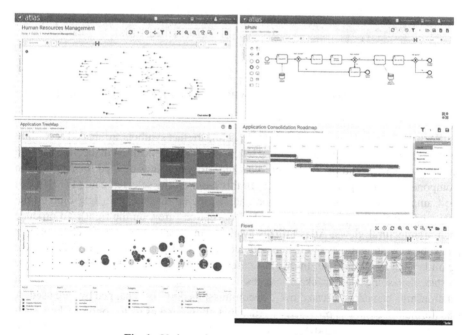

Fig. 1. Various view types supported by Atlas.

A key capability of Atlas is the generation of up-to-date architectural views with near zero effort as has been done for some cases [26, 27], including the previous generation of the tool EAMS. Users can define templates of architectural views, which are instantiated on request to particular objects. Figure 2 shows a generated view for the Human Resources (HR) Management application, presented in the middle container. Moving leftwards, services requested by the HR Management application and the applications providing such services are shown. Moving rightwards, the service realized by the HR Management application and the applications that request it are shown. Below it, various data objects used by the services are shown.

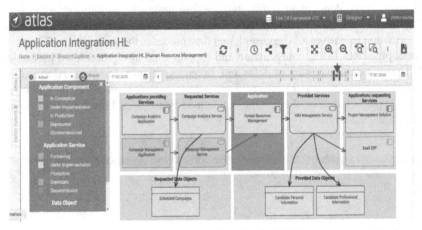

Fig. 2. High-level Application Integration Blueprint for HR Management application.

With the Lifecycle option selected (red circle), artefact symbols are shaded according to their lifetime state on the date defined by the time handler position in the time bar (top red arrow). The legend on the left presents the lifecycle states defined for Application Components and Application Services. In this case, on the selected date (17/02/2020) the Campaign Management application and service are Deprecated (light blue on the left), and the SaaS ERP application is In Conception (grey, on the right). To produce such architectural views, Atlas utilizes available information sources, such as project plans, be they simple lists of created and decommissioned artefacts or models in some notation such as ArchiMate. In this last case, since ArchiMate does not provide a way to state that some work package creates/deletes/or changes any artefact, association relationships named as "created by", "decommissioned by" or "changed by" are used. A transformation engine is provided by Atlas that allows end users to configure how each concept in an imported model (such as in ArchiMate) maps to the concepts defined in its metamodel.

End users can also define the propagation rules between project milestone dates and the artefact lifecycles that are affected (created, decommissioned, changed) by some project. One default rule for artefact creation is that objects created by a project transition to productive upon project completion. In case a project is delayed, Atlas can update the lifecycle of dependent artefacts. Finally, end users can also define the dependency rules between projects. One default rule is that a project A is dependent on Project B if it uses some artefact affected by Project B. So, whenever a project termination date is delayed, Atlas can alert the actor responsible (e.g., via email) for an impacted ongoing or planned project.

4 Solution Concept

The unlimited space available in VR can be leveraged for visualizing the growing and complex set of EA and EC models and their interrelationships simultaneously in a spatial structure. As EA and EC models grow in complexity and reflect the deeper integration of both the business and IT reality, an immersive EA environment provides an additional visualization capability to comprehend the "big picture" for structurally and hierarchically complex and interconnected diagrams and digital elements, while providing an immersive experience for digital models in a 3D space viewable from different perspectives.

Our generalized solution concept for VR-EA+TCK is shown in Fig. 3. VR-EA+TCK utilizes our generalized VR Modeling Framework (VR-MF) [10], which provides a VR-based domain-independent hypermodeling framework. VR-MF addresses four primary aspects that require special attention when modeling in VR: visualization, navigation, interaction, and data retrieval. VR-EAT [9] is our EAT repository integration solution, exemplified with Atlas integration, visualization of blueprints, and interaction capabilities. VR-EA EA [10] provides specialized direct support and mapping for EA models in VR, including both ArchiMate as well as BPMN via VR-BPMN [11]. VR-UML [28] provides support for UML® diagrams in VR, which may be of relevance to EA depending on the analysis and models. VR-EA+TCK builds on and extends these capabilities by integrating further enterprise knowledge, information, and content repositories such as a KMS and/or an ECMS.

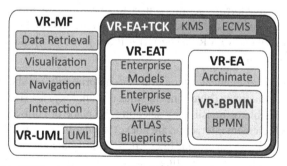

Fig. 3. The VR-EA+TCK solution concept (blue) in relation to our prior VR solution concepts (Color figure online).

As a representative EA tool and repository, Atlas provides access to diverse EA-related data in a coherent repository and meta-model and is not restricted to certain standards or notations. Blueprints (diagrams) are necessarily limited in scope to address some stakeholder concern, and are necessary and helpful for stakeholders to avoid information overload. Yet the larger picture of the entire digital enterprise and all of its elements and relations cannot be easily conveyed on a single 2D diagram or view. Furthermore, second degree relations and elements (beyond the diagram) or not readily seen. Thus, certain insights or missing elements, relations, or aspects may not be readily detected. Furthermore, any models retained in a repository are typically limited in scope to that repository, and inter-repository relations (such as between an EAT such as Atlas and an ECMS) are usually not obvious or discovered. Our VR solution seeks to address such limitations. VR-EAT details the integration with Atlas.

Visualization. As there are many possible relations between digital elements, a spherical *nexus* was chosen to visualize all elements and relations in a repository (see Fig. 4). To provide some initial ordering, layering within the sphere is available as a grouping mechanism based on similar element types using the color assigned to that type, resulting in a sphere with colored layers (intra-layer element placement is random). While the color scheme is customizable, the default color scheme is loosely based on KMDL® [29]. To assist with orientation and make interaction more intuitive by providing a context for what a model represents, labeled glass boxes readable from any angle contain a nexus based on the model of a repository (ECMS, KMS). To show inter-relations between nexuses or models, we found directly drawn additional lines between nexus spheres to lead to a large crisscross of associations that was difficult to analyze. We thus utilize a dynamically-generated nexus to show the intersection between models. As 2D-based views and diagrams remain a primary form of EA documentation, they are integrated (such as from the EAT Atlas) as 3D *hyperplanes* in proximity to its nexus for contextual support. In summary, intangible digital elements are made visible and related to one another across the enterprise spectrum.

Navigation. VR immersion requires addressing intuitively navigating the VR space while reducing the likelihood of potential VR sickness symptoms. Two navigation modes are supported in the solution concept: the default uses gliding controls, enabling users to *fly through* the VR space and get an overview of the entire model from any angle they wish. Alternatively, *teleporting* permits a user to select a destination and be instantly placed there (i.e., by moving the camera to that position); this can be disconcerting but may reduce the likelihood of VR sickness (for those prone to it) that can occur when moving through a virtual space.

Interaction. Basic user-element interaction is done primarily via the VR controllers. Views consisting of diagrams (blueprints in Atlas terminology) are stacked hyperplanes and can be made visible or invisible by selecting the plane or equivalent icon. As VR affordances and VR element interaction are not yet standardized or intuitive, a *VR-Tablet* paradigm is used (see Fig. 5) to provide interaction support and more detailed information about a selected nexus object or depicting browser-based multimedia content. It can also be used for browsing, filtering, and searching for nodes.

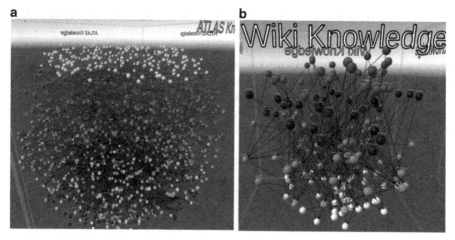

Fig. 4. VR-EA+TCK: a) Atlas EA nexus (left); b) Semantic MediaWiki nexus (right).

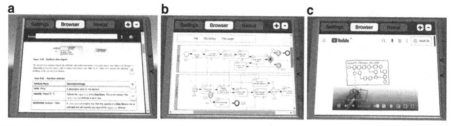

Fig. 5. VR-Tablet multimedia browser-based content: a) PDF (left), b) image (center), c) video (right).

5 Realization

Figure 6 shows our solution concept realization for VR-EA+TCK. To implement visualization, navigation, and interaction for VR-MF, Unity 2020.3 with OpenVR XR Plugin 1.1.4 is used, shown in the Unity block (top right, blue). It includes support for Nexus and Atlas Blueprint view depiction. The Data Hub (center, orange) is based on.NET and provides data integration, storage (bottom, via MongoDB 5 as BSON), and retrieval (as JSON). Atlas integration (top left, green) is cloud-based, including repository data and service access via REST queries, which retrieves JSON blueprint (diagram) data. This data is loaded into the Data Hub and saved to MongoDB in our internal BSON schema format, to permit us to transform and annotate the data as needed for VR. A command line extension (left) provides helper functions for configuration, mapping, and data loading for the Data Hub. To illustrate the ECMS/KMS VR capability, we integrated the Semantic MediaWiki (SMW). SMW (bottom right, purple) consists of MediaWiki 1.35.4 with PHP 7.4.26 and SMW 4.0.0 (run in a Docker 20.10.12 container) with MariaDB Version 10.6.5 running in a separate container. The MediaWiki Ontology is exported via the SWW script dumpRDF, which is parsed with dotNetRDF 2.7.2. Further multi-model integration - independent of the Data Hub and direct with

Unity - is shown (Fig. 6, upper right, green), and includes ArchiMate (VR-EA), BPMN (VR-BPMN), and UML (VR-UML) (not shown).

To support type and relational analysis in VR, all node types are represented as spheres in a glass meta-layer above a nexus (see Fig. 7a), differentiated by color and size indicating the relative number of instances (largest has the most). Type selection at the meta-layer selects all instances in a nexus via a glow (Fig. 7b), ghosting non-related nodes. Likewise, selecting a node highlights its type at the meta-layer, while its first-degree neighbors and relations remain shown and the rest are ghosted (Fig. 8).

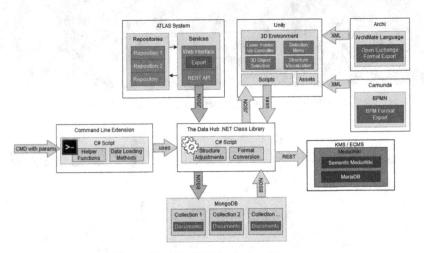

Fig. 6. VR-EA+TCK logical architecture.

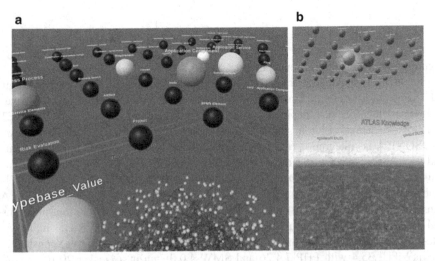

Fig. 7. a) Atlas meta-layer (left); b) type vs. node instance(s) selection highlighting (right).

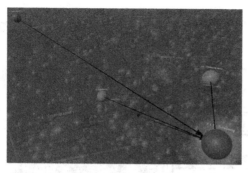

Fig. 8. Nexus node selection (glow) and first-degree neighbors and relations shown.

Atlas-specific VR integration and navigation was realized via blueprint diagram stack placement in proximity to the nexus as shown in Fig. 9. If an element on a blueprint is selected, that corresponding node in the nexus is highlighted and the rest are ghosted, while the dynamic blueprint stack on the right is updated to show all blueprints that include that element. If all elements in a blueprint are selected (Fig. 10a for the Application Management blueprint), then all nodes in the nexus are highlighted with a different colored glow and the rest are ghosted (Fig. 10b).

Fig. 9. Selecting Atlas element highlights nexus node and displays diagrams with that element.

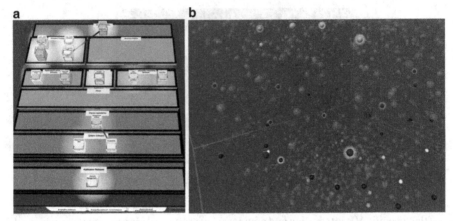

Fig. 10. a) Selecting all elements in an Atlas diagram; b) corresponding Atlas Nexus nodes highlighted.

VR-based navigation of the nexus will show details for a selected object. For VR support for ECMS/KMS, if the object is associated with a web address (wiki page), in browser mode the VR-tablet is dynamically updated with content (Fig. 11a). Figure 11b shows the wiki ontology in the meta-layer, including an actor subclass external actor.

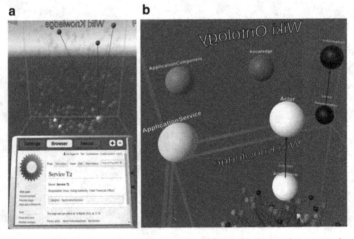

Fig. 11. Wiki knowledge nexus: a) node content in tablet (left); b) ontology meta-layer (right).

Immersive heterogeneous multi-model analysis is supported by loading multiple models in VR as shown in Fig. 12, with the ECMS/KMS Wiki Knowledge Nexus (left), EA Atlas Nexus (middle), Atlas Blueprint (right bottom, blue), and ArchiSurance Archimate model (far right).

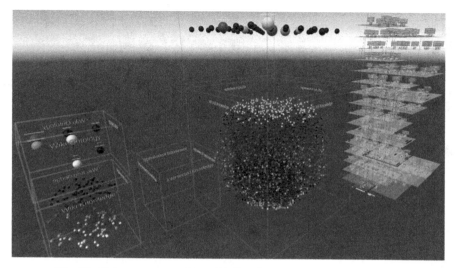

Fig. 12. Heterogeneous multi-model visualization and analysis capability.

6 Evaluation

To evaluate the practicality of the VR-EA+TCK solution concept and realization, a case study is used focusing on five illustrative enterprise analysis and decision-making scenarios: 1) ECMS/KMS Coverage, 2) Business Processes, 3) Knowledge Chains, 4) Wardley Map Value Chains, and 5) Risk and Governance Analysis.

The Atlas repository contained 66 sample core blueprints and via parameter choices results in 7843 different blueprints considering all selection combinations. This results in a total of 2034 nodes (unique entity instances) from 43 types and 2357 intra-nexus relations. As an ECMS/KMS, the Semantic MediaWiki contained semi-random Internet content, resulting in 165 nodes of 7 types with 246 intra-nexus relations.

6.1 ECMS/KMS Coverage Scenario

To support analysis and decision-making, an EA should be documented and maintained. To analyze content/knowledge coverage of an EA, VR-EA+TCK can generate an Intersected Knowledge Nexus via the VR-Tablet. It shows Atlas Nexus nodes that have (or do not have) associated content, as shown in Fig. 13. With our sample data, it consists of 92 nodes, 117 intra-nexus relations, and 142 inter-Wiki and 260 inter-Atlas relations. The right sphere half type color is from Atlas, the left sphere half type from the Wiki Knowledge Nexus; unrelated nodes in source nexuses are ghosted. The intersection set is determined by type-based string matching and can be extended for ID matching via an Atlas content ID property. Thus, the intersection of the nexus sets and their differences (missing information) via ghosting can be readily ascertained.

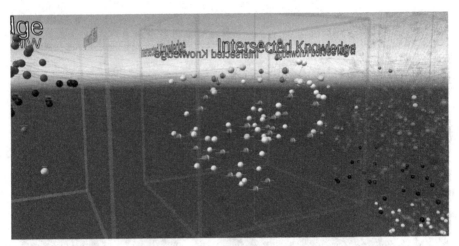

Fig. 13. Intersected knowledge nexus: relations from Atlas on the right, from Wiki on the left.

6.2 Business Process Scenario

As to analyzing business processes (BP), the models (in BPMN or another notation) typically only include primary participants as shown in Fig. 14. With VR-EA+TCK, the BP elements in a BP blueprint in Atlas can be highlighted and the BP analyzed for 1) first degree related neighbor nodes (actors, knowledge, etc.) that may influence or be influenced by this BP, or 2) dynamic access to (potentially live system) information associated with any of the associated BP nodes.

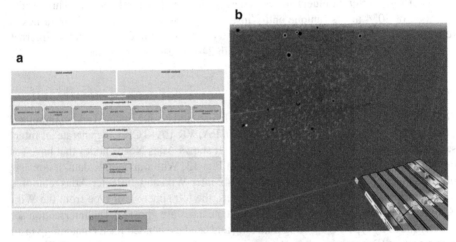

Fig. 14. Business process layered warehouse operations: a) Atlas (left); b) VR nexus (right).

6.3 Knowledge Chain Scenario

For knowledge-driven enterprises, modeling and analyzing knowledge utilization (e.g., strengths, needs) will become imperative. While KMDL® provides a notation for modeling knowledge-intensive BPs, not all knowledge or its use may be associated with BPs, and non-notation enterprise types may be involved. We thus generalize our solution to *knowledge chains* containing an open set of nodes and relations.

To demonstrate support and knowledge chain capability, we adapted a Modelangelo KMDL sample model from [30] (Fig. 15) to entities within our Atlas model (Fig. 16a). Activating KMDL mode via the VR-Tablet, KMDL nodes (11 types for our example denoted via name prefix) and chains are seen in the nexus, ghosting the rest (Fig. 16b). Available KMDL 3.0 perspectives (process, knowledge) are dynamically listed in the VR-Tablet and a subset of interest can be selected. Halo color indicates the KMDL type: white = Actor, yellow = Role, red = Information Object, green = Task/Conversion, pink/purple = Knowledge Object, orange = Requirement. As to relations (lines): green = Socialization, blue = Externalization, red = Internalization. For 2D analysis, the chain can be moved to the front glass box pane (nodes remain connected to the nexus) (Fig. 16c). This visualization offers insights into enterprise *knowledge chains*, any related elements, and how they interact and relate.

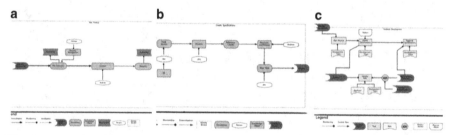

Fig. 15. Adapted KMDL sample model in Modelangelo: a) Plan Product (left), b) Create Specfication (center), c) Backend Development (right).

6.4 Wardley Map Value Chain Scenario

A Wardley Map [31] is a business strategy method that maps the business landscape in the form of a value chain. In 2D, two object properties *evolution* and *visibility* are mapped to each axis. For VR visualization, we mapped these to a 3D chain in a nexus: *evolution* has a four-level scale mapped to a halo color: 0..1 (Genesis = yellow), 1..2 (Custom Built = blue), 2..3 (Product = pink), 3..4 (Commodity = green); *visibility* has a scale 0..1 which we mapped to sphere size. After setting Wardley mode in the VR-Tablet, Wardley virtual nodes (chains or objects denoted by a string prefix and referencing Atlas nodes) are shown in the nexus, while other nodes are ghosted (Fig. 17a). If 2D analysis is preferred, the chain can be moved to the front glass box pane (nodes remain connected to the nexus) (Fig. 17b). This visualization offers insight into enterprise *value chains*, all related elements, and potential impacts.

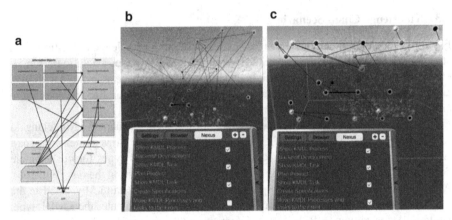

Fig. 16. Knowledge chain: a) Atlas (left), b) nexus (center), c) moved to the front glass (right).

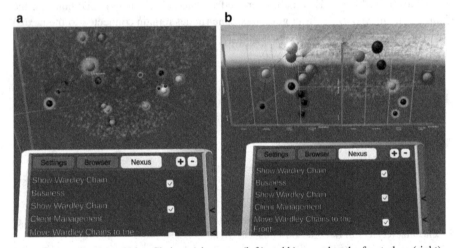

Fig. 17. Wardley Map Value Chains: a) in nexus (left) and b) moved to the front glass (right).

6.5 Risk and Governance Analysis Scenario

As the nexus displays all modeled enterprise element instances simultaneously, various analyses can be performed. In one scenario, detecting to what degree a standard such as the ISO/IEC 27005 Information Security Risk Management standards are referenced, applied, or overlooked within the enterprise (and documentation can be directly referenced via KMS) (Fig. 18a). Here we see that the standard and associated risk controls are modeled but isolated, not referenced by any other elements in the enterprise. In Fig. 18b, an employee is selected, which can be used to analyze associated roles, authority, system and physical access, teams, BPs, knowledge, Responsible Accountable Consulted Informed (RACI), and any other dependencies and influences.

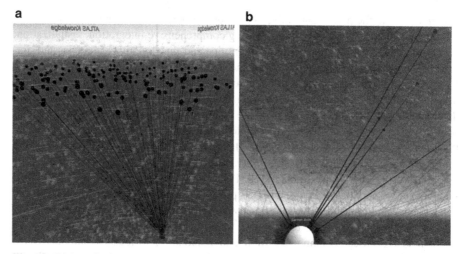

Fig. 18. Risk analysis: a) standard: ISO 27001/2 (security techniques) (left); b) person (right).

6.6 Discussion

Growing enterprise complexity and digitalization creates inherent visualization, synchronization, and documentation challenges affecting EAM analysis, decision-making, and collaboration. VR-EA+TCK brings advantageous VR factors to the EA and ECMS/KMS space. Our VR-Tablet concept provides settings to help address certain challenges or liabilities unique to VR, including limiting visual clutter and cognitive overload or ascertaining user intentions. Our evaluation demonstrated that integrating EA with ECMS/KMS in VR is viable and can support various practical EAM analysis scenarios: 1) EA-KMS Coverage via an intersection nexus showed EA elements associated with ECMS/KMS documentation and can be used to explicitly visualize and associate enterprise knowledge, 2)Business Processes exemplified how when analyzing a BP, depicted in a diagram from an EA tool such as Atlas, it can be visualized in 3D in VR, and by highlighting the involved elements in the EA nexus, additional supporting relationships, elements, and documentation and knowledge can be discovered, 3) Knowledge Chains showed how related chains of knowledge can be viewed in a nexus and comprehended in an overall enterprise context 4) Wardley Maps Value Chains illustrated how a value chain in the enterprise can be visualized within the enterprise nexus and associated elements considered, while 5) Risk and Governance Analysis showed how enterprise-wide risk-associated aspects might be discovered, such as important standards not applied, forgotten, undocumented, risk controls missing, unclarified RACI, roles, authorities, authorizations, employees, and other governance aspects depicted and analyzed.

7 Conclusion

Enterprise information, knowledge, documentation, content, and views in their various forms play an essential part in EA for gaining insights into the real digital structures and, in turn, into the digital enterprise. VR-EA+TCK contributes a unique nexus-based VR visualization solution concept, providing comprehensive integration, visualization, and synthesis of heterogenous enterprise entities and their relations, models, and diagrams simultaneously. VR-EA+TCK enhances our original heterogeneous multi-model VR-EA concept, integrating additional enterprise tool, content, and knowledge repositories (exemplified with Atlas and the Semantic MediaWiki) and including additional diagram support (Wardley and knowledge chains). Leveraging the vast VR space, it provides direct access within VR to valuable relevant related enterprise content via the browser-capable VR-Tablet and hyperplanes for Atlas-based EA diagrams. The VR implementation demonstrated its feasibility, while the evaluation case study showed its potential to support various practical EAM analysis scenarios, including ECMS/KMS knowledge intersection coverage, business processes, knowledge chains, Wardley Map value chains, and risk and governance analysis. With our solution concept, EAM activities including analysis, discovery, inquiry, reasoning, decision-making, synthesis, and assessment via VR can become accessible and included for various stakeholder groups in their daily work, towards supporting the grander enterprise modeling vision [4] with "grass-roots modeling".

The benefits of VR-EA+TCK include: comprehensive full 3D view in a nexus of all EA enterprise elements and type classifications with all relationships, ECMS/KMS integrated as a nexus to visualize knowledge elements and their relations, intersection nexus generation to support cross-nexus analysis, unlimited simultaneous EA diagrams in 3D from the Atlas tool, automatic stack-based depiction of all diagrams containing an element of interest, and simultaneous heterogeneous multi-model visualization (e.g., with VR-EA ArchiMate, VR-BPMN, or VR-UML models) in the limitless space offered by VR.

Future work includes enhancing the interactive, informational, analytical, and modeling capabilities of VR-EA+TCK, including chronological analysis, gap analysis, force-directed layout and additional visualization alternatives, and a comprehensive empirical study.

Acknowledgements. The authors would like to thank Ricardo Santos Leal for his assistance with Atlas.

References

1. Jarvis, B.: Enterprise Architecture: Understanding the Bigger Picture – A Best Practice Guide for Decision Makers in IT. The UK National Computing Centre (2003)
2. Hoogervorst, J.: Enterprise governance and enterprise engineering. Springer (2009)
3. Sousa, P., Leal, R., Sampaio, A.: Atlas: the enterprise cartography tool. In: 18th Enterprise Engineering Working Conference Forum, vol. 2229. CEUR-WS.org (2018)
4. Sandkuhl, K., et al.: From expert discipline to common practice: a vision and research agenda for extending the reach of enterprise modeling. Bus. Inf. Syst. Eng. **60**(1), 69–80 (2018). https://doi.org/10.1007/s12599-017-0516-y
5. Rickenberg, T.A., Fill, H.G., Breitner, M.H.: Enterprise content management systems as a knowledge infrastructure. Inte. J. e-Collaboration **11**(3), 49–70 (2015)

6. Venkatraman, N.: Managing IT resources as a value center, IS Executive Seminar Series. Cranfield School of Management (1996)
7. Steuer, J.: Defining virtual reality: dimensions determining telepresence. J. Commun. **42**(4), 73–93 (1992)
8. Müller, R., Kovacs, P., Schilbach, J., Zeckzer, D.: How to master challenges in experimental evaluation of 2D versus 3D software visualizations. In: 2014 IEEE VIS International Workshop on 3Dvis (3Dvis), pp. 33–36. IEEE (2014)
9. Oberhauser, R., Sousa, P., Michel, F.: VR-EAT: Visualization of Enterprise Architecture Tool Diagrams in Virtual Reality. In: Shishkov, B. (ed.) BMSD 2020. LNBIP, vol. 391, pp. 221–239. Springer, Cham (2020). https://doi.org/10.1007/978-3-030-52306-0_14
10. Oberhauser, R., Pogolski, C.: VR-EA: Virtual Reality Visualization of Enterprise Architecture Models with ArchiMate and BPMN. In: Shishkov, B. (ed.) BMSD 2019. LNBIP, vol. 356, pp. 170–187. Springer, Cham (2019). https://doi.org/10.1007/978-3-030-24854-3_11
11. Oberhauser, R., Pogolski, C., Matic, A.: VR-BPMN: Visualizing BPMN Models in Virtual Reality. In: Shishkov, B. (ed.) BMSD 2018. LNBIP, vol. 319, pp. 83–97. Springer, Cham (2018). https://doi.org/10.1007/978-3-319-94214-8_6
12. Rehring, K., Hoffmann, D., Ahlemann, F.: Put your glasses on: conceptualizing affordances of mixed and virtual reality for enterprise architecture management. Multikonferenz Wirtschaftsinformatik (2018)
13. Roth, S., Zec, M., Matthes, F.: Enterprise architecture visualization tool survey. Technical Report, sebis. Technical University Munich (2014)
14. Naranjo, D., Sánchez, M., Villalobos, J.: Towards a unified and modular approach for visual analysis of enterprise models. In: 2014 IEEE 18th International Enterprise Distributed Object Computing Conference Workshops and Demonstrations, pp. 77–86. IEEE (2014)
15. Yan, H.S.: A new complicated-knowledge representation approach based on knowledge meshes. IEEE Trans. Knowl. Data Eng. **18**(1), 47–62 (2005)
16. Górski, F., Buń, P., Zawadzki, P., Wichniarek, R.: Knowledge Management in Open Industrial Virtual Reality Applications. In: Trojanowska, J., Ciszak, O., Machado, J.M., Pavlenko, I. (eds.) MANUFACTURING 2019. LNME, pp. 104–118. Springer, Cham (2019). https://doi.org/10.1007/978-3-030-18715-6_9
17. Zenkert, J., Holland, A., Fathi, M.: Discovering contextual knowledge with associated information in dimensional structured knowledge bases. In: 2016 IEEE International Conference on Systems, Man, and Cybernetics (SMC), pp. 1923–1928. IEEE (2016)
18. Alalwan, J.A., Weistroffer, H.R.: Enterprise content management research: a comprehensive review. Journal of Enterprise Information Management (2012)
19. Escalona, M., Domínguez-Mayo, F., García-García, J., Sánchez, N., Ponce, J.: Evaluating enterprise content management tools in a real context. J. Softw. Eng. Appl. **8**, 431–453 (2015). https://doi.org/10.4236/jsea.2015.88042
20. Sehring, H.W.: Adaptive content visualization in concept-oriented content management systems. In: 2009 Computation World: Future Computing, Service Computation, Cognitive, Adaptive, Content, Patterns, pp. 659–664. IEEE (2009)
21. Dammak, H., Dkhil, A., Cherifi, A., Gardoni, M.: Enterprise content management systems: a graphical approach to improve the creativity during ideation sessions—case study of an innovation competition "24 h of innovation." Int. J. Interact. Design and Manuf. (IJIDeM) **14**(3), 939–953 (2020)
22. Sousa, P., Lima, J., Sampaio, A., Pereira, C.: An approach for creating and managing enterprise blueprints: a case for IT blueprints. In: 21st International Conference on Advanced Information Systems. LNBIP, vol. 34, pp. 70–84. Springer-Verlag (2009)
23. Tribolet, J., Sousa, P., Caetano, A.: The role of enterprise governance and cartography in enterprise engineering. Enterprise Modelling and Information Systems Architectures **9**(1), 38–49 (2014)

24. Sousa, P., Carvalho, M.: Dynamic organization's representation. linking project management with enterprise architecture. In: IEEE 20th Conf. on Business Informatics (CBI), vol. 2, pp. 170–174. IEEE (2018a)

25. Sousa, P., Cardoso, D., Colaço, J.: Managing multi-view business processes models in the Atlas tool. In: Proc. of the 19th Enterprise Engineering Working Conference Forum, vol. 2408. CEUR-WS.org (2019)

26. Sousa, P. et al.: Enterprise transformation: the serasa experian case. In: Practice-Driven Research on Enterprise Transformation (PRET 2011). LNBIP, vol. 89, pp. 134-145. Springer, Berlin, Heidelberg (2011)

27. Sousa, P., Sampaio, A. Leal, R.: A Case for a living enterprise architecture in a private bank. In: 8th Workshop on Transformation & Engineering of Enterprises (TEE 2014), vol. 1182. CEUR-WS.org (2014)

28. Oberhauser, R.: VR-UML: The Unified Modeling Language in Virtual Reality – An Immersive Modeling Experience. In: Shishkov, B. (ed.) BMSD 2021. LNBIP, vol. 422, pp. 40–58. Springer, Cham (2021). https://doi.org/10.1007/978-3-030-79976-2_3

29. Pogorzelska, B.: KMDL® v2.2 A semi-formal description language for modelling knowledge conversions. In: Gronau, N. (Ed.) Modeling and Analyzing knowledge intensive business processes with KMDL: Comprehensive insights into theory and practice, pp. 87–192. GITO mbH Verlag (2012)

30. Gronau, N.: Knowledge Modeling and Description Language 3.0 - Eine Einführung. GITO mbH Verlag, Berlin (2020)

31. Wardley, S.: Wardley Maps: The use of topographical intelligence in business strategy. Medium (10 Aug 2016). https://medium.com/wardleymaps/finding-a-path-cdb1249078c0

A Case of Social Dynamics and Social Relativism

Coen Suurmond$^{(\boxtimes)}$ (iD)

Cesuur B.V., Velp, The Netherlands
coen@cesuur.info

Abstract. The paper presents a case study of the replacement of an IT system in a production plant, in the context of a change of ownership of the plant and a renewal of its complete IT landscape as a consequence. The new systems had to be operational by a fixed date, some 8 months after formal transfer of ownership. Simultaneously with the replacement of systems the local organisation had to adapt to the views of the new parent company, exploring some workable middle ground between structures and patterns of the old and new parent company.

In the given situation where the organisation was transiting to new and partly still to be determined structures and patterns, methodologies assuming a more or less stable social world would be of little guidance. Finding – and creating – firm ground together with people from different backgrounds involved in the project was a major challenge. The paper will present the case itself, followed by a reflection on the position of several methodologies from the social relativism paradigm regarding the dynamics of evolving meanings while developing an information system. The Learning Cycle from Soft Systems Methodology will be projected on the case, to examine retrospectively the fit of SSM with the volatility of the social environment in the case.

Keywords: Case study · Social relativism paradigm · Soft system methodology

1 Introduction

In this paper a case from industry will be presented as an example of developing an information system consistent with the paradigm of social relativism. The case is particularly interesting because it concerns a production plant that was sold to a new owner, and had therefore to implement new information systems in the organisation while it was transiting to new organisational procedures and patterns. Due to the unique character of the acquisition for the new owner (scale, newness of some new product and production processes, quite different organisation culture in the acquired plant, sensitivity of the tight commercial interests with the selling parent company which would remain brand owner of the major products of the plant) and due to the tight time frame, many major changes in the organisation were taking place simultaneously, and not always with a known outcome. This fact in combination with the interdependencies between changes in different parts of the organisation created a project environment with much more uncertainties than usual. It also implies that the people involved in the project had to continuously

© Springer Nature Switzerland AG 2022
B. Shishkov (Ed.): BMSD 2022, LNBIP 453, pp. 141–157, 2022.
https://doi.org/10.1007/978-3-031-11510-3_9

evolve their understanding of developments. More specifically, it implied that people from different backgrounds had to agree on new meanings of familiar concepts.

The paper starts with a presentation of the case. First, some background of the case is provided, followed by a discussion of the character of the case. The combination of many different disciplines working simultaneously on different changes in the organisation added significantly to the complexity. The way we dealt with this will be discussed. Finding invariants and working with a fixed set of reference products contributed to developing a common background for communication and validation. We also discuss the necessity to have a broad view on information systems, not reducing analysis and design to IT-based information flows only. Section 4 presents the project itself, subdivided into three steps. The subsequent stages of the project are described, often exemplifying general issues in such projects.

Next to the presentation of the case, the paper will reflect on methodology. As indicated above, the way of working in the project can be viewed as belonging to the paradigm of social relativism. Some defining characteristics of the paradigm will be discussed, and the position of four methodologies working within this paradigm will be critically reviewed regarding these characteristics (Language Action Perspective (LAP), Organisational Semiotics (OS), DEMO, and Soft Systems Methodology (SSM)). This part will conclude with retrospectively projecting the learning cycle of SSM on the case.

2   Backgrounds of the Case

2.1   General Description

The case is about a plant that produces a wide variety of perishable fast-moving consumer food products (meat, soup, sauce) with typical shelf life from a few days up to several weeks. The main raw materials are food (fresh and frozen), spices and packaging materials. The palletised output of the plant is shipped to external warehouses by frequent shuttle services for further distribution to the customers. The plant keeps no stock of finished products. The plant operates one, two or three shifts per production line, depending on product demand, for 6 days per week. The reliability of the continuous supply chain from plant to warehouses is critical for the service level to the customers.

The project was triggered by the sale of the plant by the owner, an internationally operating company, to a company specialised in meat products. Everything related to the finished products remained with the original owner of the plant (ownership of the brands, sales, warehousing, demand planning). The two primary operational interfaces between the original owner and the new owner would be sending the weekly demand of finished products to the plant and the daily delivery and invoicing of finished products from the plant. Hence, for the original owner the difference between the old and new situations was that the output of the plant was no longer regulated by internal agreement but by a commercial contract. For the original owner all business processes related to finished products would remain the same, the only difference being that the information of the demand planning and the subsequent replenishment of their warehouses with finished goods would be an interaction with an external supplier instead of with a plant of their own.

During the transition period between the day the ownership of the plant changed and the day the IT systems of the new owner had to take over the existing business processes would be supported by the existing IT systems of the original owner. This was arranged to warrant the continuity of the availability of the products for the consumer markets, which was of course a critical issue for the brand owner. In this interim period the new owner had to prepare and implement all required changes in the organisation, its systems and its technical infrastructures. At the end of the interim period "the plugs would be pulled" and the IT systems (including all related hardware and infrastructures) of the new owner would have to take over without any interruption of production and logistic processes.

2.2 What Was to Be Achieved by the Project

The new owner intended to deploy its existing IT systems without modification as much as possible. This was partly motivated by a choice for standardisation of systems and procedures across all its factories, and partly necessitated by the sheer magnitude of the task of integrating the new plant. Integrating a host of partly new and unfamiliar kinds of product and processing embedded in a highly different organisational culture within a limited time frame and with very little tolerance for operational discontinuities left little room for trying out new solutions.

As a consequence, our company, being the preferred supplier of shop floor IT systems for the factories of the new owner, was asked to implement our systems in the newly acquired plant. As a starting point, we received a general schema of the existing landscape of IT systems in the original situation, together with a general schema of the projected landscape with the local IT systems connected to the IT systems of the new owner. We also received the available documentation about interfacing with the local systems, which was not always complete or up-to-date.

The request was to first do a preliminary investigation to scope and budget our part of the project, and to follow up with the actual implementation of our systems. The first part would be done before the formal acquisition (available time: less than 2 months), the second part would have to take place during the interim period starting with the transfer of ownership of the plant and ending with the pulling of the plugs of the systems of the original owner (available time: about 8 months).

2.3 The Project Group

In the core project group, the new owner, the plant and the IS supplier were represented by a small number of widely experienced people. Depending on the subject, specialists from the new owner, the plant or the IS supplier were involved.

Both the project as a whole and the composition of the project could be viewed as a kind of tripartite structure with three bipartite structures embedded. The tripartite structure consisted of the new owner, the plant, and our company as IS supplier. The three embedded bipartitions were (1) customer (owner + plant) 'versus' IS supplier; (2) control (owner) 'versus' production (plant + IS supplier); and (3) 'outsiders' (owner + IS supplier) 'versus' 'insiders' (plant). Please note that 'versus' should be taken as marking different backgrounds and views, not as an antagonistic relation. In fact, generally the project was characterised by a strong collaborative spirit.

My personal position in the project was determined by my expertise regarding companies and production processes in food processing, by my long-term relationship with our customer (more than 25 years), as well as my authorship of the concepts underlying our shop floor information systems for this kind of industry. My formal position in my company was business consultant at the moment of the project, twinned to a very close colleague. In fact, the project manager of the plant once remarked that he viewed us as Siamese twins. Whatever he told one of us, the other would know. This phenomenon was due to our very similar ways of looking and thinking. Kindred spirits can communicate very effectively by just short remarks such as "did you notice X?", acknowledged by a nod of the other person. Unkindred spirits would need a much longer and more verbose explanation, and reach a lesser level of understanding. This is an important but underexposed phenomenon about cooperation in organisations and projects, and our functioning as Siamese twins proved to be very fruitful in this project.

3 Preliminaries of the Project

3.1 Identifying Invariants

We started with a short preliminary survey of the existing plant, in order to get a general feel for the physical and organisational issues waiting for us in the project. This pre-project survey delivered two tangible results: the project budget, and a schema uniting the quite heterogeneous production processes in one generic picture (which proved to be very useful as a framework for similar project activities on different production lines). It also delivered an awareness of the scale of the task, especially because of the significant differences in organisational culture between the selling parent company and the new parent, the former more formalised and tangible, the latter more agile and intangible.

So, the signing of the contract would kick off a great many transition processes for the organisation of the plant (both formal and informal) and its organisational procedures. And although the general direction of the changes might sometimes be clear, many specifics of the changes were to be found out during the transition period (and after). Such a situation does not provide firm ground to undertake a project!

However, we could identify two certainties, indisputable by even the highest officers in the organisations. Firstly, it would be unacceptable for the changes to have any impact on the end products leaving the plant. This required continuity of both the production processes and in the sourcing of raw materials, no changes were allowed in this respect. Secondly, the availability of the products on the consumer market (the service level) had to be kept the same. To warrant this, the old and the new owner had agreed that the planning and information processes related to the finished products would not be changed (starting with establishing demand by the brand owner, followed by planning, production and delivery by the plant). Hence, the only change for the brand owner would be the transition from internal sourcing of finished products to external sourcing by an external supplier. In other words: the former internal transfer of goods would be replaced by a purchase transaction. To summarise: the first invariant was the unchanged finished product, and the second invariant was the planning and delivery of the finished products of the plant to the warehouses of the brand owner.

The issues regarding the continuity of the finished product and the uncertainty of all kinds of organisational issues as discussed above, imposed a bottom-up approach for the project: product, production structures and shop floor first, organisational overhead structures later.

3.2 Communication and Validation Issues in the Project

One of the dominant issues in a project is communication. Having the same mother tongue does not always guarantee understanding. In this specific project, the new owner and my company as its IT supplier for more than two decades had a long and deep common background. Communication with the people from the new plant however, was another matter. As already indicated above: different product ranges, different processes, different organisational culture, being located in a different part of the country result in a different 'language'. Given the tight timetable, the challenge was to make sure we were talking about the same things as quickly as possible, and how to minimise the risks of miscommunication.

Communication was especially problematic because of the involvement of at least four different organisations (the old owner, the new owner, the plant itself, the IT supplier), in combination with a variety of disciplines in each of the organisations involved. Within the plant alone the range was from the production line supervisors on the shop floor via production management, planning and finance up through higher management. The higher-level staff all had different counterparts in the organisations of the old and new owners. To summarise: communication would be complicated.

The counterpart to communication is validation. Without adequate communication no validation is possible; communication without validation of what is said and specified makes no sense. Hence, we had to find a mechanism for which it was sure that all parties involved would understand specifications in the same way.

3.3 Using Reference Products as Foundation for the Project

In other projects we were used to working with reference products. Because of the size of the project and its many surrounding uncertainties, we decided to apply this idea much more rigorously as a central pillar of our approach. It is not uncommon to have some specimen from the master data as running examples in analysis. Such examples are used again and again, contributing to a common background. In this project we asked from the plant to provide for each product range/production line a set of reference products. The set had to fulfil two requirements. Firstly, each individual product should represent a process variation for its production line. Secondly, the set should represent all 'relevant' process variations. The term 'relevant' is put between quotes, because here is a kind of circular argument. The reference set is meant to build a common background, to recognise what are relevant process variations requires a common background. Practically speaking, the initially selected set will be based on some initial explanation and discussion between the parties involved, and you have to allow for the possibility to adjust the set of reference products should the circumstances require so. In the course of this project, on a total set of about 50 products for all product ranges, only a few changes were made.

It is important to emphasise the difference between examples and reference products as specified above. Examples are often understood as noncommittal, informal, nothing more than an accidental illustration. We required strong commitment from the user organisation: please compile a set of reference products that represent all existing process variations on your line. The ultimate go/no-go test for your production line will be that the new system must show it will cope adequately with the full reference set, and therefore with all activities on your production line.

The prominent role of reference products in the project addressed the concerns earlier discussed in this section. Firstly, it was a major instrument in warranting continuity of the products. Secondly, it supported the "evolution of meaning" (see discussion in Sect. 5) between the core members of the project group: the newcomers got acquainted in a highly structured and detailed way manner with the local products (including item coding) and production structures (including Bill of Materials), the "locals" got acquainted with the way of thinking of the project members from the new owner and the supplier of the new shop floor systems. Thirdly, it supported the communication with the shop floor people later on in the project, because we could present our analyses, models and solutions in terms of their habitual products and processes. Fourthly, and quite importantly, amongst the many changes the local people had to go through, we could stress the continuity of their core business, the production of their well-known branded products.

3.4 Information Systems, not IT Systems

It should be emphasized that although the project was triggered by the necessity of finding a replacement of the IT systems of the former owner, the project was really about the replacing of information systems. Part of the renewal was finding a workable mix of the settled coding conventions of the plant and the equally settled conventions of the new owner (item coding as always being a major issue here!). Even more important, introducing a new IT system implies changing the ways how information relevant for business processes is communicated. The balance between information which is IT-based (formalised) and which is communicated by natural-language-based channels (less standardised, more flexible) will shift.

Although our job was specified as the renewal of the IT system, our approach was much wider. We would start with a broad view of information in business processes, asking two very simple but fundamental basic questions:

1. What information does an actor in a business process need to do their job properly?
2. What information should an actor in a business process produce to enable other actors in downstream processes to do their jobs properly?

The way the information is provided is secondary to the two basic questions (an "actor" being either a person or some equipment). For any business process, information can be communicated by dedicated IT applications, by generic Office systems, by telephone or by meetings. Training on the job, posters and pictures on the shop floor are also means for transferring information. An incidental change in a process flow will often be communicated by a direct contact between colleagues. Another example: around midnight, a token inserted in the product flow will signal a new production date on product tins, triggering a colleague two hours later to change the adjustment of the label production date in the packaging line where tins are packed into cartons.

In order to design and implement a shop floor information system, you have to understand what information is required in the process itself as well as in the downstream processes, and you have to have a view how the different information flows form a complete and consistent whole for the user. Hence, the design of an information system should encompass how all kinds of information flows work together to provide the right information in the right form on the right place (both in physical space and functional space!).

4 The Project

4.1 First Step: Analysis of Product and Production Models

The first step upon receiving the list of reference products was to analyse the bills of material (BoM) from the existing IT system for all reference products, a set of about 5000 lines. Firstly, we wanted to check the compatibility of the structure of the BoMs with our projected general process structure. Secondly, we wanted to identify process variations in the BoM of the products. Thirdly, we wanted to develop a feeling/an imagination of the production processes by means of looking at the products, the processing steps, and the ingredients.

The first outcome was that we could identify the process stages of our general process model in the existing BoMs. Basically, we had a very good fit with only minor differences, quickly resolvable. The analysis rendered some interesting process variations, especially when semi-finished products were shipped to subcontractors (to be received again after processing) or sold to other plants. Not uncommon, such anomalous situations could lead to rather awkward and incomplete solutions (or work-arounds) due to constraints in the IT systems.

Developing a feeling for the processes was done by means of reading and organising the 5000 lines of BoM details, belonging to some 50 finished products. The first organising principle was to subdivide the finished products per product range, the second principle was to mark the transitions of one production process to the next process. Doing this by eye and by hand, you get a feeling of what is going on in the process. You also get acquainted with coding and naming conventions (which make existing information more readable, because you can map the code to product/process categories), and it is a first step to familiarise yourself with the "language of the plant". We could talk with people in the plant about their products and processes in a very concrete way, and in their language (which does not imply we understood everything or even most of it, that was still a far way to go!). Altogether this first step was an effective step towards laying a firm foundation for the new system, and towards a common understanding of all parties involved.

4.2   Second Step: Linking Models to the Physical World

The analytical modelling step described above was 'fleshed out' by linking the processes to physical production processes. Assisted by layout drawings of the shop floor and examining the shop floor itself, we wanted to link our abstract processes to physical execution by looking into (1) the physical aspects of processing, transport and storing (2) the physical aspects of installation and usage of shop floor IT equipment and (3) the physical aspects of existing ways of providing information to and getting information from the shop floor.

For example one interesting finding was a configuration of two packaging lines with separate input conveyors but with shared output equipment. The physical situation of the two input conveyors belonged in our model to two different product ranges and two different production lines. So, we had to decide: either keep our model clean and easily understandable by modelling two different production lines (where practically speaking they could not be in use at the same time), or model a new complex element of a process with two different input channels and one common output channel. We chose the first option as being much simpler and much more maintainable in the future.

Matching products and product lots before you on the shop floor with IDs on an IT screen is often one of the most challenging issues in production registration. I will just mention but not discuss the many other practical issues in shop floor registration systems, such as the physical location of registration stations, their positioning relative to the product flow and the user, the way quantities are determined (pallets or big boxes are easily countable, a heap of hundreds and hundreds of small cups containing 30gr of product less so), and the way lots are created and recognised on the shop floor. The common denominator in all this: the step from office-based planning and control functions, using abstract production models, to the physical reality of the shop floor is huge. Neglecting this problem leads often to systems that are fed with plausible but unreliable production data. When systems do not fit operational reality, people on the shop floor will quickly find creative ways how to satisfy the system while minimising the impact of their actual work. The triple challenge here is to find (1) practical workable solutions that (2) not only work for the staff in the offices but that (3) also, and especially, satisfy the information needs of the shop floor itself. Self-evidently, this way of exploring possibilities and solutions is to a high degree context-sensitive.

In Sect. 3.4 two basic questions for information in business processes were formulated, asking about the information required for the job and the information to be produced from the job. The discussion above illustrates the many forms of information in processes: in physical space information is carried by products, enabling people on the shop floor which is where and enabling people at registration points to match product and lot identification on the physical product with IDs and descriptions on their screens. E.g., positioning five consecutive tins upside down can be a convention for conveying information about a lot break in a continuous flow of tins on a production line. Or the location in a storage area suggests the kind of product. Or the colour of the labels attached to raw material suggests the reception date. Or in the daily meeting people are informed that the "Wednesday colour" was out of stock, which is why by exemption the "Sunday colour" had to be used. Hence, design of an information system is partly about finding effective and efficient ways to convey information to and from operational processes;

focusing on just information flows carried and processed by IT-systems would miss a lot of relevant and often crucial information.

The product of this phase was a short document per production area (defined by the organisational responsibilities of production supervisors) describing the physical processes by short point by point statements, with peculiarities highlighted ('peculiarity' being anything that was mentioned by production staff or had otherwise struck the eye as a bit out of the ordinary, and which might have an impact on the operating of the system-to-be). This document also had more detailed drawings of shop floor layouts with the physical flows of types of materials (either food or non-food) represented by coloured arrows; the projected registration stations were marked in these layouts.

After validating the process descriptions in the document, discussions were focussed on the practicalities of (1) the position of the registration stations and (2) the feasibility of registration procedures. An example of the first kind is whether the station could be attached to a wall (existing piping might obstruct this) or assessing the risk that a passing forklift with load might hit the station. An example of the second kind could be about the ergonomics of the arrangement and the availability/visibility of relevant information for the user.

4.3 Third Step: Connecting to the World of Line Operators and Supervisors

The next step was to involve the shop floor supervisors and operators as a critical important group of stakeholders. As usual, the group was a mixed bag. Some were just curious and open-minded about the new system, some were seeing opportunities, some were reluctant and anxious about the changes. Whatever the initial attitude of the future users, an important first step in any implementation process is to focus the minds on the business processes, to see information processes as instrumental for the processes, and to see IT as instrumental for some of the information processes. The implementation of a new system must not be about systems telling users what to do and how to behave, but the other way around: about user processes that must adequately be served by systems. To paraphrase a famous saying by John F. Kennedy, the attitude should be: "Don't ask what you can do for the system, ask what the system can do for your process!". In my experience, workers on the shop floor often have an emotional stake in the smooth and proper running of 'their processes', and it helps enormously if you can address that interest.

Our preparation with supervisors and operators was based on a three-pronged approach: (1) emphasis on continuity of the primary processes, (2) focus on business processes and not on systems, (3) introducing the new systems as essentially processing existing information in slightly modified forms. Hence, we started by specifying what would <u>not</u> change: no changes in the products, no changes in the primary process, and no changes in production planning (which was done by spreadsheet and resulting in print-outs of the planning provided to the shop floor). Secondly, it was our job to understand 'their' world. We had developed production scenarios based on the combination of (a) current master data of the reference products, (b) current bills of material, and (c) recent production runs of some of the reference products. We had formatted the production scenarios in spreadsheets, broken up in the individual processes with all input and output per process calculated with realistic numbers. We presented the scenarios against the background of both the abstract processing schemes and the physical layout of the production lines. Our statement to the supervisors and operators: this is our interpretation of your existing processes, with the processing structures basically unchanged but with minor modifications according to the new production model. Our questions: Did we get it right? Did we get anything wrong in the structuring, the data, something else? Do you think this can work in your practice?

The procedure of highlighting the existing structures and the links between physical processes and information about those processes, using recognisable data, worked very well. The fierce reaction of a supervisor on a wrong amount in one of our production scenarios illustrates this. When we presented the amount of 305 g of dough per sausage in the portioning process, he reacted strongly: that is not right! It should be 298gr! We tried to find the cause of this difference, could not find it and took the problem home. The next day, we had found a possible and plausible explanation: in the portioning some auxiliary material for the sausage-skin was added, and this component amounted to some 7 g per sausage. We presented this finding to the supervisor and this was indeed what caused our mistaken calculation. We then adapted our process model and our BoM accordingly, calculated again and everything was right. This story illustrates how important it is to work with realistic and recognisable properties and numbers. The reaction of the supervisor was not triggered by his thinking or calculations, it was a spontaneous and immediate reaction to incorrect numbers. We were not discussing "our" systems in these sessions, we were discussing the user world of products and processes.

The next element in preparing for implementation was to make the users familiar with the look and feel of the new system. Before the session with the production staff of a production line, a complete set up of hardware and software would be prepared in a dedicated room. On the walls of that room print-outs of the models and layouts that were used in earlier stages were available for reference. We used the production scenarios as presented earlier by Powerpoint and spreadsheet (also simultaneously available on a big screen in the room), and showed how "those scenarios and numbers flowed through the system". Because the users were already familiar with the scenarios and the data, and because they had already checked that the scenarios were 'for real' (representing the world of their daily work), the focus in demonstrating the new system was wholly on the look and feel of the new system. Questions and answers would be about the system as such, without distracting discussions about the data.

The sessions with operators and supervisors were perhaps the most important meetings in the project: abstraction meets realisation; outsider meets insider; shop floor meets management; IT meets process. Therefore, broad participation was required: (1) as plant-insiders (1a) operators, (1b) supervisors, (1c) production department managers, (1d) general production manager; (2) as plant-outsiders (2a) business/process analysts, (2b) a production controller from the new owner, (3) implementation consultants of the IT supplier. The broad participation made it possible that questions from supervisors and operators could directly be addressed by the person(s) concerned. Discussions of the kind "but that cannot work at all in our practice!" could mostly be solved in the moment (either by explanation or adaptation), or sometimes be added to the To Do list. This procedure created a broad common background for all participants for the remainder of the implementation processes.

This initial step of the implementation phase had different meanings for different participants. For the people of the plant it was about getting acquainted with an unfamiliar way of looking at familiar products, processes and production data. For the implementation consultants, it was about getting acquainted with looking in a familiar way at unfamiliar products, processes and data. For the combination of the two groups it was getting acquainted to each other at the start of a long and intense period of a cooperative effort to bring the new IT system to operational life.

The room with the complete set-up and the accompanying information on walls and screens would remain available for further instruction and documentation purposes. This was done by the local production staff, our consultants being available for support. Short and clear operator instructions would be written first, in conformity with the existing standard procedures of the local organisation that required the availability of such instruction documents for the shop floor wherever control panels of equipment were to be used. Next, all operators would be instructed by their colleagues who had been instructed before and who had been testing the new system on their own.

5 Reflections on Methodology

5.1 Introduction

My theoretical background and philosophical stance is grounded in semiotics (Peirce [1]), speech act theory (Austin [2], Searle [3]) and Habermas' theory of communicative action with its twin concepts of system and life world (with the accompanying twin concepts of instrumental rationality and rationality based on mutual understanding) [4]. I share this background and stance with several methodologies for information systems development (ISD): Language Action Perspective (founded on speech act theory), Organisational Semiotics, DEMO (speech acts, communicative action, and semiotics amongs its foundational theories) and Soft Systems Methodology (its concept of soft systems is based on Vickers' concept of appreciative systems).

Hirschheim and Klein have analysed methodologies for ISD based on its "explicit and implicit assumptions about the nature of human organizations, the nature of the design task, and what is expected of them" [5]. Following their analysis, the four methodologies mentioned above, as well as my position, would be categorised as belonging to the social relativism paradigm. They give the following "elements used in defining IS" in this paradigm: "Subjectivity of meanings, symbolic structures affecting evolution of sense, making and sharing of meanings, metaphors" [5]. We find a kindred characterisation in Vickers' concept of an appreciative system as a system that is engaged in "attaching meaning to communication or the code by which we do so, a code which is constantly confirmed, developed or changed by use" [6].

Analysing the two characterisations, we find a static and a dynamic aspect. It is simultaneously about social norms and linguistic practices providing structure and stability to a social group, and about the continuous development of norms and practices, adapting to circumstances. The relativity of meaning to a group of language users and is aptly reflected in Wittgenstein's concept of language games [7]: in order to enter the language game, you have to learn the pre-existing rules, habits, meanings. We can recognise this aspect in the 'static' qualifications "subjectivity of meaning" and "sharing of meaning"

(Hirschheim and Klein) or "a code which is constantly confirmed ... by use" (Vickers). The dynamical aspect is about adapting to evolving environments and about finding new stability after major disturbances. This aspect is reflected in "evolution of sense" and "making of meaning" (Hirschheim and Klein) or "a code which is constantly ... developed or changed by use" (Vickers). In our case the dynamical aspects are prominently present, people involved were forced to tentatively find some workable middle ground between all sorts of different structures and conventions, evolving existing meaning and making new meaning along the way. It should be stressed that differences between our case and other cases in this respect are only gradual, not essential: introduction of a new information system in an organisation would in most cases be experienced as a major disturbance by the people involved. Therefore, the dynamic aspect should be covered in a methodology based on the paradigm of social relativism. The question to be discussed is: how do the four methodologies deal with this dynamic aspect of meaning?

Another important question to ask a methodology for ISD is what exactly is developed: is the "IS" in ISD predominantly focussed on IT-based information, or is it about all forms of information relevant for business processes in an organisation? My personal stance on this issue, and by and large the approach for information analysis in the project, is reflected in the two basic questions regarding information in business processes as formulated in Sect. 3.4: (1) what information is required to properly perform the process and (2) what information needs to be produced from the process. The questions are about information in whichever form, not just IT-based information. This view on information systems is aptly represented in the following phrasing by Avision and Fitzgerald of the view of ISAC (a very early methodology based on the principles of social relativism which was not developed further): "In ISAC terms, an information system is an organized co-operation between human beings in order to process and convey information to each other; it does not necessarily involve any form of computerization" [8]. To illustrate this point: in a sales process the buyer and seller can exchange information about the specifics of a sale in natural language (sometimes also in body language), resulting in a mutual agreement (communicative rationality) expressed in speech acts (in natural language). The agreement is based on reciprocal expectations about the fulfilment of promises, and cannot always be reduced to IDs and numbers only. Other 'soft' information might be required for order fulfilment. Hence, methodologies based on semiotics, speech act theory, and communicative action would be expected to take a broad view on information systems, and we will check to what extent this is actually the case.

5.2   Four Methodologies Based on the Social Relativism Paradigm Evaluated

On the Static and Dynamic Aspects of the Paradigm

We can discern two different worldviews in the four methodologies. SSM views the social world as something dynamical, as something that is moving from one problematical situation to the next. Unmistakable there are stable elements in this dynamic social world, otherwise we wouldn't have a social world at all. But the social world as an appreciative system is also always evolving, using codes that are "constantly confirmed, developed and changed by use" as Vickers has put it. This idea is behind the central place of the learning cycle in SSM, where existing meanings are evolving and new meanings are made [9].

The other three methodologies are approaching the social world as "being out there", waiting to be investigated and modelled. Speech Act theory is about "how to do things with words" in a given social environment, analysing how people act by means of a combination of propositional content and the intention of their utterances, thereby achieving something in the social world (respectively the locational, illocutional and perlocutional part of the speech act) [2, 3]. In a paper in 2017 Goldkuhl has criticised the focus on one person in speech act theory and LAP, and extended the perspective to establishing social relations by means of communication [10]. Still, the social relations are embedded in a pre-structured social world (as Goldkuhl himself is very much aware of, witnessed by the warning of possible bias because he has researched social relations mainly in institutionalised settings).

In DEMO, the focus on "essence" indicates its focus on stable and invariant structures (e.g.: "The most important property, however, is that this conceptual model is essential, that it shows only the essence of the enterprise" [11]). Also, the engineering metaphor that is prominent in DEMO suggests a way of think where projects are not done **in** an autonomously evolving social world, but are acting **on** a rather passive and static social world "out there".

Stamper [12] is very much aware of meaning as relative in his theory of Information Fields: "Words and other signs will have different meanings in different fields". He is also aware of the tensions resulting from people experiencing incompatible norms from different social groups they belong to. However, when Stamper writes "Our intentional speech acts lead to changes in the social world" [12] he follows up with "in business, the obvious example is the making of a contract". This is an example of the "state space" of the social world, but not a change how the social world functions.

On information Systems in a Broad or a Narrow Sense

In the seminal LAP paper by Goldkuhl and Lyytinen we find an acknowledgment of the significance of information in a broader sense, but also a reduction of information systems to IT-based systems: "The formal and closed nature of information systems implies a need for information communication channels side by side the formalized information systems" [13]. Further on, they write "Information systems development (ISD) is to force parts of professional communication into a formal language use and to realize this with a computer" [13]. In a paper from 2017 Goldkuhl writes "...there is a broader interest for how digitized information sets are elements of broader communication patterns in social settings. We need to understand non-digitized information *when it is related to digitized information*" (my italics) [10]. Hence, Goldkuhl, one of the founding fathers of LAP, is not reasoning from information in a broader sense to IT-based information, but has it the other way around.

Stamper, in his chapter on Organisational Semiotics in 1997, has been very clear on this point: "Information systems are social systems. ... Information systems have been around ever since human beings were able to use signs" [12]. In 2015, this seems to be repeated by Liu and Li in their book about OS: "An organisation is a social system in which people behave in an organised manner by conforming to a certain system of norms" [14]. However, they also write "... agents' behaviour that is governed by norms.

... Norms can be expressed in a natural language or a formal, machine-executed language. They will be incorporated into the database as integrity and consistency constraints, or programmed as software applications" [14]. This suggests a focus on IT-based systems.

The recent new edition about Enterprise Ontology by Dietz and Mulder has first a set of chapters where theories are introduced and discussed (partly founded on semiotics and Habermas' theory of communicative action), followed by a chapter on the DEMO methodology based on the theories. DEMO does not discuss information in a broader or narrower sense, but models and rules in DEMO are all formalised, for example: "The guidelines for responding to coordination facts (C-facts) are called *action rules* ... expressed in *Action Rule Specifications*" [11], and "The Process Model (PM) of an organisation is the ontological model of the state space and the transition space". [11] While the term "guidelines" suggests that responses can be flexible, everything else suggests a rather rigid formal and machine-executable model.

Only Soft Systems Methodology has an uncurtailed view on information systems as encompassing all kinds of information, best witnessed by its brilliant chapter "The Information System that Won the War" [15]. This can be considered as a practical application of Vicker's concept of an appreciative system.

Summary

The way of thinking behind three of the four methodologies discussed above seem to be leaning towards a static view on the social world, language and communication (LAP, OS, DEMO). Furthermore, their focus is on formalised information (OS: formalised norms) and hence on IT based information systems. This would have made it difficult to apply these methodologies to our case, with the proviso that the competence of the consultants doing the job might compensate any shortcomings of a methodology. Side remark: this a general problem in researching methodologies: which part of any success or failure could be ascribed to the methodology, and which part to the persons using/following/interpreting the methodology?

Only SSM does explicitly recognise the "evolving of sense" and the "making of meaning" in ISD, both in its way of thinking and in its way of working. The cyclic nature of collaborative development of meaning in the learning cycle reflects this dynamic character. Also, SSM is about information and information systems in a broad sense. In the next section we will go one step further, and project the learning cycle retrospectively on our project. As we will see, project and learning cycles fit very well together.

5.3 Soft Systems Methodology Projected on the Case

It is important to repeat that in the case studied we did not apply the insights of SSM as our approach. It was in hindsight that I realised interesting similarities of what we had been doing in the project with the learning cycle SSM approach, and it is in hindsight that I am comparing our project with the SSM approach.

From the viewpoint of the project group (representing the interests of the new owner, the plant, and our company as IS supplier) the project could be viewed as a sequence of learning cycles where (1) in each cycle some specific subjects were dealt with (some once and for all, other provisionally), and (2) a growing common understanding was developed for the social and physical reality of the plant (Table 1).

Table 1. SSM learning cycles in the project

Cycle	Real-world problematical situation	Worldview (predominant)	Model(s) used
1	Replacement of IT systems	IT Manager (new owner)	IT Systems Landscape
2	Investigating production structures	Application manager (plant)	General production model
3	Comparing product data structures	Controller (plant, new owner)	Bill-of-material structures
4	Views on production processes	Production staff (plant)	Physical layouts + Process Models
5	New IS on the shop floor	Operators (plant)	Process models + Production Scenarios

The project started with the IT manager of the new owner, asking our company to participate in the necessary renewal of the IT systems landscape (cycle 1). The replacement of IT systems was of course part of the selling of the plant, the general picture was also clear (projecting the IT structures of the new owner on the plant, and interfacing with remaining local specialised production-area control systems), the details and the circumstances were to be found out. We proceeded by step-by-step exploring firm ground, starting with the general picture of processes and Bill-of-Materials (cycles 2 and 3). In creating the general production model, the plant-view (represented by the application manager) was leading, the form of the model was such that it was both a valid representation of the plant processes and an "implementable" model of the systems of the new owner. In cycle 3 the general production model was fleshed-out by investigating the way product- and process data were structured in the IT systems of the plant, and how those structures would fit into the IT systems of the new owner. After this step we could be confident that the foundational structures (controller view) in existing and new systems could be mapped to each other. The general production model had an important role in interpreting the various configurations of production lines, and in communicating about them in a uniform – but not rigid! – manner.

Cycle 3 finished the abstract part of the project, and provided a solid footing for concretising the general structures on the shop floor, per production line. In Cycle 4 we discussed the new structures in relation to the concrete physical circumstances and the concrete management interests with the views of the production managers and supervisors. We compared their current way of working with the projected new models and new systems. Two recurring issues in the discussions were the risk of extra workload on production staff, and the reliability of production data. Abstract process models are one thing, without reliable data they are useless. One example: 40 cartons neatly aligned on a pallet are reliably countable, 1673 cups on a chaotic heap in a huge basket are not. The abstract model is identical for the two situations, the practical situation is not. Side remark: once you have captured a number in an IT system, such differences as in the example above disappear for the user; this is an important source of problems with data quality in IT systems. Another issue: it is easy to talk about "production date" and "lot break" in an abstract way. But what does this mean on the shop floor? What triggers a new production date in an 24/7 operation on a production line with a throughput time of several hours from begin to end of the line, and a production rate of 4000 units per hour? What happens when the rule for triggering the next production date (say, sharply at midnight) applies but there is only 15 min of production left? As was to be expected, various production lines had various answers to this kind of questions, the new owner also could have its opinions about such issues, and part of the learning cycle was to find answers for the new operational situation with the new information system in place.

Cycle 5 was perhaps the most interesting because of the combination of so many worldviews. As was written in the description of the case: "abstraction meets realisation; outsider meets insider; shop floor meets management; IT meets process". All the work done in the earlier cycles was synthesised in concrete reference production scenarios, leading to the confronting of all the previous the modelling work with the production worldview as represented by the operators in the production lines.

6 Conclusion

The case was certainly most interesting to work on. Practically it was challenging because of what was at stake, the size, the complexity, the uncertainties and the many simultaneous changes taking place. The complex and intensely dynamical character of the social groups involved, both inside the project and in its environment, created a way of working that had to be highly adaptable to circumstances.

Theoretically the case is interesting because of the instability of meaning and social patterns. This made the case useful for reflection on the dynamic elements of the social relativism paradigm, which led to an evaluation of four methodologies on the issue of new and evolving meaning in an organisation. Also, the four were examined on their view of an information system in an organisation: either in a broad sense encompassing all kinds of information, with IT systems embedded; or in a narrow sense as an IT-based system with social aspects analysed in relation to the IT system. It turned out that Language Action Perspective, Organisational Semiotics and DEMO lean towards a narrow view on information systems to be developed for a rather static social world. Soft Systems Methodology is quite different, taking an information system in a broad sense and developing a system in a social environment that will change while doing the project. The concept of the Learning Cycle of SSM was subsequently (and retrospectively) applied to our case, which resulted in a nice fit.

For future work it will be interesting to further analyse background theories, assumptions and ways of working of methodologies for information systems development regarding the "evolving of sense" and the "making of meaning", both as an autonomous process tacitly working in the background, as well as an instrument to be applied consciously in a project.

References

1. Short, T.L.: Peirce's Theory of Signs. Cambridge University Press, Cambridge (2007)

2. Austin, J.L.: How to Do Things with Words, 2nd edn. Harvard University Press, Cambridge MA (1978)
3. Searle, J.R.: Speech Acts. Cambridge University Press, Cambridge (1969)
4. Habermas, J.: The Theory of Communicative Action (2 Vols). Polity Press, Cambridge (1986)
5. Hirschheim, R., Klein, H.K.: Four paradigms of information systems development. In: Baskerville, R., Avison, D. (eds.) Major Currents in Information Systems, vol. II, pp. 1–30. Sage, London (2008)
6. Vickers, G.: Human Systems are Different. Harper & Row, London (1983)
7. Wittgenstein, L.: Philosophical Investigations, 4th edn. John Wiley & Sons, New York (2009)
8. Avison, D., Fitzgerald, G.: Information Systems Development – Methodologies, Techniques & Tools, 4th edn. McGraw & Hill, Maidenhead (2006)
9. Checkland, P.B., Poulter, J.: Learning for Action – A Short Definitive Account of Soft Systems Methodology and its use for Practitioners, Teachers and Students. John Wiley & Sons, Chichester (2006)
10. Goldkuhl, G.: LAP Revisited: Articulating information as social relation. http://www.vits.org/publikationer/dokument/805.pdf. Accessed 10 May 2022
11. Dietz, J.L.G., Mulder, H.B.F.: Enterprise Ontology. Springer, Berlin (2020)
12. Stamper, R.: Signs, information, norms and systems. In: Holmqvist, B., Andersen, P.B., Klein, H., Posner, R. (eds.) Signs of Work – Semiosis and Information Processing in Organisations, pp. 349–379. De Gruyter, Berlin (1996)
13. Goldkuhl, G., Lyytinen, K.: A language action view of information systems. In: Ginzberg, M., Ross, C.A. (eds.) Proceedings of the 3rd International Conference on Information Systems, TIMS/SMIS/ACM, pp. 13–29 (1982)
14. Liu, K., Li, W.: Organisational Semiotics for Business Informatics. Routledge, Abingdon (2015)
15. Checkland, P., Holwell, S.: Information, Systems, and Information Systems. Wiley, Chichester (1998)

Advantages of a Formal Specification of a Case

From Informal Description via Formal Specification to Realization

Bert de Brock$^{(\boxtimes)}$ (ID)

Faculty of Economics and Business, University of Groningen, PO Box 800,
9700 AV Groningen, The Netherlands
E.O.de.Brock@rug.nl

Abstract. Producing a complete, formal specification for an information system (IS) has several important advantages: Once we have a formal functional specification of an IS, the specification can serve as a solid starting point for several other development steps, such as generating default 'input forms', user stories, and default 'menus' per role. It also provides a potential means to prove (additional) state properties. Moreover, the specification can also serve as a 'quick reference guide' for the initiates working with the system.

In this paper we are studying the practical suitability and appropriateness of the notion of *information machine* as means for formally specifying functional requirements. In this feasibility study we illustrate this by an example which is large and subtle enough to demonstrate how our approach works. It also shows the scalability and the ease of change. The specifications are implementation-independent (as it ought to be). Nevertheless we explain and illustrate how to generate a default implementation.

Keywords: Functional requirements · Formal specifications · Information machine · Scalability · Ease of change · Generating artefacts · Implementation-independence · Property preservation · Complete induction · Proving properties · Implementation

1 Introduction

A complete, formal specification for an information system would have several important advantages: The specification can serve as a solid starting point for several other development steps, such as generating all kinds of artefacts. Moreover, it can provide a potential means to prove (additional) properties. The specification can also serve as a 'quick reference guide' for the initiates working with the system. The specification should be scalable, easy to change, and implementation-independent.

What do we need for a complete, formal specification of the functional requirements for an information system? Maybe the notion of Turing's 'discrete state machine' [1] or Mealy machine without a special start state [2], though not necessarily finite. In Sect. 2 we define the notion Information Machine (IM).

Essentially, an IM consists of a set of possible *inputs* (its *input space*), a set of possible *states* (its *state space*), an *output function* mapping pairs of an input and a

© Springer Nature Switzerland AG 2022
B. Shishkov (Ed.): BMSD 2022, LNBIP 453, pp. 158–181, 2022.
https://doi.org/10.1007/978-3-031-11510-3_10

state to an output, and a *transition function* mapping pairs of an input and a state to the corresponding next state. The *output space* consists of the set of all those outputs.

With an IM we can formalize the *functional requirements*, i.e., the functionality the system should provide [3]. In other words: What the system must be able to do. Or, more concretely, its input/output behaviour: Which inputs should the system accept and what should the corresponding outputs and state changes be? Usually, functional requirements are only specified informally, typically containing ambiguities and gaps and leading to misunderstandings. With a complete, formal specification we can master these problems.

The *state space* (plus *current state*) reflects the 'statics' of the system while the *transition function* reflects its 'dynamics'. The *output function* specifies the 'input-output behaviour' of the system. The *input space* specifies the things one can 'say to' (or 'ask from') the system, to put it simply. The inputs follow from the user wishes. In Sect. 3 we will give a complete specification of an IM for a non-trivial case.

In Sect. 3 we will give an illustrative example which is large and subtle enough to show clearly how our approach works. The section starts with an informal description of the case. From this informal description and some further (imaginary) elicitation we can deduce the user wishes. From there we are able to give a complete (mathematical) specification. We worked it out in all detail in this feasibility study because, as you know, the devil is in the details!

Thanks to the exact specification we are also able to produce a complete, straightforward implementation. We show this for SQL using the mapping rules we specified in [4] and [5]. But a translation to, say, Java could also be generated.

We are not aware of any overarching approach containing a complete, formal, semantically sound, and straightforward development path from user wishes all the way to a realization in software. The language UML (https://www.omg.org/spec/UML), for instance, is not suitable for such a formal and straightforward development path.

The rest of the paper is organized as follows: Sect. 2 contains the definition of *Information Machine* (IM), our central notion. Section 3 gives an informal description of a non-trivial case, followed by the formal specification of a corresponding IM. Section 4 discusses some generic features of the approach (*scalability* and *ease of change*) and explains how to generate certain artefacts (*input forms* per user wish, *user stories*, and *menus* per role). Section 5 introduces some means to prove (additional) state properties. Section 6 generates a default implementation for our case as an SQL-database with corresponding stored procedures. The conclusion (Sect. 7) is followed by an appendix containing the formal definitions of the mathematical expressions we used.

2 Information Machines

The notion of *information machine* (IM) turns out to be very suitable for an implementation-independent, declarative formal specification of an information system which also integrates data and transactions [6]. Informally stated, an Information Machine consists of a set of possible *inputs* (its *input space*), a set of possible *outputs* (its *output space*), a set of possible *states* (its *state space*), an *output function* mapping pairs of an input and a state to an output, and a *transition function* mapping pairs of an input and a state to the corresponding next state. The notion is related to the notion of

Turing's *discrete state machine* [1], a *Mealy machine* without a special start state [2], and Pieper's *data machine* [7].

Formally we define an **information machine** as a 5-tuple (I, O, S, G, T) consisting of:

- a set I (of *inputs*), called its *input space*
- a set O (of *outputs*), called its *output space*
- a set S (of *states*), called its *state space*
- an *output function* G: I × S → O,
  mapping pairs of an input and a state to the corresponding output
- a *transition function* T: I × S → S,
  mapping pairs of an input and a state to the corresponding next state.

The notation 'f: X → Y' indicates that f is a function from set X into set Y, i.e., that f is a function with domain X and its range being a subset of Y.

In Fig. 1, the working of an IM is shown as a 'black box' (with i ∈ I and s ∈ S):

$$i \rightarrow \boxed{s \mapsto T(i,s)} \rightarrow G(i,s)$$

Fig. 1. The working of an information machine upon input i while in state s

In words: Upon input i, the IM produces output G(i,s) and its internal state s changes into T(i,s). Both the output and the new state depend on the input as well as on the internal state. If input i represents a retrieval question ('query') then T(i,s) = s; in other words, then the state stays the same.

It is not necessary to specify the output space separately once we have specified the output function G, because the range of G can then be taken as the output space.

3 A Non-trivial Example

In the literature, examples of formal machines are usually (very) tiny. However, to show that their complete definition is also feasible in practice, we will now specify an information machine for a subtle, non-trivial case. We will subsequently.

1. Give an *informal description* of the case (in Sect. 3.1)
2. Deduce the (implicit) *user wishes* (in Sect. 3.2)
3. Define a suitable *information machine* by subsequently defining its *input space*, its *state space*, its *transition function*, and its *output function* (in Sect. 3.3)

3.1 Informal Description of the Case

Our case concerns courses, students, and their course registrations within a fictitious university. Students have a *name*, *address*, *gender*, and a unique, system-generated *student number*. Student numbers consist of (at least) 6 digits and are divisible by 11 (as a simple validation check). The system should manage those generated numbers. Courses have a unique *Course ID* (of at most 7 characters), a unique *Course name* (not more than 50 characters), a *level* (Bachelor or Master), and a *description*. Students and courses can be created, updated, and deleted. That is, the address of a student, the name of a course, and the description of a course can be updated. However, the level of a course cannot be updated, because then it will be considered as a different course.

Furthermore, (known) students can be registered – and de-registered – for (known) courses. Registration is one thing, acceptance of the registration is another, separate action the system should support: Upon registration, the registration is not (yet) accepted, by default. Upon deletion of a student, all his/her course registrations must be deleted as well (a *compound transaction*, actually a *cascading delete*).

The system must be able to produce an overview of all Bachelor courses and of all Master courses (for interested people/prospects), as well as an overview of all the courses including their number of registered students (i.e., per course).

Finally, for completeness' sake, we mention the required functionality that the system must be initializable to an 'empty' state, with suitable start values.

3.2 The User Wishes

From the informal description in Sect. 3.1 we can deduce the user wishes the system must be able to fulfil: The user must be able to:

- create, update, and delete students and courses
- register, accept, and de-register students for courses
- get an overview of all Bachelor courses and of all Master courses
- get an overview of all courses including their number of registered students

And, last but not least, the system must be initializable to an 'empty' state.

Table 1 enumerates the deduced *parameterized* user wishes (where the *elementary* user wishes are underlined).

3.3 The Sample Information Machine

In this section we subsequently specify the *input space*, the *state space*, the *transition function*, and the *output function* of an appropriate information machine.

3.3.1 The Input Space

Table 2 enumerates the *inputs* representing the parameterized user wishes. For reasons of space we use mnemonic abbreviations for the elementary user wishes. The input space is the union of all those input sets. (The union is denoted by the symbol ' ∪'.) Furthermore,

Table 1. The user wishes

UW-ID	User wish plus parameters
UW1	Initialize the system (so, no parameters)
UW2	Create Student with name x, address a, and gender e
UW3	Create Course with course ID c, name x, level y, and description d
UW4	Create Course Registration with course ID c and student number n
UW5	Delete Student with number n, including all his/her course registrations
UW6	Delete Course with course ID c
UW7	Delete Course Registration with course ID c and student number n
UW8	Update, for Student with number n, the address into a
UW9	Update, for Course with course ID c, the name into x
UW10	Update, for Course with course ID c, the description into d
UW11	Accept Course Registration with course ID c and student number n
UW12	Retrieve all Courses of level y
UW13	Retrieve Courses plus their student Counts (so, no parameters)

$\mathbb{N}$ denotes the set of all natural numbers (including 0), Str denotes the set of all character strings, and Str(n) denotes the set of all character strings of at most n characters (for any positive number n).

3.3.2 The State Space

Each state must represent a set of *courses*, a set of *students*, a set of *course registrations*, and the *next student number* to be used (a natural number). We recall that each course has a unique *course ID* (of at most 7 characters), a unique *course name* (not more than 50 characters), a *level* (Bachelor or Master), and a *description*. Each student has a unique *student number*, a *name*, an *address*, and a *gender*. Each course registration is uniquely determined by the combination of the *course ID* of a 'known' course and the

Table 2. The input space

UW-ID	Input space	
UW1	{Initialize}	
UW2	∪ {CS(x,a,e)	x ∈ Str and a ∈ Str and e ∈ {'♂', '♀'} }
UW3	∪ {CC(c,x,y,d)	c ∈ Str(7), x ∈ Str(50), y ∈ {'Ba', 'Ma'} and d ∈ Str }
UW4	∪ {CR(c,n)	c ∈ Str(7) and n ∈ $\mathbb{N}$ }
UW5	∪ {DS(n)	n ∈ $\mathbb{N}$ }
UW6	∪ {DC(c)	c ∈ Str(7) }
UW7	∪ {DR(c,n)	c ∈ Str(7) and n ∈ $\mathbb{N}$ }
UW8	∪ {USa(n,a)	n ∈ $\mathbb{N}$ and a ∈ Str }
UW9	∪ {UCn(c,x)	c ∈ Str(7) and x ∈ Str(50) }
UW10	∪ {UCd(c,d)	c ∈ Str(7) and d ∈ Str }
UW11	∪ {ACR(c,n)	c ∈ Str(7) and n ∈ $\mathbb{N}$ }
UW12	∪ {RCL(y)	y ∈ {'Ba', 'Ma'} }
UW13	∪ {RCC }	

student number of a 'known' student. (By 'known' we mean known to the system, i.e., represented in the system).

The figure below gives a concise overview of the state space. A referencing property is indicated by a '^' in front, a uniqueness constraint within a concept by a '!' in front of all properties involved, and another uniqueness constraint within the same concept by '%' in front. For layout reasons, other properties have a dot in front. The green concept represents a single entity in each state (a number) while any other concept represents a set of entities in each state.

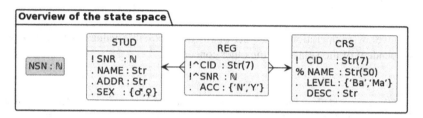

We build up and give the definition of the state space S in four steps:

1. For the student-, course-, and registration-concepts, we give an enumeration of their properties and, per property, the set of possible values:

FST =	FCR =	FREG =
{(SNR ; N),	{(CID ; Str(7)),	{(CID ; Str(7)),
(NAME ; Str),	(NAME ; Str(50)),	(SNR ; N),
(ADDR ; Str),	(LEVEL ; {'Ba', 'Ma'}),	(ACC; {'N', 'Y'}) }
(SEX ; {♂, ♀}) }	(DESC ; Str) }	

2. For those 3 concepts, we specify the acceptable subsets, including the constraints on subset level, such as *uniqueness* constraints. Below, 'u.i.' stands for 'uniquely identifying'. (See the Appendix for the definition.) Furthermore we need the notion

of a *generalized Cartesian product*. Formally: If F is a set-valued function then

$$\Pi(F) \overset{\text{def}}{=} \{f \mid f \text{ is a function over dom(F) and } f(x) \in F(x) \text{ for each } x \in \text{dom}(f)\}.$$

Loosely speaking, $\Pi(F)$ is the set of all possible choices within the frame set by F.

TST =	TCR =	TREG =
$\{ T \mid T \subseteq \Pi(FST)$ and $\{SNR\}$ is u.i. in T $\}$	$\{ T \mid T \subseteq \Pi(FCR)$ and $\{CID\}$ is u.i. in T and $\{NAME\}$ is u.i. in T $\}$	$\{ T \mid T \subseteq \Pi(FREG)$ and $\{CID, SNR\}$ is u.i. in T $\}$

3. We give an enumeration of the set of (locally) possible values per concept, i.e., independent of the values for the other concepts:

$$
\begin{array}{llll}
FTOT = \{ & (STUD \,; TST), & /* \ \ \text{Students} & \rceil \ \text{To each concept} \\
& (CRS \ \ ; TCR), & /* \ \ \text{Courses} & \mid \ \text{its set of (locally)} \\
& (REG \ \ ; TREG), & /* \ \ \text{Course registrations} & \mid \ \text{possible values} \\
& (NSN \ \ ; \mathbb{N}) \} & /* \ \ \text{Next student number} & \rfloor \ \text{is assigned}
\end{array}
$$

4. We end with the definition of the state space S, consisting of all acceptable value-combinations including constraints *between* concepts (e.g. *referential* constraints):

$$
\begin{array}{ll}
S = \{ s \mid s \in \Pi(FTOT) \text{ and} & \rceil \\
\{ t(CID) \mid t \in s(REG) \} \subseteq \{ t(CID) \mid t \in s(CRS) \} \text{ and} & \mid \ \text{The state space} \\
\{ t(SNR) \mid t \in s(REG) \} \subseteq \{ t(SNR) \mid t \in s(STUD) \} \} & \rfloor
\end{array}
$$

3.3.3 The Transition Function

Further elicitation regarding User Wish 1 revealed that by the 'empty state with suitable start values' the customer meant: no courses, no students, no registrations, and student numbers should start with 100,001 (6 digits and divisible by 11). Hence:

$$T(\underline{Initialize}, s) = \{(NSN; 100{,}001), (STUD; \varnothing), (CRS; \varnothing), (REG; \varnothing)\} \text{ for any state } s,$$

where $\varnothing$ denotes the empty set. We note that this is a *compound* transaction, i.e., several components are changed as one atomic transaction.

For each of the user wishes 2–11, the new state T(i,s) is the old state modified according to a modifying function g_s specified in Table 3, provided that it satisfies all conditions within S. Otherwise, the state stays the same, i.e., stays s. Such a modifying function g_s specifies the intended new component value(s). In most cases, g_s concerns only one component, but for the user wishes 2 and 5 it concerns two components. Those two user wishes lead to *compound* transactions, just as UW1. Table 3 specifies the modifying functions for each of the user wishes 2–11. Formally, T(i,s) = Main(S,g) (s) where the function Main(S,g) is precisely defined in the Appendix.

The user wishes 12 and 13 concern *retrievals*, hence T(i,s) = s for those inputs.

Table 3. The modifying functions

UW-ID	Input i	Modifying function indicating the new component value(s)
UW2	CS(x,a,e)	$g2_s(NSN)$ $= s(NSN) + 11$ **and** $g2_s(STUD) = s(STUD) \cup \{t1\}$ where t1 = {(SNR; s(NSN)), (NAME; x), (ADDR; a), (SEX; e) }
UW3	CC(c,x,y,d)	$g3_s(CRS)$ $= s(CRS) \cup \{t2\}$ where t2 = {(CID; c), (NAME; x), (LEVEL; y), (DESC; d)}
UW4	CR(c,n)	$g4_s(REG)$ $= s(REG) \cup \{t3\}$ where t3 = {(CID; c), (SNR; n), (ACC; 'N')}
UW5	DS(n)	$g5_s(STUD) = \{ t \mid t \in s(STUD)$ and $t(SNR) \neq n\}$ **and** $g5_s(REG)$ $= \{ t \mid t \in s(REG)$ and $t(SNR) \neq n\}$
UW6	DC(c)	$g6_s(CRS)$ $= \{ t \mid t \in s(CRS)$ and $t(CID) \neq c\}$
UW7	DR(c,n)	$g7_s(REG)$ $= \{ t \mid t \in s(REG)$ and $(t(CID); t(SNR)) \neq (c; n) \}$
UW8	USa(n,a)	$g8_s(STUD) = \{ t \mid t \in s(STUD)$ and $t(SNR) \neq n \} \cup$ $\{ t \theta \{(ADDR; a)\} \mid t \in s(STUD)$ and $t(SNR) = n \}$
UW9	UCn(c,x)	$g9_s(CRS)$ $= \{ t \mid t \in s(CRS)$ and $t(CID) \neq c \} \cup$ $\{ t \theta \{(NAME; x)\} \mid t \in s(CRS)$ and $t(CID) = c \}$
UW10	UCd(c,d)	$g10_s(CRS) = \{ t \mid t \in s(CRS)$ and $t(CID) \neq c \} \cup$ $\{ t \theta \{(DESC; d)\} \mid t \in s(CRS)$ and $t(CID) = c \}$
UW11	ACR(c,n)	$g11_s(REG) = \{ t \mid t \in s(REG)$ and $(t(CID); t(SNR)) \neq (c; n) \} \cup$ $\{ t \theta \{(ACC; 'Y')\} \mid t \in s(REG)$ and $(t(CID); t(SNR)) = (c; n) \}$

3.3.4 The Output Function

Tables 4 and 5 together specify the *output function*. It is the result after some further (limited) case analysis regarding the cases to be distinguished and their required output messages. In fact, user wishes 3 and 4 (with their *and/or*-messages) could even have had more refined output messages. Furthermore, if a user of the system wants to update or delete something, then that user might suppose that that 'something' was still in the system. Therefore, it might be useful to distinguish the cases where that 'something' was not in the system (anymore), as done in UW11 (*Accept Course Registration*). This applies in particular to the user wishes 5–10, where this distinction was not (yet) made. The column '*When*' in Table 4 refers to Table 5. In UW13, #A denotes the number of elements of set A.

Table 4. The output function

UW	Input i	Output G(i,s)	When
1	Initialize	"Done: The start value of the Next Student Number is 100,001 and all sets are empty (i.e., the set of students, of courses, and of course registrations)"	1
2	CS(x,a,e)	"Done. The student number will be " s(NSN)	1
3	CC(c,x,y,d)	"Course ID and/or course name already existed; so the state stayed the same"	3a
		"Done"	3b
4	CR(c,n)	"Registration already exists"	4a
		"Unknown course and/or student; so the state stayed the same"	4b
		"Done"	4c
5	DS(n)	"Done"	1
6	DC(c)	"There are still registrations for this course; so the state stayed the same"	6a
		"Done"	6b
7	DR(c,n)	"Done"	1
8	USa(n,a)	"Done"	1
9	UCn(c,x)	"Course name already existed; so the state stayed the same"	9a
		"Done"	9b
10	UCd(c,d)	"Done"	1
11	ACR(c,n)	"Done"	10a
		"Registration was already accepted"	10b
		"Unknown registration"	10c
12	RCL(y)	"The courses of level " y " are " { t | t $\in$ s(CRS) and t(LEVEL) = y }	1
13	RCC	"All courses plus their student counts: " { t⌈{CID, NAME, LEVEL} $\cup$ {(ST-COUNT; xx)} | t $\in$ s(CRS)} where xx = #{ r | r$\in$ s(REG) and r(CID) = t(CID) }	1

4 Some Features of a Complete, Formal Specification

The exact and complete specification of a case (in the form of an information machine) constitutes a solid starting point for other development steps, as we will discuss. We first discuss some generic features of the approach (*scalability* and *ease of change*) and then explain how to generate certain artefacts (*input forms* per user wish, *user stories*, and *menus* per role), the last two after indicating who is allowed to do what.

Table 5. Which output when?

When	When (i.e., under which condition)
1	Always (i.e., in any state s)
3a	if $c \in \{ t(CID) \mid t \in s(CRS) \}$ or $x \in \{ t(NAME) \mid t \in s(CRS) \}$
3b	otherwise
4a	if $(c;n) \in \{ (t(CID); t(SNR)) \mid t \in s(REG) \}$
4b	if $c \notin \{ t(CID) \mid t \in s(CRS) \}$ or $n \notin \{ t(SNR) \mid t \in s(STUD) \}$
4c	otherwise
6a	if $c \in \{ t(CID) \mid t \in s(REG) \}$
6b	otherwise
9a	if $x \in \{ t(NAME) \mid t \in s(CRS) \}$
9b	otherwise
10a	if $\{(CID; c), (SNR; n), (ACC; \text{'N'})\} \in s(REG)$
10b	if $\{(CID; c), (SNR; n), (ACC; \text{'Y'})\} \in s(REG)$
10c	otherwise (i.e., if $(c;n) \notin \{ (t(CID); t(SNR)) \mid t \in s(REG) \}$)

4.1 Scalability

When the number of user wishes doubles (for example), then also Tables 1, 3, and 4 will double, but the state space will probably increase less than double. Moreover, in the transition function the retrievals could be left out. So, all in all, the size probably grows at most linear in the number of user wishes.

4.2 Ease of Change

It is relatively easy to make changes in the specification (and subsequently in the implementation). By means of our 'quick reference guide' we can quickly find where, what, and how we have to change things when needed.

As a first example: On hindsight it turned out that a course can also be deleted if it has no *accepted* registrations. Hence, we must look up the user wish *Delete Course* in Table 1; so it concerns UW6. Then we must look at UW6 in the output function (Table 4), in particular the first subcase. The <u>condition</u> should change into:

$$if \ c \in \{t(CID) \mid t \in s(REG) \ and \ t(ACC) = \text{'}Y\text{'}\}$$

The <u>output</u> might change into:

"There are accepted registrations for this course; so the state stayed the same"

As a 2nd and 3rd example, on top of the first one, consider the next two change requests:

In the case of an attempt to delete a course for which there are still accepted registrations, we would also like to know <u>how many</u> accepted students, or even <u>which</u> accepted students are registered for that course.

Again, we have to look up the user wish *Delete Course* in Table 1; so UW6. Then we must look at UW6 in the output function (Table 4), in particular the first case again. That output should change into, e.g.:

"There are still " NS " **accepted registrations for this course; so the state stayed the same"** *or even into*

"The state stayed the same: There are still " NS " **accepted registrations for this course, notably:** " { t | t ∈ s(REG) ⋈ s(STUD) and t(CID) = c and t(ACC) = 'Y'}

where '⋈' denotes the natural join and NS denotes the number of accepted registrations for course c, i.e., NS = #{ t | t ∈ s(REG) and t(CID) = c and t(ACC) = 'Y'}.

So, the necessary changes (and their appropriate places) in the specification follow relatively easy from the quick reference guide, thanks to the demonstrated traceability.

4.3 Generating Input Forms

Given the parameterized user wishes we can also *generate* suitable (structures for) *input forms*, as we call them. That is, 'forms' to request to execute the user wish concerned. A **input form** conceptually consists of the parameters to be filled in by the user and contains for every such parameter an entry to fill in a value.

If a parameter has a limited list of possible values (such as *gender* or *level*, or a *registered course* or *student* in our case) then the system should allow the user to select the value from that list. This possibility might be indicated by a sign, say '▼':

_____ ▼

When we apply this to the parameterized user wishes in our running case and underline the elementary user wish then we get:

Table 6. The input forms for our case

UW-ID	Input	Input form for the parameterized user wish
UW1	Initialize	Initialize the system
UW2	CS(x,a,e)	Create a Student student name _____ address _____ gender _____ ▼
UW3	CC(c,x,y,d)	Create a Course course ID _____ course name _____ course level _____ ▼ description _____
UW4	CR(c,n)	Create a Course Registration course ID _____ ▼ student number _____ ▼
UW5	DS(n)	Delete a Student (plus all his/her course registrations) student number _____ ▼
UW6	DC(c)	Delete a Course course ID _____ ▼
UW7	DR(c,n)	Delete a Course Registration course ID _____ ▼ student number _____ ▼
UW8	USa(n,a)	Update a Student address student number _____ ▼ new address _____
UW9	UCn(c,x)	Update a Course name course ID _____ ▼ new name _____
UW10	UCd(c,d)	Update a Course description course ID _____ ▼ new description _____
UW11	ACR(c,n)	Accept a Course Registration course ID _____ ▼ student number _____ ▼
UW12	RCL(y)	Retrieve all Courses of level _____ ▼
UW13	RCC	Retrieve all Courses plus their student Counts

Forms can be 'dynamic' in several ways. E.g., based on the chosen value(s) for earlier parameter(s), the set of potential values of a parameter can become more restricted. E.g., once the course has been filled in in the input form for UW7, the set of potential students to choose from can be restricted to the students *registered for that course.*

We note that the structure of this form did not change; only the set of potential values changed while the form was filled in step by step. However, it might be that depending on a value filled in, other fields might 'pop up', as you might have experienced in daily life. A typical example might be a tax form: whether or not you have a partner, a house, a second house, an own company (etc.), it might lead to 'popping up' extra fields that must be filled in. An order form might be another example: If the order type is not *'Internal'* but *'Commercial'*, something like a *contract section* might pop up. For a thorough treatment of dynamic forms, we refer to [5].

4.4 Indicating Who is Allowed to Do What

Not everybody is allowed to do everything. In general, we have to indicate which 'roles' are allowed to execute which user wishes.

For instance, in our running case only the system administrator is allowed to initialize the system. On the other hand, everybody is allowed to see all courses. Table 7 contains a complete overview for our running case (where CSA stands for Central Student Administration). Altogether, 8 roles are distinguished.

Table 7. Who is allowed to do what?

UW-ID	Elementary user wish	Authorized role(s)
UW1	Initialize the system	Sysadmin
UW2	Create a Student	CSA-employee
UW3	Create a Course	Program director
UW4	Create a Course Registration	Student, Secretary
UW5	Delete a Student	CSA-employee
UW6	Delete a Course	Program director
UW7	Delete a Course Registration	Student, Secretary, Course coordinator
UW8	Update a Student address	Student, CSA-employee
UW9	Update a Course name	Program director
UW10	Update a Course description	Course coordinator
UW11	Accept a Course Registration	Course coordinator
UW12	Retrieve all Courses of a given level	Guest
UW13	Retrieve all Courses plus their Counts	Dean, Program director

4.5 Generating User Stories

Once we know which role is allowed to do what, we can simply *generate* the corresponding user stories, using the template below (without a benefit part). See [8] for more background on user stories.

As a < role >, **I want to** < elementary user wish >

Based on Table 7 there are 18 user stories (because some UWs have more than 1 role).

4.6 Generating Menus Per Role

From Table 7 we can also simply generate the 'menu' for each role:

Sysadmin	**Dean**
Initialize the system	Retrieve all Courses plus their Counts
Guest	**Secretary**
Retrieve all Courses of a given level	Create a Course Registration
	Delete a Course Registration
Program director	**Course coordinator**
Create a Course	Update a Course description
Update a Course name	Accept a Course Registration
Delete a Course	Delete a Course Registration
Retrieve all Courses plus their Counts	
Student	**CSA-employee**
Create a Course Registration	Create a Student
Delete a Course Registration	Update a Student address
Update a Student address	Delete a Student (plus registrations)

5 Means to Prove (Additional) State Properties

The exact specification of a case in the form of an information machine (IM) provides a starting point for other parts as well, as we will (continue to) show in this section.

In this section we introduce a potential means to prove (additional) state properties of an IM: Section 5.1 defines the notions of *property preservation* and *complete induction*. In Section 5.2 we apply it to our sample IM and prove some of its 'silent' properties.

5.1 Property Preservation and Complete Induction Within an IM

Informally, an IM *preserves* a state property ⇔ whenever that property holds in a state of that IM then it also holds in any potentially subsequent state of that IM. Such a property is also known as an **invariant** of that IM. We define *property preservation* within an information machine formally as follows:

> An information machine (I, O, S, G, T)
> **preserves** state property P ⇔ P(s) implies P(T(i,s)) for all i ∈ I and s ∈ S

If an information machine M starts in a state s_0 which has state property P (s_0, P(s_0) holds), and M *preserves* that state property P then, consequently, M will always be in a state with that state property (**complete induction**).

5.2 Provable Properties of Our Sample IM

Now we give some examples of state properties that hold for our sample IM after initialization. In the 4 properties (P1 – P4), the relevant state parts are marked grey. Properties P2 and P4 are properties that were *required by the customer* (Sect. 3.1). Property P1 is an *auxiliary* property used to prove P2. Similarly, Property P3 is an *auxiliary* property used to prove P4. (A mathematician would call P1 and P3 *lemmas*.)

P1(s): s(NSN), the next student nr, consists of (at least) 6 digits and is divisible by 11
P2(s): t(SNR) consists of (at least) 6 digits and is divisible by 11, for each t ∈ s(STUD)
P3(s): s(NSN) > t(SNR) for each t ∈ s(STUD)
P4(s): {SNR} is uniquely identifying (u.i.) in s(STUD);

i.e., if t ≠ t′ then t(SNR) ≠ t′(SNR) for all t,t′ ∈ s(STUD)

After initialization the state s_0 is {(NSN; 100,001), (STUD; ∅), (CRS; ∅), (REG;∅)} according to the specification in Sect. 3.3.3. So, per property P we must prove that

(A) s_0, the state after initialization, has property P and
(B)   our sample IM preserves property P

Proofs:

We start with some general considerations:

Property P1 is about s(NSN).
Besides UW1 (initialization), only UW2 might influence it: See the specs in Section 3.3.3.

Properties P2-P4 are about s(STUD) and P3 is about s(NSN) too.
Besides UW1, only UW2, UW5, and UW8 might influence them: See Section 3.3.3.

The other user wishes do not influence any STUD-entry or NSN-value.

Now we will prove (A) and (B) for each of the four properties P1 – P4 individually.
(We note that the proofs for P2 – P4 are similar.)

P1(s):

(A) P1(s_0) holds because s_0(NSN) = 100,001, so s_0(NSN) consists of (at least) 6 digits
  and is divisible by 11: 100,001/11 = 9,091.
(B) For UW2, the value of T(i,s) at NSN is defined as $g2_s$(NSN),
  which in turn is defined as s(NSN) + 11; see Table 3.
  So, if s(NSN) consists of (at least) 6 digits and is divisible by 11
  then so does s(NSN) + 11, which is T(i,s) (NSN).
  The other user wishes do not introduce or change any NSN-value.
  In conclusion: if s(NSN) consists of (at least) 6 digits and is divisible by 11
  then so does T(i,s) (NSN).
  Therefore, P1 holds for T(i,s) *for all i ∈ I and s ∈ S.*

P2(s):

(A) P2(s_0) holds, simply because s_0(STUD) = ∅.
(B) For UW2, the value of T(i,s) at STUD is defined as $g2_s$(STUD),
  which in turn is defined as s(STUD) ∪ {t1}, where t1(SNR) = s(NSN); see Table 3.
  But s(NSN) consists of (at least) 6 digits and is divisible by 11, according to property
  P1.
  Hence, if t(SNR) consists of (at least) 6 digits and is divisible by 11 for each t ∈
  s(STUD),
  then that also holds for each t ∈ s(STUD) ∪ {t1}, which in turn is T(i,s) at STUD.
  So, then P2 also holds for T(i,s) for any input i via UW2.
  UW5 can delete a STUD-entry, and UW8 can update a STUD-address,
  but then P2 still holds.
  The other user wishes do not influence any STUD-entry.
  Therefore, P2 holds for T(i,s) *for all i ∈ I and s ∈ S.*

P3(s):

(A) P3(s_0) holds, simply because s_0(STUD) = ∅.
(B) For UW2, in Table 3, T(i,s) at NSN is defined as $g2_s$(NSN)
  which is defined as s(NSN) + 11, and T(i,s) at STUD is defined as $g2_s$(STUD)
  which is defined as s(STUD) ∪ {t1}, where t1(SNR) = s(NSN).
  So, T(i,s) (NSN) = s(NSN) + 11 > s(NSN) = t1(SNR).
  Therefore, if P3(s) holds, i.e., if s(NSN) > t(SNR) for each t ∈ s(STUD)
  then also T(i,s) (NSN) > t(SNR) for each t ∈ T(i,s) (STUD).
  Hence, then P3 also holds for T(i,s) for any input i via UW2.
  UW5 can delete a STUD-entry and UW8 can update a STUD-address,
  but then P3 still holds.
  The other user wishes do not influence any STUD-entry or NSN-value.
  Therefore, P3 holds for T(i,s) *for all i ∈ I and s ∈ S.*

P4(s):

(A) P4(s_0) holds, simply because s_0(STUD) = ∅.
(B) For UW2, in Table 3, T(i,s) (STUD) = $g2_s$(STUD) = s(STUD) ∪ {t1}
  where t1(SNR) = s(NSN).
  But according to P3, s(NSN) > t(SNR) for each t ∈ s(STUD).
  So, t1(SNR) = s(NSN) ≠ t(SNR) for each t ∈ s(STUD).
  Therefore, the SNR-value of t1 is 'new'.
  Hence, {SNR} is u.i. in T(i,s) (STUD) for any input i via UW2.
  UW5 can delete a STUD-entry and UW8 can update a STUD-address,
  but then P4 still holds.
  The other user wishes do not influence the STUD-value.
  Therefore, P4 holds for T(i,s) *for all i ∈ I and s ∈ S.*

Let us look at the original customer description again:

'Students have [...] a unique, system-generated student number. Student numbers consist of (at least) 6 digits and are divisible by 11 (as a simple validation check). The system should manage those generated numbers'

Properties P2 and P4 confirm this. And, indeed, the system generates and manages those student numbers, as originally required.

A subtle, general question is: Should a requirement/property be specified in the state space or is it enough if it follows from the transitions that are (not) possible in the IM? For example, in the definition of the state space, we stipulated that {SNR} should be u.i. but, as just shown, that property also follows from the (im)possibilities of the (current) machine itself, even without using that requirement in the state space specification. So, that requirement seems redundant in the state space definition. However, it is an invariant of the *currently* defined machine, which might be disturbed by adding new user wishes (e.g., *'Create a student with a freely chosen student number'*). Therefore we also added that important requirement in the state space definition itself.

6   A Default Implementation

In this section we work out a default implementation for our case, namely as an SQL-database with so-called *stored procedures* (because SQL-databases are much used in practice). SQL is a standard language for databases, although each Database Management System might have its own dialect. For more background, see [9, 10]. To cite the US standards agency NIST (https://www.itl.nist.gov/div897/ctg/dm/sql_info.html):

The basic structure is a table, consisting of rows and columns. Data definition includes declaring the name of each table to be included in a database, the names and data types of all columns of each table, constraints on the values in and among columns [...] Tables can be accessed by inserting new rows, deleting or updating existing rows, or selecting rows that satisfy a given search condition for output. [...] Referential integrity allows specification of primary and foreign keys with the requirement that no foreign key row may be inserted or updated unless a matching primary key row exists. Check clauses allow specification of inter-column constraints to be maintained by the database system.

Since we have a formal specification, it is pretty straightforward to transform it to an SQL-database with stored procedures. We follow the formal specification given in Sect. 3.3. The *state space* is transformed to a database in SQL (Sect. 6.1) while the *transition function* and *output function* in combination are transformed to stored procedures in SQL (Sect. 6.2). We end with the formats for 'calling' the stored procedures (Sect. 6.3).

6.1   The State Space

A state space can be specified using the DDL (Data Definition Language) of SQL. In general, the mapping of a state space to SQL runs as follows:

- First, a declaration CREATE DATABASE < database name > is introduced
- Each concept translates to a *table*
- Each property of a concept translates to an *attribute* (a.k.a. *column* or *field*) in that table, followed by the corresponding *data type*, which represents the set of allowed values. Besides the available basic data types, 'sub data types' can be defined by 'creating' so-called *domains* (using a *check* constraint).
- The data type of a property is followed by 'NOT NULL' if a value is always *required* (never absent) for that property, else followed by 'NULL' (so if a value is *optional*, i.e., might be absent)
- Each remaining constraint within a row in a table, be it a constraint on one column (not yet covered by its data type or domain) or among its columns, translates to a *check* constraint (a.k.a. *check clause*)
- Each uniqueness condition translates to a *primary key* constraint or a *unique* constraint, each specified by one or more properties. Each table should have one primary key
- Each reference condition translates to a *foreign key* constraint
- Each extra constraint *between* rows within a table or *between* tables translates to an *assertion*
- In SQL, table names and attribute names cannot contain hyphens ('-') or spaces. In practice, they are often replaced by underscores ('_')

The formal specification of the sample state space was given in Sect. 3.3.2 and was built up in four steps. The details of step 1 (properties & possible values) can be found back in the CREATE TABLE declarations and the preceding CREATE DOMAIN declarations. The details of step 2 can be found back in the PRIMARY KEY and UNIQUE constraints. The (naming) details of step 3 can be found back in the TABLE and VARIABLE names. The details of step 4 can be found back in the FOREIGN KEY constraints.

```
CREATE DATABASE Registration_Example

CREATE DOMAIN Gender_set AS CHAR(1)
CHECK( @VALUE IN ('♂', '♀') )

CREATE DOMAIN Level_set AS CHAR(2)
CHECK( @VALUE IN ('Ba', 'Ma') )

CREATE DOMAIN YesNo_set AS CHAR(1)
CHECK( @VALUE IN ('N', 'Y') )

CREATE TABLE   STUD
(SNR     INTEGER        NOT NULL,
 NAME    VARCHAR        NOT NULL,
 ADDR    VARCHAR        NOT NULL,
 SEX     Gender_set     NOT NULL,

 CONSTRAINT K1 PRIMARY KEY (SNR)
)

CREATE TABLE   CRS
(CID     VARCHAR(7)     NOT NULL,
 NAME    VARCHAR(50)    NOT NULL,
 LEVEL   Level_set      NOT NULL,
 DESC    VARCHAR        NOT NULL,

 CONSTRAINT K2 PRIMARY KEY (CID),
 UNIQUE(NAME)
)

CREATE TABLE   REG
(CID     VARCHAR(7)     NOT NULL,
 SNR     INTEGER        NOT NULL,
 ACC     YesNo_set      NOT NULL,

 CONSTRAINT K3 PRIMARY KEY (CID,SNR),
 CONSTRAINT R1 FOREIGN KEY (CID) REFERENCES CRS(CID),
 CONSTRAINT R2 FOREIGN KEY (SNR) REFERENCES STUD(SNR)
)

CREATE VARIABLE   NSN   AS INTEGER
```

The CREATE VARIABLE is actually pseudo-SQL. Since SQL is 'table oriented', we could create a table for storing global parameters such as NSN, e.g., a table with two fields: the *name* and the *value* of the parameter, with the field '*name*' being the primary key of that table. The global parameter NSN will then be one of the entries.

6.2   The Combined Transition Function and Output Function

In general, a transition function and output function will be implemented in combination, via so-called *stored procedures* in SQL. In principle, each user wish is represented by a (stored) procedure which could be named after the user wish it represents (aiding further traceability). The procedures have the following form:

```
CREATE PROCEDURE UWx  <input parameters plus their datatype>,
                      @output varchar OUTPUT
AS BEGIN
   <SQL-statement(s)>
   END
```

As the name already suggests, the text parameter @output is used for the output (so, related to the output function). If the procedure consists of only one SQL-statement, the BEGIN ... END is redundant (but we always add it for clarity).

For each user wish, the transition function and output function are combined in one stored procedure in SQL. Therefore we will have 13 stored procedures. The formal specifications of the transition function and output function were given in Sects. 3.3.3 and 3.3.4. We present only a few illustrative examples: *Initialization* (UW1), the other *compound transactions* (UW2 and UW5) including a *cascading delete* (UW5), an *insert* (attempt) with refined output messaging (UW4), an *update* (UW11), and a *retrieval* (UW13). We indicate the procedure names in green. Note that the procedures follow the analysis-structure of the transition and output function.

As mentioned earlier, user wishes 3 and 4 (with their 'and/or'-messages) could have had more refined output messages. For UW4 we will still do it in the shown procedure (although we should have adapted it first in the specification).

```
CREATE PROCEDURE UW1 @output varchar OUTPUT
AS BEGIN
   BEGIN TRANSACTION
      DELETE FROM REG      -- This Delete must come before the other deletes
      DELETE FROM CRS
      DELETE FROM STUD
      SELECT NSN = 100,001
      SELECT @output = 'Done: The start value of the next student number
                        is 100,001 and all sets are empty (i.e., the set of
                        students, of courses, and of course registrations) '
   COMMIT TRANSACTION
   END


CREATE PROCEDURE UW2 @x varchar, @a varchar, @e Gender_set,
                     @output varchar OUTPUT
AS BEGIN
   BEGIN TRANSACTION
      INSERT INTO STUD(SNR, NAME, ADDR, SEX) VALUES(NSN,@x,@a,@e)
      SELECT @output = 'Done. The student number will be ' + NSN
      SELECT NSN = NSN + 11
   COMMIT TRANSACTION
END


CREATE PROCEDURE UW4 @c varchar(7), @n integer,
                     @output varchar OUTPUT
AS BEGIN
   SELECT @output = ''    -- Invariant: @output = '' ⇔ till now no reason to
refuse
   IF @c NOT IN (SELECT CID FROM CRS)
      THEN SELECT @output = 'Unknown course. '
   IF @n NOT IN (SELECT SNR FROM STUD)
      THEN SELECT @output = @output + 'Unknown student. '
   IF @output = ''
      THEN IF @c IN (SELECT CID FROM REG WHERE SNR = @n)
              THEN SELECT @output = 'Registration already exists. '
   IF @output = ''
      THEN BEGIN  INSERT  INTO  REG(CID,  SNR,  ACC)  VALUES(@c,
@n, 'N')
                  SELECT @output = 'Done '
           END
      ELSE SELECT @output = @output + 'So the state stayed the same '
   END


CREATE PROCEDURE UW5 @n integer, @output varchar OUTPUT
AS BEGIN
   BEGIN TRANSACTION
      DELETE FROM REG  WHERE SNR = @n   -- This Delete must come first
      DELETE FROM STUD WHERE SNR = @n
      SELECT @output = 'Done '
   COMMIT TRANSACTION
   END
```

```
CREATE PROCEDURE UW11 @c varchar(7), @n integer,
                      @output varchar OUTPUT
AS BEGIN
   IF @c NOT IN (SELECT CID FROM REG WHERE SNR = @n)
   THEN SELECT @output = 'Unknown registration.'
   ELSE IF (SELECT ACC FROM REG WHERE CID = @c AND SNR = @n) = 'Y'
        THEN SELECT @output = 'Registration was already accepted'
        ELSE BEGIN   UPDATE REG SET ACC = 'Y'
                        WHERE CID = @c AND SNR = @n
                     SELECT @output = 'Done'
             END
   END
END


CREATE PROCEDURE UW13 @output varchar OUTPUT
AS BEGIN
   SELECT @output = 'All courses:'
   SELECT t.CID, t.NAME, t.LEVEL, count(t.SNR) AS ST_COUNT
   FROM   REG r, CRS t  WHERE r.CID = t.CID
   GROUP BY CID
   END
END
```

6.3 Format for Calling the Procedures

We give the formats for 'calling' the stored procedures (for executing and/or testing). We give three examples: one with no parameters, one with three text parameters, and one with a text parameter and an integer parameter.

```
EXECUTE UW1
EXECUTE UW2 @x = '…', @a = '…', @e = '…'
EXECUTE UW4 @c = '…', @n = …
```

7 In Conclusion

In this feasibility study we showed that producing a complete formal (mathematical) specification of the functional requirements for a system has several important advantages. Once we have such a specification, it can serve as a 'quick reference guide' for initiates and as a solid starting point for other development actions, e.g., for generating default 'input forms'. When we determine which roles are allowed to apply which user wishes, we can generate user stories and default 'menus' per role. Moreover, a mathematical specification also provides a potential means to prove additional state properties, as we showed. We gave an illustrative example which was large and subtle enough to demonstrate how our approach works, for example to show its scalability and the ease of change. The specifications were implementation-independent.

Thanks to the exact specification we are also able to produce a complete, straightforward implementation. In this paper, we showed it for SQL. Essentially, the state space was implemented with CREATE TABLE statements while the transition function and output function were implemented (in combination) via so-called *stored procedures* in SQL. Compound transactions were implemented using SQL's transaction concept. Mapping it to an imperative language (e.g., Java) constitutes future work.

We are not aware of a similar rigorous, straightforward, and encompassing mathematical specification approach being semantically sound.

Appendix: Explanation of Some Mathematical Expressions

This appendix informally explains some mathematical notions and notations we used. The notions in Part A might be familiar to you. The notions in Part B are subtle and might be unfamiliar, but they are crucial to define transactions in a *declarative* manner.

Part A
$\{ x | x \in A \text{ and } C(x) \}$: the set of all elements of the set A that satisfy condition C

$A - B$: $\{ x | x \in A \text{ and } x \notin B \}$, i.e., the set of all elements of A that are not in B

$(x; y)$: the ordered pair with first coordinate x and second coordinate y

function: set of ordered pairs in which each first coordinate occurs only once

dom(f): the set of all first coordinates of the function f (called *the domain of* f)

function over A: function for which the set A is its domain

$f(x)$ or $f.x$ or f at x or f_x: the second coordinate of the ordered pair in function f with first coordinate x (a.k.a. *the value of* f *at* x)

$f \restriction B$: the function f restricted to the set B (i.e., the set of all $(x;y) \in f$ for which $x \in B$)

set-valued function: function for which each value (i.e., each 2nd coordinate) is a set

If A is a set and T is a set of functions over A (a.k.a. a *table* over A) and $B \subseteq A$ then:

B is uniquely identifying in T $\Leftrightarrow$ for each $t \in T$ and $t' \in T$: if $t \restriction B = t' \restriction B$ then $t = t'$; i.e., each 'B-value' occurs at most once in T. ('u.i.' abbreviates 'uniquely identifying').

Part B
If s and g are functions, then $s \, \theta \, g$ is the function over $\text{dom}(s) \cup \text{dom}(g)$ which is equal to g on dom(g) and equal to s on dom(s) – dom(g). Formally:

$$s \, \theta \, g \, (x) \stackrel{\text{def}}{=} \begin{cases} s(x) & \text{for } x \in \text{dom}(s) - \text{dom}(g) \\ g(x) & \text{for } x \in \text{dom}(g) \end{cases}$$

We call $s \, \theta \, g$
the modification of s *by* g

Hence, in $s \, \theta \, g$, the 'modifying' function g 'overrules' s on their common domain.

If S is a set of functions and g is a function over S (i.e., $\text{dom}(g) = S$) and for each s $\in S$ g_s is a function then $\underline{\text{Main}(S,g)}$ is the function over S defined for each $s \in S$ as:

$$\text{Main}(S,g) \, (s) \stackrel{\text{def}}{=} \begin{cases} s \, \theta \, g_s & \text{if } s \, \theta \, g_s \in S \\ s & \text{otherwise} \end{cases}$$

We call Main(S,g)
the transaction according to g

In words: The function Main(S,g) assigns to each $s \in S$ the state $s \theta g_s$ if $s \theta g_s$ is in S, i.e., satisfies all conditions within S; otherwise, the state stays the same, i.e., stays s.

Note that Main(S,g) is a function from S *into* S again. Hence, Main(S,g) always specifies an allowed state! The function Main(S,g) specifies a *rollback* effect.

We note that, for each $E \in \text{dom}(g_s)$, $g_s(E)$ represents the intended new E-value while the value stays the same for every other E, i.e., for every $E \in \text{dom}(s) - \text{dom}(g_s)$.

References

1. Turing, A.M.: Computing Machinery and Intelligence. Mind **49**, 433–460 (1950). Accessed on 03 May 2022
2. Mealy, G.H.: A method for synthesizing sequential circuits. Bell Syst. Tech. J. **34**, 1045–1079 (1955). Accessed on 03 May 2022
3. SWEBOK: Software Engineering Body of Knowledge. (2014) Accessed on 03 May 2022
4. de Brock, E.O.: Foundations of Semantic Databases. Prentice Hall (1995).
5. de Brock, E.O.: Developing Information Systems Accurately - A Wholistic Approach. Springer books (2022).
6. de Brock, E.O.: Declarative modelling of transactions for IS development. In: Shishkov, B. (ed.), Int. Symposium on Business Modeling and Software Design (BMSD), Lecture Notes in Business Information Processing, vol. 356, pp. 114–133 (2019). Accessed on 03 May 2022
7. Pieper, F.T.A.M.: Data machines and interfaces. Ph.D. thesis, TU Eindhoven (1989). Accessed on 03 May 2022
8. Lucassen, G.: Understanding User Stories. Ph.D. thesis, Utrecht University (2017). Accessed on 03 May 2022
9. Ullman, J.D. et al.: Database Systems: The Complete Book. 2nd edn. Pearson (2009). Accessed on 03 May 2022
10. Elmasri, R., Navathe, S.B.: Fundamentals of Database Systems. Pearson (2016). Accessed on 03 May 2022

An Architecture for Attesting to the Provenance of Ontologies Using Blockchain Technologies

Simon Curty[1]([⊠])[iD], Hans-Georg Fill[1][iD], Rafael S. Gonçalves[2][iD], and Mark A. Musen[3][iD]

[1] Digitalization and Information Systems Group, University of Fribourg, Fribourg, Switzerland
{simon.curty,hans-georg.fill}@unifr.ch
[2] Center for Computational Biomedicine, Harvard Medical School, Boston, USA
rafael_goncalves@hms.harvard.edu
[3] Stanford Center for Biomedical Informatics, Stanford University, Stanford, USA
musen@stanford.edu

Abstract. When applying ontologies in practice, human and machine agents need to ensure that their provenance is trustworthy and it can be relied upon the contained concepts. This is particularly crucial for sensitive tasks such as in medical diagnostics or for safety-criticial applications. In this paper, we propose an architecture for the decentralized attestation and verification of the integrity and validity of ontologies using blockchain technologies. Blockchains are an immutable, tamper-resistant and decentralized storage where all transactions are digitally signed. Thus, they permit tracing the provenance of concepts and identify responsible actors. For a proof-of-concept we extended the WebProtégé editor so that domain experts can attest to the provenance of ontologies via their Ethereum blockchain account, subsequently permitting other actors to reason about the validity and integrity of ontologies. For evaluating the applicability of this approach, we explore a use case in the biomedical domain and perform a cost analysis for the public Ethereum blockchain. It is shown that the attestation procedure is technically feasible and offers a new strategy for placing trust in ontologies.

Keywords: Ontology · Attestation · Blockchain · WebProtégé

1 Introduction

Since the first conceptions of a semantic web, trust has been a central issue due to the decentralized and inconsistent nature of the web itself [4,19]. With the recent integration of linked data, knowledge representations, inferencing mechanisms and machine learning, it has become essential both for human and machine agents to know about the provenance of data and derived information [17,23,31]. Thereby, ontologies play a central role as a formal knowledge

© Springer Nature Switzerland AG 2022
B. Shishkov (Ed.): BMSD 2022, LNBIP 453, pp. 182–199, 2022.
https://doi.org/10.1007/978-3-031-11510-3_11

resource. Besides *policy-based trust* that regulates the origin and access to information, e.g. through authentication, *reputation-based trust* has played a major role in decentralized settings, where past interactions and/or ratings by users determine the level of trust [7]. According to O'Hara et al. [39], it can be distinguished between five strategies for ensuring trust: *optimism* where trustful information is regarded as default; *pessimism*: where trust is restricted unless a reason for trust is given; *centralized*: where trust is achieved through centralized institutions; *investigation*: where trustworthiness is achieved through active self-evaluation; and *transitivity*: where it is being relied on other agents.

With the recent popularization of blockchain technologies, another technique for ensuring trust according to the transitive and investigative strategy has been added. Through blockchains as append-only, immutable, decentralized and distributed data stores, trust is achieved through full transparency of the recorded, digitally-signed transactions that are verified through peer-to-peer consensus protocols. These properties qualify blockchain technology for applications where trust in the correctness and integrity of information is essential and shall be publicly verifiable without a central party. Previously proposed techniques for facilitating trust in ontologies, typically reverted to canonical representations that are digitally signed, e.g. [11]. However, this trust information must be shared to be of any use. Through its fundamental properties, blockchain technologies provide means to incorporate these aspects in one decentralized trusted system.

Extending upon previous work [13], where we showcased a first demonstration, we therefore explore in which way blockchain technologies can contribute to the integrity and trust in ontologies through so-called attestations, i.e. verifiable, transparent proofs of the existence of information and derive an architecture for this purpose. Reverting to blockchains yields multiple benefits. First, for domains where the quality of information is of utmost importance, the attestation of ontologies by qualified parties enables the transparent and decentralized guarantee of the correctness of information upon *human judgment*. For example, ontologies in bio-medical domains may be attested by a board of specialists independently of a central organization. A machine learning algorithm is then able to verify via the attestation that this ontology has been approved and is safe to be used for diagnosis without a third-party or central platform. Second, appended records in a blockchain cannot be re-ordered, enabling creation of decentralized immutable *timestamps* for information. Third, the *evolution* of ontologies may be tracked transparently, such that it is evident who committed what change and at what point in time, as information in a blockchain is traceable. Fourth, ontologies may contain sensitive information not suitable to be shared among all parties. It may, however, be necessary to prove the presence of information, for example, to fulfill compliance requirements. In such a scenario, *zero-knowledge proofs* may be used as no information needs to be disclosed.

Furthermore, the collaborative nature of authoring ontologies requires toolsets supporting multiple users. We thus describe a prototypical implementation of an attestation approach using the Stanford WebProtégé editor that has been extended with a plug-in for the Ethereum blockchain. For evaluating the applicability of the attestation procedure, we show its application in a use case of the biomedical domain. We conduct a performance evaluation and a cost analysis for the public Ethereum mainnet.

The remainder of this paper is structured as follows: In Sect. 2 we discuss related work. In Sect. 3 we introduce fundamental technologies and concepts relevant for our approach. The architecture itself and its implementation are presented in Sects. 4 and 5. We evaluate our approach in Sect. 6. Finally, we discuss the benefits and limitations of the approach in Sect. 7 and conclude with an outline of future research in Sect. 8.

2 Related Work

In this section we briefly review previous work on trust in the context of semantic web, digital signatures and the integrity of ontologies, collaborative ontology authoring and ontologies and blockchains.

2.1 Trust in the Context of Semantic Web

Early approaches for assessing trust in semantic web relied on *reputation* or *transitivity* based strategies where trustworthiness is derived by placing trust in other users and their assessments, e.g. [40]. Later work often followed the *investigation strategy* [39], i.e. where trust is placed in knowledge sources upon active self-evaluation. In this direction, Heymans et al. proposed for example a logic programming-based framework for software agents operating on the semantic web [25]. These agents form a *trusted web*, capable of reasoning about the reliability of knowledge sources.

Due to the distributed nature of the semantic web, sources may become unavailable, causing inconsistencies in inferred knowledge. Schenk et al. [43] therefore proposed trust levels, allowing for *caching* mechanisms to offset the unavailability of sources. Another approach for determining trust based on the consistency of knowledge bases involving uncertain information was presented in [19]. In this work, an inconsistency tolerant trust computation model has been described based on Bayesian description logic, which is capable of computing a degree of inconsistency of a knowledge base.

In semantic web environments, documents are typically annotated based on ontologies in a peer-to-peer setting. Thereby, peers may use different vocabularies, requiring the alignment of these ontologies for answering queries truthfully. Atencia et al. thus proposed a probabilistic model for calculating trust in query answers in such a P2P setting [3]. As shown by Nolle et al., inconsistencies can also be a chance to gather further information [36]. For this purpose, they described an approach for calculating a measure of trust in federated knowledge bases relying on statistical conflict assertions.

Another strategy often found is the *centralized* strategy, where trust is placed in institutions that host knowledge bases. This applies for example to platforms such as NCBO BioPortal [37,52], that provides access to a large amount of principled biomedical ontologies and is maintained by Stanford University, or DBPedia as maintained by the DBPedia Association, which provides an open knowledge graph extracted from Wikipedia [30].

2.2 Digital Signatures and Integrity of Ontologies

In today's web, digital signatures are widely used for message authentication and for ensuring data integrity and non-repudiation. In the context of the semantic web, digital signatures may be used for achieving *policy-based trust*. As a foundation for deriving signatures for RDF graphs, Carroll proposed a canonicalization of RDF graphs without changing their semantics, which allows the graphs to be signed in $O(n\log(n))$ as the signing of arbitrary RDF graphs cannot be done in polynomial time [11]. Later work extended the original approach and introduced the ability to sign individual statements of an RDF graph [51].

In a collaborative environment, the ability to sign only parts of a document is a beneficial feature. An approach to compute a digest of RDF graphs for content identifiers without the need for canonicalization was discussed by Sayers and Karp [42]. Based on these previous works, Kasten et al. [29] presented a framework for signing RDF and OWL graphs, with the capability of signing individual sub-graphs. The use of variations of a Merkle tree for hashing RDF graphs has been proposed in [46]. A Merkle tree is a tree of hashes, where leaves are hashes of data blocks and non-leaf nodes are hashes of child nodes [33]. The root of the tree is a hash representation of the underlying data. Thus, any modification of the data will result in a different root hash. This property allows one to verify the integrity of data. However, a drawback of Merkle trees, is that insertions require reconstruction of the entire tree. This poses a disadvantage for the purpose of integrity verification of evolving knowledge, for example, when monitoring ontology evolution and tracking changes. Sutton and Samavi therefore proposed data structures based on Merkle trees for RDF datasets that support insertions [46].

2.3 Collaborative Ontology Authoring

Real-world ontologies, such as the ones from BioPortal [37,52], are typically created in a collaborative fashion. Already in the early days of the semantic web, efforts have been made for providing tools for collaborative ontology development [27,44]. Since then, these tools have evolved and matured. A popular ontology editor is *Protégé* [35,49], which offers solutions to many challenges that come with collaborative workflows. This includes functionalities for engaging in discussions with other authors, the ability to annotate elements and for tracking changes in ontologies. In recent years, a cloud-based editor in the form of *WebProtégé* has been developed [28,50]. It presents an evolution of the Protégé desktop platform, developed to make use of modern web infrastructure.

2.4 Blockchains and Ontologies

Blockchain technologies are currently widely discussed and have led to innovative solutions in various fields [8]. Multiple benefits have been previously identified for applying blockchains in the semantic web [10], e.g., for using RDF as the data storage format on blockchains and thus providing a decentralized, immutable, tamper-proof data storage for RDF graphs [45]. Another approach has been proposed in [16]. There, the concept of *knowledge blockchains* is applied for the transparent monitoring of ontology evolution and proving the existence of concepts without disclosing them using so-called zero-knowledge proofs. A hybrid approach for storing RDF triplets for use in edge networks was presented in [48], where triplets are stored in a distributed off-chain RDF store but access is controlled by smart contracts. A blockchain-based architecture for the distribution of knowledge graphs was proposed in [1]. There, linked open data is stored on a blockchain where updates are driven by a community-based consensus. Other works discuss the benefits of applying techniques of the semantic web to blockchains, e.g., in [47] the authors propose a mechanism to index transactions of blockchains as linked data conforming to a vocabulary described by the BLONDiE ontology [24].

In conclusion, previous publications have discussed approaches for establishing trust in ontologies using investigative, centralized, transitive and reputation-based strategies, for digitally signing ontologies and for the collaborative authoring of ontologies and as well as the storage of ontologies on blockchains. What is however missing is a decentralized, light-weight approach for the collaborative attestation of ontologies for ensuring their trustful provenance.

3   Foundations

In this section we briefly introduce fundamental concepts and technologies relevant for describing our approach. This includes a formal definition of cryptographic hash functions and the fundamental properties of blockchain technologies.

3.1   Cryprographic Hash Functions

A hash function $h : M \to D$ maps a message of arbitrary length to a fixed length digest, such that, given the length function l: $\forall m, m' \in M : l(h(m)) = l(h(m'))$ and $\not\forall m, m' \in M : l(m) = l(m')$. That is, the length of the message digest is always the same, no matter the length of the hashed message. However, in a cryptographic system, additional properties are desired [41]:

- *Pre-image resistance*: Calculating the message from the digest is practically infeasible, that is, for a given d the original message m, such that $d = h(m)$ cannot be computed reliably in polynomial time by a probabilistic function.
- *Second pre-image resistance*: It is practically infeasible to find a message m' for a given m such that $h(m) = h(m'), m \neq m'$.
- *Collision resistance*: It is practically infeasible to find two arbitrary messages m and m' such that $h(m) = h(m'), m \neq m'$.

Furthermore, calculating the digest for any given message should be cheap to compute, that is, there exists a polynomial algorithm to calculate the digest for any input. However, to impede pre-image attacks, there should not be a correlation between the similarity of messages and their digests. In summary, one would want a cryptographic hash function to map any distinct input x to distinct outputs y, but not to be able to calculate x given y. This is for example achieved by the SHA-256 hash function [15] or Keccak-256 [5] as used by Ethereum.

3.2 Digital Signatures

Digital signatures are used to verify authenticity, integrity and non-repudiation of documents or messages. Authenticity refers to the origin of the document, that is, a receiving party can verify that the signed document was actually authored by a known party. The integrity of a document is given, when a receiving party can verify that it was not altered en route by a third party. Non-repudiation guarantees that the signing party cannot dispute authorship of the signed data. Digital signatures are based on the *public key cryptosystem*, also employed in asymmetric encryption of messages. In a public key cryptosystem, a pair of *keys* are used for encryption. The pair consists of a public and a private key. The public key is to be distributed and accessible to other parties, while the private key must be kept secret. The way public keys are published and linked to user identities is application-specific. Messages are signed by encrypting a cryptographic hash of the data with the signer's private key and attaching this information to the original message. The recipient of the message retrieves the attached information and the original message. To verify the signature, the signed hash is decrypted using the signer's public key. Finally, the decrypted hash is compared to a hash of the message calculated by the recipient. If they are identical, the digital signature is valid and the message has not been altered.

3.3 Blockchain Technologies

The term *blockchain* refers to a family of technologies and concepts for storing data in a decentralized, immutable and tamper-proof manner. In the following we only outline the major characteristics of blockchains as required for presenting our approach – for further details we refer the reader to the literature [2,18].

A blockchain can be described as an electronic ledger of transactions distributed over multiple locations. Participants in a blockchain operate a node with a replication of the whole blockchain database as part of a peer-to-peer network. Through this network, participants are able to send transactions to each other. Depending on the blockchain system, a transaction can include a transfer of funds, data or even the deployment of executable software code in the form of *smart contracts* [2]. For preventing fraud and establishing trust, participants can read and validate all transactions.

For initiating a transaction, a participant submits the transaction to a node where it is stored in a pool of *unverified* transactions. Thereby, every transaction is digitally signed by the participant, i.e. the cryptographic hash of the transaction data is signed with the participant's private key. The node then propagates the transaction to its peers for validation using specific consensus protocols. Nodes that validate transactions are called *validators*[1]. Validators choose unverified transactions from the pool and verify the signature of the initiator. In some systems, additional constraints may need to be fulfilled due to the consensus protocols, e.g. for randomly choosing a validator to prevent fraudulent validators in public blockchains such as Bitcoin or Ethereum. Based on the public key of the initiator, it can be verified, that (i) the transaction data has not been altered and (ii) the sender is in fact the initiator and not an impostor. The validated transactions are then added to the blockchain in the form of an append-only block data structure and linked to the previous block by referencing the hash value of its content. Consequently, the consensus protocols and the validation process make it impossible for a fraudulent participant to change any transaction data, for example, the recipient of a funds transfer. On the other hand, the initiator can neither roll back the transaction nor dispute any involvement.

4   Architecture for Blockchain-based Attestation of Ontologies

We now advance to the description of our blockchain-based attestation architecture for ontologies for ensuring their trustful provenance. An *attestation* describes a cryptographically verifiable claim about the existence of information [22]. In blockchain-based settings, these attestations can be recorded on a blockchain in the course of a digitally-signed transaction. In this way, a blockchain participant can issue a claim about the existence of information that can be verified. In contrast to traditional RDF signatures, it is not necessary to share the claim separately. In practice, such claims are conducted by first calculating the hash value of the information using a hash function. This hash value is then included in a blockchain transaction that is digitally signed and recorded on the blockchain. Subsequently, everyone with access to the blockchain can inspect the transaction, verify who has signed it and retrieve the hash value. By re-calculating the hash value for a given information and comparing it to the stored hash value, the attestation claim can be verified.

For applying attestations to ontologies in a collaborative ontology authoring environment, we have designed the architecture shown in Fig. 1. The architecture is composed of two main components: (i) on–chain smart contracts and (ii) a client–server-based ontology editor. The choice of blockchain platform greatly affects the level of decentralization, data visibility and costs, due to the specific properties and network configurations of different platforms. The proposed architecture requires an account-centric blockchain capable of executing smart contracts, i.e. Turing-complete programs that are stored and executed via transactions [2]. Deployed on-chain is an attestation smart contract, responsible for recording and verifying attestation claims.

---

[1] Validators are sometimes also called *miners*.

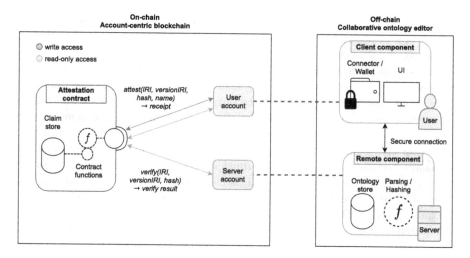

Fig. 1. Architecture of the attestation approach showing a client-server based ontology editor and the on-chain components.

The remote component of the ontology editor includes an ontology store as well as a component for parsing ontologies and calculating digest values. The server further has access to the blockchain and the attestation contract functions via a dedicated account. However, this account is not used to attest to the provenance of ontologies, but for verification only. Different versions of an ontology may have been published such that an ontology's revision is identified by the tuple (IRI, version IRI). Calculation of the ontology's hash value is done by a component on the server so that the client is not required to download the entire ontology for processing each attestation claim. The concrete hashing approach influences additional capabilities of the system, e.g., a merkle-tree–based hashing allows for conducting so-called *zero-knowledge proofs*. This may be used for example to verify that an ontology with a specific IRI containing privacy-sensitive information has been attested and contains specific concepts, without the need to disclose what these are.

Each user holds a personal blockchain account, not linked to the ontology editor. These accounts reside on the blockchain itself and the user alone holds authority over its management. That is, the blockchain accounts are completely independent of the user profiles of the editor. The user accesses this account by connecting to the blockchain network with a wallet application, through which attestation transactions are authorized upon demand.

5   Realization Using Ethereum and WebProtégé

For the prototypical realization of the described architecture, we reverted to WebProtégé [28] and the Ethereum blockchain [9]. The choice of Ethereum and related implementation details are further elaborated in Sect. 5.2. The two main components of WebProtégé are the web server and the client application, running in the user's browser. Ontologies are stored in a database on the server. When the user opens a saved ontology in the editor, the server fetches the ontology and transforms it from the database representation into the OWL 2 model. Thereby, only those parts of an ontology instance are transmitted asynchronously to the client that are necessary for the current actions of the user. Instead of transmitting the entire ontology to the client, hash calculation is done on the server, as detailed in Sect. 5.1. However, creating, signing and transacting the attestation claim must be done by the client as the authority over personal blockchain accounts should not be transferred away from the user. In order to integrate the attestation approach, some changes had to be made to key classes of WebProtégé in addition to extending it with a plugin in the form of an attestation portlet. Therefore, an open-source fork of the project was created and made publicly available where the attestation approach has been integrated [12]. Further documentation is available in the repository, as well as a pre-built docker image.

5.1   Calculating an Ontology Digest

OWL Ontologies differ from arbitrary text documents in that (i) the order of statements, e.g., triples in an RDF representation, do not change semantics, and (ii) other ontologies may be referenced by use of *imports*. These properties must be considered for hash calculation. There are multiple formats for representing OWL 2 ontologies such as the Turtle syntax or OWL/XML. Some hashing approaches require a specific format, canonical form or pre-processing of the ontology. If specific properties, such as proof of membership, are required, an appropriate hashing approach must be chosen. The OWL API [26] is a Java library for processing OWL 2 ontologies. It provides a mechanism for generating a hash code for OWL elements. The hash code implementation applies the *visitor design pattern* [20] for traversing the OWL 2 element structure. This is accomplished as follows. An OWL 2 ontology consists of *axioms* A_X, *annotations* A_O, as well as a term vocabulary, i.e. the entities. The set of entities is called the *signature* S of an ontology [34]. These sets are merged to a set $U = \bigcup \{S, A_X, A_O\}$ and the hash code of the resulting set is calculated as $hc(U) = \sum_{a \in U} visit(a)$, where *visit* is the concrete visitor function of a structure element provided by the API[2]. The resulting hash code is then converted to a fixed-length hexadecimal hash and used as ontology digest for the attestation claim. This method does not require a canonical form, i.e., representing the ontology as sequence of RDF triples with some deterministic ordering. However, as no cryptographic hash function is currently used, this method is not secure, i.e., not suitable for conducting zero-knowledge proofs. An extension of the hash function using a secure version will be considered for a future version as it will require the adaptation of the OWL-API.

---

[2] The visitor implementation is found here: http://owlcs.github.io/owlapi/apidocs_4/org/semanticweb/owlapi/util/HashCode.html.

5.2   Attestation Contract and Blockchain Integration

A key part of the prototype is a smart contract on the standard Ethereum blockchain. Ethereum was chosen due to its popularity, tooling support and its capability to execute Turing-complete smart contracts. Using the public mainnet has the advantage, that besides the WebProtégé Server, no additional infrastructure must be operated. The proposed approach can be adapted to other blockchain-based systems, as will be discussed in Sect. 7. The smart contract takes the role of a storage for the ontology hashes and as an API for their verification. When storing a hash on a blockchain, a signed transaction is sent to the address of the smart contract. For verifying that an ontology was attested, only the contract address, the network and the method for hashing must be known. In the prototype implementation, the contract address is known to the server, and we assume the network, including the procedure to connect to it, is known to the user. The users provide their own Ethereum account for interacting with the blockchain. User profiles in WebProtégé are not directly linked to blockchain accounts. This approach requires the users to connect their browser to the blockchain network. For this purpose we integrated a wallet browser plugin in the form of Metamask[3] to handle user login and network interactions.

The process for conducting attestations is shown by the sequence diagram in Fig. 2. Thereby it is assumed that some domain expert wants to attest to the provenance of an ontology and triggers the attestation process through the UI in the web browser. The client requests the necessary data from the server and the Metamask wallet plugin prompts the domain expert to login and select the relevant blockchain network. After the connection to the network has been established, the domain expert is prompted to authorize a transaction to the smart contract. With the transaction call, the ontology hash and information about the signer are sent. The smart contract stores the attestation and returns a receipt. Finally, the success of the attestation is reported to the domain expert.

6   Evaluation

Since our implementation is focused on offering a practical solution for an attestation process, we briefly describe an illustrative use case for its practical application. Additionally, we conduct a performance-based evaluation of the hashing and a cost analysis for the Ethereum mainnet. With the prototypical implementation presented in the previous chapter, the technical feasibility of the proposed architecture has been shown.

6.1   Use Case for Biomedical Ontology Authoring

In the biomedical domain ontologies play an important role. As of today, NCBO BioPortal hosts more than 850 ontologies with more than 10 mio. classes. This knowledge repository is highly valuable not only for human users but often serves

---

[3] A crypto wallet & gateway to blockchain apps - https://metamask.io/.

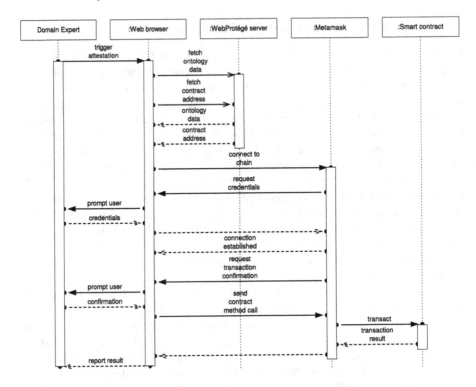

Fig. 2. Sequence diagram of the attestation process.

as a basis for machine learning approaches, e.g. [21]. In addition, various applications, such as specific annotation or recommender services provide easy access to the ontologies [32]. Importing parts of other ontologies, and thereby re-using enclosed concepts, is a common practice when engineering biomedical ontologies. Re-using parts of ontologies has the advantage of reducing maintenance efforts and allows users to focus on concepts specific to their ontology [38]. This highlights the importance of ensuring trust in ontologies. With the proposed attestation approach, we believe that the quality of services operating on biomedical ontologies as well as the trust in the contained concepts can be enhanced by means of a combination of the transitive and investigative trust strategy (see Sect. 1). By providing an immutable and tamper-proof attestation of an ontology by a domain expert or a board of specialists, the quality of an ontology can be verified both by human as well as machine agents even if it not hosted by an official body, e.g. a gene ontology (GO) version not issued by the GO consortium. Thus, it could be verified, which exact ontology version a machine learning algorithm has used and how the contained information is further propagated, e.g. [17,21]. It would also enable users who wish to re-use existing ontology concepts to verify whether an ontology has been approved by domain experts.

6.2 Performance

The process of attestation involves calculating the ontology digest and transacting the claim. Since the digest is of fixed length (see Sects. 3.1 and 5.1), the size of an ontology does not affect the size of an attestation claim. Thus, the validation and confirmation time for a transaction with an attestation claim largely depends on the current performance of the blockchain network, e.g., the Ethereum mainnet, but neither on the file size of an ontology nor the number of contained concepts, e.g., the number of classes. Therefore, the confirmation time for transactions is not part of the evaluation.

Table 1. Selected OWL ontologies from BioPortal. The ten largest in terms of classes as of Sep. 2021 were retrieved.

Acronym	Num. classes	Num. entities	Hash time [ms]
IOBC	126'842	2'123'338	2811
RETO	147'738	2'213'776	2595
REXO	158'239	2'350'454	2622
UPHENO	159'981	1'466'043	2346
NIFSTD	160'818	1'905'381	2490
GEXO	166'254	2'466'421	2991
NCIT	167'138	2'984'569	4609
BIOMODELS	187'520	2'093'464	2684
RH-MESH	305'349	1'959'445	2494
DRON	578'391	3'012'069	4106

In order to evaluate the suitability of the hashing approach for real world ontologies, we conduct performance tests using ontologies from BioPortal, shown in Table 1. The top ten OWL ontologies in terms of the number of classes[4] as of Sep. 2021 were chosen. The tests were run on an Intel i7 Skylake @2.6 GHz CPU on Ubuntu 21.04 and the ontologies were loaded into memory before the measurements were taken to minimize the impact of file system delays. The testing script is implemented in Java, using the JUnit5 testing framework. For each ontology, 20 measurements were taken and the trimmed mean [6] calculated – with 5% of upper and lower bounds removed to account for uncontrollable factors, such as OS operations. Figure 3 shows the results of the performance evaluation. While the time needed to calculate a digest increases and correlates with the number of structural elements, i.e. entities, expressions, axioms and annotations, it remains on an acceptable level for this kind of application. The more so as the transaction confirmation time in the Ethereum mainnet is often magnitudes higher.

---

[4] Filtering by size on BioPortal orders ontologies by number of classes.

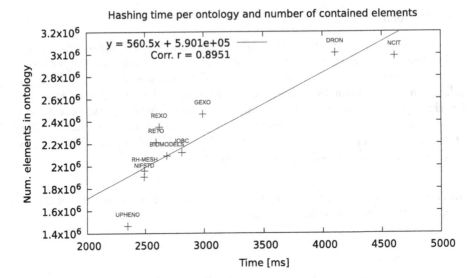

Fig. 3. Time needed to calculate a digest with the OWL API increases linearly with the number of elements in an ontology.

6.3 Cost Analysis

A major drawback of using public blockchains and smart contracts such as found on the Ethereum main network is that execution is slow and expensive compared to traditional, centralized systems, especially when either the size of the transaction data is large or the computations of a contract call are complex. This is mainly due to the decentralized consensus protocols used in public blockchains.

In Ethereum, size and computational complexity of transactions are measured in an energy unit, called *Gas*. This is a fee payed by the originator in the cryptocurrency Ether and depends on the complexity of commands to be executed [2] by Ethereum's virtual machine. The Ether price of a unit of gas is influenced by the transaction volume. Figure 4 shows historical transaction fees in USD for an attestation in comparison to a baseline, a contract storing a 256bit integer value. E.g., on June 1, 2021, an ontology attestation would have cost USD 8.62 (vs. baseline of USD 3.25). Prior to the London Upgrade[5] the transaction cost in USD is calculated as follows: *gas limit* ∗ *gas unit price* ∗ *ether price*, where *gas limit* is the estimated gas cost of an attestation transaction, *gas unit price* the average daily price of a single unit of gas and *ether price* the average daily price of one ether in USD. The historical Ethereum data was obtained from Etherscan[6]. With the London Upgrade, a *priority fee* is added to the *gas unit price* as incentive for the validators to include the transaction in a block – a higher priority fee accelerates transaction confirmation. For this cost analysis we include a priority fee of 2 Gwei. Both gas and ether price are volatile. As such,

---

[5] London Upgrade – https://ethereum.org/en/history/#london.

[6] Etherscan – https://etherscan.io.

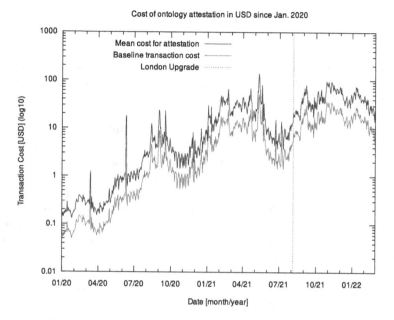

Fig. 4. Transaction costs for attestations based on the price for ETH. The attested ontology only has a minor influence on the incurred costs as the digest length is fixed but the IRI and the signer's name are not. With the London Upgrade the way costs are calculated have been changed.

the transaction cost may change significantly in a short period of time. However, Ethereum is in the process of adopting the proof-of-stake consensus mechanism[7], enabling higher transaction throughput and better energy efficiency.

7   Discussion

The approach we described for attesting to the provenance of ontologies describes a novel solution for placing trust in knowledge bases. In contrast to previously described approaches such as in [10,16], we do not store complete ontologies on a blockchain but rather the attestation claims in the form of hash values that are bound to the identities of blockchain users. As such, the approach pursues a *transitive* trust strategy, where trust is placed in resources upon the digitally verifiable certification of peer users of the blockchain. As the identities of users in today's public blockchain systems are pseudonymous, i.e. they are not bound to physical identities, additional measures need to be taken for retrieving the real identity of an attesting user in the sense of an investigative trust strategy. This could for example be achieved by publishing one's public key of the blockchain account on the website of a trusted institution. While this resembles the

---

[7] See https://ethereum.org/en/developers/docs/consensus-mechanisms/pos/.

traditional trust centralization strategy, it does not require the central storage of ontologies and permits the decentralized verification of the attestations.

Although we propose a working approach, it's not without limitations. The currently implemented hashing approach does not yet make use of the full potential of hashing an ontology. In the future the hashing could be adapted towards the use of Merkle-Trees or compression trees, which would permit more fine granular application of zero-knowledge proofs [16,46] as well as the consideration of change-tracking information, which would permit to attest to the nature of changes. The prototype currently does not support zero-knowledge proofs, proof of membership, partial or incremental attestation of ontologies. Further, the smart contract currently does not support the attestation by multiple users but only returns the most recent attestation of an ontology version for verification, i.e. collaborative ontology attestations are not yet supported. However, due to the nature of blockchains, all previous attestations can be inspected in the history of transactions. While we focus on the public Ethereum main network as deployment choice, multiple blockchain-based options exist. The approach can be adapted to other public blockchains, e.g., Avalanche[8], an Ethereum compatible proof-of-stake blockchain promising lower transaction costs compared to Ethereum. Permissioned blockchain networks in the form of a consortium infrastructure may be used as alternative to public networks. In such a consortium infrastructure, access is restricted to authorized and validated participants, sharing the effort to operate the network, e.g., by operating a node. This implies a difference in IT infrastructure and user enrollment [14]. However, instead of building such an infrastructure specific to this purpose, one may revert to existing consortial blockchains such as the Bloxberg infrastructure[9] for decentralized services for the scientific community.

8 Conclusion

In this paper we described an architecture for attesting to the provenance of ontologies using the Ethereum blockchain. The approach has been evaluated through a prototypical implementation and a performance evaluation of the attestation approach by applying it to real-world ontologies in the biomedical domain. Future work will include the investigation of alternative hashing procedures for ontologies for enabling zero-knowledge proofs on a more fine granular level and the extension of the smart contract implementation towards supporting attestations by multiple users.

Acknowledgments. The research on this paper has been partially financed by the Swiss National Science Fund grant number 196889.

---

[8] Avalanche - https://www.avax.network/.

[9] Bloxberg infrastructure - https://bloxberg.org/.

References

1. Aebeloe, C., Montoya, G., Hose, K.: ColChain: collaborative linked data networks. In: WWW 2021: The Web Conference 2021, Virtual Event/Ljubljana, Slovenia, 19–23 April 2021, pp. 1385–1396. ACM/IW3C2 (2021). https://doi.org/10.1145/3442381.3450037
2. Antonopoulos, A.M., Wood, G.: Mastering Ethereum: Building Smart Contracts and DApps. O'Reilly Media, Sebastopol (2018)
3. Atencia, M., Euzenat, J., Pirrò, G., Rousset, M.-C.: Alignment-based trust for resource finding in semantic P2P networks. In: Aroyo, L., et al. (eds.) ISWC 2011. LNCS, vol. 7031, pp. 51–66. Springer, Heidelberg (2011). https://doi.org/10.1007/978-3-642-25073-6_4
4. Berners-Lee, T., Hendler, J., Lassila, O.: The semantic web. Sci. Am. **284**(5), 34–43 (2001)
5. Bertoni, G., Daemen, J., Peeters, M., Van Assche, G.: The Keccak reference. Technical report, Team Keccak, January 2011. https://keccak.team/files/Keccak-reference-3.0.pdf
6. Bolstad, W.M., Curran, J.M.: Displaying and summarizing data. In: Introduction to Bayesian Statistics, 3rd edn., pp. 31–57. Wiley (2016)
7. Bonatti, P., Duma, C., Olmedilla, D., Shahmehri, N.: An integration of reputation-based and policy-based trust management. Networks **2**(14), 10 (2007)
8. Braun-Dubler, N., et al.: Blockchain: Capabilities, Economic Viability, and the Socio-Technical Environment. vdf AG of ETH Zurich (2020)
9. Buterin, V.: A Next-Generation Smart Contract and Decentralized Application Platform (2013). https://ethereum.org/en/whitepaper/
10. Cano-Benito, J., Cimmino, A., García-Castro, R.: Towards blockchain and semantic web. In: Abramowicz, W., Corchuelo, R. (eds.) BIS 2019. LNBIP, vol. 373, pp. 220–231. Springer, Cham (2019). https://doi.org/10.1007/978-3-030-36691-9_19
11. Carroll, J.J.: Signing RDF graphs. In: Fensel, D., Sycara, K., Mylopoulos, J. (eds.) ISWC 2003. LNCS, vol. 2870, pp. 369–384. Springer, Heidelberg (2003). https://doi.org/10.1007/978-3-540-39718-2_24
12. Curty, S.: WebProtégé Attestation: Prototype source code archive (2021). https://doi.org/10.5281/zenodo.5765038
13. Curty, S., Fill, H.G., Gonçalves, R.S., Musen, M.A.: A WebProtégé plugin for attesting to the provenance of ontologies on the Ethereum blockchain. In: Proceedings of the ISWC 2021 Posters, Demos and Industry Tracks. CEUR Workshop Proceedings, vol. 2980 (2021). http://ceur-ws.org/Vol-2980/paper329.pdf
14. Curty, S., Härer, F., Fill, H.G.: Towards the comparison of blockchain-based applications using enterprise modeling. In: Lukyanenko, R., Samuel, B.M., Sturm, A. (eds.) Proceedings of the ER Demos and Posters 2021. CEUR Workshop Proceedings, vol. 2958, pp. 31–36 (2021). http://ceur-ws.org/Vol-2958/paper6.pdf
15. Dang, Q.H.: Secure hash standard. Technical report, NIST FIPS 180-4, National Institute of Standards and Technology, July 2015. https://doi.org/10.6028/NIST.FIPS.180-4
16. Fill, H.G.: Applying the concept of knowledge blockchains to ontologies. In: AAAI 2019 Spring Symposium. CEUR-WS.org (2019)
17. Fill, H., Härer, F.: Supporting trust in hybrid intelligence systems using blockchains. In: AAAI 2020 Spring Symposium. CEUR-WS.org (2020)
18. Fill, H.G., Meier, A.: Blockchain Kompakt. Springer, Heidelberg (2020). https://doi.org/10.1007/978-3-658-27461-0

19. Fokoue, A., Srivatsa, M., Young, R.: Assessing trust in uncertain information. In: Patel-Schneider, P.F., et al. (eds.) ISWC 2010. LNCS, vol. 6496, pp. 209–224. Springer, Heidelberg (2010). https://doi.org/10.1007/978-3-642-17746-0_14
20. Gamma, E., Vlissides, J., Helm, R., Johnson, R.: Design Patterns: Elements of Reusable Object-Oriented Software. Addison-Wesley (1995)
21. Grigoriu, A., Zaveri, A., Weiss, G., Dumontier, M.: Siena: semi-automatic semantic enhancement of datasets using concept recognition. J. Biomed. Semant. 12(1), 1–12 (2021)
22. Härer, F., Fill, H.: Decentralized attestation of conceptual models using the Ethereum blockchain. In: IEEE CBI Conference, vol. 01, pp. 104–113 (2019)
23. van Harmelen, F., ten Teije, A.: A boxology of design patterns for hybrid learning and reasoning systems. J. Web Eng. 18(1–3), 97–124 (2019)
24. Hector, U.R., Boris, C.L.: BLONDiE: blockchain ontology with dynamic extensibility. arXiv:2008.09518 [cs], August 2020
25. Heymans, S., Van Nieuwenborgh, D., Vermeir, D.: Preferential reasoning on a web of trust. In: Gil, Y., Motta, E., Benjamins, V.R., Musen, M.A. (eds.) ISWC 2005. LNCS, vol. 3729, pp. 368–382. Springer, Heidelberg (2005). https://doi.org/10.1007/11574620_28
26. Horridge, M.: OWL API main repository (2020). https://github.com/owlcs/owlapi
27. Horridge, M., Gonçalves, R.S., Nyulas, C.I., Tudorache, T., Musen, M.A.: Webprotégé 3.0 - collaborative OWL ontology engineering in the cloud. In: ISWC 2018 Posters & Demonstrations, Industry and Blue Sky Ideas Tracks, vol. 2180. CEUR-WS.org (2018)
28. Horridge, M., Gonçalves, R.S., Nyulas, C.I., Tudorache, T., Musen, M.A.: WebProtégé: a cloud-based ontology editor. In: World Wide Web Conference, pp. 686–689. ACM (2019)
29. Kasten, A., Scherp, A., Schauß, P.: A framework for iterative signing of graph data on the web. In: Presutti, V., d'Amato, C., Gandon, F., d'Aquin, M., Staab, S., Tordai, A. (eds.) ESWC 2014. LNCS, vol. 8465, pp. 146–160. Springer, Cham (2014). https://doi.org/10.1007/978-3-319-07443-6_11
30. Lehmann, J., et al.: DBpedia-a large-scale, multilingual knowledge base extracted from Wikipedia. Semant. Web 6(2), 167–195 (2015)
31. Martin, A., et al. (eds.): AAAI 2022 Spring Symposium on Machine Learning and Knowledge Engineering for Hybrid Intelligence, Stanford University, USA, 21–23 March 2022, CEUR Workshop Proceedings, vol. 3121 (2022). http://ceur-ws.org/Vol-3121
32. Martínez-Romero, M., Jonquet, C., O'Connor, M.J., Graybeal, J., Pazos, A., Musen, M.A.: NCBO ontology recommender 2.0: an enhanced approach for biomedical ontology recommendation. J. Biomed. Semant. 8(1), 21 (2017)
33. Merkle, R.C.: A digital signature based on a conventional encryption function. In: Pomerance, C. (ed.) CRYPTO 1987. LNCS, vol. 293, pp. 369–378. Springer, Heidelberg (1988). https://doi.org/10.1007/3-540-48184-2_32
34. Motik, B., et al.: OWL 2 Web Ontology Language Structural Specification and Functional-Style Syntax, 2nd edn., December 2012. https://www.w3.org/TR/owl2-syntax/
35. Musen, M.A.: The protégé project: a look back and a look forward. AI Matters 1(4), 4–12 (2015)
36. Nolle, A., Chekol, M.W., Meilicke, C., Nemirovski, G., Stuckenschmidt, H.: Automated fine-grained trust assessment in federated knowledge bases. In: d'Amato, C., et al. (eds.) ISWC 2017. LNCS, vol. 10587, pp. 490–506. Springer, Cham (2017). https://doi.org/10.1007/978-3-319-68288-4_29

37. Noy, N.F., et al.: BioPortal: ontologies and integrated data resources at the click of a mouse. Nucleic Acids Res. **37**, W170–W173 (2009)
38. Ochs, C., Perl, Y., Geller, J., Arabandi, S., Tudorache, T., Musen, M.A.: An empirical analysis of ontology reuse in BioPortal. J. Biomed. Inform. **71**, 165–177 (2017)
39. O'Hara, K., Alani, H., Kalfoglou, Y., Shadbolt, N.: Trust strategies for the semantic web. In: Proceedings of the ISWC*04 Workshop on Trust, Security, and Reputation on the Semantic Web. CEUR, vol. 127 (2004)
40. Richardson, M., Agrawal, R., Domingos, P.: Trust management for the semantic web. In: Fensel, D., Sycara, K., Mylopoulos, J. (eds.) ISWC 2003. LNCS, vol. 2870, pp. 351–368. Springer, Heidelberg (2003). https://doi.org/10.1007/978-3-540-39718-2_23
41. Rubinstein-Salzedo, S.: The RSA cryptosystem. In: Rubinstein-Salzedo, S. (ed.) Cryptography. SUMS, pp. 113–126. Springer, Cham (2018). https://doi.org/10.1007/978-3-319-94818-8_12
42. Sayers, C., Karp, A.: Computing the digest of an RDF graph. Technical report, HP Laboratories Palo Alto (2004). https://www.hpl.hp.com/techreports/2003/HPL-2003-235R1.pdf. Accessed 09 Apr 2021
43. Schenk, S.: On the semantics of trust and caching in the semantic web. In: Sheth, A., et al. (eds.) ISWC 2008. LNCS, vol. 5318, pp. 533–549. Springer, Heidelberg (2008). https://doi.org/10.1007/978-3-540-88564-1_34
44. Simperl, E., Luczak-Rösch, M.: Collaborative ontology engineering: a survey. Knowl. Eng. Rev. **29**(1), 101–131 (2014). https://doi.org/10.1017/S0269888913000192
45. Sopek, M., et al.: GraphChain: a distributed database with explicit semantics and chained RDF graphs. In: The Web Conference 2018, pp. 1171–1178. ACM (2018)
46. Sutton, A., Samavi, R.: Integrity proofs for RDF graphs. Open J. Semant. Web **6**, 1–18 (2019)
47. Third, A., Domingue, J.: Linked data indexing of distributed ledgers. In: Proceedings of the 26th International Conference on World Wide Web Companion, pp. 1431–1436. International WWW Conferences Steering Committee, April 2017. https://doi.org/10.1145/3041021.3053895
48. Le-Tuan, A., Hingu, D., Hauswirth, M., Le-Phuoc, D.: Incorporating blockchain into RDF store at the lightweight edge devices. In: Acosta, M., Cudré-Mauroux, P., Maleshkova, M., Pellegrini, T., Sack, H., Sure-Vetter, Y. (eds.) SEMANTiCS 2019. LNCS, vol. 11702, pp. 369–375. Springer, Cham (2019). https://doi.org/10.1007/978-3-030-33220-4_27
49. Tudorache, T., Noy, N.F., Tu, S., Musen, M.A.: Supporting collaborative ontology development in Protégé. In: Sheth, A., et al. (eds.) ISWC 2008. LNCS, vol. 5318, pp. 17–32. Springer, Heidelberg (2008). https://doi.org/10.1007/978-3-540-88564-1_2
50. Tudorache, T., Vendetti, J., Noy, N.: Web-Protege: a lightweight OWL ontology editor for the web. In: Fifth OWLED Workshop on OWL: Experiences and Directions, January 2008
51. Tummarello, G., Morbidoni, C., Puliti, P., Piazza, F.: Signing individual fragments of an RDF graph. In: Special Interest Tracks and Posters of the 14th International Conference on World Wide Web - WWW, pp. 1020–1021. ACM, January 2005
52. Whetzel, P.L., et al.: BioPortal: enhanced functionality via new Web services from the National Center for Biomedical Ontology to access and use ontologies in software applications. Nucleic Acids Res. **39**(Web-Server-Issue), 541–545 (2011). https://doi.org/10.1093/nar/gkr469

Trends for the DevOps Security. A Systematic Literature Review

Tiina Leppänen, Anne Honkaranta[(✉)], and Andrei Costin

University of Jyväskylä, Jyväskylä, Finland
anne.honkaranta@gmail.com, ancostin@jyu.fi

Abstract. Due to technical advances, old ways for securing DevOps software development have become obsolete. Thus, researchers and practitioners need new insights into the security challenges and practices of DevOps development. This paper reviews the data extraction and analysis phase and results of a Systematic Literature Review (SLR) study that was carried out in 2019. The outcome is an updated list of security challenges and practices for DevOps software development. Both reviews shows that the most essential challenges for the DevOps security deal with the complexity of the development pipelines and the overall complexity of the cloud and microservice environments. The security activities identified were classified by using the BSIMM maturity model for software security as a framework. Our review shows that DevOps security research focuses mostly on deployment phase and technical aspects of software security. We compared the security activities identified in our study with the ones identified by the BSIMM development company in their 2020 review of 128 practitioners' security practices and found matching practices and similar trends.

Keywords: DevOps · Security · Systematic Literature Review

1 Introduction

Over the past decade, the increasing "need for speed" for faster software release cycles has increased the popularity of Agile methodologies [1]. DevOps, *"a set of practices intended to reduce the time between committing a change to a system and the change being placed into normal production, while ensuring high quality"* [2], is the cornerstone for agile and fast software development. One enabler for DevOps's fast deliveries is automated delivery pipelines [4–6]. In addition, DevOps blends the development and operations (e.g., maintenance of the software) together [3].

The software community has largely adopted DevOps; it was estimated that in 2020, even 74% of database professionals used it. In an article from the *Harvard Business Review* 80% of the respondents considered DevOps as essential for their organizations, and 69% reported using DevOps either selectively or solely for their software development [8]. DevOps also appeals to the builders of software because of its emphasis on the collaborative culture and positive impact on career, and for providing the tools to build higher quality software [9].

© Springer Nature Switzerland AG 2022
B. Shishkov (Ed.): BMSD 2022, LNBIP 453, pp. 200–217, 2022.
https://doi.org/10.1007/978-3-031-11510-3_12

Security breaches are reported daily on the news [10], and several identified security incidents as well as the rate of cyber-attacks are rising, which underlines the need for enhancing security of the contemporary software [4]. Traditional security approaches have focused on "gluing" software security as the final step in software development [11]. This approach turns the focus of the security on the firewalls, intrusion detection/prevention and antivirus software, instead of incorporating the security into the software itself [11]. Building secure software is not a "glue-on" activity but requires complex operations to ensure that software cannot be easily attacked [12] and does not contain vulnerabilities [3].

Software configurations have grown more complex than ever, and the contemporary approaches for securing software have become outdated [3]. Thus, developers and researchers lack information about 1) security challenges and 2) new features that their peers are utilizing in secure software development. This paper provides information about the topics by presenting updated results of a Systematic Literature Review (SLR) which was conducted in 2019 [13]. The challenges for DevOps security were identified using typification, whereas the activities for securing software were presented by using the Building Security in Maturity Model (BSIMM) by Synopsis Corporation as a framework [15, 21].

The current paper contributes by:

- reviewing the data extraction phase and findings of an original SLR study,
- discussing the findings, i.e., challenges and practices for DevOps security, and
- updating the security activities identified in primary studies to the latest version of the BSIMM software security maturity model.

The current paper also compares updated DevOps security activities from the research literature with the findings of BSIMM project study in 2020, which covered 128 organizations and their security postures in practice.

Section two introduces the SLR and snowballing methods, and BSIMM security maturity model, which is used as a framework for presenting the security activities identified from the preliminary studies. Section three describes the original SLR and the review process. The challenges for DevOps security and the security activities identified in the SLR are presented in section four. Section four also provides a comparison between the BSIMM project [15] Top 10 security activities and security trends identified by the BSIMM project [48] and the Top 14 list of security activities from our SRL study. Section five discusses the findings and proposes avenues for further research.

For the remainder of the current paper, the original SLR by [13] is referred to as "the original SLR study," and our review of the study is referred as "the review of the original SLR study."

2 Systematic Literature Review (SLR), Snowballing, and the BSIMM Framework

2.1 Systematic Literature Review (SLR)

An SLR provides a way to review the results provided by the research in a rigorous way [14]. An SLR is not focused on gathering relevant findings related to a research question;

it also seeks to provide evidence-based guidelines for practitioners. Systematic reviews are laborious by their very nature, but they may provide accumulative information about the phenomena under scrutiny.

According to Kitchenham's original guidelines [14, 16], the objective of an SLR is to identify all relevant research regarding the research questions. Unlike other literature review methods, an SLR may be utilized throughout the entire research process, including during formulating the research questions, searching for the relevant research, extracting data from the previous research, analyzing the findings, and providing guidelines for practitioners [16]. SLRs have been adopted in other scientific domains, such as criminology, social policy, economics, nursing, and software engineering [16].

An SLR uses specific concepts to separate the research papers that are analyzed and the literature reviews, such as the SLR itself. The research papers that are scrutinized in the SLR are called the *primary studies*, while the SLR itself is called *the secondary study* [17].

MacDonell et al. [18] evaluated the reliability of SLRs by comparing the results of two studies carried out by two independent groups of researchers. The SLR was proven to be a robust and trustworthy method for literature reviews. According to [17] an SRL study starts with identification of what needs to be known and summing it up into the form of the research questions. After that, a method for searching for the primary studies is formed. The search method should contain clear inclusion and exclusion rules. For example, it may be stated that certain digital libraries are included, while some others are excluded. After the search has been carried out the initial result set of primary studies is narrowed down by carefully examining the names, abstracts, and contents of the primary studies [17].

Once the result set is selected, an analysis tool should be prepared for data extraction [17]. It is important that the data analysis and extraction is tested by multiple researchers to ensure that the findings are valid and repeatable, and that the data extraction framework is properly understood and used [17]. The results of the analysis should be revisited and compared with other similar studies to ensure validity. Ways to enhance the analysis should also be carefully considered during the analysis [17].

The SLR methodology is developed by medical practitioners thus it has an unordinary step in analysis: the researchers should develop and share practical guidelines from the study with other practitioners [17]. The outcome of the study is the study report or a research paper.

The SLR methodology also emphasizes that the research report should include the method and search strategy that was used, how the inclusion and exclusion rules were utilized, and how the fellow researchers extracted the data and other potentially relevant aspects of the study [17].

It may be difficult to identify all relevant research by manual or automated database searches [19]. Many expert researchers know that a key for finding the most relevant research is to follow the references used by other researchers. The more particular research item is referenced by others, the more valuable it may be for the research. *The snowballing* method proposes that the list of references within each primary study should be further explored, and potential references listed from it should be examined. This is called backward snowballing [19, 20]. Forward snowballing aims to identify those papers that cite papers in the results. The cited papers may be identified, for example, by using Google Scholar. The set of papers citing the original reference paper is subjected to a second round of backward and forward snowballing [19]. The snowballing goes on for as long as a strong paper is present [19, 20].

2.2 The BSIMM Framework

Measuring software security only by "look and feel" is a challenging task. Instead of trying to compare software that solves the same problem, models for identifying and measuring activities supporting security have been developed [12]. The Building Security in Maturity Model (BSIMM) [15, 21] by Synopsis Corporation is a framework that can be used as a tool for measuring the security of software, to compare as security plan with other organizations' security initiatives, and for building a roadmap for enhancing security measures. BSIMM also provides a vocabulary for describing security activities. [21].

BSIMM contains four high-level domains that, in turn, contain three practices each. These top levels of the framework are illustrated in Table 1 [15]. Each practice contains 7–12 observed and related activities, comprising of 122 security activities in total. All the activities can be used in an organization rarely or intensively [15]. Frequently observed activities are designated as level 1, less frequently observed activities are designated as level 2, and infrequently observed activities are designated as level 3 [15, 21].

Table 1. The domains and practices of the BSIMM model [15].

Domain 1: governance	Domain 2: intelligence	Domain 3: SSDL touchpoints	Domain 4: deployment
Strategy & metrics	Attack models	Architecture analysis	Penetration testing
Compliance & policy	Security features & design	Code review	Software environment
Training	Standards & requirements	Security testing	Configuration Management/ Vulnerability management

The first version of BSIMM was created in 2008. The original SLR mapping was done using BSIMM version 9, which was released in 2018. The BSIMM framework has evolved since then from version 9 to version 12. The main changes include the addition of DevOps in version 10 [22] (i.e., DevOps was not a part of the BSIMM framework used in the original SLR study), "shift left" (an emphasis on the application security at the earliest stages of the software development) transforming to "shift everywhere" in version 11 [23], and additional activities regarding vulnerabilities and malicious code with automated security tools in version 12 [15].

The total amount of security activities in the BSIMM framework has grown from 116 in version 9 to 122 in version 12. In addition to the increase in quantity, activities have been modified to reflect the advances in technology [15].

In addition to the BSIMM, several other frameworks provide a common measuring stick for security. Two were developed by the OWASP Foundation (Open Web Application Security Project®), a non-profit foundation that works to improve the security of software and is familiar to most application security professionals.

The "OWASP Software Maturity Model" [24], which has been referred to as SAMM or OpenSAMM, is an open framework for organizations to analyze and improve their software security posture. Although the BSIMM model is descriptive by its very nature, the SAMM model measures maturity against a prescriptive set of security practices. Because the BSIMM can be used to understand how organizations can introduce security into their processes, SAMM supports the understanding of how security level can be improved in organizations' products. [25] The DSOMM (the OWASP Devsecops Maturity Model) [26] aims to tackle security in agile and DevOps software development.

The BSIMM was chosen as the framework for presenting the research results related to the security activities by [13, pp. 23] because "it has been developed using the largest set of data collected about software security anywhere." [12] also utilized the BSIMM on his security assessments covering 20 public and six private sector organizations.

3 The Original Literature Review and the Review Process

[13] had a broader scope in her research than the one selected for the current paper. The original research questions were defined as follows [13]:

- RQ1: What are the challenges of security in DevOps as reported by the authors of primary studies?
- RQ2: Which security activities are associated with DevOps in the literature?
- RQ3: How are the CAMS (culture, automation, measurement and sharing) principles reflected in secure DevOps research?

Our research was limited by time and scope; thus, the third original research question was not reviewed in the review.

3.1 The Search Process and Selected Primary Studies

The original SLR study proceeded using the SLR guidelines given by [14] and [17]. To find relevant primary studies for analysis, [13] created a search strategy based on search terms that were then used as a search string. She decided to include research articles and conference papers in the result set and exclude books and writings of opinion. The search terms used by the researcher are presented in Table 2.

The search for primary sources was conducted in April 2019 in four digital libraries: Science Direct, ACM Digital Library, IEEE Xplore, and Springer Link. [13] justified this selection by pointing out that these digital libraries were utilized for other literature review studies of software development and design, for example, [27, 28]. [13] reported

Table 2. The keywords and phrases used in the search for primary studies [13, pp. 28].

Topic	Search terms derived from topics
Main research topic	devops & secur*
Variations	devsecops, secdevops, devopssec

that she inserted the search terms in title and/or in abstract data fields. The publication year of the search results was not limited. The result of the first search round was 292 articles [13].

[13] narrowed the resulting set of primary studies down twice. In the first round, the articles' titles and abstracts were scrutinized regarding the research questions. The resulting primary studies were narrowed down to 38 primary studies. In the second round, all the articles in the result set were read, and the inclusion and exclusion criteria mentioned above was used to select the remaining 16 articles. Backward and forward snowballing processes following the guidelines provided by [19] produced two new primary studies. In the review process, this phase was not repeated because the original result set of primary studies was not available.

The final set for review in the original SLR study consisted of the 18 primary studies. They are referenced in this review as [3, 12, 29–44]. As our review of the SLR was limited by time and scope, the review started by adopting the result set of the 18 primary studies from the original SLR study.

3.2 Data Extraction from the Primary Studies

The original SLR study was conducted in a following way. First, [13] analyzed the primary studies and extracted the challenges by using typification. Typification is a method in which specific keywords and phrases are searched from the text. There were 27 challenges identified in the first round of analysis, and after a review of the list of the challenges and wordings in the research papers, the researcher typified the challenges into nine separate themes [13].

The second research question was studied using the BSIMM framework. Even though the BSIMM is a maturity model, it was used as a framework for plotting security activities identified from the primary studies to the BSIMM security activities [13] crafted a spreadsheet containing the BSIMM domains, related security practices, and activities.

After all primary studies were read and analyzed, there were total of 139 distinct security activities recorded, and these were sorted into 47 groups. These groups, in turn, were plotted against the security practices and activities of the BSIMM framework. If the counterpart for an activity was found in the BSIMM framework, the number of the study was added to the BSIMM practice's activity field, along with possible notes from [13]. The result was a table containing the BSIMM domains and practices; each practice field contained a list of the BSIMM security activities identified from the studies.

The review of the original SLR study was carried out as follows. First, the researchers prepared an Excel spreadsheet for data extraction containing a list of the original primary studies ordered as in the original SLR study. In addition, two columns were created:

one for the most essential findings extracted by the researchers and another in which the security challenges and activities identified in the original SLR study were copied. Finally, two additional columns provided space for the review comments and change proposals related to the original challenges and identified security activities.

Two primary studies were randomly selected for review. A trial data extraction comparing the results with the original SLR study was carried out by two authors of this paper. Some remarks for data interpretation and documenting were formulated for enhancing the process. The researchers split the papers in the result set into half, and each performed an individual review of the papers.

First, the findings related to the security challenges for DevOps were reviewed and analyzed together. Three new challenges were identified, as described in the following chapter. Second, the findings related to the security activities were scrutinized. It was soon noticed that something did not add up with the findings, and it was discovered that the BSIMM framework had been changed from to the one that has been used in the original study; hence the findings regarding BSIMM version 9, and the current version (12) were studied for gathering the findings. Data extraction was laborious, and the use of the BSIMM framework interpretation was quite challenging in some cases. The findings were analyzed together, and the differences were documented on a spreadsheet. The differences in our analysis are presented and discussed in the following chapter, which shows the findings of the original SLR study, and the findings of the review as plotted to the newest version of the BSIMM framework.

4   The Findings

This chapter discusses our findings about the similarities and differences between the original and new findings, along with the possible causes for these differing interpretations.

4.1   Challenges for DevOps

Figure 1 summarizes the challenges identified in the original SLR study and the current review. New challenges are marked with *.

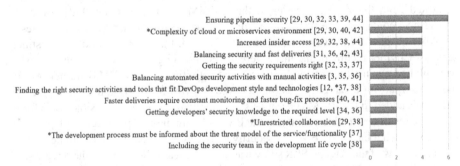

Fig. 1. Security challenges in DevOps after the review of the original SLR study.

Many of the primary studies were carried out in cloud environments, which are complex and fast evolving by their nature. Fast development stresses the need for balancing between quality, security, and speed. Many papers noted that new technologies and tools, such as microservices and containers, are not designed primarily for security in mind, and their use in the pipelines requires that novel kinds of security risks related to them are identified appropriately. Therefore, *Ensuring pipeline security* was the challenge that was brought up in six articles. The *Complexity of cloud or microservices* environment is related to the complexity of the contemporary cloud services, too, and it is apparent in four of the primary studies. Although these challenges are remarkable, they are not specific to the DevOps method.

Balancing security and fast deliveries, on the other hand, is quite tightly tied into the DevOps method. Fast deliveries are the core and foremost reason for the creation of the DevOps method. Automation is required for quickening security procedures, but the outcome of this automation may not be as good as anticipated [38]. One challenge with fast deliveries is also how to get the security team to do their work at the right time and promptly.

Primary study [29] focused on an insider threat, which is obviously a security concern, while the team accessing the development environment is larger with the appearance of the operations team. Furthermore, the DevOps culture embraces the idea that developers and operations personnel both become multi-talented and may work in both roles, creating an increased number of insiders in the environment who also have larger access to the components in the environment. The insider threat was bought up by many other papers, too (e.g., primary studies [3] and [38]).

Insider threat caused by the co-existence of both "Devs" and "Ops" personnel having broad access to the software development environments and the increased speed for development are perhaps the most prominent features of DevOps development leading to characterizing the security practices in preliminary studies [12] and [38] as "Finding the right security activities and tools that fit the DevOps development style and technologies".

4.2 Security Practices and Activities for DevOps

The security activities identified in the original SLR study and updated and mapped to BSIMM framework version 12 [15] during the research review by the current authors are presented in the tables below. The total amount of security practices (139) and ranking between the BSIMM domains did not change as a result of this review. The numbers in brackets after the BSIMM practice column name show the total number of primary studies mentioning the security practice. The numbers in brackets after the BSIMM activity names refer to the identifier of the primary study (listed in Chapter 3.1). An article with no equivalency to the original SLR is marked with strikethrough (e.g., ~~40~~). A new finding is emphasized (e.g., **3**), and an article not openly available is underlined (e.g., <u>35</u>).

The *Governance* domain presented in Table 3 includes activities that belong to the organization, management, and measurement practices of a software security initiative. Because primary study [3] emphasized the meaning of education and training as being especially important in secure agile development during planning and getting input from the learning phase, that article was added in *Conduct software security awareness training activity* (T1.1).

Table 3. Security activities used in the BSIMM *Governance* domain.

BSIMM practice (23) > (24)	BSIMM observed and related activities
Strategy and metrics (8) *no change*	[SM1.4] Implement lifecycle instrumentation and use to define governance. [34, 36, 37, 43] [SM2.2] Verify release conditions with measurements and track exceptions. [37] [SM2.3] Create or grow a satellite. [3, 12] [SM2.6] Require a security sign-off prior to software release. [37]
Compliance & policy (13) *no change*	[CP1.1] Unify regulatory pressures [37, 38] [CP1.3] Create policy. [31, 32, 38, 42–44] [CP2.1] Build PII data inventory. [12] [CP2.3] Implement and track controls for compliance. [37, 38] [CP2.4] Include software security SLA in all vendor contracts. [40] [CP3.2] Impose policy on vendors. [40]
Training (2) > (3)	[T1.1] Conduct software security awareness training. [3, 38] [T3.5] Establish SSG office hours. [12]

The *Intelligence* domain contains software security practices and activities whose results end up in collections of corporate knowledge. This domain received the least mentions of all the domains. The results are presented in Table 4. Two articles were removed because they did not cover the attack patterns nor open-source related activities directly. The changes in BSIMM activity names and their purpose were also reanalyzed.

Table 4. Security activities used in the BSIMM *Intelligence* domain.

BSIMM practice (21) > (18)	BSIMM observed and related activities
Attack models (10) > (9)	[AM1.2] Create a data classification scheme and inventory. [29, 41] [AM1.3] Identify potential attackers. [29, 36] [AM1.5] Gather and use attack intelligence. [35, 36] [AM2.1] Build attack patterns and abuse cases tied to potential attackers. [29, 41] [AM2.2] Create technology specific attack patterns. [30] [AM2.7] Build an internal forum to discuss attacks. [12, 29]

(continued)

Table 4. (*continued*)

BSIMM practice (21) > (18)	BSIMM observed and related activities
Security features & design (2) *no change*	[SFD1.1] Integrate and deliver security features. [42] [SFD2.1] Leverage secure-by-design components and services. [42]
Standards & requirements (9) > (7)	[SR1.3] Translate compliance constraints to requirements. [32, ~~38, 41~~] [SR2.4] Identify open source. [35, 36, ~~38~~] [SR3.1] Control open-source risk. [12, 35, ~~38~~]

The *Secure Software Development Lifecycle (SSDL) touchpoints* domain covers practices included in all software security methodologies. In our review of the original SLR study, the total number of articles in the *Intelligence* domain increased by three (see Table 5). Primary study [34] proposed several security tools relating to the use of architecture analysis processes and automated deployment that was also covered in the research by primary study [3]. On the other hand, primary study [43] mentioned difficulties with automated testing and presented CAVAS workflow with automated steps but did not explicitly cover the usage of automated tools. This article was excluded from the results.

Table 5. Security activities used in the BSIMM *SSDL touchpoints* domain.

BSIMM practice (36) > (39)	BSIMM observed and related activities
Architecture analysis (13) > (14)	[AA1.1] Perform security feature review. [29, 30, 33, 36, 37, 38, 40, 41, 43] [AA2.1] Define and use AA processes. [**34**, 37, 38, 41] [AA3.3] Make the SSG available as an AA resources or mentor. [37]
Code review (12) > (14)	[CR1.4] Use automated tools along with manual review. [3, 30, 36, 37, 38] [CR1.5] Make code review mandatory for all projects. [36, 37] [CR1.6] Use centralized reporting to close the knowledge loop. [36] [CR2.6] Use automated tools with tailored rules. [**3**, 31, **34**, 35, 36] [CR2.7] Use a top N bugs list (real data preferred). [30]
Security testing (11) *no change*	[ST1.3] Drive tests with security requirements and security features. [30, 31, 33, 34, 38, 43] [ST2.4] Share security results with QA. [36] [ST2.5] Include security tests in QA automation. [34, 36] [ST3.3] Drive tests with risk analysis results. [41] [ST3.5] Begin to build and apply adversarial security tests (abuse cases). [34]

The domain with the most mentions, *Deployment*, includes practices that relate to traditional network security and software maintenance. The most often mentioned practice and activity are also in this domain (see Table 6). *Use application behavior monitoring and diagnostics* (SE3.3) was mentioned in 10 of the primary studies. This result is well aligned with DevOps' principle of measuring what is needed to keep the heart of DevOps beating. The value of monitoring and using data from deployed applications is crucial in automated pipelines. Article [44] was added in the *Penetration testing* practice. The research in this article focused on continuous delivery, and penetration testing activity was recommended for assessing the security of web applications. In the *Software Environment* practice, two articles were removed because they did not cover activities of concern.

Table 6. Security activities used in the BSIMM *Deployment* domain.

BSIMM practice (59) > (58)	BSIMM observed and related activities
Penetration testing (4) > (5)	[PT1.2] Feed results to defect management and mitigation system. [31] [PT1.3] Use penetration testing tools internally. [31, 36, 37, **44**]
Software environment (43) > (41)	[SE1.1] Use application input monitoring. [12, 40, 42] [SE1.2] Ensure host and network security basics are in place. [29–33, 39, 40, ~~42~~, 43] [SE2.5] Use application containers to support security goals. [29, 32, 39, 43] [SE2.6] Ensure cloud security basics. [3, 40–44] [SE2.7] Use orchestration for containers and virtualized environments. [32, 34, 39, 40, 42–44] [SE3.3] Use application behavior monitoring and diagnostics. [3, 12, 31, 33, 34, 38, 40–43] [SE3.6] Enhance application inventory with operations bill of materials. [30, 35]
Configuration management & vulnerability management (12) *no change*	[CMVM1.1] Create or interface with incident response. [12] [CMVM1.2] Identify software defects found in operations monitoring and feed them back to development. [3, 12, 36, 40] [CMVM2.1] Have emergency codebase response. [12] [CMVM2.2] Track software bugs found in operations through the fix process. [3, 36] [CMVM2.3] Develop an operations inventory of applications. [12, 35] [CMVM3.3] Simulate software crises. [12, 33]

The BSIMM security activities that received more than four mentions were introduced in more detailed level in the original SLR study [13] on a list of the top 13 activities. In this review, that list has been updated to contain 14 items (see Fig. 2). There were no changes in the top seven security activities. *Use automated tools along with manual review* (CR1.4) and *Use automated tools with tailored rules* (CR2.6) got both one new mention improving their rankings compared with the original top 13 list. In turn, *Use application containers* (SE2.5) and *Use application input monitoring* (SE1.1) were activities that lost one mention each.

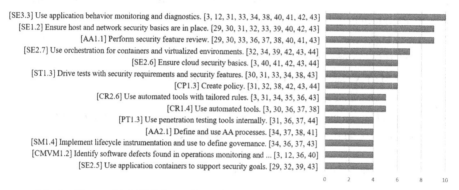

Fig. 2. The top 14 BSIMM security activities after the review of the original SLR.

The results of the current review align with the original SLR study [13] that contemporary research has focused strongly on technology and how it is secured in the DevOps infrastructures. Some of the selected research articles were purely concentrated on certain cloud computing technologies (e.g., containers, multicloud environments). As in the original SLR study, the results of the current review showed that 42% of the security activities applied to the primary studies were related to the deployment domain.

Adopting DevOps has been found to be a challenging task because of the vast amount of information, practices, and tools related to it [46]. DevOps heavily emphasizes the relevance of building a collaborative, sharing, and transparent culture. Regardless of these principles, *Training and Security* and *Design* practices received the fewest mentions.

4.3 Findings of the SLR Review Versus the Findings of the BSIMM Top 10 Security Activities

Synopsys Software, the company that created the BSIMM framework, assessed the security of hundreds of companies by using the BSIMM framework. In its latest research project, 128 organizations were scrutinized using the BSIMM framework [15]. The BSIMM project published an overview containing statistics and findings for the whole project [15].

The security activities top 14 list resulting from our SLR review has four matches with the BSIMM Top 10 list identified from the 128 participating organizations. The matching security activities are presented in Table 7.

Implement lifecycle instrumentation and use to define governance (SM1.4) which was ranked as 11th in the current SLR review is in the first place in the BSIMM Top 10 list of practitioner's security activities. *Ensure host and network security basics are in*

Table 7. BSIMM12 top 10 activities compared with the findings in the current review.

#	BSIMM12 top 10	This review
1	[SM1.4] Implement lifecycle instrumentation and use to define governance	11th
2	[SE1.2] Ensure host and network security basics are in place	2nd *(Exact match)*
3	[CP1.2] Identify PII obligations	–
4	[AA1.1] Perform security feature review	3rd *(Good match)*
5	[PT1.1] Use external penetration testers to find problems	–
6	[CMVM1.1] Create or interface with incident response	–
7	[SFD1.1] Integrate and deliver security features	–
8	[CR1.4] Use automated tools	8th *(Exact match)*
9	[ST1.1] Ensure QA performs edge/boundary value condition testing	–
10	[SR1.3] Translate compliance constraints to requirements	–

place (SE1.2) was an exact match in second place in both lists. *Perform security feature review* (AA1.1) was ranked in fourth place in the BSIMM Top 10 list, and in third in the current SLR review. This confirms that the most appreciated BSIMM security activities by the practitioner organizations were also considered important by the researchers. For example, activity *Use automated tools* (CR1.4) was an exact match in these rankings.

The first two security activities in the BSIMM12 top 10 list, *Implement lifecycle instrumentation and use to define governance* (SM1.4) and *Ensure host and network security basics are in place* (SE1.2) reside in the *Governance* domain. This indicates the importance of practices that help organize, manage, and measure secure software processes in a proactive way and throughout the lifecycle of the software. *Identify PII obligations* (CP1.2) was not covered in any of the primary studies of our SLR review, even though the implementation of the GDPR received a lot of attention and forced software providers to develop novel protective measures for personal information processing.

Both rankings emphasize that the most utilized security activities focus on the technology domains of the BSIMM framework. To be more exact, the top 10 of the most mentioned BSIMM activities in our SLR review can be divided into two categories: *Deployment* and *SSDL Touchpoints* domains.

The company that published the BSIMM12 Top10 report has also published an overview of DevOps trends that were identified as emerging in the BSIMM12 project. The review reminds that too few security tools allow security gaps, but too many are a burden for the developers, and may freeze the pace of software development which remains as the ultimate target for DevOps. [48].

The new BSIMM review [48] identifies some interesting, totally new trends for security as:

- ransomware and supply chain disruptions, which call upon for increased scrutiny of software security
- increasing the capabilities for cloud security
- security teams are increasingly collaborating with DevOps practitioners, lending staff and knowledge to them instead of mandating security postures, and
- security testing as an automated activity seems to have doubled its size.

The new BSIMM review [48] points out activities that have gained a remarkable growth in the past 24 months when compared with our SRL review top 14 list: 1) *Use orchestration for containers and virtualized environments* (SE2.7) – over 500% increase in mentions in the security activities, ranked as fourth in our SLR review top 14 list, 2) *Ensure cloud security basics* (SE2.6) – over 500% increase in mentions in the security activities, which was fifth in our SRL review top 14 list, and 3) *Use application containers to support security goals* (SE2.5) – over 200% increase in mentions in the security activities, which was 14th in our SRL review top 14 list. In overall it seems that research on DevOps security is more focused on *Software development environment* practice, while the practitioners' security activities cover more of the BSIMM framework's different practices.

5   Discussion and Avenues for Further Research

The current study reviewed the method and findings of an original SLR study conducted in 2019 which discovered the challenges and the cures for DevOps security. Since the original study was carried out, the BSIMM framework has changed mainly in the areas of DevOps and automated security tools. New activities were added to reflect the impact of DevOps security, and existing ones were updated to reflect how organizations are implementing them.

The contribution of the current review was the cross-validation and assessment of the original SLR study by reviewing the original 18 primary research studies identified by Koskinen [13], and as a result updating the challenges for DevOps, and mapping the security activities identified to the newest version of the BSIMM software security maturity model as a framework. We also mapped our findings with the BSIMM project's results from a study covering 128 organizations.

Mapping the security activities identified from the primary studies to the BSIMM framework was challenging. Our findings were well aligned with the original SLR study. As the main finding and common trend of the SLR and the BSIMM analysis of the organizations was the technology focus, the key differences were the diversity of domains and practices. The results of SLR indicate strong focus on software environment practices, while the BSIMM analysis of the organizations covers 10 different practices in the list of top 10 activities. The current study showed that research on DevOps security is mostly challenged by complexity in the management of the pipelines and overall security of the complexity of cloud and microservice environments. The BSIMM framework security activities *Use application behavior monitoring and diagnostics* and *Ensure host and network security basics are in place* were the most mentioned security activities on the primary studies. The BSIMM top 10 security activities list from 2020 show that

Implement lifecycle instrumentation and use to define governance was the most popular security activity while *Ensure host and network security basics are in place* came in second place. Interestingly, our SLR study's top 14 and the BSIMM project top 10 security activities had three matches; in addition to *Ensure host and network security basics are in place, Implement lifecycle instrumentation and use to define governance* and *Use automated tools* were mentioned in both listings. The BSIMM review [48] had identified ransomware and collaboration with security practitioners and DevOps specialists as activities that are gaining attention. It still seems that both the practitioners and researchers were mostly focused on the technical aspects of software security, the researchers perhaps even more than the practitioners.

We identified several potential avenues for further research. [47] carried out an SLR for detecting the challenges for security in the DevOps work. They applied the Preference Ranking Organization Method for Enrichment Evaluation (PROMETHEE) technique to prioritize the 18 challenges identified in the study. A framework like PROMETHEE would help to organize the challenges identified by our study in a more ordered way. It would also be interesting to compare the challenges of our SLR study with the challenges identified by [47], which would be possible if both listings of challenges were presented with the same framework.

The original SLR study was conducted in 2019. We conducted a new search on the research databases that were used to identify the preliminary studies for this SLR, finding 27 potential new studies that could be analyzed to update the findings.

The extraction of data from the primary sources was conducted by two researchers in our review study. Yet there is a possibility to false interpretations, as always when humans are analyzing abstract evidence such as research papers. Our SLR was also limited by time, thus we did not have the chance to update and enlarge the primary studies with the new 27 studies that were identified.

We hope that practitioners and researchers interested in SLR, DevOps and security find the current paper useful for their endeavors.

Acknowledgements. Authors wish to thank the two anonymous reviewers for their invaluable comments and feedback that helped greatly to improve the quality of paper. Specifically, the other reviewer offered a very thorough review with many good comments, ideas, and suggestions.

References

1. Lwakatare, L., et al.: Devops in practice: a multiple case study of five companies. Inf. Softw. Technol. **114**, 217–230 (2019)
2. Bass, L., Weber, I., Zhu, L.: DevOps: A Software Architect's Perspective. Addison-Wesley Professional (2015)
3. Jaatun, M., Cruzes, D., Luna, J.: DevOps for better software security in the cloud. Invited paper. In: ARES '17. Proceedings of the 12th International Conference on Availability, Reliability and Security 2017, Article no. 69, pp. 1–6. ACM (2017)
4. Hsu, T.: Hands-On Security in DevOps: Ensure Continuous Security, Deployment, and Delivery with DevSecOps. Packt Publishing Ltd. (2018)
5. Humble, J., Farley, D.: Continuous Delivery: Reliable Software Releases through Build, Test, and Deployment Automation. Pearson Education (2010)

6. Konersmann, M., Fitzgerald, B., Goedicke, M., Holmström Olsson, H., Bosch, J., Krusche, S.: Rapid continuous software engineering-state of the practice and open research questions: report on the 6th international workshop on Rapid Continuous Software Engineering (RCoSE 2020). ACM SIGSOFT Softw. Eng. Notes **46**(1), 25–27 (2021)
7. RedGate Software The state of database devops 2021 report. https://www.red-gate.com/sol utions/database-devops/report-2021
8. Vizard, M.: Survey finds wide gap between DevOps adoption and success. https://devops. com/survey-finds-wide-gap-between-devops-adoption-and-success/
9. Atlassian survey 2020 - DevOps trends. https://www.atlassian.com/whitepapers/devops-sur vey-2020
10. Williams, L., McGraw, G., Migues, S.: Engineering security vulnerability prevention, detection, and response. IEEE Softw. **35**(5), 76–80 (2018)
11. Mohammed, N., Niazi, M., Alshayeb, M., Mahmood, S.: Exploring software security approaches in software development lifecycle: a systematic mapping study. Comput. Stan. Interfaces **50**, 107–115 (2017)
12. Jaatun, M.: Software security activities that support incident management in secure DevOps. In: Proceedings of the 13th International Conference on Availability, Reliability and Security, pp. 1–6. ACM (2018)
13. Koskinen, A.: Devsecops: Building Security into the Core of Devops. University of Jyväskylä, Jyväskylä, Finland (2019)
14. Kitchenham, B.: Procedures for Performing Systematic Reviews, vol. 33, pp. 1–26. Keele University, UK (2004)
15. SynopsysSoftware: BSIMM12, 2021 Insights Trends Report. https://www.bsimm.com/
16. Kitchenham, B., Brereton, O., Budgen, D., Turner, M., Bailey, J., Linkman, S.: Systematic literature reviews in software engineering–a systematic literature review. Inf. Softw. Technol. **51**(1), 7–15 (2009)
17. Brereton, P., Kitchenham, B.A., Budgen, D., Turner, M., Khalil, M.: Lessons from applying the systematic literature review process within the software engineering domain. J. Syst. Softw. **80**(4), 571–583 (2007)
18. MacDonell, S., Shepperd, M., Kitchenham, B., Mendes, E.: How reliable are systematic reviews in empirical software engineering? IEEE Trans. Softw. Eng. **36**(5), 676–687 (2010)
19. Wohlin, C.: Guidelines for snowballing in systematic literature studies and a replication in software engineering. In: EASE '14. Proceedings of the 18th International Conference on Evaluation and Assessment in Software Engineering, pp. 1–10. ACM (2014)
20. Jalali, S., Wohlin, C.: Systematic literature studies: database searches vs. backward snow-balling. In: Proceedings of the 2012 ACM-IEEE International Symposium on Empirical Software Engineering and Measurement, pp. 29–38. IEEE (2012)
21. Glas, B.; Comparing BSIMM SAMM. https://owaspsamm.org/blog/2020/10/29/comparing-bsimm-and-samm/
22. Mello, J.: BSIMM10. DevOps is changing how software teams approach security. https://tec hbeacon.com/security/bsimm-10-devops-changing-how-software-teams-approach-security
23. SynopsysSoftware.   https://news.synopsys.com/2020-09-15-Synopsys-Publishes-BSI MM11-Study-Highlighting-Fundamental-Shifts-in-Software-Security-Initiatives-in-Res ponse-to-DevOps-and-Digital-Transformation
24. OWASP Foundation: OWASP software assurance maturity model. https://owasp.org/www-project-samm/
25. Pagel, T.: Overview of (DevSecOps) OWASP projects. https://owasp.org/www-chapter-ger many/stammtische/frankfurt/assets/slides/48OWASPFrankfurtStammtisch1.pdf
26. OWASP DevSecOps maturity model. https://owasp.org/www-project-devsecops-maturity-model/

27. Felderer, M., Fourneret, E.: A systematic classification of security regression testing approaches. Int. J. Softw. Tools Technol. Transfer **17**(3), 305–319 (2015)

28. Souza, E., Moreira, A., Goulão, M.: Deriving architectural models from requirements specifications: a systematic mapping study. Inf. Softw. Technol. **109**, 26–39 (2019)

29. Ahmadvand, M., Pretschner, A., Ball, K., Eyring, D.: Integrity protection against insiders in microservice-based infrastructures: From threats to a security framework. In: Mazzara, M., Ober, I., Salaün, G. (eds.) STAF 2018. LNCS, vol. 11176, pp. 573–588. Springer, Cham (2018). https://doi.org/10.1007/978-3-030-04771-9_43

30. Bass, L., Holz, R., Rimba, P., Tran, A., Zhu, L.: Securing a deployment pipeline. In: 2015 IEEE/ACM 3rd International Workshop on Release Engineering, pp. 4–7. IEEE (2015)

31. Beigi-Mohammadi, N., et al.: A DevOps framework for quality-driven self-protection in Web software systems. In: Proceedings of the 28th Annual International Conference on Computer Science and Software Engineering, pp. 270–274. IBM Corp. (2018)

32. Diekmann, C., Naab, J., Korsten, A., Carle, G.: Agile network access control in the container age. IEEE Trans. Netw. Serv. Manage. **16**(1), 41–55 (2018)

33. Düllmann, T., Paule, C., van Hoorn, A.: Exploiting DevOps practices for dependable and secure continuous delivery pipelines. In: 2018 IEEE/ACM 4th International Workshop on Rapid Continuous Software Engineering (RCOSE), pp. 27–30. IEEE (2018)

34. Tigli, J.Y., Winter, T., Muntés-Mulero, V., Metzger, A., Velasco, E., Aguirre, A.: ENACT: development, operation, and quality assurance of trustworthy smart IoT systems. In: Software Engineering Aspects of Continuous Development and New Paradigms of Software Production and Deployment: First International Workshop, DEVOPS 2018, vol. 11350, p. 112. Springer, Heidelberg, 5–6 Mar 2018 (2019)

35. Mackey, T.: Building open source security into agile application builds. Netw. Secur. **2018**(4), 5–8 (2018)

36. Mansfield-Devine, S.: DevOps: finding room for security. Netw. Secur. **2018**(7), 15–20 (2018)

37. Michener, J., Clager, A.: Mitigating an oxymoron: compliance in a DevOps environments. In: 2016 IEEE 40th Annual Computer Software and Applications Conference (COMPSAC), vol. 1, pp. 396–398. IEEE (2016)

38. Rahman, A., Williams, L.: Software security in DevOps: synthesizing practitioners' perceptions and practices. In: 2016 IEEE/ACM International Workshop on Continuous Software Evolution and Delivery (CSED), pp. 70–76. IEEE (2016)

39. Raj, A., Kumar, A., Pai, S., Gopal, A.: Enhancing security of docker using Linux hardening techniques. In: 2016 2nd International Conference on Applied and Theoretical Computing and Communication Technology (iCATccT), pp. 94–99. IEEE (2016)

40. Rios, E., Iturbe, E., Mallouli, W., Rak, M.: Dynamic security assurance in multi-cloud DevOps. In: 2017 IEEE Conference On Communications And Network Security (CNS), pp. 467–475. IEEE (2017)

41. Schoenen, S., Mann, Z.Á., Metzger, A.: Using risk patterns to identify violations of data protection policies in cloud systems. In: Braubach, L., Murillo, J.M., Kaviani, N., Lama, M., Burgueño, L., Moha, N., Oriol, M. (eds.) ICSOC 2017. LNCS, vol. 10797, pp. 296–307. Springer, Cham (2018). https://doi.org/10.1007/978-3-319-91764-1_24

42. Thanh, T., Covaci,S., Magedanz. T., Gouvas, P., Zafeiropoulos, A.: Embedding security and privacy into the development and operation of cloud applications and services. In: 2016 17th International Telecommunications Network Strategy and Planning Symposium (NETWORKS), pp. 31–36. IEEE (2016)

43. Torkura, K.A., Sukmana, M.I.H., Cheng, F., Meinel, C.: Cavas: Neutralizing application and container security vulnerabilities in the cloud native era. In: Beyah, R., Chang, B., Li, Y., Zhu, S. (eds.) SecureComm 2018. LNICSSITE, vol. 254, pp. 471–490. Springer, Cham (2018). https://doi.org/10.1007/978-3-030-01701-9_26

44. Ullah, F., Raft, A., Shahin, M., Zahedi, M., Babar, M.: Security support in continuous deployment pipeline. In: Proceedings of 21th International Conference on Evaluation of Novel Approaches to Software Engineering, 12 p. Cornell University Archive (2017)

45. SynopsysSoftware: BSIMM12.explanation of the activities. https://www.bsimm.com/framework/governance/compliance-and-policy.html

46. Luz, W.P., Pinto, G., Bonifácio, R.: Adopting DevOps in the real world: a theory, a model, and a case study. J. Syst. Softw. **157**, 110384 (2019)

47. Rafi, S., Yu, W., Akbar, M.A., Alsanad, A., Gumaei, A.: Prioritization based taxonomy of DevOps security challenges using PROMETHEE. IEEE Access **8**, 105426–105446 (2020)

48. SynopsysSoftware: BSIMM12 Digest:The CISO's Guide to Next-Gen AppSec. https://www.synopsys.com/software-integrity/resources/ebooks/ciso-guide-modern-appsec.html

Short Papers

Errors in the Process of Modeling Business Processes

Norbert Gronau(⊠) 🆔

University of Potsdam, Hedy-Lamarr-Platz, 14482 Potsdam, Germany
ngronau@lswi.de

Abstract. Process models are the basic ingredient for many attempts to improve business processes. The graphical depiction of otherwise not observable behavior in an enterprise is one of the most important techniques in the digital society. They help to enable decision making in the design of processes and workflows. Nevertheless it is not easy to correctly model business processes. Some approaches try to detect errors by an automated analysis of the process model. This contribution focuses on the creation of the first model from scratch. Which errors occur most frequently and how can these be avoided?

Keywords: Business process modeling · Errors in modeling · Process of modeling

1 Introduction

Business process management strives for efficient use of resources to create value and benefits for internal and external customers while meeting time, cost, quality and satisfaction goals [1]. For the graphical representations of processes methods like BPMN [2] or EPC [3] are used. These are followed by rules for the creation of process models, whose compliance can also be enforced. However, the modeler has the freedom to deviate from them. Also an understanding of the concept of modeling is necessary. Therefore especially people unexperienced in process modeling have difficulties to find the appropriate level of abstraction, the right shapes and edges to express what should be expressed and so on.

A successful implementation of business process modeling in the organization needs not only avid readers of business process models but also as many people as are available to create these models. Experts are rare and expensive. Consultants leave the company. Software solutions can store the models but not the stories behind the models. So it is desirably to have laymen and laywomen which are able to model business processes without too many mistakes. In the huge body of knowledge created by the research community on business process modeling there are seldom any mentions of the errors which can occur during the process of process modeling.

There this contribution starts. We want to know where novices in process modeling are making mistakes and—ideally—why. This paper covers some earlier attempts to distinguish errors in process modeling. We also try to pinpoint these errors to certain

© Springer Nature Switzerland AG 2022
B. Shishkov (Ed.): BMSD 2022, LNBIP 453, pp. 221–229, 2022.
https://doi.org/10.1007/978-3-031-11510-3_13

steps in the process of process modeling. We have to mention that there is not a single "right" model of a business process. Abstractions can be made in different ways, and choices what to include at what level of detail, and what not to include can be done in different ways, and still be right. So there is not a single 'right model'. Therefore we had to be careful what an error is and what a wrong model consists of. To overcome this deficit we concentrate in this contribution on basic choices of the modeler like choosing the right symbols, edges, naming and joining.

To answer the research question mentioned above we conducted an experiment with 85 undergraduate students at a German university. The results show what typical errors are and state some hypotheses why these mistakes are made. In an outlook we propose some directions for further investigation.

2   The process of Process Modeling

"The process of modeling is most likely more important ... than the final models" [4]

Process modeling has to be disciplined, standardized and consistent to facilitate process visibility for a heterogeneous group of stakeholders (from the CXO to the end-user). It has to be able to provide a bridge between IT capabilities and business requirements [4]. Soffer et al. [5] distinguish between the forming of a mental model of the domain by the modeler and the mapping of the mental model to modeling constructs. Pinggera et al. [6] define the process of process modeling consisting of three phases:

Comprehension. In this phase a modeler tries to understand the requirements to be modeled as well as the model that has been created so far. Consequently, she fills her working memory with knowledge stemming from the requirements and the process model itself. The amount of information stored in working memory depends on the modeler's abilities and her knowledge organization.

Modeling. The modeler uses the information acquired and stored in her working memory now to adapt the process model. The number of modeling steps depend from the utilization of the modeler's working memory influences. If these are insufficient the modeler has to revisit the requirements for acquiring more information.

Reconciliation. After the modeling phase, modelers reorganize the process model (e.g., renaming of activities) and utilize the process model's secondary notation (e.g., notation of layout, typographic cues) to enhance the process model's understandability [3, 7]. However, the number of reconciliation phases in the process of process modeling is influenced by a modeler's ability of placing elements correctly when creating them, alleviating the need for additional layouting. Furthermore, the factual use of secondary notation is subject to the modeler's personal style [7]. The improved understandability supports the comprehension phase of the subsequent iteration, as the process model becomes more comprehensible for the modeler when coming back to it [7]. In particular, during the subsequent comprehension phase the modeler has to identify the part of the model to work on next. A better laid out model helps identifying a suitable area of the model, causing less distraction and therefore enables the modeler to store more information in working memory that can be incorporated in the process model. Another approach to describe the process of process modeling was attempted by Krogstie [8]. He distinguishes a preparation phase, a constant cycle of model expansion and model consolidation, followed by a phase of suspension when modeling stops.

From the approaches mentioned above the following process model of process modeling was derived, using PMDL [1] (Fig. 1).

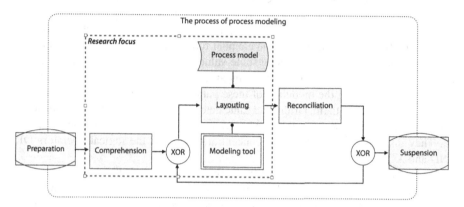

Fig. 1. The process of process modeling.

We focus in our research described in this paper on the steps to create a first process model, without further reconciliation.

3 Error Detection in Business Process Models

There are numerous errors that can occur in business process models. There are syntactical, semantical and pragmatic errors. You can find errors in data representation, process representation, and stakeholder representation in process models. There are consistency errors within the models, and errors relating the models to the system. These all are different in how easy they are to detect, and how easy they are to solve. Some could be detected automatically, some not.

Kherbouche et al. propose an approach to automate the checking of some structural errors such as deadlocks, livelocks, and multiple terminations in BPMN process models based on model checking [2] or on transferring the model into a Prolog structure [9]. Vanderfeesten et al. [10] investigate the question whether errors appear by chance in a process model, or if there is some way to use business process metrics to predict the error probability using 600 EPC models from a software vendor.

Oca et al. [11] conducted a systematic literature review of studies on business process **modeling quality**. Hornung et al. [12] developed a recommender system to improve the modeling process in the modeling tool. Other related work focus on improving the understanding of prior created process models [13].

The quality of process models encompass syntactic, semantic and pragmatic criteria [8]. While pragmatic criteria are difficult to judge, syntactic and semantic criteria can be used to assess the quality of a business process model. Krogstie provides a comprehensive list of quality measures for business models, but there is no attention to the quality of the modeling process itself.

Pfeiffer and Niehaves [14] call the graphical arrangements of model elements and their connections among each other **model element structure**. The actual meaning of the modeling constructs in the application domain is called **terminological structure**. Gruhn and Laue see some error patterns in EPC models like identical elements which lead to unnecessary complexity (4 patterns), contradictory labeling of elements which lead to an impossible flow through the system (3 patterns), a mismatch between the allowed number of elements prior to an element further down and the actual number of elements depicted (1 pattern), missing some values in the data range while checking a number (1 pattern) and using the wrong element for expressing a condition (one pattern). But instead of avoiding the modeling of these patterns in the first place the authors try to automatically detect them. Gruhn and Laue detect error patterns similar to the GOTO programming in software engineering when control flow blocks are not properly nested [9]. They distinguish several pattern concentrating around the logical operators OR, AND and XOR.

Especially a BPM project spanning more than one site needs the support of dozens of modelers to ensure a comparable level of model quality [15]. Claes et al. note that the complexity of the process model and the modelers competence are the major factors concerning process model quality. They tried to improve the process of modeling by giving more structure, movement and speed [15]. Claes et al. used an experimental setting to record the interaction between test persons and the modeling tool for a given description which had to be modeled as a simple BPMN process. Their experiment focused on the depiction of the model with a tool and not on the comprehension phase. Small BPMN models are easy to supervise but many types of errors will not be made with a simple example. Thereby there is a a chance that not all errors that are typically made in real-world situations, which are almost always complex, could be generated.

In our contribution we do not focus on errors which can be identified automatically. We also do not list errors in wrong representation of real world elements in model elements nor the wrong degree of detailing. We solely focus on the step from the first comprehension of the real world extract to the first usage of the elements of the modeling language.

4 Empirical Study - The Experiment

The text of the task for the test persons is shown as following:.

In a snowboard production, the raw material is first brought from the warehouse to the buffer in front of machine 3 by the warehouse clerk Ralf. The machine operator Shakira is informed about the delivered material and then starts manufacturing the snowboards. At her machine, the edges of the snowboards are cut off. To do this, Shakira places the snowboard raw material in the machine and releases the corresponding cutting program in the CNC programming unit of the machine. After 4 minutes, the cutting is done. Shakira places the finished cut board on the pickup pile.

Ralf or another warehouse operator then picks up the finished cut board and brings it to the central waiting buffer.

As soon as Dina, the machine operator of machine 4, gives a signal, one of the warehouse operators brings a finished cut board to machine 4. Here the shaping of the board takes place. Each board must remain in the machine for 8 minutes and is then placed on the cooling stack by Dina. From there, a warehouse worker picks it up on occasion and takes it to another hall for packing.

Please represent the following facts in a process model. Use __process interfaces,__ __tasks, information systems, roles__ and __physical objects__. Consider only the process section of manufacturing.

All participants was given an introduction into process modeling and into the modeling technique to use. All participants of the experiment had two weeks to compete their assignment. There was no limitation for the test persons, which tools they should use to depict the process model. So the results spanned very different process models from drawings on checkered paper to printouts from full-fledged modeling tools (see Fig. 2).

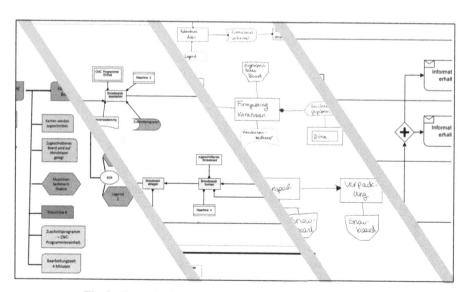

Fig. 2. Examples for process models from different test persons.

All process models were graded by the same process expert to avoid the influence of different judgments. When there were more objects identified from the text and depicted, there was no deduction.

The process models were graded in the following manner: It was counted how many of the necessary model elements (tasks, roles, physical objects, process interfaces and information systems) actually made it into the model. Then the naming of all objects in the model was judged. If for instance the name of a person was used instead of the name of the role, this was considered as a mistake. Another mistake occurred, when the task was not properly named. For the naming an overall grade was given from 0 (no naming or nearly all wrong) to 100 (all elements correctly named).

The use of another modeling technique as proposed was not leading to a lesser grading. On the level of investigation here the step from the real world extract to one modeling technique seems to be as difficult as to another one.

Finally the joining of the model elements was graded. Were the correct edges used? Had the edges between the tasks arrows to indicate the control flow? Were there elements without edges? Were the correct elements joint together (e.g. an information system cannot be joined directly with a role).

5 Results

Performing the experiment we want to address the following questions:

- Are there modeling concepts which are easier to grasp then other?
- Are there more mistakes in the naming of elements or in the correct joining?

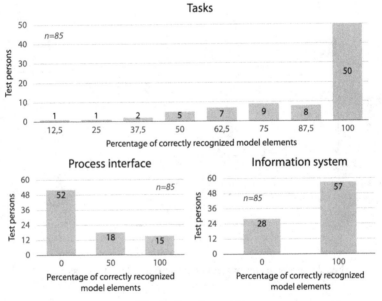

Fig. 3. Results, part 1.

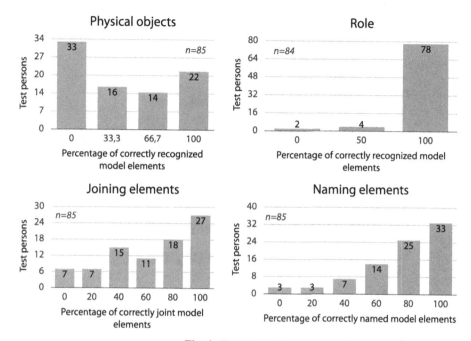

Fig. 4. Results, part 2.

Figures 3 and 4 show the detailed results concerning the elements used in the process models. Each graph is to be read in the following way: On the x-axis the percentage of correct model elements is shown and on the y-axis the number of test persons is shown, which achieved exactly this percentage. 50 of the 85 participants were able to recognize all tasks in the original text, while only 4 participants were not even able to recognize half of the required elements correctly. The latter is called "halfway results" because it gives us an estimate how many persons are able to create a model that is at least more than 50% a correct depiction of the reality.

In Fig. 4 we see that the results of correct joining and naming are not evenly distributed. More test persons than not were able to correctly join and name the elements of the process model.

Figure 5 shows a summary of the key figures "Overall correct modeling" and "Halfway modeling" compared to the elements used in the process model. It can be seen that process model elements like role, task and information system (in declining order) are more easily to be recognized by the participants than physical objects and process interfaces. While a process interface is a purely theoretical concept without representation in reality it is not easy to explain why physical objects pose much more problems for modeling beginners than other objects in process models.

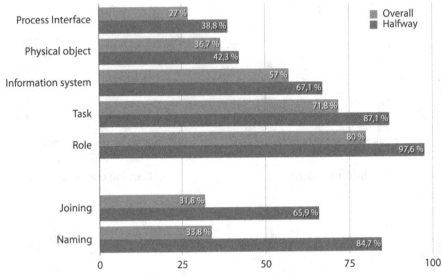

Fig. 5. Some modeling key figures.

6 Summary and outlook

Is it very complicated to create a somehow appropriate process model from scratch after 15 min of instruction? No, it is not. The halfway figures in our experiment show that nearly 85% of the participants were able to name many relevant model elements and two thirds of them were even able to use the correct joining edges. So our experiment has shown that business process modeling is feasible for the majority of business workers today.

Is there an ideal way to create a first process model from a real world description? Perhaps not. All resulting models will be less than perfect. Therefore modeling editors which suggest improvements for the first model or detect errors automatically and inform the user in a decent manner make a lot of sense.

There are a lot of aspects we didn't cover in our work. We did not distinguish between different groups of participants concerning education, age or gender. Also we did not try to segment the process of modeling by nudging the participants to use tools which would help them to create besser models. One of these tools might be a table in which all occurring model elements from the text can be filled in. We also did not investigate whether this intervention would have different grades of improvement with participants with different backgrounds.

Another research question we were not able to answer is the psychology of creating an intellectual concept of an element of reality. This seems to be the core of modeling and has to be further investigated.

References

1. Gronau, N.: Business Process Management in Industry and Administration, 3rd ed. Berlin (2022) (in German)
2. Kherbouche, O.M., Ahmad, A., Basson, H.: Detecting structural errors in BPMN process models. In: 2012 15th International Multitopic Conference (INMIC), pp. 425–431. IEEE (Dec 2012)
3. Mendling, J., Neumann, G., van der Aalst, W.: Understanding the occurrence of errors in process models based on metrics. In: Meersman, R., Tari, Z. (eds.) On the Move to Meaningful Internet Systems 2007: CoopIS, DOA, ODBASE, GADA, and IS, pp. 113–130. Springer Berlin Heidelberg, Berlin, Heidelberg (2007). https://doi.org/10.1007/978-3-540-76848-7_9
4. Rosemann, M.: Potential pitfalls of process modeling: part A. Bus. Process Manag. J. 12(2), 249–254 (2006). https://doi.org/10.1108/14637150610657567
5. Soffer, P., Kaner, M., Wand, Y.: Towards understanding the process of process modeling: theoretical and empirical considerations. In: Proc. ER-BPM' 11, LNBIP 99, pp. 357–369 (2012)
6. Pinggera, J., et al.: Tracing the process of process modeling with modeling phase diagrams. In: Daniel, F., Barkaoui, K., Dustdar, S. (eds.) Business Process Management Workshops: BPM 2011 International Workshops, Clermont-Ferrand, France, August 29, 2011, Revised Selected Papers, Part I, pp. 370–382. Springer Berlin Heidelberg, Berlin, Heidelberg (2012). https://doi.org/10.1007/978-3-642-28108-2_36
7. Petre, M.: Why looking isn't always seeing: readership skills and graphical programming. Commun. ACM 33–44 (1995)
8. Krogstie, J.: Quality of business process models. In: Krogstie, J. (ed.) Quality in Business Process Modeling, pp. 53–102. Springer International Publishing, Cham (2016). https://doi.org/10.1007/978-3-319-42512-2_2
9. Gruhn, V., Laue, R.: Detecting common errors in event-driven process chains by label analysis. Enterprise Modeling and Information Systems Architectures (EMISAJ) 6(1), 3–15 (2011)
10. Vanderfeesten, I., Cardoso, J., Mendling, J., Reijers, H.A., Van der Aalst, W.: Quality metrics for business process models. BPM and Workflow Handbook 144, 179–190 (2007)
11. Oca, I.M.-M., Snoeck, M., Reijers, H.A., Rodríguez-Morffi, A.: A systematic literature review of studies on business process modeling quality. Inf. Soft. Technol. (2014). https://doi.org/10.1016/j.infsof.2014.07.011
12. Hornung, T., Koschmider, A., Lausen, G.: Recommendation based process modeling support: Method and user experience. In: International Conference on Conceptual Modeling, pp. 265–278. Springer, Berlin, Heidelberg (2008)
13. Figl, K., Laue, R.: Cognitive complexity in business process modeling. In: International Conference on Advanced Information Systems Engineering, pp. 452–466. Springer, Berlin, Heidelberg (2011)
14. Pfeiffer, D., Niehaves, B.: Evaluation of conceptual models – a structuralist approach. In: Proceedings of the 13th European Conference on Information Systems, Information Systems in a Rapidly Changing Economy. ECIS 2005, Regensburg (2005)
15. Claes, J., et al.: Tying process model quality to the modeling process: the impact of structuring, movement, and speed. In: International Conference on Business Process Management, pp. 33–48. Springer, Berlin, Heidelberg (2012)

Use Cases for Augmented Reality Applications in Enterprise Modeling: A Morphological Analysis

Fabian Muff[(✉)] and Hans-Georg Fill

Research Group Digitalization and Information Systems, University of Fribourg,
Fribourg, Switzerland
{fabian.muff,hans-georg.fill}@unifr.ch

Abstract. With the more-widespread availability and cost effectiveness of advanced computer vision technologies, first attempts have
recently been made for applying augmented reality in enterprise modeling. Despite these first steps, a systematic analysis of the potential
opportunities of this technology for enterprise modeling has so far not
been conducted. Therefore, we describe in this paper the results of a
morphological analysis that has been performed in a series of expert
workshops for deriving according use cases. Based on the technological
dimensions of augmented reality and the traditional dimensions of enterprise modeling, we show the potential of this combination by means of
three selected use cases.

Keywords: Enterprise modeling · Augmented reality · Use cases

1 Introduction

Enterprise modeling is a widely-used method in business and information systems engineering [19]. Its goal is to capture and analyze the knowledge of an
enterprise by reverting to conceptual models. By using such models, the knowledge of domain experts can be formally represented [3,5]. A traditional limitation
of enterprise modeling originates from the necessary formal knowledge acquisition, also referred to as the knowledge acquisition bottleneck [10]. In many cases,
models are created by experts manually. This in turn requires prior experience by
the experts with enterprise modeling. Thus, for further lowering the barriers to
engage in enterprise modeling, the vision of enterprise modeling as an *everyday
business practice* that does not require specific know-how has been formulated
by Sandkuhl et al. [16].

One approach that could make enterprise modeling more accessible for non-
modeling experts is the use of augmented reality (AR) [12]. AR is a technology
for embedding virtual objects and information into the user's field of view by
using different sensors. This sensor data can then be used to enhance the acquisition, analysis and application of enterprise models in various ways. In the literature, already some approaches for combining augmented reality with enterprise

© Springer Nature Switzerland AG 2022
B. Shishkov (Ed.): BMSD 2022, LNBIP 453, pp. 230–239, 2022.
https://doi.org/10.1007/978-3-031-11510-3_14

modeling have been described [4,11,17]. However, no systematic elaboration of potential use cases has so far been conducted. Therefore, the research question that we aim to address in this paper is 'Which use cases can be derived theoretically for combining enterprise modeling and augmented reality?'. For answering this question, we will present selected results of a morphological analysis [23], that revealed interesting use cases for enterprise modeling in the area of classical augmented reality, AR for the elicitation and transfer of knowledge from and to the real world, and AR for creative collaboration.

The remainder of the paper is structured as follows. In Sect. 2 we outline the foundations of augmented reality and related work. In Sect. 3 we explain the morphological analysis as our research methodology and in Sect. 4 we will discuss the selected use cases. The paper ends with a conclusion in Sect. 5.

2   Foundations

In this section we briefly present the foundations of augmented reality for achieving a common understanding. Further, we investigate the state-of-the-art in related work for combining enterprise modeling and augmented reality.

2.1   Augmented Reality

Augmented reality is a technology that allows virtual images generated by a computer to be embedded in the real environment [22]. A commonly-used definition of AR is given by Azuma [2]. He describes AR as a technology that combines the real and virtual world and is interactive in real time. This also involves generating a three-dimensional reference of virtual and real objects based on interactions.

With the help of sensors, a superimposition of the real and the virtual world can be achieved, while the real environment can still be perceived. This perception of the environment is one of the strengths of augmented reality applications. Out of the information that we receive from the different sensors, it is not just possible to draw conclusions about the alignment of the real and the virtual world. We can also reason about the contextual situation of the user [13]. The output of information can be of visual, acoustic, or haptic nature. Typically, the output in AR is presented through visual means. Therefore, a *Head Mounted Display* (HMD) or a mobile output device such as a smartphone or tablet is used.

2.2   Previous Work on AR and Enterprise Modeling

The application of augmented reality has been explored in various fields. Recent examples include personal information systems, industrial and military applications, medical applications, AR for entertainment, or AR for the workplace [21].

In respect to AR and enterprise modeling, the already mentioned advantage of the perception of the user's environment comes into focus. Since the data from the AR sensors permits to reason about a user's context, a wide range of potential applications opens up. For example, enterprise modeling and AR could be joined for the real-time elicitation of business processes, the mapping of real-world entities to models, or for remote collaborative modeling.

Metzger et al. [11] designed and implemented a system for interacting with virtual process models by using smart glasses. Their approach permits to create and modify event-driven process chain models in augmented reality while executing a process. Thereafter, the documented processes can be used for instruction and training purposes. The presented use case is in the air conditioning and heating sector, where a runtime modeling system based on HMD AR could help technicians increase the quality of service.

Seiger et al. [17] presented the *HoloFlows* prototype to use HMDs for augmented reality for simplifying the modeling and configuration of basic *Internet of Things* (IoT) workflows. The approach eases the modeling of standard IoT processes by using AR. The use case domain is home/building automation. A related direction has been pursued by Ariano et al. [1]. They present a use case for smartphone-based AR home automation.

Grambow et al. [7] propose a method for integrating context-aware AR into intelligent business processes to support and guide manufacturing staff in their duties. As use case they showed a machine modification scenario in an industrial context where the process of adding a component to a computer is guided in AR based on an annotated BPMN process [7].

Similarly, Gronau and Grum [8] presented an integration of AR technologies in process modeling based on the existing *Knowledge Modeling Description Language* (KMDL). Thereby, additional information about a process step can be visualized at the location where the task takes place. They presented three use cases in the area of business process modeling where non-transparent processes can be supported by showing static or dynamic information about the process in augmented reality during execution.

Rehring et al. [15] presented an approach for supporting decision making about enterprise architecture (EA). The presented prototype lets the user visualize multi-dimensional enterprise architecture models in HMD-based AR to better understand the different layers of the model. The user can interact with the model by means of hand gestures or voice commands. They showed a use case for making decisions based on AR enterprise architecture models.

In summary, most of the previous approaches concentrate on a particular scenario and show the feasibility of their concepts in some use case. However, a systematic elaboration of upcoming potentials and opportunities by combining augmented reality and enterprise modeling has so far not been conducted.

3   Research Methodology

For the systematic derivation of potential use cases that combine augmented reality and enterprise modeling, we revert to a *morphological analysis* as research methodology. Its modern form of general morphological analysis has been proposed by Zwicky [23]. He describes morphological research as a possibility of seeing and recognizing connections in the totality of material objects, phenomena, ideas and conceptions, as well as a human activity for constructive creation.

In a previous paper, Grum and Gronau [9] had used the methodology of morphological analysis by presenting a morphological schema for bi-directional AR modeling. However, their morphological analysis focused more on the modeling activity itself and not on the derivation of new use cases like in our work. For the derivation of our morphological schema, we conducted expert workshops as an additional research methodology [18]. In three workshops with five experts, the morphological schema, as well as the use cases proposed in the next section were derived.

4   Use Cases for AR in Enterprise Modeling

For the derivation of new use cases in the area of enterprise modeling and augmented reality we designed two morphological schemes – see Fig. 1. The morphological schemes represent the two areas AR and enterprise modeling as *origins*. These are refined into *parameter dimensions*. Each of the dimensions has different characteristics, denoted as *values*. The dimensions and the according values were defined at the beginning of the workshops by analyzing the properties of the two origins.

Origin	Dimension	Values			
AR	GPS Position	Yes	No ◆○▲		
	Indoor Position	Yes	No ◆○▲		
	Relative Position	Yes ◆○▲	No		
	Orientation	User / Device ◆○▲	Device Orientation		
	Eye Tracking	Yes	No ◆○▲		
	Type of Device	HMD ◆○▲	Tablet	Smartphone	Artificial Lenses
	Audio Input	Yes ◆○▲	No		
	Audio Output	Yes ◆○▲	No		
	Acceleration Data	Yes ◆○▲	No		
	Depth Camera	Yes ◆○▲	No		
	Camera	Yes ◆○▲	No		
	Gesture Recognition	Yes ◆○▲	No		
	3D Controllers	Yes	No ◆○▲		
	Internet Connectivity	Yes ◆○▲	No		
	Collaboration	Yes ◆○▲	No		
Enterprise Modeling	Level	Strategic Level ◆	Business Process Level ○	IT Level ▲	
	Knowledge Elicitation	Formal ◆○▲	Semi-Formal ◆○▲		
	Simulation	Yes ◆○▲	No ◆○▲		
	Human Understanding	Expert Level ◆○▲	Laymen Level ◆○▲		
	Machine Processing	Yes ◆○▲	No ◆○▲		
	State	As-Is ◆○▲	To-Be ◆○▲		

Fig. 1. Morphological schema for the different perspective dimensions: strategic perspective (◆), business process perspective (○), and IT perspective (▲)

4.1   Description of the Solution Space

For the origin *augmented reality*, we included the dimensions visible in the upper part of Fig. 1, which are commonly found in state-of-the-art AR devices.

For the origin enterprise modeling, we first specified the major focus of a solution in terms of the *perspective* [6]. Possible values are the *Strategic Perspective*, e.g., including business models, performance indicator models, capability models, or product models. Second, the *Business Process Perspective*, e.g., comprising business process models, organizational models, or skill models. And finally, the *IT Perspective*, e.g., including IT service models, IT Architecture Models, or SLA Models. In addition, we defined the remaining enterprise modeling dimensions visible in the lower part of Fig. 1. By combining different values across dimensions, an enormous number of total combinations is possible. The combination of all possible values shown in Fig. 1, would yield a total of 6.291.456 solutions. Since an analysis of such a high number of solutions is not feasible in practice, we limited the solution space.

4.2   Limiting the Solution Space

For the origin *augmented reality*, we limited the origin to the use of head-mounted displays (HMD). In particular, we considered only the characteristics of the popular Microsoft HoloLens[1]. This excludes by default the use of GPS positions, indoor positions, eye tracking and 3D controllers – see upper part of Fig. 1.

These dimensions are thus held constant and thereby reduce the number of possible solutions. For the origin *enterprise modeling*, we chose to analyze the values of the perspective dimension separately. Thereby, we keep one perspective constant and vary only the remaining dimensions. This resulted in the reduced solution space as shown by the colored signs in Fig. 1.

With the restriction to the AR Hololens for the first origin and to the three perspectives in the second origin, the total number of possibilities is reduced to 96 combinations. In the following sections we will present the outcome of our workshops, in which we analyzed these combinations and derived new use cases for the combination of EM and AR. Due to the limitations of space we will restrict this to three selected use cases.

Each *Perspective* can profit in a different way from AR. In the *Strategic Perspective* remote or on-site collaboration without any additional equipment can be enabled. For example, strategic white boards and post-its are no longer required. In the *Business Process Perspective* AR can be used for the elicitation and transfer of knowledge from and to the real world. Last, the *IT-Perspective* can profit from classical AR by augmenting real objects with additional information that would not be visible for the user without AR. In the following we will look at an example use case on each level that could profit from AR.

---

[1] https://www.microsoft.com/en-us/hololens.

4.3 Exemplary Use Case for the Strategic Perspective

In the first expert workshop, the *Perspective* dimension has been set to the *Strategic Perspective*. In the following we describe a use case for the collaborative modeling of a *Business Model Canvas* (BMC) [14,20]. The advantage of using AR in this scenario is that multiple users can collaborate remotely or on-site, and physical tools are no longer needed because all BMC components can be visualized virtually.

Since there exists no formal definition of a BMC, the dimension of *Knowledge Elicitation* is set to *Semi-Formal*. There is no *Simulation* available for the classical BMC and the *Human Understanding* dimension is oriented towards laymen rather than expert modelers. The dimension *Machine Processing* is set to *Yes*. Further, a BMC is mostly about a desirable state in the future, which is why the value of the *State* dimension is *To-Be*. The values of the different dimensions for the strategic perspective are marked in Fig. 2 with blue rhombuses.

Origin	Dimension	Values			
AR HoloLens	GPS Position	Yes	No ♦○▲		
	Indoor Position	Yes	No ♦○▲		
	Relative Position	Yes ♦○▲	No		
	Orientation	User / Device ♦○▲	Device Orientation		
	Eye Tracking	Yes	No ♦○▲		
	Type of Device	HMD ♦○▲	Tablet	Smartphone	Artificial Lenses
	Audio Input	Yes ♦○▲	No		
	Audio Output	Yes ♦○▲	No		
	Acceleration Data	Yes ♦○▲	No		
	Depth Camera	Yes ♦○▲	No		
	Camera	Yes ♦○▲	No		
	Gesture Recognition	Yes ♦○▲	No		
	3D Controllers	Yes	No ♦○▲		
	Internet Connectivity	Yes ♦○▲	No		
	Collaboration	Yes ♦○▲	No		
Enterprise Modeling	Perspective	Strategic Perspective ♦	Business Process Perspective ○	IT Perspective ▲	
	Knowledge Elicitation	Formal	Semi-Formal ♦○▲		
	Simulation	Yes	No ♦○▲		
	Human Understanding	Expert Level ▲	Laymen Level ♦○		
	Machine Processing	Yes ♦○	No ▲		
	State	As-Is ▲	To-Be ♦○		

Fig. 2. Morphological schema for the use case on the strategic perspective (♦), the business process perspective (○) and the IT perspective (▲) with the restriction to the Microsoft HoloLens. (Color figure online)

Regarding the AR HoloLens origin, we exclude several dimensions marked from the upper part of Fig. 2. In terms of collaboration, multiple users have access to the same modeling canvas – dimension of *Collaboration*. Since the canvas could be virtually projected using an AR device, the participants can be in different locations for remote modeling and analysis. Therefore, the morphological schema is set to *Relative Positioning* and *User/Device* orientation. To retrieve information about the objects in the real environment and the movement of the user, *Acceleration Data*, *Depth Cameras* and normal *Cameras* are used in the HMD.

In respect to interacting with models, various options are available. Any part of the model could be manipulated through voice commands or hand gestures –

dimensions of *Gesture Recognition* and *Audio Input*. One could navigate through the model and modify parts of the model using a voice assistant – dimensions of *Audio Input/Output*. In addition, camera sensors may be used, e.g., for digitizing documents or notes and integrating them directly in the model – again the dimension of *Camera*. Additional information on the models - e.g., financial data - could be provided through external services using *Internet Connectivity*.

In summary, the use of AR for creating business model canvases could ease remote collaboration on new business models by letting users have the impression to be in the same room when brainstorming for new ideas. Additionally, such an approach would be more flexible, since there is no need for physical design tools anymore.

4.4   Exemplary Use Case for the Business Process Perspective

The *Business Process Perspective* includes all enterprise modeling activities related to business processes. The following example use case is about the elicitation, subsequent execution and monitoring of a future industrial manufacturing process using BPMN in combination with AR. Using AR in business processes can enable the elicitation and transfer of knowledge from and to the real world by perceiving the real world and by augmenting the environment with virtual information. The characteristics of the morphological schema for the business process perspective use case are marked as green circles in Fig. 2.

The knowledge elicitation is set to *Semi-Formal* as it is common for *BPMN* models. Further, the use case is not about *Simulation* and the dimension on *Human Understanding* is more on *Laymen Level* than for experts. The model can be processed by machines – dimension of *Machine Processing*. Since the use case is about the elicitation of a future process, the *State* dimension is *To-Be*.

Concerning the AR HoloLens origin, we exclude the same dimensions as in Sect. 4.3. For capturing the process, an expert uses the AR device. A scanned marker sets the origin and all positions are calculated relative to this. This relates to the dimension of *Relative Positioning* and to *User/Device* orientation and *Acceleration Data*. In addition, activities are recognized using camera sensors. This relates to the dimensions of *Camera* and *Depth Camera*. The user can define tasks of a process and label them as desired using a voice assistant and hand gestures – dimension of *Audio Input/Output* and *Gesture Recognition*. Further, correct sequences, control rules, information flows and responsibilities can be defined through voice commands. Furthermore, the work environment is captured by the AR sensors and objects such as machines or environment conditions are added to the model via annotations – again *Camera* and *Depth Camera*. Through semantic analysis of this information for the respective process step, additional actions or measures can be inferred and suggested to be included in the model – for example, workplace safety measures, see e.g. [13]. In this use case as well, the device needs an internet connection.

The captured process can now be used to support employees during real-time assistance during process execution. The user thereby receives visual or acoustic instructions about the current task. If a user needs hints about the information flow or the responsibilities, he can ask for them by voice commands and the according information will be visualized – *Audio Input* dimension. In addition, holographic overlays on objects are visualized, assuming they were defined during the process elicitation, e.g., through video recordings and object recognition. These show the user the exact procedure for accomplishing a specific task. For example, the movement of a wrench is displayed at the specified position in the form of a pre-recorded video.

Within the business process perspective, this use case shows numerous opportunities for enhancing process management by using AR. The main advantage over conventional approaches is certainly the direct elicitation and the transfer of knowledge from and to the real world.

4.5 Exemplary Use Case for the IT Perspective

The *IT Perspective* contains all enterprise models concerning IT-services and IT-infrastructure. In the following we considered a scenario where ArchiMate models of the hardware infrastructure are mapped to physical devices for conducting inspections. In such a scenario, the classic features of AR can provide added value by visualizing additional information about real-world objects that the user would not see otherwise. The according characteristics of the morphological schema for this use case are marked as red triangles in Fig. 2.

As in the two other perspectives, the dimension of *Knowledge Elicitation* is *Semi-Formal*. There is no *Simulation* and the dimension of *Human Understanding* is set to *Expert Level*, since the users must have a good understanding of IT-architecture modeling. In the use case there is no *Machine Processing*. Since the IT-architecture is already in place, the *State* is descriptive, and therefore this dimension is set to *As-Is*. In respect to the AR HoloLens origin, we exclude the same dimensions as in the two use cases above. For the use case, the user has to be at the physical location of the hardware infrastructure, e.g., a server room. Subsequently, the ArchiMate objects are mapped to the physical devices by means of *Relative Positioning* and the movements of the user are tracked with *User/Device* orientation and *Acceleration Data*. The sensors of the device capture the server racks and display the available information – dimension of *Depth* and normal *Camera*. The user can then select from a list the IT-services that are running on this server by means of hand gestures or voice command – dimensions of *Audio Input* and *Gesture Recognition*. The user may retrieve further details by using a voice assistant, i.e., *Audio Input/Output*. Further, she can inspect all ArchiMate levels for a particular device. By using gesture navigation and voice commands, the user can select the different views and perceive relations to other layers – again *Audio Input* and *Gesture Recognition*.

Further, sensors of the AR device can retrieve information about the environment and with the help of semantic reasoning, additional information can be inferred. Here, we assume that *Internet Connectivity* is required. For example, the system can provide information about heat clusters and the problem area is visualized via the AR device. The models can be visualized in AR for collaborating with other users and for discussing the model – dimension of *Collaboration*.

With this use case, technical experts in IT infrastructure may get a better overview of the whole system, including dependencies between physical components and software services running on them. Thus, problems and risks may be identified faster and the infrastructure can be optimized in the real environment, e.g., regarding heat conditions caused by particular services. Without the visualization in the real environment, perceiving such information can be very difficult, which is why AR could add some real value in this scenario.

5   Conclusion and Outlook

In this paper, we derived a variety of use cases by conducting a morphological analysis and workshops on combining augmented reality and enterprise modeling. In doing so, we have demonstrated the potential and possibilities of combining AR and enterprise modeling. Using the morphological analysis helped reduce bias and avoid the exclusion of options based on subjective reflections during the expert workshops. As examples, we have presented three selected use cases for the *Business Process Perspective*, the *Strategic Perspective* and the *IT Perspective*.

In the future we plan to derive further use cases with the help of industry experts and to derive the most important requirements for the implementation of these use cases. Further, we plan to implement some of the use cases in prototypical applications.

References

1. Ariano, R., Manca, M., Paternó, F., Santoro, C.: Smartphone-based augmented reality for end-user creation of home automations, Behav. Inf. Technol. 1–7 (2022). https://doi.org/10.1080/0144929X.2021.2017482
2. Azuma, R.T.: A survey of augmented reality. Presence: Teleoperators Virtual Environ. **6**(4), 355–385 (1997)
3. Cairó Battistutti, O., Bork, D.: Tacit to explicit knowledge conversion. Cogn. Process. **18**(4), 461–477 (2017). https://doi.org/10.1007/s10339-017-0825-6
4. Brunschwig, L., Campos-Lopez, R., Guerra, E., de Lara, J.: Towards domain-specific modelling environments based on augmented reality. In: 2021 IEEE/ACM 43rd International Conference on Software Engineering: New Ideas and Emerging Results (ICSE-NIER), pp. 56–60. IEEE (2021)
5. Fill, H.-G., Härer, F., Muff, F., Curty, S.: Towards augmented enterprise models as low-code interfaces to digital systems. In: Shishkov, B. (ed.) BMSD 2021. LNBIP, vol. 422, pp. 343–352. Springer, Cham (2021). https://doi.org/10.1007/978-3-030-79976-2_22
6. Frank, U.: Multi-perspective enterprise modeling: foundational concepts, prospects and future research challenges. Softw. Syst. Model. **13**(3), 941–962 (2012). https://doi.org/10.1007/s10270-012-0273-9
7. Grambow, G., Hieber, D., Oberhauser, R., Pogolski, C.: Leveraging augmented reality to support context- aware tasks in alignment with business processes. In: Proceedings of Virtual Reality International Conference (VRIC), vol. 21, no. 1, 17–20 (2021)

8. Gronau, N., Grum, M.: Integration of augmented reality technologies in process modeling - the augmentation of real world scenarios with the KMDL. In: Proceedings of the Seventh International Symposium on Business Modeling and Software Design, pp. 206–215. SCITEPRESS - Science and Technology Publications (2017)
9. Grum, M., Gronau, N.: Process modeling within augmented reality. In: Shishkov, B. (ed.) BMSD 2018. LNBIP, vol. 319, pp. 98–115. Springer, Cham (2018). https://doi.org/10.1007/978-3-319-94214-8_7
10. Hoppenbrouwers, S.J.B.A., Lucas, P.J.F.: Attacking the knowledge acquisition bottleneck through games-for-modelling. In: Proceedings of AISB 2009 Workshop "AI and Games", Edinburgh, April 2009
11. Metzger, D., Niemöller, C., Jannaber, S., Berkemeier, L., Brenning, L., Thomas, O.: The next generation? Design and implementation of a smart glasses-based modelling system. Enterp. Model. Inf. Syst. Archit. Int. J. Concept. Model. 13(18), 1–25 (2018)
12. Muff, F., Fill, H.: Initial concepts for augmented and virtual reality-based enterprise modeling. In: ER Demos and Posters 2021 - International Conference on Conceptual Modeling (ER 2021), vol. 2958, pp. 49–54. CEUR-WS (2021)
13. Muff, F., Fill, H.: A framework for context-dependent augmented reality applications using machine learning and ontological reasoning. In: AAAI Spring Symposium on Machine Learning and Knowledge Engineering for Hybrid Intelligence, vol. 3121. CEUR-WS (2022)
14. Osterwalder, A., Pigneur, Y., Clark, T.: Business Model Generation: A Handbook for Visionaries, Game Changers, and Challengers. Wiley, Hoboken (2010)
15. Rehring, K., Greulich, M., Bredenfeld, L., Ahlemann, F.: Let's get in touch - decision making about enterprise architecture using 3D visualization in augmented reality. In: HICSS Conference, pp. 1–10 (2019)
16. Sandkuhl, K., et al.: From expert discipline to common practice: a vision and research agenda for extending the reach of enterprise modeling. Bus. Inf. Syst. Eng. 60(1), 69–80 (2018)
17. Seiger, R., Kühn, R., Korzetz, M., Aßmann, U.: Holoflows: modelling of processes for the internet of things in mixed reality. Softw. Syst. Model. 20(5), 1465–1489 (2021)
18. Thoring, K., Müller, R.M., Badke-Schaub, P.: Workshops as a research method: guidelines for designing and evaluating artifacts through workshops. In: 53rd Hawaii International Conference on System Sciences, pp. 1–10 (2020)
19. Vernadat, F.: Enterprise modelling: research review and outlook. Comput. Ind. 122, 103265 (2020)
20. Wieland, M., Fill, H.: A domain-specific modeling method for supporting the generation of business plans. In: Modellierung 2020. LNI, vol. P-302, pp. 45–60. GI (2020)
21. Xue, L., Parker, C.J., McCormick, H.: A virtual reality and retailing literature review: current focus, underlying themes and future directions. In: tom Dieck, M.C., Jung, T. (eds.) Augmented Reality and Virtual Reality. PI, pp. 27–41. Springer, Cham (2019). https://doi.org/10.1007/978-3-030-06246-0_3
22. Zhou, F., Duh, H.B.L., Billinghurst, M.: Trends in augmented reality tracking, interaction and display: a review of ten years of ISMAR. In: International Symposium on Mixed and Augmented Reality, pp. 193–202. IEEE (2008)
23. Zwicky, F.: Morphologische Forschung: Wesen und Wandel materieller und geistiger struktureller Zusammenhänge. Schriftenreihe der Fritz-Zwicky-Stiftung, Baeschlin (1989)

On the Context-Aware Servicing of User Needs: Extracting and Managing Context Information Supported by Rules and Predictions

Boris Shishkov[1,2,3(✉)] and Marten van Sinderen[4]

[1] Institute of Mathematics and Informatics, Bulgarian Academy of Sciences, Sofia, Bulgaria
[2] Faculty of Information Sciences, University of Library Studies and Information Technologies, Sofia, Bulgaria
[3] Institute IICREST, Sofia, Bulgaria
b.b.shishkov@iicrest.org
[4] Faculty of Electrical Engineering, Mathematics and Computer Science, University of Twente, Enschede, The Netherlands
m.j.vansinderen@utwente.nl

Abstract. The desired context-aware servicing of user needs assumes adequately capturing the user situation, which in turn is often done using sensors. In most cases, the sensor-driven extraction of context information is done counting on pre-defined rules that concern Boolean expressions directly referring to data values for the sake of evaluating the user situation. Further, sensors would be of limited use when considering context indicators (such as intentions) that are not "physical". Inspired by those challenges, we address the training-data-driven extraction of context information, opting for considering Bayesian Modeling and particularly the Naïve Bayesian Classification Approach because it is: (i) effective as it concerns predictions that are based on training data; (ii) rarely misleading in comparatively "simple" cases, which holds for most real-life cases, as opposed to natural-science-related cases where numerous possible outcomes may apply to any situation; (iii) easily applicable in terms of hardware and software capabilities. Hence, we study the adequacy and usefulness of applying probabilistic approaches together with rules, in establishing and managing the extraction of context information that in turn is needed for the appropriate context-aware servicing of user needs.

Keywords: Context-awareness · User needs · User situation · Bayesian modeling

1 Introduction

Context-awareness [1] is receiving much attention in numerous application domains - from mobile health monitoring [2] to drone-driven monitoring in areas affected by disruptive events [3]. Information Systems (IS) incorporate context-awareness in order to automatically adapt to changes in their system and social environment. The increasing

© Springer Nature Switzerland AG 2022
B. Shishkov (Ed.): BMSD 2022, LNBIP 453, pp. 240–248, 2022.
https://doi.org/10.1007/978-3-031-11510-3_15

IS complexity demands such capabilities but at the same time careless design of context-awareness can introduce new risks because the services delivered by IS concern the context - it is possible that an IS derives a wrong conclusion regarding its context, e.g., due to faulty measurements, misinterpretation of the data, or incorrect reasoning based on the data; then those services would affect the context with possibly serious consequences (here the impact is not limited to users, but may extend to other elements of the context, such as machines, processes, and so on). Hence, we argue that it is important to have correctly functioning IS that are capable of properly and continuously establishing the context and adapting to it accordingly – this is adaptive service delivery and context-awareness is essentially related to it.

Extending previous work on a conceptual framework [4], this paper presents work-in-progress on improving context-aware servicing of user needs. What is left beyond our scope are adaptations that may concern system internal processes and public values [5]. Hence, we face the essential challenge of adequately capturing the **user situation**, such that **situation-specific services** can be provided accordingly. **Sensor technology** is of key importance in this regard [6]: in many cases sensors are capable of providing useful low-level data that in turn can go (in some cases) through fusion algorithms (because sometimes many sensors have to be used in combination and their output needs to be converged), interpretations, and so on, for the sake of extracting higher-level information that is useful for the system in adapting its behavior. We argue that what is to be taken into account with respect to the extraction of context information is as follows: (i) Data can be represented and communicated in different ways; (ii) The quality of data can be such that it does not allow reliable inference; (iii) Data can be about different domains which have to be semantically integrated.

We have identified two challenges in this regard:

- Challenge 1: The extraction of context information is not always possible with pre-defined rules (this is what is done in many cases) that use Boolean expressions; they directly refer to data values to evaluate user situations. Sometimes such rules would become too complex, would not be effective, or cannot be anticipated at design time.
- Challenge 2: We are to count on context indicators in establishing the user situation but this is not always a matter of "physical" things (that can be "easily" captured), such as vital signs, location, and so on; it is sometimes a matter of "mental" things, such as intentions and capturing such indicators is considered difficult.

In our view, **data analytics** [7] can be applied to develop algorithms for performing the extraction task based on *training data*. In some cases, this would not only replace or complement rules (referring to Challenge 1) but would also allow for capturing "non-physical" context indicators (referring to Challenge 2). Observing the current scientific literature, we would lean towards probabilistic approaches (in general), opting for considering Bayesian Modeling and particularly the **Naïve Bayesian Classification Approach** [8] because it is: **(i)** effective as it concerns *predictions that are based on training data*; **(ii)** *rarely misleading in comparatively "simple" cases*, which holds for most real-life cases, as opposed to natural-science-related cases where numerous possible outcomes may apply to any situation; **(iii)** *easily applicable* in terms of *hardware* and *software* capabilities. Hence, we study the adequacy and usefulness of applying probabilistic approaches together with rules, in establishing and managing the extraction of context information that in turn is needed for the appropriate context-aware servicing of user needs.

After providing relevant background information in Sect. 2, we will present in Sect. 3 an analysis that considers context indicators and corresponding capturing mechanisms. Our proposed solution directions will be outlined in Sect. 4 and we will conclude the paper in Sect. 5.

2 Background

As for the notion of "system", we refer to the SYSTEMICS conceptualization of Mario Bunge [9–11]:

$$C(\sigma) = \{x \in \Gamma | x \prec \partial\}$$
$$E(\sigma) = \{x \in \Gamma | x \notin C(\sigma) \land \exists y; y \in C(\sigma) \land (x \triangleright y \lor y \triangleright x)\}$$
$$S(\sigma) = \{\langle x, y \rangle | (x \triangleright y \lor y \triangleright x) \land (x, y \in C(\sigma) \lor (x \in C(\sigma) \land y \in E(\sigma)))\},$$

envisioning *composition* (C), *environment* (E), and *structure* (S) – see above. A system comprises *entities* and those entities are featuring the SYSTEM COMPOSITION. The way they are related among each other defines the SYSTEM STRUCTURE. Finally, the entities that are outside the system but interact with entities that are inside the system (driven by the system *goal*) represent the SYSTEM ENVIRONMENT. For the sake of brevity, we are not going to discuss those notions in more detail. What needs to be noted with regard to the current paper is that we use the term "context-aware system", envisioning either purely software systems (composed of software components), or IS ("information system" is a broader notion compared to "software system" because it reflects not only software entities but also hardware entities, human agents, and so on), or just organizational (human-centric) systems.

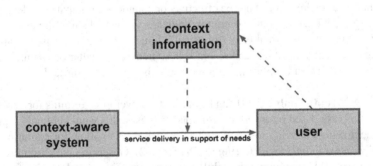

Fig. 1. A vision of context-aware servicing

In a' 19 paper, we have carried out a literature review [12] that was taken into account in our constructing a context-awareness conceptual framework [4]. Referring to it, we view a context-aware system as delivering services to users in support of corresponding user needs (see Fig. 1), adapting this to the user situation. In establishing it, it is essential to adequately extract and manage information that concerns the user. Hence, as the figure suggests, the context-aware service delivery counts on context information (see the dashed line at the central part of the figure). As mentioned above, this information concerns the user (see the dashed line at the right side of the figure) in the sense that user-related contextual details are used to establish the situation of the user.

As stated already, in the current paper we only consider the perspective of maximizing the user-perceived effectiveness (hence, adapting the delivered services to the situation of the user), and we are not focusing on service adaptations driven by desires to optimize system-internal processes and/or to conform to relevant public values.

Because of the limited scope of this paper, we are not providing further elaboration in the current section and we "step" on what was done in two previous papers [4, 12].

3   Context Indicators

According to Hincks: "Contextual indicators often (although not always) take the form of quantifiable variables which are used to help describe and measure wider social, environmental, economic, physical, and demographic contexts in which a particular phenomenon is operating" [13]. By "context indicators" we mean types of details that are relevant to possible situation types we are interested in. Take as an example the tele-health-monitoring of persons where two situation types are considered, namely: "Normal situation" and "Emergency situation". Then we could consider vital signs (such as blood pressure, pulse, and so on) reflected in corresponding values (captured at a point in time) as indicator for "what is going on" – in this case: whether the situation is normal or urgent.

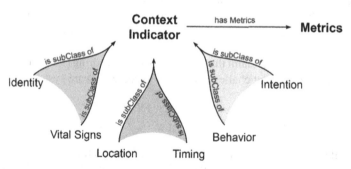

Fig. 2. Clustering context indicators

Inspired by our experience and not claiming exhaustiveness we have identified several key indicator types, namely: *identity*, *vital signs*, *location*, *timing*, *behavior*, and *intention*, visualizing this (using OWL notations [14]) – see Fig. 2.

Further, we have provided a clustering accordingly – see the three colored areas on the figure. The first cluster (from left to right) concerns things that characterize the user himself/herself, such as identity and vital signs. The second cluster concerns "environmental" (with regard to the user) features, such as location and timing. The third cluster concerns the physical/mental "activity" of the user, such as behavior and intention. Finally, these all are to be measurable things, such that we are able to "extract" values that would indicate for corresponding situations.

Hence, an important question is how to deal with those measurements. Our observation is that:

- There are many sensor-driven ways of establishing the identity of a person, for example: fingerprint/iris scanners, ID card readers, and so on. Then depending on who the user is, the context-aware system could adapt its behavior accordingly.
- There are blood pressure sensors, pulse sensors and other sensors that are helpful in vital-signs-related measurements, done for establishing the situation of the user.
- It is easy establishing the location of a person and/or time-stamping his/her activity, just counting on the location/timing services of the person's smartphone. Then the context-aware system could adapt its behavior based on the location of the user and/or taking into account the timing.
- Often it is possible capturing the behavior of a person by means of sensors – sensing that a person enters a gym, sensing that the person is sleeping, sensing that the person is using his/her smartphone, sensing that the person is typing, and so on. Sometimes it is even possible "measuring" the behavior of a person – for example, measuring the accuracy or stress in typing, by analyzing the keyboard/mouse pressings/movements. Then depending on the behavior type (and possibly also on the corresponding condition of the user) the context-aware system could adapt its behavior accordingly.
- Nevertheless, it would be much more difficult "measuring" intentions because sensors are mostly powerful in capturing "physical" things, such as the ones considered above.

Still, **intentions** are important in this regard because often the user situation is much related to what the user intends to do. Depending on this, we would have particular user needs that in turn would need to be addressed in a corresponding way by the context-aware system.

Hence, we reinforce our claim that capturing (and measuring) "mental" things, such as intentions, is an important challenge relevant to context-aware systems.

4 Solution Directions

Addressing the challenges that were stated in the Introduction and elaborated in the previous section, we assume that "mental" things, such as intentions, are hard to capture (and measure) by means of sensors and supported by rules that use Boolean expressions. Just to give an example: the blood pressure of a person is measured by means of sensors, and there is a simple rule that directs us – if the value is above a threshold, then the situation is considered "urgent"; otherwise, the situation is considered "normal". This would not work for "mental" things firstly because we have no sensors to capture/measure them (How to capture intentions?) and secondly, because "mental" things are not always straightforwardly relatable to user situations, which in turn means that rules using Boolean expressions cannot help (How could a laptop replacement intention work out if the person is running low on finances, for example?).

This draws our attention to **statistics**, taking into account that *anything dealing with the collection, processing, analysis, or interpretation of numerical data* belongs to the domain of statistics [15]. On top of that, we are interested in considering: (i) **probabilities**, acknowledging that very many current real-life processes are *probabilistic* (as opposed to *deterministic*) [16]; (ii) **current data analytics**, acknowledging the possibilities of today to acquire huge volumes of (sensor) data and derive classifications, clusterings, associations, and so on [7]. Finally, we consider **Bayesian Data Analysis** as an intersection of those influences, where *statistics, probabilities, and data analytics are brought together for the sake of predicting a situation* [17].

As mentioned and motivated in the Introduction, we opt for considering the **Naïve Bayesian Classification Approach** in this regard – this approach takes as a basis a number of attribute vectors $X_i = (x_{i1}, x_{i2}, .. x_{in})$; each vector depicts n measurements concerning n corresponding attributes (applied for each of the vectors X_i); there are m hypotheses considered with regard to this vector space, namely: Hypothesis 1 (C_1), Hypothesis 2 (C_2). Hypothesis m (C_m), called "classes"; finally, we know the *class* for each vector X_i; then the approach allows us to predict the *class* for each new vector $V = (v_1, v_2, .. v_n)$ for which v_i reflects attribute values concerning the same n attributes mentioned above [7, 8]. For the sake of brevity, we will not go in more detail concerning the approach. Moreover, we have discussed it as well as the corresponding *Bayes' theorem* in one of our previous papers [12].

Taking a CONCEPTUAL PERSPECTIVE, we *justify* the relevance of the approach as follows:

- We may consider the classes (see above) as reflections of corresponding user needs;
- We may assume that acquiring attribute values (that concern "other users") is realistic because in many cases we currently have technical/technological means of achieving this;
- We could therefore predict user needs based on such values, trusting the approach that in turn is based on the abovementioned theorem.

For the sake of ILLUSTRATION, we provide partial exemplification, considering a simple and popular example, namely the *AllElectronics* example, presented and discussed in [7] – see Fig. 3.

The figure depicts, with regard to 14 customers, 14 corresponding attribute-value vectors featuring values for the following four attributes: "age", "income", "student", and "credit_rating". It is depicted as well whether or not each of the 14 customers has purchased a computer – this points to two corresponding hypotheses - effectively H0 and "not H0", labelled as C_1 and C_2, respectively (so, we can see that the first customer has not purchased a computer, the second customer has not purchased a computer either, the third customer has purchased a computer, and so on).

The goal in our example is to classify the data tuple **X**: {**senior,high, no, fair**}. This is what we do (see below), applying the Naïve Bayesian Classification Approach.

According to the approach, we need to maximize $P(X|C_i) \times P(C_i)$, $i = 1, 2$ where $P(C_1) = P$ (buys_computer = yes); $P(C_2) = P$ (buys_computer = no); "P" stands for "probability".

age	income	student	credit_rating	Class: buys_computer
1 youth	high	no	fair	NO
2 youth	high	no	excellent	NO
3 middle_aged	high	no	fair	YES
4 senior	medium	no	fair	YES
5 senior	low	yes	fair	YES
6 senior	low	yes	excellent	NO
7 middle_aged	low	yes	excellent	YES
8 youth	medium	no	fair	NO
9 youth	low	yes	fair	YES
10 senior	medium	yes	fair	YES
11 youth	medium	yes	excellent	YES
12 middle_aged	medium	no	excellent	YES
13 middle_aged	high	yes	fair	YES
14 senior	medium	no	excellent	NO

Fig. 3. Class-labelled training tuples from the AllElectronics customer database [7]

Further: $P(X|C_1) = P(X \mid$ buys_computer=yes); $P(X|C_2) = P(X \mid$ buys_computer=no).

P(buys_computer=yes) = 9/14 = 0,643; P(buys_computer=no) = 5/14 = 0,357.

$P(X \mid$ buys_computer=yes) =

= P (age = senior | buys_computer=yes) x

x P (income = high | buys_computer=yes) x

x P (student = no | buys_computer=yes) x

x P (credit_rating = fair | buys_computer=yes) =

= 3/9 x 2/9 x 3/9 x 6/9 = 0,016.

$P(X \mid$ buys_computer=no) =

= P (age = senior | buys_computer=no) x

x P (income = high | buys_computer=no) x

x P (student = no | buys_computer=no) x

x P (credit_rating = fair | buys_computer=no) =

= 2/5 x 2/5 x 4/5 x 2/5 = 0,051

We need to maximize $P(X|C_i)$ x $P(C_i)$ => we compare:

(i) 0,016 x 0,643 = 0,010 and **(ii)** 0,051 x 0,357 = 0,018.

Since **(ii)** is bigger than **(i)** (that is because 0,018 > 0,010) we point to:

HYPOTHESIS C_2: buys_computer=no.

Said otherwise, the classifier predicts **buys_computer=no** for tuple **X**.

Imagine that the sales managers at the AllElectronics store anticipate particular user needs concerning those customers who would most probably purchase a computer and different user needs concerning those customers who most probably would not purchase a computer – the former would be treated with special attention and offered detailed information featuring the best computer offers while the latter would be "left" with the broad variety of items offered at the store. This actually means adapting the AllElectronics' "behavior" based on the user needs that are predicted using training data.

Thus, servicing user needs in a context-aware way is not only possible when establishing the user situation by means of sensors and applying rules accordingly but is also possible by means of data analytics and probabilistic modeling, when the user situation is predicted using training data.

5 Conclusions

Context-awareness essentially concerns adaptive service delivery, for which three adaptation perspectives are possible, viz. serving (i) user needs; (ii) system needs; and (iii) public values. Addressing (i) in the current paper, we have essentially focused on the goal of adequately capturing the user situation, such that situation-specific services can be provided accordingly, acknowledging the key importance of sensor technology + rules in this regard and identifying two challenges: (a) The extraction of context information is not always possible with pre-defined rules that use Boolean expressions; (b) Often capturing of such "mental" context indicators, such as intentions, is considered difficult.

We have put those challenges "against" our conceptual model featuring the context-aware servicing of user needs (which model is rooted in previous studies), considering on top of that context indicators, offering a relevant analysis and clustering.

On that basis, we have stated and justified a claim that the *Bayesian Data Analysis (BDA)* could be useful in some cases when it is possible to predict (using training data) the user needs. This is considered a helpful alternative in situations when using sensors poses limitations and/or when the extraction of (sensor-based) context information is not so easy supported by pre-defined rules.

BDA (and particularly the Naïve Bayesian Classification Approach) is capable of classifying a data tuple (featuring attribute values) with regard to pre-defined hypotheses (classes), by using the attribute values (and corresponding class "values") of other data tuples as training data and we see different classes as pointing to corresponding user needs. Hence, we are capable of PREDICTING user needs using as training data the "historic" data featuring previous users. We have partially illustrated this by means of a small example – we have considered the famous AllElectronics example.

The limitations of our work are three-fold:

- We have not conceptualized sufficiently our views to establish/elaborate in what situations sensors would be the best solution and in what situation predictions would be the best solutions.
- We have only considered a simple example where just two classes are considered (H0 and "not H0"), not addressing cases where the consideration of many hypotheses would be needed.

- We have not discussed the "probabilistic risk" behind the classifier's prediction – obviously "52% vs 48%" is different compared to "82% vs 18%" but the classifier does not offer such "sensitivity".

Hence, we plan as future work to: (1) study in depth in what situations it would be more appropriate to count on sensors and in what situations it would be more appropriate counting on predictions; (2) address situations featuring more hypotheses (classes); (3) carry out a case study for the sake of acquiring more empirical insight, related to our research.

References

1. Dey, A., Abowd, G., Salber, D.: A conceptual framework and a toolkit for supporting the rapid prototyping of context-aware applications. Hum.-Comput. Interact. **16**(2) (December) (2001)
2. Wegdam, M.: Awareness: a project on context aware mobile networks and services. In: Proc.: 14th Mobile & Wireless Communications Summit. EURASIP (2005)
3. Shishkov, B., Branzov, T., Ivanova, K., Verbraeck A.: Using drones for resilience: a system of systems perspective. In: Proc.: 10th International Conference on Telecommunications and Remote Sensing (ICTRS 2021). Association for Computing Machinery, New York, NY, USA (2021)
4. Shishkov, B. (ed.): BMSD 2021. LNBIP, vol. 422. Springer, Cham (2021). https://doi.org/10.1007/978-3-030-79976-2
5. Shishkov, B. (ed.): BMSD 2017. LNBIP, vol. 309. Springer, Cham (2018). https://doi.org/10.1007/978-3-319-78428-1
6. Kopják, J., Sebestyén, G.: Comparison of data collecting methods in wireless mesh sensor networks. In: IEEE 16th World Symposium on Applied Machine Intelligence and Informatics (SAMI), Kosice and Her-lany, Slovakia (2018)
7. Han, J., Kamber, M., Pei, J.: Data Mining: Concepts and Techniques, 3rd edn. Morgan Kaufmann Publ. Inc., San Francisco, CA, USA (2011)
8. Webb, G.I.: Naïve bayes. In: Sammut, C., Webb, G.I. (eds.) Encyclopedia of Machine Learning. Springer, Boston, MA, USA (2011)
9. Bunge, M.A.: Treatise on Basic Philosophy, vol. 4, A World of Systems. D. Reidel Publishing Company, Dordrecht.
10. Dietz, J.L.G.: Enterprise Ontology, Theory and Methodology. Springer, Heidelberg (2006)
11. Shishkov, B.: Designing Enterprise Information Systems: Merging Enterprise Modeling and Software Specification. Springer International Publishing, Cham (2020)
12. Shishkov, B. (ed.): BMSD 2019. LNBIP, vol. 356. Springer, Cham (2019). https://doi.org/10.1007/978-3-030-24854-3
13. Michalos, A.C. (ed.): Encyclopedia of Quality of Life and Well-Being Research. Springer, Dordrecht (2014). https://doi.org/10.1007/978-94-007-0753-5
14. OWL. https://www.w3.org/OWL (2022)
15. Freud, J.E.: Modern Elementary Statistics. Prentice Hall, Englewood Cliffs (1987)
16. Jaynes, E.T.: Probability Theory: The Logic of Science. Cambridge University Press, New York, NY, USA (2003)
17. Gelman, A., Carlin, J.B., Stern, H.S., Dunson, D.B., Vehtari, A., Rubin, D.B.: Bayesian Data Analysis. Chapman and Hall/CRC, UK (2013)

Towards Identification of Privacy Requirements with Systems Thinking

Tuisku Sarrala[1]([✉]), Tommi Mikkonen[1], Anh Nguyen Duc[2],
and Pekka Abrahamsson[1]

[1] University of Jyväskylä, PO Box 35, 40014 Jyväskylä, Finland
tuisku.rad.sarrala@student.jyu.fi,
{tommi.j.mikkonen,pekka.abrahamsson}@jyu.fi
[2] Department of Business and IT, University of South-Eastern Norway,
PO Box 4, 3199 Borre, Norway
Anh.Nguyen.duc@usn.no

Abstract. Implementing privacy as software functions is required by privacy regulation. Achieving this requires shared understanding between business process owners and software engineers, who implement it. Current literature reveals a major gap between privacy requirements and how engineers interpret privacy. Furthermore, as today's sociotechnical systems are increasingly complex and ever-evolving, unknown privacy issues can emerge from them as a side-effect. Understanding privacy and identifying privacy threats are pre-requisites for deciding on and implementing the right functionality in software. However, current methods for privacy threat identification do not cover all aspects of privacy, suit complex sociotechnical systems or requirements engineering, or support engineers forming a mental model of privacy. We claim that this situation can be improved by applying a systems thinking approach to privacy threat identification. In this paper, we elaborate the problem and propose a research agenda that will help close the gap between privacy requirements and technical software functionality.

Keywords: Privacy by design · Privacy engineering · Privacy threat modelling · Privacy mental model · Systems thinking

1 Introduction

Privacy is a common concern for today's businesses as almost all businesses have to deal with personal data at some scale. Although privacy is a public value, in many contexts it is not a matter of choice to implement privacy in software, but a necessity imposed by laws and regulation (e.g. [1]). How to satisfy legal requirements when designing software (software being the technical manifestation of the business processes that handle personal data) is a nontrivial question for both research and practice. Today's business processes are complex, software is complex, and business process owners and software engineers lack shared

© Springer Nature Switzerland AG 2022
B. Shishkov (Ed.): BMSD 2022, LNBIP 453, pp. 249–258, 2022.
https://doi.org/10.1007/978-3-031-11510-3_16

understanding and cooperation around operationalising privacy in the technical software functionalities. Both as a cause and an effect of the struggles, privacy is often seen as an afterthought in software development projects [2].

Not only business process owners need to understand privacy in relation to the business processes, but also software engineers need to share this understanding to design, implement, and maintain privacy-related functions in software systems [3]. Changes to the software can create privacy threats as a side effect. Engineers need to be able to understand and identify emergent privacy threats at their end and involve the business when necessary. This paper focuses on the engineers. It has been shown that there is a major gap between privacy requirements and how software engineers' perceive and interpret privacy [4]. This issue has received little research attention.

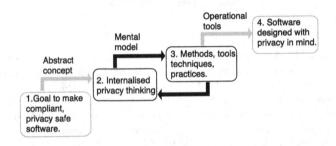

Fig. 1. A gap (shown in black) in the development and deployment of privacy-by-design for software design. The figure has been contextualised from method adoption framework of [5]

The gap between the development and deployment of privacy-by-design for software design is illustrated through Fig. 1. The figure depicts the necessary components of successful development and deployment of privacy-by-design for software design.

Privacy as a high-level concept and a goal (Step 1) has been widely adopted by organisations and can be assumed to be well known for engineers [4]. Operational methods, tools and techniques exist (Step 3), such as privacy engineering methods and privacy standards. However, the "internalised privacy thinking" step (Step 2) between goal and operation is poorly supported, which hinders the use of provided operational tools. In addition, current operational tools do not support well the forming a mental model of privacy. Hence, the learning loop between 2 and 3 that develops privacy practice is no well supported. As a result of the gap, engineers proceed directly to the provided operational tools, without the help of a mental model of what privacy means in the context. Engineers end up having to interpret privacy requirements while lacking the skills to do so [4]. Having a mental model is essential for new practices [6], like for engineers to effectively operationalise privacy-safe business processes in the software design. When the gap is present, there is a risk of mismatch between what was intended and what was built. Thus, the goal represented on Step 4 is not reached.

To close this gap, we need to focus on a critical and difficult privacy-by-design task for engineers, that includes collaboration with business and understanding of privacy in the context: the identification and addressing of *systemic* [9] privacy threats. This activity is a pre-requisite for risk-based privacy-by-design: deciding on and implementing the right technical software functionality. With systemic privacy threats, we mean threats that arise from the interplay of the software's business purposes, technology in use, and people who it touches, without forgetting its wider context [1,20]. The ever-evolving unbounded nature of software makes this task even harder, since engineers to need be able to understand what emergent, unknown privacy threats may arise from the software system's interacting and ever-changing aspects [7].

So far this activity, identifying systemic privacy threats, has not been well supported in the described context. Current methods and tools either take a reductionist approach that does not suit complex software contexts; only target either engineers or business; omit aspects of privacy threats such as the technology or impact to people; focus on direct compliance requirements do not consider threats of systemic nature at all; or do not support forming a mental model of privacy.

We look to systems thinking to address the described gap, focusing on the task and tools for privacy threat modelling. Systems thinking is aimed at understanding complex targets such as today's ever-evolving unbounded software systems [8]. It commonly promotes focus on the whole rather than parts, the dynamic behaviour of the system, relationships and interconnections, and how system behaviours (such as threats) arise from the system's structure. Systems thinking commonly utilises conceptual modelling. Complexity of the scenario (in one's mind, in order to work with it) is reduced by conceptual modelling [8]. This in turn builds a mental model for the observer, an internal representation of the real world, and improves their overall ability to deal with the complex scenario [10,11].

The rest of the paper is organised as follows. Section 2 considers the concepts of privacy and privacy threats as well as complexity and systems thinking. Section 3 discusses existing approaches. Section 4 presents the research agenda. Finally, towards the end of the paper, Sect. 5 draws some final conclusions.

2 Background

Privacy as a Value and a Requirement. Turning abstract elements like values or a goals into system functionality is a known struggle [12]. Public values such as privacy have made their way into non-functional requirements (NFRs), but it is argued [13] that they should be treated differently since they are essentially values, not requirements. An important point with public values as NFRs is that they are cross-cutting concerns that should cover all parts of the design. Shishkov and Mendling propose a metamodel [13] in which value consideration targets business process models, based on which software functionality can be specified. Therefore, ideally, public values are operationalised directly into functional solutions rather than separately gathered through requirements engineering process and scattered in relevant places.

For some values, the pressure to include them comes from the public, but some are legislated for. Next, we discuss the regulatory issues in the EU, but it is noted that similar legal frameworks exist elsewhere in the world. In the EU, commonly agreed public values are written in the EU Charter of Fundamental Rights. Two of the rights, data protection and privacy, have been particularly prominent in the area of software development in recent times. Data protection is known through its implementation as the General Data Protection Regulation (GDPR) [1]. This paper considers in particular the values of data protection and privacy through the requirements of the GDPR. The term privacy is used.

Privacy as a value differs from others and deserves particular attention in the context of software design due to several reasons:

- Privacy directly and concretely relates to software design, when personal data is used in software.
- Lack of privacy has direct human impact; it can result in real harms to people, even death [20].
- Privacy and especially privacy threats are wide complex concepts, challenging to understand in the context of today's complex sociotechnical software.
- There are known challenges implementing privacy in software functionality [4].
- Unlike many values, privacy is not a choice but a legal requirement, with accountability requirement and potential sanctions for non-compliance [1].

Attempts have been made to turn the GDPR into a list of NFRs which then are turned into functionality by engineers [14]. This approach of gathering privacy NFRs from legal and adding it to the requirements list is far from ideal. Since the GDPR requirements are cross-cutting, they must be evident everywhere in the software's design and because of privacy being essentially a value, it should ideally be built in the business processes. This paper is concerned of the process of arriving at functionality that have privacy requirements built in. This implements the idea of data protection by design and is in line with the observations of Shiskov and Mendling [13].

The GDPR contains only some clear requirements but also the requirements to do data protection by design (DPbD) and to consider impacts to people. The clear requirements are simpler to incorporate in business process models and are commonplace seen as NFRs. For example, tracking of sensitive data, controlling data transfers outside of the EU and ensuring conditions for consent. By nature, they are already more "technical", and can be excused to be listed as the NFR. However, the DPbD and impact assessment are processes that are meant to produce privacy-aware functionality for the software, and are difficult to satisfy without an understanding of privacy in both business and technical viewpoints and a way to assess very complex situations. This is where privacy threat modelling is essential.

Going back to public values, to operationalise a value, one needs to identify possible threats to it. In this case, these are privacy harms. The GDPR requires these harms to be understood very widely in the DPbD and impact assessment. They may be physical, material or non-material damage to people as a result of processing personal data [1,20]. Being subject to unethical data processing is one. It is expected that they arise from interplay of different elements in the situation, meaning that they are systemic threats. Because of this wide concept of a privacy threat extending far outside of the business processes, they are especially difficult to identify. Understanding of the threats and impacts arising from the personal data utilising business processes as whole should result in an understanding of what particular business processes should be varied for privacy and how. They can then be expressed as a privacy-safe business processes variants, that can then be turned directly into functionality. However, since privacy issues have a clear technology aspect and business processes manifest as software, these privacy-by-design activities cannot take place in the business side alone. Engineers and their understanding is essential.

Software Complexity and Systems Thinking. Today's software systems are complex. Since they increasingly revolve around people, they should essentially be viewed as social systems [16]. This raises their complexity and means that they have no clear boundary.

From the viewpoint of Lehman's SPE-classification of computer programs with respect to their evolution, these are E-type systems: constantly evolving, embedded in their environment and aiming to satisfy their users' varying needs [15]. An underpinning idea in systems thinking is that such systems are best approached through holistic synthesis—aiming to understand the whole—instead of reductionist analysis, trying to understand their parts in isolation and aggregating the results [16]. The approach to understand them should be flexible to match their complexity. Ashby's law of requisite variety means that if the target has high variety, such as complex ever-evolving software, the variety of the intervention has to match it [17,18].

Systems thinking [8] is a way to approach complexity, commonly through focusing on the whole rather than parts, dynamic interconnections of the parts and behaviour of the whole arising from that as well as the system's structure. Iterative approaches are common and the problem situation is often probed by different techniques and from different angles, for example multiple cause diagramming, rich pictures, systems maps, and multiple-perspective techniques [9]. Sense-making, understanding and learning have an important role in systems thinking [9]. Systems thinking approach and developing one's own thinking go hand in hand, which is an area widely researched by Senge [19].

3   Existing Approaches for Privacy Modelling

Our main interest is on tools that consider privacy, impact to people from the processing of personal data and tools that are placed in the requirements engineering context. Privacy threats arise from the interplay of business purposes and technical aspects as well as people and the wider context, so ideally all of these, and the interplay aspect, are present. Applications of systems thinking to threat and impact assessments are also relevant.

The GDPR [1] includes the *data protection impact assessment* requirement, which includes the requirement to understand systemic privacy threats. It does not elaborate how exactly to uncover the privacy threats. Although technical experts are recommended to take part, it is a generic, not requirements engineering process. Data protection authorities have published versions of the process but the privacy threat identification stage lacks detailed methodology [20]. Impact assessments in general promote learning about the situation [21].

Value-sensitive design includes techniques that aim to incorporate public values in software designs [22], for example Security and Privacy Threat Discovery Cards [23]. These tools and guidelines consider privacy along other impacts in systemic manner, taking the wider context into account. The techniques offered under the value-sensitive design brand are not particularly attached to the requirements engineering context. *Technology assessment* has a wider scope and is used for example in medical and new innovative technology contexts [24]. Recent topic of artificial intelligence ethics has inspired *ethics tools* such as ECCOLA [25], which is a method for incorporating ethics in requirements engineering. ECCOLA involves the listed aspects; however, its privacy considerations are not developed far enough.

Various operational tools and methods exist for *privacy engineering*, such as PRIAM [26], the "design science approach" [27], LINDDUN [28] and Elevation of privacy cards [29]. Wider impact to people is not considered. These methods commonly take a reductionist approach involving techniques such as detailed mapping, making them inflexible and resource heavy for complex targets [21], although the last two allow for a lighter application as well. Reductionist approaches by their nature are not equipped to uncover systemic privacy threats, but rather address the more straightforward compliance requirements. Also, they lack the benefits of learning and mental model development that systems thinking approach has. Systems thinking has been widely used for identifying *systemic threats and solutions to global problems*, such as climate change [30], and for public policy development.

The gap between privacy requirements and engineers' understanding of privacy may be addressed by training and education. However, our focus is on the practical task and learning through doing and through cooperation. Therefore, pure privacy training and education is not in the scope of this paper.

4   Research Agenda

Based on the above background, research is needed to improve operationalising privacy requirements in technical software functionality. We argue that a systems thinking approach should be explored as a possible way forward. We believe that the targeting privacy threat modelling task would improve deciding on and implementing the right functionality for privacy and result in ever-improving privacy mental model for the users, engineers especially.

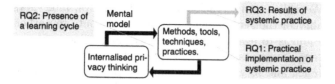

Fig. 2. Research questions illustrated against the identified gap

The agenda aims at answering to the following research questions, which have been illustrated in Fig. 2 against the identified gap between privacy requirements and implementing privacy in software:

- **RQ1:** *Through what kind of practical implementation could systems thinking approach be included in the privacy threat identification processes?* RQ1 targets the practical implementation. It addresses the practical need of engineers and benefits them, and for the academic community, widens the understanding of how systems thinking approach could be brought into this setting. Answering RQ1 would help to understand what features of system thinking approach produce desirable effects.
- **RQ2:** *How does using systems thinking approach in the privacy threat identification process impact on the forming of a mental model of privacy in engineers?* RQ2 contributes to RQ1 by checking that the implementation does what it is envisioned to: builds a mental model. Should strong learning effect be evident, that knowledge could be applied and further researched in the areas of privacy awareness and training. Even without evidence of learning, RQ3 would let us find out how well the tool would support the task of operationalising privacy in software functionality.
- **RQ3:** *What is the impact on arriving at software functionality for privacy in terms of efficiency, effectiveness and efficacy, if a systems thinking approach is used in process of uncovering systemic privacy threats?* RQ3 contributes to RQ1 by checking that the output is meaningful privacy threat information for deciding on software functionality. RQ3 would let us find out how well the tool would support the task of operationalising privacy in software functionality.

To answer RQ1, the practical implementation of systems thinking, we plan to carry out a literature review to describe and explore current practices in operationalising privacy in software design; those in particular that involve privacy threat identification or systems thinking approach. We will also review systems thinking approaches to identify suitable features for inclusion in privacy threat identification. With the gathered understanding, we plan to insert systems thinking approach in privacy threat identification in the requirements engineering setting and test its effects. In practice, this means creating a tool with systemic features and testing and developing it in an iterative manner using action learning approach.

To answer RQ2, the presence of a learning cycle, we plan to run quasi-experimental studies of engineers using the tool against traditional, non-systemic approaches. We will use observational method, surveys, interviews and analysis of the quality of the requirements elicitation outputs to gather data of the learning. The aim is to evaluate the tool's learning value to engineers in their requirements engineering task, and to explain the relationship between systems thinking approach and privacy mental model forming in this setting.

To answer RQ3, the output of systems thinking practice, we plan to run quasi-experimental studies as in RQ2, to describe and explain how taking a systems thinking approach impacts the results that the tool produces. Mainly qualitative data in the form of privacy threats and requirements will be gathered and analysed. The effectiveness, efficiency and efficacy of the tool will be evaluated.

In general, an action learning approach will be taken to begin answering the research questions. Action learning approach suits the practical aim of helping engineers. Action learning suits research that is about system thinking approach; ideally this results in double loop learning, where learning happens both about the target and the learning itself, and the approach is modified on the way to better respond to the changing situation. In this case, we could see an action learning cycle taking the research forward about how to include action learning (in the form of systems approach) into privacy threat modelling practices.

5   Conclusion

This paper was framed around the wider challenge of turning the NFRs and cross-cutting concern for privacy into technical functionality in software. We traced this to the lack of shared understanding and cooperation between business and engineering, and focused on the major gap in engineers' understanding of privacy. Privacy threat modelling was identified as a concrete activity through which overall improvements could be made.

We made a distinction between straightforward privacy requirements and systemic privacy threats. The identification of systemic privacy threats is essential for deciding and implementing the right functionality in software. Recognising also the increasing complexity of software, we argued that applying systems thinking approach to privacy threat modelling would bring improvement. Systems thinking is well suited at understanding complex situations such as privacy issues in today's ever-evolving software, improving one's mental model in the process. We expect that improvement at the engineers' end will benefit business process owners alike.

Our future research plans include investigating practical tools for privacy threat modelling, the presence of a learning cycle while using them, and the practical outcomes for requirements engineering. Therefore, our contribution comprises of (i) a presentation of a critical problem in business and software design to address and (ii) a tentative solution with a formulated research agenda to address the problem.

Acknowledgements. This research was partially funded by Business Finland under ITEA 18033 Mad@Work.

References

1. Regulation (EU) 2016/679 General Data Protection Regulation (GDPR). Regulation (EU) 2016/679 of the European Parliament and of the Council of 27 April 2016, on the protection of natural persons with regard to the processing of personal data and on the free movement of such data, and repealing Directive 95/46/EC. Official Journal Of The European Union L119/1 (2016). http://eur-lex.europa.eu/legal-content/FI/TXT/?uri=CELEX%253A32016R0679

2. Kostova, B., Gürses, S.,Troncoso, C.: Privacy engineering meets software engineering. On the challenges of engineering privacy by design. ArXiv:2007.08613 [cs], 16 July 2020. http://arxiv.org/abs/2007.08613

3. Sinnhofer, A.D., Oppermann, F.J., Potzmader, K., Orthacker, C., Steger, C., Kreiner, C.: Increasing the visibility of requirements based on combined variability management. In: Shishkov, B. (ed.) BMSD 2018. LNBIP, vol. 319, pp. 203–220. Springer, Cham (2018). https://doi.org/10.1007/978-3-319-94214-8_13

4. Hadar, I., et al.: Privacy by designers: software developers' privacy mindset. Empir. Softw. Eng.. **23**, 259–289 (2018)

5. Ebert, C., Abrahamsson, P., Oza, N.: Lean software development. IEEE Comput. Archit. Lett. **29**, 22–25 (2012)

6. Senge, P.M.: Mental models. Plann. Rev. **20**(2), 4–44 (1992). https://doi.org/10.1108/eb054349

7. Anthonysamy, P., Rashid, A., Chitchyan, R., Lancaster, S.: Privacy requirements: present & future. In: 2017 IEEE/ACM 39th International Conference on Software Engineering: Software Engineering in Society Track (ICSE-SEIS) (2017). https://ieeexplore.ieee.org/document/7961663

8. Arnold, R., Wade, J.: A definition of systems thinking: a systems approach. Proc. Comput. Sci. **44**, 669–678 (2015)

9. Monat, J., Gannon, T.: What is systems thinking? A review of selected literature plus recommendations. Am. J. Syst. Sci. **59**, 11–26 (2015). http://resources21.org/cl/files/project264_5674/Overv

10. Richardson, G., Andersen, D., Maxwell, T., Stewart, T.: Foundations of mental model research. In: Proceedings of the 1994 International System Dynamics Conference, pp. 181–192 (1994)

11. Jones, N., Ross, H., Lynam, T., Perez, P., Leitch, A.: Mental models: an interdisciplinary synthesis of theory and methods. Ecol. Soc. (2011). https://www.jstor.org/stable/26268859

12. Chung, L., Nixon, B., Yu, E., Mylopoulos, J.: Non-functional Requirements in Software Engineering. Springer, Heidelberg (2012). https://doi.org/10.1007/978-1-4615-5269-7

13. Shishkov, B., Mendling, J.: Business process variability and public values. In: Shishkov, B. (ed.) BMSD 2018. LNBIP, vol. 319, pp. 401–411. Springer, Cham (2018). https://doi.org/10.1007/978-3-319-94214-8_31

14. Miri, M., Foomany, F.H., Mohammed, N.: Complying with GDPR: an agile case study. ISACA J. **2**, 1–7 (2018)

15. Lehman, M.: Program evolution. Inf. Process. Manag. **20**, 19–36 (1984)

16. Ackoff, R.: Systems thinking and thinking systems. Syst. Dyn. Rev. **10**, 175–188 (1994)

17. Ashby, W.: Requisite variety and its implications for the control of complex systems. Cybernetica **1**, 83–99 (1958). http://pcp.vub.ac.be/Books/AshbyReqVar.pdf

18. Braithwaite, J., Braithwaite, J., Wears, R., Hollnagel, E.: Resilient Health Care. Volume 3, Reconciling Work-as-Imagined and Work-as-Done. CRC Press (2016). https://www.finna.fi/Record/jamk.993205274806251

19. Senge, P., Sterman, J.: Systems thinking and organizational learning: acting locally and thinking globally in the organization of the future. Eur. J. Oper. Res. **59**, 137–150 (1992)

20. Privacy Impact Assessment PIA Knowledge Base (2018). https://www.cnil.fr/sites/default/files/atoms/files/cnil-pia-3-en-knowledgebases.pdf

21. Raab, C.: Information privacy, impact assessment, and the place of ethics. Comput. Law Secur. Rev. **37**, 105404 (2020)

22. Hendry, D.: Designing Tech Policy: Instructional Case Studies for Technologists and Policymakers. UW Tech Policy Lab (2020)

23. Denning, T., Friedman, B., Kohno, T.: Security and privacy threat discovery cards. University of Washington (2013). http://securitycards.cs.washington.edu/assets/security-cards-deck-with-croplines.pdf

24. Nemoto, E., Issaoui, R., Korbee, D., Jaroudi, I., Fournier, G.: How to measure the impacts of shared automated electric vehicles on urban mobility. Transp. Res. Part D: Transp. Environ. **93**, 102766 (2021). https://www.sciencedirect.com/science/article/pii/S1361920921000705

25. Vakkuri, V., Kemell, K., Abrahamsson, P.: ECCOLA - a method for implementing ethically aligned AI systems. In: Proceedings - 46th Euromicro Conference on Software Engineering and Advanced Applications, SEAA 2020, pp. 195–204 (2020)

26. De, S., Métayer, D.: PRIAM: A Privacy Risk Analysis Methodology. Springer, Heidelberg (2016). http://link.springer.com/10.1007/978-3-319-47072-615

27. Oetzel, M., Spiekermann, S.: A systematic methodology for privacy impact assessments: a design science approach. Eur. J. Inf. Syst. **23**, 126–150 (2014). https://www.tandfonline.com/doi/full/10.1057/ejis.2013.18. ISBN 1476-9344

28. Yskout, K., Heyman, T., Landuyt, D., Sion, L., Wuyts, K., Joosen, W.: Threat modeling: from infancy to maturity. In: Proceedings - 2020 ACM/IEEE 42nd International Conference on Software Engineering: New Ideas and Emerging Results, ICSE-NIER 2020, pp. 9–12 (2020)

29. F-Secure Elevation of Privacy, Privacy Cards for Software Developers (2018). https://github.com/F-Secure/elevation-of-privacy. Issue: 1.1, vol. 2021

30. Li, H., Wang, X., Zhao, X., Qi, Y.: Understanding systemic risk induced by climate change. Adv. Clim. Change Res. **12**, 384–394 (2021). https://www.sciencedirect.com/science/article/pii/S1674927821000782

Toward a Reference Architecture for User-Oriented Open Government Data Portals

Ahmad Luthfi[1]([⊠]) [iD] and Marijn Janssen[2] [iD]

[1] Department of Informatics, Universitas Islam Indonesia, Jalan Kaliurang KM. 14,5 Sleman, Yogyakarta 55584, Indonesia
ahmad.luthfi@uii.ac.id
[2] Delft University of Technology, Delft, The Netherlands
m.f.w.h.a.janssen@tudelft.nl

Abstract. Governments have established Open Government Data Portals (OGDP) to open various types of datasets that can be used to increase transparency, accountability, and innovation. OGDP is becoming a strategic program for citizen engagement and empowering users. Nevertheless, many OGDP architectures focus merely on publishing data and do not support the actual data use. Therefore, this paper aims to develop a reference architecture (RA) that takes a broader set of requirements aimed at enabling the use of open data into account. The RA consists of recommended structures and integrations of the end-to-end user interactions and services. In this research, we use the DKAN open data management platform as the basis to design a full suite of cataloguing and visualising the end-to-end user interactions. Five layers are proposed providing functionalities for using data. Whereas most portals are focused on releasing data, our RA is focused on empowering users by providing functionalities for the use of data.

Keywords: Reference architecture · Open data · Portal · DKAN · End-user

1 Introduction

Governments provide and maintain vast amounts of datasets in the Open Government Data Portal (OGDP). The government has started implementing open data initiatives and also setting up open data portals to make these data available in the open by default and in reusable formats [1, 2]. The OGDP is an online management platform that assists end-to-end users in accessing the categorical datasets provided by the government organisation [3, 4]. These categorical datasets such as transportation, education, funding, geospatial, city taxes, energy, and COVID-19 outbreaks present the data openly and freely to the end-users. The OGDP encloses information of interest to the end-users, such as data scientists, data stewards, researchers and university students, business owners, non-profit organisations, and journalists. Theoretically, the simplest OGDP is a dataset catalogue with instructions for how end-users can access, search, download, and use the data in various file formats, such as CSV, PDF, XML, and JSON [5, 6].

© Springer Nature Switzerland AG 2022
B. Shishkov (Ed.): BMSD 2022, LNBIP 453, pp. 259–267, 2022.
https://doi.org/10.1007/978-3-031-11510-3_17

Yet, the usage of OGDP lags behind as the primary focus on opening data and the user view is given less attention [7]. In order to build successful open data portals, systematic evaluation is necessary to understand them better, assess the types of value they generate and identify what services need to be made to improve them. However, many non-trivial procedures must be considered in the course of execution of the (OGD) movement, including using the OGDP management platform and classifying the end-to-end user's interactions. Several characteristics of good OGDP refers to (1) the use of open standards and access to the dataset without human complicity [8, 9], (2) the straightforward and unsupervised portal to understand for the end-to-end users [10], and (3) data should be presented in clear structures and metadata [4, 10].

Ideally, OGDP should not be a practical or technical burden for end-to-end users. Therefore, the objective of this paper is to develop a RA for OGDP that aims to facilitate the use of OGD. The RA consists of five main layers which focus on different aspects of enabling the use of OGD. The five main layers of the RA developed in this paper include data collection, data lake, data management, data analysis and modelling, and data visualisation. These five major layers are supposed to support and relate to each other to orchestrate the use of OGDP. Furthermore, to ensure the complicity of end-to-end users in the implementation of the OGDP, we included the involvement of several open data stakeholders, such as data scientists, data engineers, researchers, data stewards, business owners, communities, data enthusiasts, and parents. These types of OGDP stakeholders represent the end-user-oriented in collecting, managing, analysing, and using open data.

In general terms, a RA in the field of software architecture refers to a list of functions and several indications and their interactions with each other [11]. Reference architectures for a domain capture the fundamental sub-systems shared by all systems within that domain as well as their interrelationships [12]. A RA is useful for both maintenance and design. It can improve understanding of a system, and it can be used to set up new systems and re-engineer existing systems [13]. In this study, an OGDP reference architecture can be defined as a fundamental architecture that captures relationships between the five main layers of developing OGDP, including the involvement of representative stakeholders.

This research may contribute to government organisations and respected researchers' understanding of the RA for the OGDP development and provide recommendations related to its RA development. The paper is structured as follows: Sect. 1 presents the current issues and problems, Sect. 2 reviews related literature background, Sect. 3 proposes the research approach, Sect. 4 summarises the RA. Finally, Sect. 5 concludes the paper.

2 Theoretical Background

Open data portals are a web-based system that collects data from a variety of sources in various forms and publish data to be used by users interacting with a user interface dashboard [14]. Open data portals must be considered rigorous architectures and infrastructures as interactions between governments and external users. They should be able to allow or disable operations and establish a range of possible data uses, and unlocking the promise of open data requires the capacity to locate relevant data [14, 15]. Therefore, one endeavour to make these datasets more accessible and easier to reuse is to provide an open data gateway of available datasets [4, 9].

Despite the excitement generated by the availability of an ever-increasing amount of freely available data in the open data portal, several critical problems, such as unstructured metadata and data sources, have emerged to address the emerging issue of low quality in the available data portal, which is a severe disadvantage that might derail the open data portal development [2, 3, 16]. Similarly, there is a wide range of content, functionality, and technical standards among the various data management systems used by open data portals [14, 17]. For that reason, a re-designing and benchmarking framework or available data architecture are required to understand quality issues in open data portals better and investigate the impact of improvement approaches [9, 18].

A reference architecture frequently consists of a list of system functions and some indication of their end-user interfaces and their interactions with each other [13]. Reference architectures explain how to use specific patterns and methods to tackle specific types of challenges [19]. As a result, it can be used to reference the individual designs that businesses or organisations will use to solve their deficiencies [11, 13].

In the domain of OGDP, a RA is an abstract design that provides a frame of open data reference, common vocabulary, reusable structures, and end-user best practices compiled in rigorous layers for designing specific instances. Besides, multiple stakeholders of the OGDP, from data engineers to data analysts, should be able to access and comprehend the defined RA layers. Therefore, a RA should be explicit and technically tangible [13]. At the same time, the task at hand is to design a RA that is both generic and actual while still including specific information [11].

3 Research Approach

This research aims to develop a RA for OGDP. First and foremost, the challenge faced in this study was derived from the previous study literature. Therefore, we use a Systematic Literature Review (SLR), which follows three primary sequential steps: data collection and identification, screening for eligibility, and deductive and inductive coding [20]. The objective of this SLR process is to define some terminologies using three main Boolean keywords operator: "open government data portal" AND "reference architecture". In this step, the inclusion was limited to English-language scientific journals using Scopus based gateway. Based on the data collection step using the Boolean operator, we acquired (n = 137 articles). Furthermore, we filtered our prior 137 articles by screening abstracts without explicit reference to "end-to-end user" (n = 88 articles). In the final step, we filtered the full-text version by excluding articles without comparing their research objective and empirical research. We finally found (n = 24) eligible papers by performing this PRISMA protocol.

The findings of this literature study were used to develop an OGDP RA. Thereafter, we also conducted content analysis for some references related to Open Data Portal management and platforms, such as Comprehensive Knowledge Archive Network (CKAN), Git Data Publisher, Socrata, OpenDataSoft, and Drupal-based Knowledge Archive Network (DKAN) Platform. This study aims to design interactions and relationships between open data portal communication and end-users. Therefore, we selected and followed the

DKAN Platform because: (1) it is an open data platform that enables data providers like governments to easily share data with the general public with a comprehensive set of cataloging, publishing, and visualization tools [21], and it is suitable to create an independent interconnection between the proposed RA and the roles of the OGDP users [21]. Although DKAN is criticised and has shortcomings, we opted for using DKAN as a starting point as many portals make use of this platform [22]. The RA can then be used to extend the DKAN platform. The DKAN platform that is used as the basis consist of three main elements [21, 23]: (1) DKAN Dataset Content Types, which contains the actual dataset and resource types and fields to develop layer 1 (data collection) and layer 2 (data lake), (2) The DKAN Dataset Representational State Transfer (REST) API and management, which defines the REST interface to integrate and protect data in the ODGP (layer 3), (3) The DKAN Dataset Groups, which combine both dataset analysis and site users including data visualisation (layer 4 and 5).

4 OGDP Reference Architecture

Implementing a RA within an organisation can boost productivity by using a proven solution and providing governance to ensure the consistency and applicability of the technology. Theoretically, a RA aids as an elementary guide to developing Information Technology (IT) systems and infrastructures. Therefore, in this paper, the RA proposed the highest level of abstraction and architectural guidance in developing OGDP rather than describing a system in detail or providing a detailed diagram of the interconnection among the layers and actors involved.

This study proposed the OGDP reference architecture consisting of five main layers that represent the data science life cycle: data collection, data lake, data management, data analysis and model, and data visualisation. In Fig. 1, we show the RA we derived. It consists of five major sub-systems plus their relationships focused on enabling the use of open data. These five layers were represented the DKAN open data management platform. Basically, there will be two primary roles of the representative stakeholders in this RA. First, the internal open data stakeholders such as data engineer, data steward, and data analyst are able to access, modify, and configure the selected datasets. In this part, the internal stakeholders can collect, store, manage, analyse, and visualise the dataset based on the specific role. For example, in the layer 1 (data collection), data engineer can extract, transform, and load the dataset to generate several specific file formats such as PDF, CSV, XLS, XML, and JSON. At the same time, data engineer can also manage the dataset to create a metadata, DKAN architecture, and ensure the security of the data. Second, the external open data stakeholders such as researchers, business owners, journalists, communities, and other potential public actors' domain, they all can access, download, and reuse the provided datasets in the OGDP. For example, in the layer 4 (data visualisation), journalists can find and view the selected categorical dataset related to the weather forecast to report the updated news. In this layer, OGDP provides a quantitative-based visualisation through the charts, graphs, and maps. At the same time, the OGDP also serves the dataset into a qualitative-based visualisation by figuring it via infographics, word clouds, and sentiment mapping.

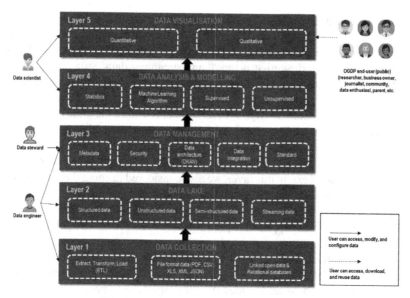

Fig. 1. Reference architecture of the OGDP

- **Layer 1. Data Collection**
  The primary layer of the OGDP reference architecture is data collection. In this layer, data providers collect, monitor, and analyse accurate data from various sources. As part of data collection, data providers have to specify what types of data will be collected, where they will obtain data, and how they will collect it. We defined three sub-systems in this first level: (1) extract, transform, load (ETL). The ETL process is an integration process that compiles data from multiple sources into a single, consistent data store that can then be uploaded to a data warehouse. Thus, in this layer, the objective of the ETL process is to enhance data quality by performing data cleansing before loading the data into the data lake; (2) file format data that refers to a standard of file extension to arrange logically within a file. File formats also describe the structure and type of data that can be stored in a file. There may be a header, metadata, and saved content in a typical file structure. In the case of OGDP, there have been several file formats structured by the data providers, such as Comma-separated Values (CSV), eXtensible Markup Language (XML), Portable Document Format (PDF), Microsoft Excel Format (XLS), Keyhole Markup Language (KML), JavaScript Object Notation (JSON), GeoJSON; (3) linked open data and relational database. In this sub-system, the OGDP should be able to integrate the data with other sources (other OGDPs) to provide specific context. The benefit derives from the open linked data that end-users like researchers and journalists can discover more expected and related data while accessing the OGDP.
- **Layer 2. Data Lake**
  In the second layer, data lake is used to collect and integrate data from the first layer. Essentially, a data lake is a central repository containing many raw data in its original format. In general, data lakes differ from traditional data warehouses in that

they use flat architectures and object storage to store data [24]. The most important aspect of data lakes is open format, avoiding the lock-in that comes with proprietary systems like data warehouses. We identified four sub-systems in this data lake layer: structured, unstructured, semi-structured, and streaming data. Structured data refers to data that can be analysed effectively because its elements can be addressed easily. For instance, a structured table with rows and columns can store all the information that can be found in database SQL. Therefore, fields within the table can be mapped easily and have relational keys. Furthermore, unlike structured data, unstructured data lacks a predefined structure. Consequently, it's unsuitable for mainstream relational databases. However, since many data providers have unstructured data formats, such as PDF, DOCX, and Text, in this layer, we also considered keeping these types of data in the data lake. As such, unstructured data can be stored and managed on alternative platforms. It is more prevalent in IT systems, and businesses use it in various business intelligence and analytics application platforms. At this level, we also studied the semi-structured data. Semi-structured data has some organisation properties that make it easier to analyse, but it does not reside in a relational database. Some processes can be stored in relational databases (in XML format, for example), even if semi-structured data is challenging to store. Besides the three important sub-systems (structured, unstructured, and semi-structured data), we also provide the diverse data sources and format known as streaming data. Nowadays, the Internet of Things (IoT) connects devices in various situations, including cars, factories, homes, retail establishments, and wearables. These all things collected by sensors in IoT produce many types of streaming data, such as videos, images, geospatial, and e-commerce data. Therefore, we provide the streaming data sub-system to represent the need to store the stream processing the real-time data.

- **Layer 3. Data Management**

The data management layer represents the techniques for organising, structuring, securing, integrating, and keeping an organisation's data. As government organisations generate and consume data at unprecedented rates, data management solutions are becoming increasingly important for making sense of massive amounts of data. After discussing the prior two layers (data collection and data lake), we now provided five main sub-systems in the data management layer: metadata, security, data architecture, data integration, and standard. In implementing the OGDP, technically, we entail establishing policies and procedures to ensure that information can be effectively integrated, accessed, shared, linked, analysed, and maintained throughout the government institutions. To do so, metadata management can help data engineers to provide the basic knowledge in identifying and classifying the collected data. At the same time, the security aspect is also an important issue in the OGDP. The OGDP is an open-access platform that anyone can access freely without restriction. Opening more data to the public domain can reap many advantages. However, protecting the data in the OGDP is not trivial. Therefore, we ensure that the security elements should be included in this data management layer. We need to configure and protect several high-level services for external access over the Internet at the hardware level, such as security firewalls, API services, and data connectors. In the meantime, we are also required to protect the data by performing pseudonymous algorithms on user access levels and proposing a regular assessment of the OGDP system. Furthermore, the data management layer also deals with the data architecture for developing and organising the OGDP. In this sub-system, we used DKAN Open Data Platform as an open-source management platform with a comprehensive set of cataloguing, publishing, and visualisation tools, and therefore, government organisations can simply share data with the general public. DKAN is a Drupal-based open data portal built on Comprehensive Knowledge Archive Network (CKAN), the first extensively utilised open data portal with a mature and rigorous upgrade system. Therefore, DKAN can support the open data providers in developing an OGDP to organise and customise the collected data.

- **Layer 4. Data Analysis and Modelling**
  In the fourth layer, we designed an essential step in developing the OGDP, namely data analysis and modelling. Data analysis is analysing, cleansing, manipulating and modelling data to identify usable information, inform conclusions, and assist decision-making [14]. This layer proposed four main sub-systems: statistics, Machine Learning (ML) algorithms, and supervised and unsupervised approaches. These data analysis methods aim to interpret and understand the results of such techniques and methods for data collection to make data analysis straightforward, more precise, or accurate, and all the equipment and outcomes. In the case of OGDP, statistical analysis can be used to generate predictive analysis using the collected data by performing text analytics, for instance. In the supervised machine learning, several algorithms can be used such as linear regression, classification, Naïve Bayesian Model, Random Forest Model, and Neural Networks. While in the unsupervised machine learning, the algorithms include exclusive, overlapping, hierarchical, and probabilistic clustering. These are all methods that can support the data analysis to become more accurate at predicting outcomes of the collected data. At the same time, this proposed RA can support semi-supervised learning and reinforcement learning. Therefore, this layer can promote a small amount of labelled dataset, and perform actions from trial-and-error of data analysis.

- **Layer 5. Data Visualisation**
  Data visualisation is the last layer of this study's proposed ODGPS's reference architecture. Data visualisation is the presentation layer for the external OGDP end-user, such as researchers, business owners, journalists, communities, and data enthusiasts. In this layer, the end-user can freely access, download, and reuse the provided data in the OGDP platform. Therefore, this layer is crucial and should be defined and designed comprehensively. The way OGDP developers approach data visualisation can greatly impact how thought-provoking and far-reaching the end-user's conclusions are. Data visualisation done correctly allows others to understand insights faster, simpler, and deeper, resulting in increased knowledge retention and a higher possibility of action being performed as a result. In this layer, we divided the sub-systems of the data visualisation into two main parts, namely quantitative and qualitative visualisation. Quantitative refers to numerical-based visualisation displayed through graphs, charts, tables, and maps. Meanwhile, qualitative data visualisation indicates the textual in building connections and landing context. Some example methods that can be selected to generate qualitative data visualisation are world clouds, sentiment mapping, info-graphics, and timelines graphics. Therefore, by using quantitative and qualitative data visualisation, the OGDP end-users are able to examine the data to obtain additional insights regarding the information or messages within OGDP.

Moreover, regarding the end-to-end user design that we approached in the prior introduction part of this paper, the involvement of the internal and external users can be seen in Fig. 1. Several studies about developing a RA in information systems and software domains did not explicitly include the end-to-end user as the primary component. The end-to-end user in the OGDP reference architecture presents the roles and responsibilities of each user, including their privilege in using the OGDP. This paper identified several actors like data engineers, data stewards, and data scientists (Fig. 1). For example, data engineers can access, modify, and configure the data in layer 1 (data collection), layer 2 (data lake), and layer 3 (data management). In contrast, data scientists are responsible for managing layer 4 (data analysis and modelling) and layer 5 (data visualisation). In addition, external end-users, such as researchers, business owners, journalists, community, data enthusiasts, and parents, can all access, download, and reuse the categorical dataset in the OGDP supported by the data visualisation layer.

5 Conclusion

We started our study from the issues of the quality and non-trivial procedures of the open data portals in general and their existing system architecture to maintain categorical datasets. OGDP should not be a practical or technical burden for end-to-end users. Therefore, the objective of this paper is to develop a RA for OGDP. The RA was based on DKAN as most of the existing portals are DKAN-based. This facilitates the extensions of existing OGDP to make them more user-oriented. Five main layers of the RA were formed in this paper, including data collection, data lake, data management, data analysis and modelling, and data visualisation. These major layers are expected to support and relate to each other to enable and orchestrate the use of open data. In addition, to make certain the involvement of end-to-end users in the implementation of the OGDP, we also involved a number of open data stakeholders, such as data scientists, data engineers, researchers, data stewards, business owners, communities, data enthusiasts, and parents.

Our next step will be to put the RA into practice. The proposed reference architecture of the OGDP in this study should be generalised with care, not only using a single DKAN open data platform. DKAN has shortcomings, and its metadata model is relatively simple. For further research, we recommend using and combining other open data platforms, such as Socrata, Git Data Publisher, and OpenDataSoft, to comprehensively capture the data management layers and their interaction among the stakeholders. Furthermore, we recommend developing more comprehensive meta-data models to advance the easy discovery and use of the OGDP.

References

1. Ubaldi, B.: Open Government Data: Towards Empirical Analysis of Open Government Data Initiatives. OECD Working Papers on Public Governance, vol. 22, p. 60 (2013)
2. Lourenço, R.P.: Open Government Portals Assessment: A Transparency for Accountability Perspective. In: EGOV 2013, Koblenz, Germany (2013)
3. Ivanov, M., Varga, M., Bach, M.P.: Government open data portal: how government strategies should be more open. In: 7th International Conference: An Enterprise Odyssey: Leadership, Innovation and Development for Responsible Economy, Zadar, Croatia (2014)

4. Lněnička, M., Máchová, R.: Open (big) data and the importance of data catalogs and portals for the public sector. In: The 3rd International Global Virtual Conference (GV-CONF 2015) (2015)

5. Luthfi, A., Janssen, M.: A conceptual model of decision-making support for opening data. In: 7th International Conference, E-Democracy 2017, pp. 95–105. Springer CCIS 792, Athens, Greece (2017)

6. Luthfi, A., et al.: Bayesian-belief networks for supporting decision-making of the opening data by the customs. In: EGOV-CeDEM-ePart 2020. Linköping University, Sweden (2020)

7. Janssen, M., Charalabidis, Y., Zuiderwijk, A.: Benefits, adoption barriers and myths of open data and open government. Inf. Syst. Manag. 29(4), 258–268 (2012)

8. Lourenço, R.P.: An analysis of open government portals: a perspective of transparency for accountability. Gov. Inf. Q. 32(3), 323–332 (2015)

9. Máchová, R., Lněnička, M.: Evaluating the quality of open data portals on the national level. J. Theor. Appl. Elect. Comm. Res. 12(1), 21–44 (2016)

10. Alhawawsha, M., Panchenko, T.: Open Data Platform Architecture and Its Advantages for an Open E-Government, in Advances in Computer Science for Engineering and Education III (2021)

11. Cloutier, R., et al.: The concept of reference architectures. Syst. Eng. 13(1), 14–27 (2010)

12. Grosskurth, A., Godfreyz, M.W.: A reference architecture for web browsers. J. Softw. Maint. Evol. Res. Pract. 1(1), 1–7 (2006)

13. Martínez-Fernández, S., et al.: Aggregating empirical evidence about the benefits and drawbacks of software reference architectures. In: ACM IEEE International Symposium on Empirical Software Engineering and Measurement (ESEM) (2015)

14. Lněnička, M.: An in-depth analysis of open data portals as an emerging public e-service. Int. J. Soc. Behav. Educ. Econ. Bus. Ind. Eng. 9(2), 589–599 (2015)

15. Kostovski, M., Jovanovik, M., Trajanovic, D.: Open data portal based on semantic web technologies. In: 7th South East European Doctoral Student Conference (2012)

16. Kučera, J., Chlapek, D., Nečaský, M.: Open government data catalogs: current approaches and quality perspective. In: International Conference on Electronic Government and the Information Systems Perspective, Prague, Czech Republic (2013)

17. Juana-Espinosa, S.: Open government data portals in the European Union: a dataset from 2015 to 2017. Data Brief 29 (2020)

18. Umbrich, J., Neumaier, S., Polleres, A.: Quality assessment and evolution of open data portals. In: 3rd International Conference on Future Internet of Things and Cloud (2015)

19. Wahyudi, A., Matheus, R., Janssen, M.: Benefits and challenges of a reference architecture for processing statistical data. In: 16th Conference on e-Business, e-Services and e-Society (I3E). Springer, Delhi, India (2017)

20. Biesbroek, R., et al.: Data, concepts and methods for large-n comparative climate change adaptation policy research: a systematic literature review. WIREs Clim. Change 9, 1–15 (2018)

21. Aky̋urek, H., et al.: Maturity and usability of open data in North Rhine-Westphalia. In: International Conference on Digital Government Researc, Delft, the Netherlands (2018)

22. Zuiderwijk, A., Jeffery, K., Janssen, M.: The potential of metadata for linked open data and its value for users and publishers. eJ. eDemocracy Open Gov. (JeDEM) 4(2), 222–244 (2012)

23. Seto, T., Sekimoto, Y.: The construction of open data portal using DKAN for integrate to multiple Japanese local government open data. In: Free and Open Source Software for Geospatial (FOSS4G) Conference Proceedings (2016)

24. Giebler, C., et al.: Leveraging the Data Lake: current state and challenges. In: International Conference on Big Data Analytics and Knowledge Discovery, Stuttgart, Germany (2019)

KnowGo: An Adaptive Learning-Based Multi-model Framework for Dynamic Automotive Risk Assessment

Paul Mundt[1], Indika Kumara[2,3]([⊠]), Willem-Jan Van Den Heuvel[2,3], Damian Andrew Tamburri[2,4], and Andreas S. Andreou[5]

[1] Adaptant Labs, Adaptant Solutions AG, Berlin, Germany
`paul.mundt@adaptant.io`
[2] Jheronimus Academy of Data Science, Sint Janssingel 92, 5211 DA 's-Hertogenbosch, The Netherlands
[3] Tilburg University, Warandelaan 2, 5037 AB Tilburg, The Netherlands
{`i.p.k.weerasinghadewage,w.j.a.m.vdnHeuvel`}`@tilburguniversity.edu`
[4] Eindhoven University of Technology, 5612 AZ Eindhoven, The Netherlands
`d.a.tamburri@tue.nl`
[5] Cyprus University of Technology, 3036 Limassol, Cyprus
`andreas.andreou@cut.ac.cy`

Abstract. In autonomous driving systems, the level of monitoring and control expected from the vehicle and the driver change in accordance with the level of automation, creating a dynamic risk environment where risks change according to the level of automation. Moreover, the input data and their essential features for a given risk model can also be inconsistent, heterogeneous, and volatile. Therefore, risk assessment systems must adapt to changes in the automation level and input data content to ensure that both the risk criteria and weighting reflect the actual system state, which can change at any time. This paper introduces *KnowGo*, a learning-based dynamic risk assessment framework that provides a risk prediction architecture that can be dynamically reconfigured in terms of risk criterion, risk model selection, and weighting in response to dynamic changes in the operational environment. We validated the *KnowGo* framework with five types of risk scoring models implemented using data-driven and rule-based methods.

Keywords: Dynamic risk assessment · Adaptive systems · Autonomous vehicles · Meta-learning · Multi-model · Dynamic software architecture

1 Introduction

Emerging data-driven business services in the insurance and transportation industries, such as usage-based insurance and risk-based pricing, require the

European Commission grant no. 825480 (H2020), SODALITE and no. 857420 (H2020), DESTINI.

B. Shishkov (Ed.): BMSD 2022, LNBIP 453, pp. 268–278, 2022.
https://doi.org/10.1007/978-3-031-11510-3_18

accurate assessment of the risk exhibited by a driver or vehicle on a given journey or overtime. For example, fleet managers can use the risk score as an indicator of driver safety or as a basis for driver coaching. Likewise, insurance companies can use it to calculate premium changes over time more accurately, allowing them to target discounts at careful or more experienced drivers and penalties at more aggressive ones.

Assessing automotive risk in real-time is problematic due to several complexities [2,15]. First, the same risk factor can have different implications depending on the level of automation and the driving situation. For example, harsh braking when a driver is fully in control may be assessed as high risk as it could result from distracted or defensive driving, each having different implications for the driving behavior while posing a similar level of situational risk to the vehicle. When operating at higher levels of automation in which the vehicle is either fully or partially in control, the same risk may be evaluated at a much lower level, with the expectation that any such occurrences are purely defensive in nature. Second, there exist different levels of vehicle automation [6], and during the same journey, the automation level of a vehicle can change multiple times. Thus, the risk assessment needs to adapt to the changes in the automation level [2].

Recently, learning-based approaches have been developed to support dynamic risk assessment (DRA), where risk-relevant metrics of the current driving situation are monitored and used as input for risk prediction/scoring models [2,5,13,14]. However, the proposed approaches exhibit several limitations. First, they use a single, static machine learning model and assume that data points are consistently obtainable, measurable, and of similar granularity. Second, they do not consider the changes to the level of automation during a journey. As a result, a static risk scoring model is often insufficient to produce accurate results over a more extended period. Furthermore, different data sources capture different perspectives of the risk assessment, and thus the representative risk predictors can be produced when each data source is used separately.

In this paper, to address the above-mentioned limitations of the existing studies, we present the *KnowGo Score* framework, which supports dynamic selection, tuning, and fusion of multiple risk scoring models. *KnowGo Score* allows using multiple risk scoring models, each using different data sources and risk assessment criteria. At runtime, *KnowGo Score* can monitor the current driving situation (per vehicle), select the most appropriate set of risk scoring models for a given automation level and availability of data, and combine the predictions made by the selected models to generate a weighted risk assessment. The implementation of the framework is available as a partially open-source product[1]. We assessed the practicability and usefulness of the framework by using a set of risk predictors and a vehicle/driving simulator.

This paper is structured as follows: Sect. 2 summarizes state of the art in the data-driven automotive DRA while highlighting their research limitations. Section 3 presents our *KnowGo Score* DRA framework in detail. Finally, Sect. 4 evaluates our framework, and Sect. 5 concludes the paper while outlining future research directions.

---

[1] https://knowgo.io/products/knowgo-score/.

2   Related Work

The data-driven approaches have been applied to predict automotive risk levels at runtime [2,13,15,18]. Feth *et al.* employed a Convolutional Neural Network (CNN) to predict the risk level of a driving situation based on the camera images of that particular situation [2]. They created the data set for training CNN models by simulating different driving situations with a driving simulator and assigning a risk metric to those situations. Then, they modeled the risk prediction as a regression problem. Kato [18] also used a CNN model but modeled the risk prediction as a classification problem. In [13], the Support Vector Machine (SVM) was used to predict the severity and controllability rating classes based on the measured data from the sensors. SINADRA [15] provides a framework for creating situation-aware dynamic risk assessment monitors. It uses a Bayesian Network Model for inferring a risk index from monitored risk factors. Katrakazas *et al.* [7] proposed a data-driven method that can estimate collision risk by considering road network safety information and inter-vehicle dependencies. They first used the ML classifiers to predict the network-level collision risk. They then calculated collision probabilities by integrating the predicted risk with inter-vehicle dependencies using dynamic Bayesian networks.

Liu *et al.* [10] used the real-time traffic features extracted from the Tweets to build probabilistic graphs that capture the causal relationships among the features and collision results. Next, a Bayesian network model based on those graphs is used to estimate the collision probabilities. Gao *et al.* [3] proposed a CNN model that can combine the information from both driving scene video data and kinematics data (*e.g.,* vehicle velocity and acceleration) to predict hazardous driving situations. Lin *et al.* [9] employed a set of classical ML and deep neural networks to predict accident risk locations (*e.g.,* intersections) using traffic accident data. The features in the data set include speed limit, road width, types of signs, pavement edge line, road patterns, and crossroads. They found road the first three features have the most impact on accidents.

The single static model approaches often assume that the input data are homogeneous, and the data points are consistently obtainable, measurable, and of similar granularity. However, this assumption does not always hold in practice. Machine learning models tuned to a given data set and features can, therefore, quickly become inadequate, which was also observed by some learning-based approaches for dynamic environments [17]. Another critical limitation of the learning-based risk prediction approaches is that they do not consider the changes in automation levels during a journey and the simultaneous co-existence of multiple vehicles at different automation levels.

3   KnowGo Automotive Risk Score Framework

To address the aforementioned limitations of the existing works, we propose the *KnowGo Score* framework, a system for assessing automotive risks at runtime. It implements a novel learning-based DRA architecture that enables dynamic

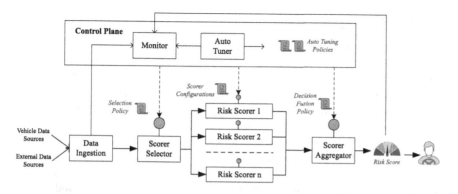

Fig. 1. Architecture of Dynamic Automotive Risk Assessment Framework

selection, tuning, and fusion of risk scoring models. Moreover, the framework allows multiple risk scorers to co-exist to support the heterogeneity in the risk assessment data sources. An accurate set of risk scoring models are dynamically selected based on the real-time data, and the decisions made by individual scorers are combined by applying decision fusion methods [11]. The rest of this section discusses the *KnowGo Score* framework in detail.

3.1 Overall Framework Architecture

Figure 1 depicts the architecture of the *KnowGo Score* framework, which consists of a set of *Risk Scorers* that can be dynamically enacted and managed. Each risk scorer calculates a risk index using one or more risk metrics based on the multi-dimensional input data from one or more data sources. The data can be injected into the system in real-time through the *Data Ingestion* component, which is a message-oriented middleware. *Scorer Selector* and *Control Plane* are the immediate consumers of the ingested data. The former component uses the contextual data extracted from the raw data, *e.g.*, automation level, and data source type, to choose the risk scorers for a set of data points. For this purpose, it uses a scorer selection policy that maps contextual attributes to risk scorers. The individual risk scorers predict risks as they receive the input data and send the predicted risk scores to the *Scorer Aggregator*, which in turn calculates the weighted average per automaton level, and produces the final averaged risk score. The decision fusion policy of the *Scorer Aggregator* defines risk scorers and scorer-specific weights suitable for assessing identified risks in the current vehicle state. At runtime, the *Monitor* at the control plane can observe the vehicle system state continuously and notify the *Auto Tuner* of state changes that impact risk assessment. These can include but are not limited to changes in automation level, legal jurisdiction, and driver privacy preferences. In response to state notifications, *Auto Tuner* can provide *Scorer Aggregator* and *Scorer Aggregator* with the updated policies for selecting scorers and fusing risk predictions. Each component of the *KnowGo Score* framework is implemented as a microservice that offers REST or event-driven APIs.

3.2   Risk Scoring Models

Individual risk scorers can be implemented using a range of data-driven techniques and rule-based techniques. As the scorers are not tightly coupled with the scoring framework itself, they are not limited by their choice of the implementation method. They may choose to use whichever technique is most appropriate for them. Section 4.1 describes the risk scorers currently available in the *KnowGo Score* framework. The *KnowGo Score* framework also supports adding and removing risk scorers at runtime via a plugin framework, where each scorer must implement the scorer interface defined by the framework.

The *KnowGo Score* system consists of general-purpose risk scorers and vehicle-specific scorers. The latter models can leverage additional vehicle manufacturer-provided data points. Risk Scorers are further broken down into three categories:*Independent Scorers*, *Dependent Scorers*, and *Augmented Scorers*. *Independent Scorers* are self-contained scoring models that can derive a risk score based on the input received, such as simple linear and logistic regression models. *Dependent Scorers* are scorers with finish-to-start dependency on one or more scorers in order to establish context for their risk assessment, if available. For example, a risk scorer can use driver alertness and obstacle detection to infer whether a harsh braking or swerving event is defensive or a result of driver inattentiveness. *Augmented Scorers* are scorers that extend the input data with external data to provide additional context for their risk assessment, such as using vehicle geolocation to obtain weather and road condition data.

3.3   Meta Risk Scoring Methods

Scorer Aggregator uses decision fusion methods to combine decisions made by individual risk scorers. The final fusion output (*i.e.*, the overall automotive risk) depends on the prediction accuracy of the risk scorers and the fusion algorithm. There exist various fusion algorithms, including averaging and voting methods, data-driven models (*e.g.*, classical machine learning and deep neural networks), and rule-based methods [11,16]. In this study, we selected the averaging method, which is simple, intuitive, and used for integrating the decisions made by regression models [12].

We considered three variations of the averaging scheme: simple averaging, weighted averaging, and confidence weighted averaging. In the simple averaging method, the average value of the predictions of individual risk scorers is calculated for each trigger interval. In the weighted averaging scheme, the prediction of each risk scorer is multiplied by the weight given for the scorer, and then their average is taken. Finally, the confidence weighted averaging scheme further normalizes the scorer-specific weights by multiplying the weight with the prediction confidence rate, ensuring that uncertain predictions are not given the same weighting in the final risk score calculation as more confident ones. The formula for the confidence weighted averaging is:

$$W = \frac{\sum_{i=1}^{n} b_i c_i w_i X_i}{\sum_{i=1}^{n} b_i c_i w_i} \tag{1}$$

```
rule "from_3_to_4"
  when
    $f1 : AutomationLevelChangedEvent(preLevel == 3, newLevel == 4)
  then
    metaScorerAPI.reconfigure(new String [] {"JourneyDuration:10:40",
                        "HarshBraking:10:40", "NightDriving:10:40",
                        "DriverAlertness:10:40", "WeatherConditions:10:40"});
  end
```

Fig. 2. A Snippet of the Rules Used by Auto Tuner

where b_i is the scorer-specific bias given for an individual driver or vehicle, c_i the confidence of a given prediction by a specific scorer, w_i the scorer-specific weighting, and X_i the scorer-specific risk score.

Weighting enables end-users to express their preferences on risk scoring models and their contributions. For example, in the case where a vehicle is switched to the autonomous driving mode, the weighting of a driver monitoring risk scorer can be increased or decreased, proportional to the autonomous driving level, establishing a direct correlation between the degree of risk of inattentive or distracted behavior by the driver with the level of automation. This change in weighting similarly allows driver alerting to adapt and escalate/deescalate in severity. A driver or vehicle-specific bias may also be applied to increase or decrease the impact of individual scorers.

3.4 Auto-tuning

Auto Tuner decides and carries out the desired reconfigurations or tunings to the *Scorer Selector* and *Scorer Aggregator*. To allow the end-users to define the tuning decisions, we provide an ECA (Event-Condition-Action) policy language. A policy consists of a set of ECA rules. The rule-based systems are one of the most popular approaches to implementing self-adaptive systems [4]. The *Auto Tuner* continuously receives the vehicle state data, including the changes in the automation level and driver preferences, from the *Monitor* component. The reception of the vehicle data can trigger auto-tuning rules, which in turn enact the necessary changes to the behaviors of the *Scorer Selector* and *Scorer Aggregator* through their REST APIs. Currently, the changes are limited to the configurations of the decision fusion methods used by them, *i.e.,* changing the selection of risk scorers and their weights and confidence levels. Figure 2 shows an example of a rule that reacts to the event *AutomationLevelChangedEvent* by adjusting the weights and confidence levels of the individual risk scorers.

4   Implementation and Evaluation

We set the following research questions for evaluating *KnowGo Score*:

RQ1 - To what extent can risk scorers predict the automotive risk accurately?
RQ2 - To what extent can auto-tuning of risk scoring help to accurately predict risk as automation level changes?

Table 1. General-purpose Risk Scorers in the KnowGo Score System

Risk Scorer (Default Weight)	Description	Data Points Used
Night Driving (50)	Determine the extent of a journey that has taken place in night-time conditions	Sunset/Sunrise times at location GPS location and timestamp
Journey Duration (50)	Determine the duration of a journey, and calculate its risk relative to Regulation (EC) No 561/2006	Journey start/stop times, journey duration (for in-progress journeys)
Weather Conditions (65)	Determine the weather conditions during a journey and assess whether a vehicle is appropriately configured for the conditions	GPS location and timestamp, Vehicle make/model, Weather conditions, Instrumentation status
Driver Alertness (75)	Determine if a driver is drowsy or distracted. Includes heart rate monitoring, eyelid closure, and gaze estimation	In-cabin video, Heart rate from wearable sensor, gyroscope readings
Harsh Braking/ Acceleration (50)	Determine the extent to which harsh braking and acceleration events have occurred during the course of a journey	Accelerator/brake pedal positions and timestamps, gyroscope and accelerometer readings

4.1   Framework Implementation

We developed the *KnowGo Score* framework[2] using Python. To implement the risk scoring microservices, we used *Flask* micro web framework, *scikit-learn* machine learning library, and *OpenCV* computer vision library. We used the Drools business rule management system to implement the rule-based auto-tuning engine. All components are containerized with *Docker*. The framework can be deployed and managed on a *Kubernetes* cluster over Edge and/or Cloud infrastructures. To simplify the deployment and runtime adaptation processes, we used the SODALITE framework [1,8].

Table 1 and Table 2 provide a brief overview of the risk scorers implemented, including their data sources and their mappings to SAE(Society of Automotive Engineers) automation levels. As appropriate, we use both ML-based and non-ML algorithms. The domain experts at the KnowGo company decided on the risk calculation algorithm for each risk scorer. As regards ML algorithms, we selected a wide range of learning algorithms used by the research literature [2,9]: Linear Regression (Journey Duration), Logistic Regression (Harsh Braking/Acceleration), and Convolutional Neural Network (CNN) (Driver Alertness). The non-ML scorers include the Night Driving scorer and Weather Conditions scorer.

---

[2] https://knowgo.io/products/knowgo-score/.

Table 2. Mapping of SAE Automation Levels to Risk Scorers and Weights

Level	Risk Scorer (Default Adjusted Weight)	Justification
0	Driver Alertness (75), Journey Duration (50) Harsh Braking/ Acceleration (50)	No driver support, defaults unchanged
1	Driver Alertness (75), Journey Duration (50) Harsh Braking/ Acceleration (40)	Possible acceleration/braking or steering assistance to the driver
2	Driver Alertness (75), Journey Duration (50) Harsh Braking/ Acceleration (30)	Acceleration/braking and steering assistance provided by vehicle
3	Driver Alertness (85), Journey Duration (25) Harsh Braking/ Acceleration (15)	Vehicle takes over driving tasks, driver must maintain situational awareness, risk of automation complacency
4	Driver Alertness (5), Journey Duration (15) Harsh Braking/ Acceleration (15)	Vehicle maintains situational awareness, driver involvement significantly reduced
5	Harsh Braking/Acceleration (15), Journey Duration (15)	No driver involvement, fully autonomous

4.2   Dataset Generation

As it is challenging to collect a large amount of data for multi-user and multi-autonomy scenarios in a real driving environment, as in [2,13], we used a simulation environment to generate sufficient data for training and evaluating risk score prediction models. A range of journeys, events, and instrumentation readings under several different driving conditions and styles have been generated with the *KnowGo Vehicle Simulator*[3], an open-source connected car simulator designed to generate realistic streaming vehicle telemetry. The simulator can also track and expose changes to the level of automation to enable the generation of journeys with events spanning across multiple levels of automation.

4.3   RQ1: Accuracy of Risk Scorers

Table 3 shows the average overall accuracy of the scoring models, including *Scorer Aggregator*. The accuracy of the *Scorer Aggregator* is directly influenced by its included scoring models, and is brought up or down with the introduction of additional models. As both the automation level and the overall model confidence directly impact the per-model weighting, lower confidence results in lower overall impact on the final risk score, ensuring that the impact of reduced accuracy for a given model can be better absorbed by the system without having a significant

---

[3] https://github.com/knowgoio/knowgo-vehicle-simulator.

Table 3. Predictive Accuracy of the Risk Scorers

Risk Scorer	Model	Accuracy
Journey Duration	Linear Regression	72.05
Harsh Braking/Acceleration	Logistic Regression	95
Night Driving	Non-ML	100
Weather Conditions	Non-ML	100
Driver Alertness	Multi-model, Linear SVM, CNN	75
Scorer Aggregator	**Performance-weighted-voting**	**93.75**

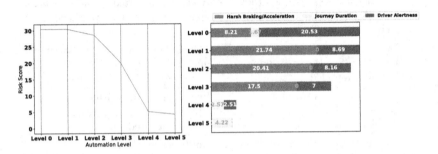

Fig. 3. (a) Risk Score vs Automation Level, (b) Scorer Contribution

impact on the underlying score. A mixture of models including ML and non-ML ones exhibiting a high degree of accuracy further ensure that confidence variance can be handled while keeping the overall confidence high.

4.4   RQ2: Effectiveness of Auto-tuning of Risk Scorers

Figure 3 shows the changes in the risk score in response to changes in automation levels and the contribution of the risk scorers at each level. This experiment only used ML-based risk scorers. In (a), we observe that the risk level for a journey drops in proportion to the level of automation. Per the scorer selection and weighting outlined in the previous section, the overall risk drops off considerably as the driver's role is diminished. A notable exception is level 3, in which the driver must be alert and ready to intervene, and the risk of automation complacency emerges. In (b), we see that driver alertness has significantly more impact at level 3 than at higher levels. Journey duration risks are lessened on a per-level basis, as this reflects the journey duration risk for the time spent within a specific level of automation, which is later compounded. By the time the journey is long enough for this to become more of a risk, higher levels of automation have taken over, and the risk is mitigated.

5 Conclusion

This paper proposes, *KnowGo Score*, a novel dynamic automotive risk assessment framework based on runtime selection and fusion of risk prediction models. It supports assessing the automotive risk levels in a dynamic environment, where automation level and input data frequently change over time. To improve the accuracy of the overall automotive risk assessment, the framework employs multiple risk scoring models that use different data sources and learning algorithms. A scheme for selecting and ranking scoring models according to changing data points and automation levels is presented. A partially open-source implementation of the *KnowGo Score* is available. With a set of risk predictors and a vehicle simulator, the practicability and usefulness of the framework were assessed. We plan to extend our risk assessment framework for future work by supporting different meta-learning approaches and incorporating more adaptation capabilities such as switching off/on or scaling up/down models on demand. We will also investigate monitoring and adapting to complex situations or context changes.

References

1. Di Nitto, E., et al.: An approach to support automated deployment of applications on heterogeneous Cloud-HPC infrastructures. In: 2020 22nd International Symposium on Symbolic and Numeric Algorithms for Scientific Computing (SYNASC), pp. 133–140 (2020)
2. Feth, P.: Dynamic Behavior Risk Assessment for Autonomous Systems. Ph.D. thesis, Kaiserslautern University of Technology, Germany (2020)
3. Gao, Z., Ou, M., Liu, Y., Zheng, J.Y.: Perceiving driving hazards in a data-fusion way using multi-modal net and semantic driving trajectory. In: 2020 International Conference on Sensing, Diagnostics, Prognostics, and Control, pp. 322–328 (2020)
4. Ghahremani, S., Giese, H., Vogel, T.: Efficient utility-driven self-healing employing adaptation rules for large dynamic architectures. In: 2017 IEEE International Conference on Autonomic Computing (ICAC), pp. 59–68 (2017)
5. Hegde, J., Rokseth, B.: Applications of machine learning methods for engineering risk assessment - a review. Saf. Sci. **122**, 104492 (2020)
6. SAE International: Taxonomy and definitions for terms related to driving automation systems for on-road motor vehicles. SAE (2018)
7. Katrakazas, C., Quddus, M., Chen, W.H.: A new integrated collision risk assessment methodology for autonomous vehicles. Accid. Anal. Prev. **127**, 61–79 (2019)
8. Kumara, I., et al.: SODALITE@RT: orchestrating applications on cloud-edge infrastructures. J. Grid Comput. **19**(3), 29 (2021). https://doi.org/10.1007/s10723-021-09572-0
9. Lin, D.J., Chen, M.Y., Chiang, H.S., Sharma, P.K.: Intelligent traffic accident prediction model for internet of vehicles with deep learning approach. IEEE Trans. Intell. Transp. Syst. 1–10 (2021)
10. Liu, X., Lan, Y., Zhou, Y., Shen, C., Guan, X.: A real-time explainable traffic collision inference framework based on probabilistic graph theory. Knowl.-Based Syst. **212**, 106442 (2021)
11. Mangai, U.G., Samanta, S., Das, S., Chowdhury, P.R.: A survey of decision fusion and feature fusion strategies for pattern classification. IETE Tech. Rev. **27**(4), 293–307 (2010)

12. Mendes-Moreira, J., Soares, C., Jorge, A.M., Sousa, J.F.D.: Ensemble approaches for regression: a survey. ACM Comput. Surv. **45**(1), 1–40 (2012)
13. Patel, A., Liggesmeyer, P.: Machine learning based dynamic risk assessment for autonomous vehicles. In: International Symposium on Connected and Autonomous Vehicles (SoCAV) (2021)
14. Rabe, M., Milz, S., Mader, P.: Development methodologies for safety critical machine learning applications in the automotive domain: a survey. In: Proceedings of the IEEE/CVF Conference on Computer Vision and Pattern Recognition (CVPR) Workshops, pp. 129–141 (2021)
15. Reich, J., Trapp, M.: SINADRA: towards a framework for assurable situation-aware dynamic risk assessment of autonomous vehicles. In: 2020 16th European Dependable Computing Conference (EDCC), pp. 47–50 (2020)
16. Sinha, A., Chen, H., Danu, D., Kirubarajan, T., Farooq, M.: Estimation and decision fusion: a survey. Neurocomputing **71**(13), 2650–2656 (2008)
17. Stefana, E., Paltrinieri, N.: Prometaus: a proactive meta-learning uncertainty-based framework to select models for dynamic risk management. Saf. Sci. **138**, 105238 (2021)
18. Wang, Y., Kato, J.: Collision risk rating of traffic scene from dashboard cameras. In: 2017 International Conference on Digital Image Computing: Techniques and Applications (DICTA), pp. 1–6 (2017)

OSRM-CCTV: CCTV-Aware Routing and Navigation System for Privacy and Safety

Lauri Sintonen, Hannu Turtiainen, Andrei Costin$^{(\boxtimes)}$, Timo Hämäläinen, and Tuomo Lahtinen

Faculty of Information Technology, University of Jyväskylä,
P.O. Box 35, 40014 Jyväskylä, Finland
{lauri.m.j.sintonen,tuomo.t.lahtinen}@student.jyu.fi,
{turthzu,ancostin,timoh}@jyu.fi
https://jyu.fi/it/

Abstract. For the last several decades, the increased, widespread, unwarranted, and unaccountable use of closed-circuit television cameras (CCTV) globally has raised concerns about privacy risks.

Recent CCTV camera features, such as Artificial Intelligence (AI)-based facial recognition, only increase concerns.

Therefore, *CCTV-aware solutions* must exist that provide privacy, safety, and cybersecurity features. We argue that a significant step forward in privacy is to provide privacy and safety options for areas where cameras are present in routing and navigation systems. However, no routing and navigation system, whether online or offline, provides corresponding CCTV-aware functionality.

In this paper, we introduce *OSRM-CCTV* – the first CCTV-aware routing system designed and built for privacy, anonymity, and safety applications. We demonstrate the effectiveness and usability of the system on a handful of examples. To help validate our work as well as further to encourage the development and broad adoption of the system, we release *OSRM-CCTV* as open-source.

Keywords: Privacy-enhancing technologies · PET · Anonymity · Usable security and privacy · Research on surveillance and censorship · Privacy · Anonymity · Surveillance · Safety · Routing · Navigation · Mapping · OSM · OSRM · Open-source

1 Introduction

In the modern world, public spaces of many cities are being surveilled by close-circuit television (CCTV) cameras to a considerable extent. It is estimated that globally there are around 770 million CCTV cameras in use and that their

---

L. Sintonen—An extended version of our paper is also available [38].
A. Costin—Original idea author.

© Springer Nature Switzerland AG 2022
B. Shishkov (Ed.): BMSD 2022, LNBIP 453, pp. 279–288, 2022.
https://doi.org/10.1007/978-3-031-11510-3_19

amount could rise to one billion during the year 2021 [5,7]. As an example, there are approximately half a million CCTV cameras in London, and an average person living there is recorded on camera 300 times everyday [6]. In the United States, people likely get recorded by a CCTV camera over fifty times per day [15]. In 2019, a person documented 49 CCTV cameras on the way to work in New York City [34] and described it as dystopian. In addition, the discourse on CCTV surveillance has ethical dimensions as, for example, CCTV surveillance is sometimes covert and people often believe that they are not under CCTV surveillance when they are [13].

Considering the amount of CCTV cameras having been installed globally and the fact that people can be detected and recorded by them, adding face recognition to the pattern opens up an unsettling possibility to also automatically identify people by CCTV cameras [1,14,42]. Moreover, CCTV cameras, Digital Video Recorders (DVR), and Video Surveillance Systems (VSS) are notoriously known to be vulnerable to cybersecurity attacks and hacks [8]. Therefore it is reasonable to assume that the CCTV cameras overlooking public places and routes may be under the control of unauthorized persons hence posing a direct threat to privacy.

In this context, we argue that it is essential to create *CCTV-aware* solutions and technologies that allow people at least a slight option to choose between being under CCTV surveillance (or not!) whenever they walk, cycle, or drive in public spaces. We approach the question from the perspective of routing and navigation. While there is a substantial amount of existing routing solutions and technologies [4,22,29–31,40], to the best of our knowledge, none of them focuses on the issue at hand to provide a *CCTV-aware* routing solution.

In this paper, we propose one such *CCTV-aware* solution. Our *CCTV-aware* solution enables two modes of routing. Firstly, *privacy-mode* which aids in maintaining privacy by choosing a route where CCTV cameras are avoided. *Privacy-mode* is strict in the sense that it will never choose a route that leads through the field-of-view (FoV) of a CCTV camera. Avoiding CCTV cameras would be desirable anytime when privacy or anonymity is essential. Secondly, *safety-mode* aids in maintaining safety by choosing a weighted route that leads through the fields of vision of CCTV cameras. *Safety-mode* is called safe because sometimes (e.g., at night and for the preference of staying physically safe), one would prefer to be detected and recorded by CCTV cameras.

It is worth mentioning that neither of these routing modes is guaranteed to ultimately maintain either privacy or safety, as described in this paper. This drawback is mainly because of the lack of up-to-date and accurate data about CCTV cameras. The relevant data in question would contain information about different attributes of for example, the CCTV camera model and lens, the radius, the angle of view, and the direction of the CCTV cameras, and data like this is unavailable more often than not. Currently, to our knowledge, there is no automated way to gather data about CCTV cameras to be used in our *CCTV-aware* approach. However, regarding the collection of relevant data, we have also developed and demonstrated the first Computer Vision (CV) models that can be used to detect CCTV cameras in images (e.g., street-level/street view, indoors). For example, our CV models achieve an accuracy of up to 98.7% [41], and we are currently in the process of mapping large areas around the globe. Our main contributions with this work are:

1. To the best of our knowledge, first to propose, implement, and evaluate CCTV-aware routing for privacy, anonymity, and safety applications.
2. We demonstrate the usefulness and the feasibility of CCTV-aware routing applied to synthetic and real-world examples.
3. We release the relevant artifacts (e.g., code, data, documentation) as open-source: https://github.com/Fuziih/osrm-cctv.

The rest of the paper is organized as follows. In Sect. 2 we present earlier work that has been done to allow different types of routing. Then, in Sect. 3 we provide an outline of how we have implemented our *CCTV-aware* solution. Next, in Sect. 4 we describe how our *CCTV-aware* solution functions where we present different examples of both *privacy-mode* and *security-mode* on a synthetic evaluation map where different routing scenarios can be demonstrated. We also present one example based on real data. We conclude this paper with Sect. 5.

2   Related Work

OpenStreetMap (OSM) is a collaborative open-source project which aims to supply free and editable maps of the world. Many reputable projects [4, 22, 29–31, 40] (e.g., routing solutions and technologies for different use-cases) base their work on the OSM. Most routing solutions focus on everyday driving, cycling, and walking schemes. In addition to this, there are some less common/popular yet useful solutions, such as finding wheel-chair accessible routes [11, 16, 44], finding curvy roads [10], and solutions that calculate routes based on the day arc [9, 25, 28].

Recently, Siriaraya et al. [39] argued that in the modern contemporary society, pedestrians prefer to set "alternative routing criteria" rather than the more common routing criteria such as duration and length. The authors refer to this as "routing based on different qualities", i.e., *qualitative-aware routing*. The authors identified five routing quality categories: safety, well-being, effort, exploration, and pleasure. Correspondingly to our work, the safety category is acknowledged by the authors as the need for avoiding areas with a high occurrence of past criminal activities. Although the privacy category is not mentioned nor categorized, it could be accommodated into the safety category of [39].

When pursuing to achieve a *CCTV-aware* routing solution, inspiration was drawn from the day arc routing solutions. For example, Olaverri Monreal et al. [28] created a sun-avoiding routing solution, and Ma [24, 25] developed a solution to either avoid or face the sun during travel. Recently, Leilani et al. [9] provided a routing solution that considers tree shading. The routing solutions in these works could be used to establish our *CCTV-aware* routing; however, there are a few pitfalls with that approach. Firstly, the data requirements for these solutions are pretty specific, and reaching them could prove problematic. Secondly, as an *OSM* "Way"object is defined as a collection of nodes, a line, and the width is saved only as a key-value tag [21,33], this fundamental issue would need to be addressed.

Privacy and safety routing has been previously researched to a specific yet limited degree. Bao et al. [3] proposed a routing solution with multiple safe pedestrian routing conditions. Hirozaku et al. [26] took into account street lights for safer walking routes. Keller and Mazimpaka [17] employed crowd-sourcing in their efforts to create safe routing. Lastly, Tessio et al. [27] were set on finding ways for users to find routing through green areas, social places, and quieter streets. Lahtinen et al. [18] investigated just the initial feasibility of CCTV-aware routing solutions and the quantitative impact on the routing options.

However, none of the previous works address the privacy, anonymity, and safety routing approaches given the exponential growth of CCTV cameras and video surveillance presence in public spaces and routes [34]. We try to close this gap with this work as it is also part of our bigger vision revolving around CCTV cameras, video surveillance, digital privacy, and anonymity. Therefore, we present that related work as well. First, we designed a Computer Vision (CV) model for detecting CCTV and video surveillance cameras in images and video frames [41]. Second, to improve and accelerate the training of our CV model [41], we created from scratch a novel image annotation tool *BRIMA* [20] which is a browser extension that provides an effortless way to map CCTV cameras using services such as Google Maps Street View [12], Yandex [43] or Baidu [2]. Third, we published an initial feasibility-study work where we mapped 450 CCTV cameras in the city of Jyväskylä Finland, and conducted routine experiments concluding that our system is feasible for further exploration and development, as it supports both the *privacy-first* and *safety-first* approaches [19]. Finally, more insight regarding this paper can be found at our preprint article [38].

3   Implementation Details

This section is a brief description of the data manipulation process that is used to enable *CCTV-aware* routing with two alternative modes called *privacy-mode* and *safety-mode*. The routing process is two-fold. First, *OSM* data is processed so that the resulting *OSM* file contains 1) the CCTV cameras as nodes, 2) entrance and exit nodes of the areas that intersect with the fields-of-view (FoV) of CCTV cameras, and 3) ways that are not merely lines without a width but ones that have an actual width on the map. *OSM* Way objects do not have an actual width as they are defined as a collection of nodes, and the width is saved only as a key-value tag [21,33]. Having an actual width is essential in enabling *CCTV-aware* routing because if a CCTV camera surveils only a part of one side of a way, one should still be able to traverse the other side of that way, and width is needed to allow this possibility. Second, *privacy-mode* and *safety-mode* are briefly described.

3.1   Data Processing

The data processing phase of our *CCTV-aware* routing solution can be divided into two parts. First, manipulating OSM file to contain CCTV data and second, preparing final OSM data for routing with *OSRM-CCTV*.

In essence, manipulating OpenStreetMap (OSM) data means using an existing *OSM XML* [32] file and writing a new one based on a Comma-Separated Value (CSV) file, which includes the properties of the cameras that are to be added to the resulting *OSM XML* file. These properties are GPS coordinates (e.g., latitude, longitude), type, radius, angle, and direction of vision of each new camera.

The resulting *OSM XML* file will include the new CCTV cameras as nodes. Also, the intersection points of routable ways and the field-of-view (FoV) of the CCTV cameras are represented as nodes in the ways. These nodes are marked with an access tag that indicate surveillance. Depending on the selected routing mode, the router would avoid the access tags that indicate surveillance or pursue routing through these nodes. Finally, the ways in the resulting *OSM XML* are split in three whenever there is a CCTV camera nearby. The three split ways represent the left, the middle, and the right side of the way.

The second part of the data processing, preparing data for routing with *OSRM-CCTV*, is executed by *OSRM-CCTV*, which involves parts for extracting, partitioning, and customizing both the *OSM* file (resulting from the first part of the data processing phase) and the profile file, which determines which mode is used – *privacy* or *safety*. Extracting, partitioning, and customizing are performed to create all the necessary files for running *OSRM-CCTV* router.

3.2   Privacy-Mode and Safety-Mode

Our *CCTV-aware* routing solution has two alternative modes called *privacy-mode* and *safety-mode*. Their functioning utilizes the entrance and exit nodes in the ways that intersect with the fields of vision of CCTV cameras. Not allowing to traverse through these nodes and the field-of-view (FoV) of a CCTV camera would maintain privacy; hence, *privacy-mode* is being used. *Privacy-mode* is implemented as a *Lua* profile [37] by blacklisting access tags that indicate surveillance. *Safety-mode* works vice versa. *Safety-mode* does not blacklist the access tags in the *Lua* profile, but it is instead enabled by using traffic updates [36] of the standard *OSRM* functionality. These traffic updates are used to weigh the calculations so that the route will run through areas with more CCTV cameras. These calculations use weights that are added to the *OSM* file in the data manipulation phase before running the router.

4   Evaluation

In this section, we present the evaluation of the two routing modes, *privacy-mode* and *safety-mode*, using some relevant example images. We use a synthetic evaluation map as well as a real map on the city of Jyväskylä, Finland. For every use-case presented in this section, more examples can be found at our longer preprint paper [38]. Using the default settings that we used, *Open Street Routing Machine (OSRM)* tries to find the shortest route like for example Google Maps does. Here, we do not present the default behavior of *OSRM* but only the functioning of the two routing modes. In addition to the synthetic map, we present examples using a real map.

4.1 Privacy-Mode

Privacy-mode aims to maintain privacy by avoiding surveilled areas. It never routes through a field-of-view (FoV) of a CCTV camera. If only a part of a way is under surveillance, the routing chooses the other side of that way. Here, the other side means one of the split ways parallel to the original one in the middle.

First, in Fig. 1 the calculated route is the shortest one that is not under surveillance. Figure 2 illustrates a more complicated route where many CCTV cameras surveil different parts of the map, but there is still a route that has no cameras, and it is shorter than the longest possible route. If all possible routes are under surveillance, *privacy-mode* would choose no route.

Fig. 1. All the shortest ways are blocked by a CCTV camera. The longest possible route must be used.

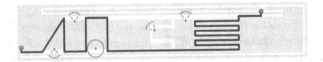

Fig. 2. A more complicated situation where various parts of the map under surveillance.

4.2 Safety-Mode

In this section, example images of the evaluation of *safety-mode* are shown. A safe route in *safety-mode* means a route that is under the surveillance of CCTV cameras. In principle, a route leading through the fields of vision of more cameras would mean a safer route. *Safety-mode* is not simply the *privacy-mode* reversed, and it does not always choose a surveilled route, but it works more selectively.

The standard *OSRM* [23,35] provides traffic updates [36] which are used to weigh preferable routes based on the amount of CCTV cameras surveilling the way. If a route is too long, the weighing can cause *OSRM-CCTV* to generate a route that has no camera surveillance.

In Fig. 3, one of the ways is surveilled by one more camera than the next one. *OSRM-CCTV* chooses the route that has more CCTV cameras surveilling it. Figure 4 shows a similar case to prove that the chosen route is the one under the surveillance of more CCTV cameras. It is worth to mention that because of using weights *safety-mode* does not prefer too long a route over a safe route.

Fig. 3. *OSRM-CCTV* routes through the way under the surveillance of more CCTV cameras.

Fig. 4. Similar to Fig. 3, *OSRM-CCTV* routes through the way under the surveillance of more CCTV cameras.

4.3   Real-World Examples

In this section, we present one example of how the *safety-mode* of our *CCTV-aware* approach operates in the downtown of the city of Jyväskylä, Finland. The location was chosen because we have mapped around 450 CCTV cameras around the city of Jyväskylä [19]. The mapped data contains, for example, the coordinates and the type of the cameras. The type can be either *round* or *directed*. The *round* type corresponds to a camera with a circular, 360° angle of view. The *directed* type corresponds to a camera with a less than the 360° angle of view. In our current data and for our evaluations, the radii, the angles of view, and the directions have been added randomly with a script.

Figure 5 shows the same scenario run with *safety-mode*. *OSRM-CCTV* finds a route that goes through the fields of vision of multiple CCTV cameras.

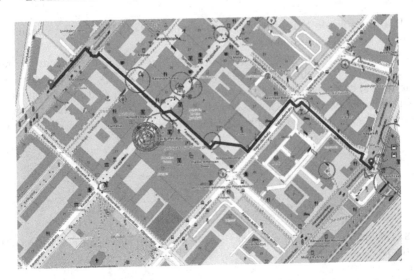

Fig. 5. *OSRM-CCTV* run with *safety-mode* chooses its route to route through the fields of vision of multiple CCTV cameras in the downtown of Jyväskylä, Finland.

5   Conclusion

In this paper, we propose, implement and briefly present examples of our evaluations of a *CCTV-aware* privacy- and safety-oriented routing solution. To the best of our knowledge, this is the first work where a *CCTV-aware* approach to routing has been conceptualized and proposed. For the routing engine, we start from the existing open-source *Open Street Routing Machine (OSRM)* routing framework. Subsequently, we customize it and open-source release *OSRM-CCTV* – a CCTV-aware routing modification based on *OSRM*.

References

1. Axis: Identification and recognition. https://www.axis.com/files/feature_articles/ar_id_and_recognition_53836_en_1309_lo.pdf
2. Baidu. map.baidu.com
3. Bao, S., Nitta, T., Ishikawa, K., Yanagisawa, M., Togawa, N.: A safe and comprehensive route finding method for pedestrian based on lighting and landmark. In: 2016 IEEE 5th Global Conference on Consumer Electronics, pp. 1–5 (2016)
4. Bast, H., et al.: Route planning in transportation networks. In: Kliemann, L., Sanders, P. (eds.) Algorithm Engineering. LNCS, vol. 9220, pp. 19–80. Springer, Cham (2016). https://doi.org/10.1007/978-3-319-49487-6_2
5. Bischoff, P.: Surveillance camera statistics: which city has the most CCTV cameras? (2021). https://www.comparitech.com/blog/vpn-privacy/the-worlds-most-surveilled-cities/
6. Caught on Camera: How many CCTV cameras in London? https://www.caughtoncamera.net/news/how-many-cctv-cameras-in-london/

7. Cosgrove, E.: One billion surveillance cameras will be watching around the world in 2021. https://cnbc.com/2019/12/06/one-billion-surveillance-cameras-will-be-watching-globally-in-2021.html

8. Costin, A.: Security of CCTV and video surveillance systems: threats, vulnerabilities, attacks, and mitigations. In: 6th International Workshop on Trustworthy Embedded Devices (TrustED) (2016)

9. Deilami, K., et al.: Allowing users to benefit from tree shading: using a smartphone app to allow adaptive route planning during extreme heat. Forests **11**(9), 998 (2020)

10. Franco, A.: What is curvature? (2016). https://roadcurvature.com/. Accessed 1 Nov 2020

11. GIScience, H.I.f.G.T.H. (2020). https://openrouteservice.org/

12. Google. https://www.google.com/maps

13. von Hirsch, A.: The Ethics of Public Television Surveillance. Ethical and Social Perspectives on Situational Crime Prevention. Hart Publishing (2000)

14. Hu, W., Tan, T., Wang, L., Maybank, S.: A survey on visual surveillance of object motion and behaviors. IEEE Trans. Syst. Man Cybern. Part C (Appl. Rev.) **34**(3), 334–352 (2004)

15. Karas, B.: Americans vastly underestimate being recorded on CCTV. https://ipvm.com/reports/america-cctv-recording

16. Kasemsuppakorn, P., Karimi, H.A.: Personalised routing for wheelchair navigation. J. Locat. Based Serv. **3**(1), 24–54 (2009). https://doi.org/10.1080/17489720902837936

17. Keler, A., Mazimpaka, J.D.: Safety-aware routing for motorised tourists based on open data and VGI. J. Locat. Based Serv. **10**(1), 64–77 (2016)

18. Lahtinen, T., Sintonen, L., Turtiainen, H., Costin, A.: Feasibility study on CCTV-aware routing and navigation for privacy, anonymity, and safety. Jyvaskyla - Case-study of the First City to Benefit from CCTV-aware Technology (Preprint) (2020)

19. Lahtinen, T., Sintonen, L., Turtiainen, H., Costin, A.: Towards CCTV-aware routing and navigation for privacy, anonymity, and safety-feasibility study in jyväskylä. In: 2021 28th Conference of Open Innovations Association (FRUCT), pp. 252–263. IEEE (2021)

20. Lahtinen, T., Turtiainen, H., Costin, A.: BRIMA: low-overhead BRowser-only IMage annotation tool. In: Proceedings of the IEEE International Conference on Image Processing (2021, to appear)

21. Lucas-Smith, M.: Is the OSM data model creaking? https://2019.stateofthemap.org/sessions/DW7WW8/

22. Luxen, D., Vetter, C.: Real-time routing with OpenStreetMap data. In: Proceedings of the 19th ACM SIGSPATIAL International Conference on Advances in Geographic Information Systems (2011)

23. Luxen, D., Vetter, C.: Real-time routing with OpenStreetMap data. In: Proceedings of the 19th ACM SIGSPATIAL International Conference on Advances in Geographic Information Systems, GIS 2011, pp. 513–516. ACM, New York (2011). http://doi.acm.org/10.1145/2093973.2094062

24. Ma, K.: Parasol: shade model and routing algorithm for comfortable travel outdoors. https://github.com/keithfma/parasol

25. Ma, K.: Parasol navigation: optimizing walking routes to keep you in the sun or shade (2018). https://www.allnans.com/jekyll/update/2018/08/07/introducing-parasol.html

26. Miura, H., Takeshima, S., Matsuda, N., Taki, H.: A study on navigation system for pedestrians based on street illuminations. In: König, A., Dengel, A., Hinkelmann, K., Kise, K., Howlett, R.J., Jain, L.C. (eds.) KES 2011. LNCS (LNAI), vol. 6883, pp. 49–55. Springer, Heidelberg (2011). https://doi.org/10.1007/978-3-642-23854-3_6

27. Novack, T., Wang, Z., Zipf, A.: A system for generating customized pleasant pedestrian routes based on OpenStreetMap data. Sensors **18**(11), 3794 (2018)

28. Olaverri Monreal, C., Pichler, M., Krizek, G., Naumann, S.: Shadow as route quality parameter in a pedestrian-tailored mobile application. IEEE Intell. Transp. Syst. Mag. **8**, 15–27 (2016)

29. OpenStreetMap: Routing/offline routers. https://wiki.openstreetmap.org/wiki/Routing/offline_routers

30. OpenStreetMap: Routing/online routers. https://wiki.openstreetmap.org/wiki/Routing/online_routers

31. OpenStreetMap Wiki: List of OSM-based services – OpenStreetMap Wiki (2020). https://wiki.openstreetmap.org/w/index.php?title=List_of_OSM-based_services&oldid=2052956. Accessed 1 Nov 2020

32. OpenStreetMap Wiki: Osm xml—openstreetmap wiki (2020). https://wiki.openstreetmap.org/w/index.php?title=OSM_XML&oldid=2027286. Accessed 5 Nov 2020

33. OpenStreetMap Wiki: Way—openstreetmap wiki (2020). https://wiki.openstreetmap.org/w/index.php?title=Way&oldid=2045405. Accessed 2 Nov 2020

34. Pasley, J.: I documented every surveillance camera on my way to work in New York City, and it revealed a dystopian reality, December 2019. https://www.businessinsider.com/how-many-security-cameras-in-new-york-city-2019-12

35. Project-OSRM: Open Source Routing Machine (OSRM) - a modern C++ routing engine for shortest paths in road networks. http://project-osrm.org/

36. Project-OSRM: Traffic (2019). https://github.com/Project-OSRM/osrm-backend/wiki/Traffic

37. Project-OSRM: Osrm profiles (2020). https://github.com/Project-OSRM/osrm-backend/blob/master/docs/profiles.md

38. Sintonen, L., Turtiainen, H., Costin, A., Hamalainen, T., Lahtinen, T.: OSRM-CCTV: open-source CCTV-aware routing and navigation system for privacy, anonymity and safety (Preprint). arXiv preprint arXiv:2108.09369 (2021)

39. Siriaraya, P., et al.: Beyond the shortest route: a survey on quality-aware route navigation for pedestrians. IEEE Access **8**, 135569–135590 (2020)

40. Szczerba, R.J., Galkowski, P., Glicktein, I.S., Ternullo, N.: Robust algorithm for real-time route planning. IEEE Trans. Aerosp. Electron. Syst. **36**(3), 869–878 (2000)

41. Turtiainen, H., Costin, A., Hamalainen, T., Lahtinen, T.: Towards large-scale, automated, accurate detection of CCTV camera objects using computer vision. Applications and implications for privacy, safety, and cybersecurity (Preprint). arXiv preprint arXiv:2006.03870 (2020)

42. Wheeler, F.W., Weiss, R.L., Tu, P.H.: Face recognition at a distance system for surveillance applications. In: 2010 Fourth IEEE International Conference on Biometrics: Theory, Applications and Systems (BTAS), pp. 1–8. IEEE (2010)

43. Yandex. https://yandex.eu/maps/

44. Zipf, A., Mobasheri, A., Rousell, A., Hahmann, S.: Crowdsourcing for individual needs-the case of routing and navigation for mobility-impaired persons. In: European Handbook of Crowdsourced Geographic Information, pp. 325–337 (2016)

CCTV-Exposure: System for Measuring User's Privacy Exposure to CCTV Cameras

Hannu Turtiainen, Andrei Costin$^{(\boxtimes)}$, and Timo Hämäläinen

Faculty of Information Technology, University of Jyväskylä,
P.O. Box 35, 40014 Jyväskylä, Finland
{turthzu,ancostin,timoh}@jyu.fi
https://jyu.fi/it/

Abstract. In this work, we present CCTV-Exposure – the first CCTV-aware solution to evaluate potential privacy exposure to closed-circuit television (CCTV) cameras. The objective was to develop a toolset for quantifying human exposure to CCTV cameras from a privacy perspective. Our novel approach is trajectory analysis of the individuals, coupled with a database of geo-location mapped CCTV cameras annotated with minimal yet sufficient meta-information. For this purpose, CCTV-Exposure model based on a Global Positioning System (GPS) tracking was applied to estimate individual privacy exposure in different scenarios. The current investigation provides an application example and validation of the modeling approach. The methodology and toolset developed and implemented in this work provide time-sequence and location-sequence of the exposure events, thus making possible association of the exposure with the individual activities and cameras, and delivers main statistics on individual's exposure to CCTV cameras with high spatio-temporal resolution.

Keywords: Privacy · Privacy measurements · Privacy-enhancing technologies · PET · Video surveillance · CCTV surveillance · CCTV exposure · Experimentation · Open-source · GPS location track · GPX

1 Introduction

In the modern world, public spaces of many cities are being surveilled by closed-circuit television (CCTV) cameras to a considerable extent. It is estimated that globally there are around 1 billion CCTV cameras in use today [3,5]. In the United States, people are likely recorded by a CCTV camera over fifty times per day [11]. In 2019, a person documented 49 CCTV cameras on the way to work in New York City [15] and described it as dystopian.

H. Turtiainen—An extended version of our paper is also available [18].
A. Costin—Original idea author.

© Springer Nature Switzerland AG 2022
B. Shishkov (Ed.): BMSD 2022, LNBIP 453, pp. 289–298, 2022.
https://doi.org/10.1007/978-3-031-11510-3_20

The discourse on CCTV surveillance has ethical dimensions. Von Hirsch argues that CCTV surveillance is sometimes covert, and often people believe that they are not under CCTV surveillance when they are [9]. Furthermore, according to a 2016 survey, an average citizen of the United States is assumed to be recorded by four or fewer CCTV cameras per day, while the actual figure is likely over ten times larger [11]. Considering the amount of CCTV cameras having been installed globally and the fact that people can be detected and recorded by them, adding face recognition to the pattern opens up an unsettling possibility to also automatically identify people by CCTV cameras [1,10,20]. Moreover, CCTV cameras, Digital Video Recorders (DVRs), and Video Surveillance Systems (VSSs) are notoriously known to be vulnerable to cybersecurity attacks and hacks [6]. Therefore, it is reasonable to assume that the CCTV cameras overlooking public places may be under the control of unauthorized persons hence posing a direct threat to privacy.

In this context, we argue that it is essential to create *CCTV-aware* solutions and technologies that allow people the discretion to be under surveillance or not in public places. We approach the question from the perspective of estimating individual users' exposure to CCTV cameras based on their real-time or historical geo-location (e.g., position, tracks, routes). While there is a substantial amount of studies related to exposure to various "harmful environments" [2,4,7,8,14,17], to the best of our knowledge, none of the existing works focuses on the exposure to privacy invasion by CCTV cameras when this is seen as a "harmful environment" for individual privacy.

Nevertheless, when shared responsibly and for practical purposes, the users' GPS data can also be used for Privacy Enhancing Technologies (PET), as we present in this paper. In this paper, we propose one such *CCTV-aware* solution, namely CCTV-Exposure. When compared to exposure to "harmful environments" such as exposure to radiation, the CCTV-Exposure system is intended to act like a "CCTV dosage meter" for travel activities of privacy-minded individuals.

Our contributions with this work are:

1. We propose, implement, and demonstrate a system aimed at measuring individuals' privacy exposure to CCTV cameras using analysis of historical and real-time GPS data
2. For evaluation and further improvements, we release (upon peer-review acceptance) the relevant artifacts (e.g., code, data, documentation) as open-source: https://github.com/Fuziih/cctv-exposure

The rest of this paper is organized as follows. We briefly introduce related work in Sect. 2. We present in Sect. 3 our algorithms as well as design and implementation details. Then, in Sect. 4 we introduce results and their evaluation. Finally, we conclude this paper with Sect. 5.

2   Related Work

To date, to the best of our knowledge, none of the works (systems, implementations, surveys) have addressed the research question related to individuals' privacy exposure to CCTV and video surveillance, as we do in this paper. However, we briefly introduce closely related state-of-the-art and related work in adjacent fields below.

Turtiainen et al. [19] were the first to propose and develop a dedicated computer vision (CV) model – CCTVCV – designed specifically to detect CCTV cameras from street view and other images, with the primary intended purpose of building various privacy-enhancing technologies (PET), tools, and large-scale datasets (e.g., global mapping of CCTV cameras in public spaces). Building on the applicative ideas from Turtiainen et al. [19], Sintonen et al. [16] developed and proposed OSRM-CCTV, which is the first of its kind route planning and management. PET solution offers pro-active route planning optimized for individual privacy and public safety. Subsequently, Lahtinen et al. [12] applied and validated an early prototype of OSRM-CCTV to demonstrate the feasibility of OSRM-CCTV in real cities (e.g., Jyväskylä, Finland), and to study the impact of CCTV cameras on users' route planning when privacy or safety is a crucial factor. Our present work is different yet complementary to these studies [12,16].

Using GPS data to measure human exposure in different cases is nothing new to the general research field. Dias and Tchepel [7] used GPS data collected from test subjects' mobile phones to measure the users' exposure to air pollution. Their study was conducted in the Leiria area in Portugal, and their pollution data were estimated via Transport Emission Model for Line Sources (TREM) model and meteorological data. Dias and Tchepel claim that due to pollution concentration variation within "microenvironments", their exposure model will yield a meaningfully better understanding of individual's pollution exposure in urban areas in contrast to traditional background pollution measurements. Correspondingly, Tchepel et al. [17] measured human exposure to benzene in the Leiria area in Portugal. Several other studies (such as [2,4,14]) have also measured exposure to air pollutants using GPS data. Global positioning system data are also valuable for creating large datasets of human mobility data. These datasets can be used in conjunction with machine learning and artificial intelligence technologies, for example, to predict crowd flows. Luca et al. [13] surveyed on that subject. However, they concluded that at the time of publishing in December 2020, state-of-the-art models for predicting human mobility suffer from several limitations, for example, data privacy concerns and the geographical constraints for the trained models.

Global positioning system devices and data sending units are also used in tracking wildlife. Hinton et al. [8] measured Cesium-137 exposure on wildlife in the Chornobyl exclusion zone in Ukraine from November 2014 to May 2015. They attached a GPS monitoring unit and a dosimeter to eight free-ranging wolves in the area for data gathering. The gathered dosage data was used to analyze the soil Cesium-137 levels in relation to the temporal and spatial data collected from the GPS units.

3 Design and Implementation

Our CCTV-Exposure system is written in Python3 with minimal requirements, as only GPXpy[1] and NumPy[2] are used to reduce any code and dependency overhead. We also implemented the module in Rust (v. 1.60). The Rust implementation is similar and equivalent to our Python3 counterpart; however, it does not allow the use of non-timestamped GPX files due to parser limitations.

At present, and for this paper's evaluation, our system accepts only GPX files as input. However, an application programming interface (API) input is an option that we leave to be implemented in future work. A required argument for the module is the camera database file. For our testing, we used the camera coverage radius and the field-of-view specified in the camera database file; however, these values can be overridden with input arguments by the user.

We decided to use Euclidean distance to perform faster computations instead of the more accurate Haversine distance. However, the module allows option specification to easily switch between Euclidian and Haversine distances and add alternative distance measurement implementations. The core module performs all calculations in meters (for distance) and seconds (for time). For this reason, we ignore the curvature of the earth to quicken the calculations, as well as simplify the model. Our synthetic tests show that for GPX tracks of several kilometers, the cumulative error is negligible when assuming realistic (e.g., hundreds of meters to several kilometers) human geo-location tracks within CCTV-fitted public spaces.

The gist of the module is to loop over all tracks and segments read from the GPX input file. It is important to note that the input GPX file can (and should) be wholly anonymized and scrubbed of any Personally-Identifiable Information (PII), as CCTV-Exposure aims to enhance and preserve privacy as one of its core principles. A GPX file can have multiple tracks, which can have multiple segments, and each segment is specified in the GPX file via a set of points (i.e., exact GPS locations, with optional timestamp). We refer to these points throughout the rest of this paper as *GPX points*. The core module loops over each GPX point and identifies "in-range cameras" for each iterated point. An "in-range camera" for a GPX point means a CCTV camera (from the available and loaded database of geo-location mapped CCTV cameras) whose field-of-view (whether directed or 360) covers or intersects with the GPX point. Afterward, the module:

- loops all GPX points which we concluded above to be "within the visual reach" of their "in-range cameras."
- splits the distance between the point and their adjacent point for more granular inspection and calculation (see Sect. 3.1)

For output interoperability, we use JavaScript Object Notation (JSON) formatted output. We provide distance and time exposure metrics as well as per camera information to the user.

---

[1] https://pypi.org/project/GPXpy/, https://github.com/tkrajina/GPXpy.
[2] https://numpy.org/.

For this proof-of-concept module, we loaded our database of geo-location mapped CCTV cameras from a comma-separated values (CSV) file and then looped over all of them for each point.

3.1   Interpolated Points - Points Between GPX Points

To increase the accuracy of our calculations, for each GPX point that a camera is in range of, we split the distance to *interpolated points*. *Interpolated points* are not present in GPX data and are a result of our internal calculations to increase both the granularity of analysis and accuracy of the exposure estimate. A variable splits the distance we call *resolution*. The default resolution for our experiments was 0.5 meters; however, the resolution can configure into the system for lower or higher granularity and accuracy purposes. This value is a critical parameter to adjust due to the inherent uncertainty of the GPS data and the variability of data accuracy (GPS drift). The interpolated points are illustrated in Fig. 1a. We go through the GPX points with cameras and calculate how far back from the present GPX point the field-of-view of the camera in question reaches (i.e., how many interpolated points). From the answer, we can accurately (within resolution) calculate the distance and time spent in the field-of-view of the individual camera.

After the backward iteration, we loop the GPX points again but focus on going forward from the GPX points, where each camera stops in range. This way, we cover the whole union of camera field-of-view and the route in the process. Figure 1c stages the idea behind the back-and-forth coverage system. Also in Fig. 1b, calculated interpolated points are demonstrated. In the example, both blue GPX points are in the red camera's range; therefore, there's no need for granular calculation between the points.

4   Evaluation and Results

The Jyväskylä city area in Central Finland was chosen as the experiment location for this study. As of writing, it is the seventh-largest city in Finland by population. The immediate city center area is relatively compact and rather CCTV congested. The camera mapping was conducted in the summer of 2020 [12,16], and the routes for this study were captured in early 2022.

4.1   Evaluation Methodology

We tested four tool-generated 'synthetic' GPX files, and four Garmin recorded 'real-world scenario' files as routes for evaluation of CCTV-Exposure. Map examples of the routes are depicted in Fig. 3. The 'synthetic' GPX files were created using GPSVisualizer[3], and timestamps were added to them using GoToes GPX editing tool[4]. Our Garmin EDGE 810 recorded the files in Garmin's FIT format,

---

[3] https://www.gpsvisualizer.com.
[4] https://gotoes.org.

 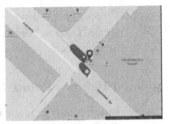

(a) **CCTV-Exposure** interpolated point system: blue markers are GPX points and red markers are interpolated points between them.

(b) **CCTV-Exposure** interpolated points measured: interpolated points in yellow, camera in red, GPX points in blue.

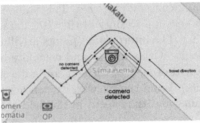

(c) **CCTV-Exposure** granular calculation

Fig. 1. Interpolated point depiction.

which were subsequently converted into GPX using a converter from AllTrails[5]. The real-world scenario files provide a bit more exciting data as the timestamps are more varied due to changes in the recorded speed of the person; therefore, the exposure time and distance will yield differing results. However, the Garmin device used in this test had some accuracy issues during recording.

Certain Assumptions and Limitations. In our current test setup, we were limited by our camera dataset containing only 450 cameras [12] around the city center of Jyväskylä (Finland). However, there is an active work-in-progress to expand this dataset rapidly in various parts of the world.

For our testing, for all the cameras in our database, we set by default ten (10) meters for the camera "privacy invasion" radius, i.e., the radius on which we assume any CCTV camera in the database can successfully record hard- and soft-biometrics of an individual with subsequent potential recognition or identification. This radius setting is highly conservative and emulates the "worst-case scenario" (i.e., limited visibility range from a CCTV camera perspective).

Moreover, our CCTV camera dataset (and any other public dataset we have seen) has limitations as these datasets do not have 100% accurate characteristics

---

[5] https://www.alltrails.com/converter.

of each camera in the dataset. One core reason for this is that we can detect the presence of the camera (e.g., using CCTVCV [19] or crowdsourcing); however, we (and any similar third-party project) will not know certain information about each camera, such as:

1. exact camera model – this would also be challenging to perform visually by humans (due to low resolution and lack of markings) and via computer vision (as this would require the equivalent of "face recognition" accuracy and system, but for CCTV cameras).
2. exact owner/operator of the camera(s) – these contacts are generally missing but could (or perhaps **should**, as required by GDPR?) provide much more meta-information about the camera; we have a work-in-progress towards achieving this meta-information collection via crowdsourcing; however, we leave this challenge as future work.

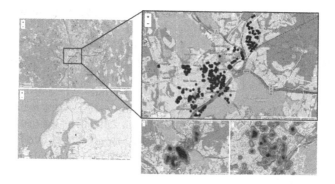

Fig. 2. CCTV cameras dataset mapped in the city of Jyväskylä [12], and used for evaluation of CCTV-Exposure.

4.2   Exposure Results

In Table 1, we disclose the exposure metrics for the test routes. Our synthetic routes' average CCTV exposure distance and time were 3.7% of the total routes. Our real-world routes (captured by the authors with Garmin devices in the city center of Jyväskylä) indicated an average CCTV exposure of 12.5% relative to segments' distance, and 15.1% close to segments' time, respectively.

Our synthetic routes had a more sparse point distribution, thus resulting in lesser exposure metrics. Our real-world recordings, however, produced more accurate data.

Based on these results, and especially on the real-world recorded routes, it is pretty safe to say that avoiding CCTV cameras around the city center of Jyväskylä (Finland) proves to be a challenge. These observations are in line with the conclusions from Lahtinen et al. [12], where the authors implemented and studied CCTV-aware route-planning for "preventive privacy analysis".

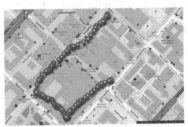

(a) Example of a synthetic route traveling through the narrow side of the city.

(b) Example of a recorded route in the city center.

Fig. 3. Example routes used in evaluation of CCTV-Exposure.

Table 1. Exposure results for the routes used during preliminary evaluation.

Route	Distance − m	Unique cams − num	Exposure dist. − %	Exposure time − %
syn1.gpx	1538	2	2.6% (41m / 1538m)	2.6% (0:00:29 / 0:18:29)
syn2.gpx	497	1	3.7% (18m / 497m)	3.7% (0:00:20 / 0:09:15)
syn3.gpx	571	1	3.5% (20m / 571m)	3.5% (0:00:14 / 0:06:50)
syn4.gpx	897	3	4.8% (43m / 897m)	4.8% (0:00:32 / 0:11:08)
real1.gpx	633	13	25.4% (161m / 633m)	36.0% (0:02:55 / 0:08:05)
real2.gpx	614	14	17.4% (107m / 614m)	17.4% (0:01:16 / 0:07:15)
real3.gpx	597	9	4.7% (28m / 597m)	4.5% (0:00:18 / 0:06:41)
real4.gpx	775	1	2.3% (18m / 775m)	2.6% (0:00:15 / 0:09:17)

It is important to note, however, that due to the systematic lack of previous works, ground truth datasets, and baseline recommended exposure levels related to "CCTV privacy invasion", the evaluation numbers should be interpreted with care because they represent a best-effort estimate of the privacy exposure to the CCTV cameras based on the limited CCTV camera datasets and the error-prone GPS tracks.

5 Conclusion

In this paper, we presented CCTV-Exposure – an open-source system for measuring users' privacy exposure to mapped CCTV cameras based on geo-location, GPX, and historic tracks. We evaluated the CCTV-Exposure on multiple GPS tracks in Jyväskylä, where we also had a comprehensive CCTV camera mapping database of 450 cameras. Our evaluations demonstrate the effectiveness, performance, and practicality of CCTV-Exposure when tasked with measuring CCTV exposure of users based on their real-time or historical geo-location and GPS tracks.

As this is some early yet promising implementation and evaluation, certain limitations and challenges have been identified. They present a fertile ground for further research that we leave as future work. First, performance optimization and accuracy validation of CCTV-Exposure will benefit from collecting more extensive and more complete CCTV databases while being validated on larger and more diverse datasets. Second, CCTV-Exposure will benefit from being validated with larger and more diverse user-base and stakeholders' scenarios. Third, CCTV-Exposure, as well as OSRM-CCTV, would both benefit from a holistic integration into an end-to-end CCTV-aware system.

For evaluation and further improvements, as well as to encourage researchers and practitioners to explore this digital privacy-related field, we release (upon peer-review acceptance) the relevant artifacts (e.g., code, data, documentation) as open-source: https://github.com/Fuziih/cctv-exposure.

Acknowledgement. Part of this research was supported by a grant from the *Decision of the Research Dean on research funding within the Faculty (17.06.2020)* of the Faculty of Information Technology of the University of Jyväskylä (The authors thank Dr. Andrei Costin for facilitating and managing the grant). Hannu Turtiainen also thanks the Finnish Cultural Foundation / Suomen Kulttuurirahasto (https://skr.fi/en) for supporting his Ph.D. dissertation work and research (under grant decision no. 00221059) and the Faculty of Information Technology of the University of Jyvaskyla (JYU), in particular, Prof. Timo Hämäläinen, for partly supporting and supervising his Ph.D. work at JYU in 2021–2022. Map images in Figs. 1a, 1b, 2, and 1 are generated with Folium (for Python) library (https://python-visualization.github.io/folium/) using OpenStreetMap data (https://www.openstreetmap.org). Map image in Fig. 1c is generated in GPSVisualizer.com (https://www.gpsvisualizer.com) also using OpenStreetMap data.

References

1. Axis: identification and recognition. https://www.axis.com/files/feature_articles/ar_id_and_recognition_53836_en_1309_lo.pdf
2. Beekhuizen, J., Kromhout, H., Huss, A., Vermeulen, R.: Performance of GPS-devices for environmental exposure assessment. J. Expo. Sci. Environ. Epidemiol. **23**(5), 498–505 (2013)
3. Bischoff, P.: Surveillance camera statistics: which city has the most CCTV cameras? May 2021. https://www.comparitech.com/blog/vpn-privacy/the-worlds-most-surveilled-cities/
4. Breen, M.S., et al.: GPS-based microenvironment tracker (MicroTrac) model to estimate time-location of individuals for air pollution exposure assessments: model evaluation in central north Carolina. J. Expo. Sci. Environ. Epidemiol. **24**(4), 412–420 (2014)
5. Cosgrove, E.: One billion surveillance cameras will be watching around the world in (2021). https://cnbc.com/2019/12/06/one-billion-surveillance-cameras-will-be-watching-globally-in-2021.html
6. Costin, A.: Security of CCTV and video surveillance systems: threats, vulnerabilities, attacks, and mitigations. In: 6th International Workshop on Trustworthy Embedded Devices (TrustED) (2016)

7. Dias, D., Tchepel, O.: Modelling of human exposure to air pollution in the urban environment: a GPS-based approach. Environ. Sci. Pollut. Res. **21**(5), 3558–3571 (2014). https://doi.org/10.1007/s11356-013-2277-6

8. Hinton, T.G., et al.: GPS-coupled contaminant monitors on free-ranging Chernobyl wolves challenge a fundamental assumption in exposure assessments. Environ. Int. **133**, 105152 (2019)

9. von Hirsch, A.: The ethics of public television surveillance. Ethical Soc. Perspect. Situational Crime Prev. (2000)

10. Hu, W., Tan, T., Wang, L., Maybank, S.: A survey on visual surveillance of object motion and behaviors. IEEE Trans. Syst. Man Cybern. Part C (Appl. Rev.) **34**(3), 334–352 (2004)

11. Karas, B.: Americans vastly underestimate being recorded on CCTV. https://ipvm.com/reports/america-cctv-recording

12. Lahtinen, T., Sintonen, L., Turtiainen, H., Costin, A.: Towards CCTV-aware routing and navigation for privacy, anonymity, and safety-feasibility study in Jyväskylä. In: 28th Conference of Open Innovations Association (FRUCT), pp. 252–263. IEEE (2021)

13. Luca, M., Barlacchi, G., Lepri, B., Pappalardo, L.: Deep learning for human mobility: a survey on data and models. arXiv preprint arXiv:2012.02825 (2020)

14. Ma, J., Tao, Y., Kwan, M.P., Chai, Y.: Assessing mobility-based real-time air pollution exposure in space and time using smart sensors and GPS trajectories in Beijing. Ann. Am. Assoc. Geogr. **110**(2), 434–448 (2020)

15. Pasley, J.: I documented every surveillance camera on my way to work in New York City, and it revealed a dystopian reality, December 2019. https://www.businessinsider.com/how-many-security-cameras-in-new-york-city-2019-12

16. Sintonen, L., Turtiainen, H., Costin, A., Hamalainen, T., Lahtinen, T.: OSRM-CCTV: open-source CCTV-aware routing and navigation system for privacy, anonymity and safety (Preprint). arXiv preprint arXiv:2108.09369 (2021)

17. Tchepel, O., Dias, D., Costa, C., Santos, B.F., Teixeira, J.P.: Modeling of human exposure to benzene in urban environments. J. Toxicol. Environ. Health A **77**(14–16), 777–795 (2014)

18. Turtiainen, H., Costin, A., Hamalainen, T.: CCTV-Exposure: an open-source system for measuring user's privacy exposure to mapped CCTV cameras based on geo-location (Extended Version). arXiv preprint (2022)

19. Turtiainen, H., Costin, A., Lahtinen, T., Sintonen, L., Hamalainen, T.: Towards large-scale, automated, accurate detection of CCTV camera objects using computer vision. Applications and implications for privacy, safety, and cybersecurity. (Preprint). arXiv preprint arXiv:2006.03870 (2020)

20. Wheeler, F.W., Weiss, R.L., Tu, P.H.: Face recognition at a distance system for surveillance applications. In: Fourth IEEE International Conference on Biometrics: Theory, Applications and Systems (BTAS). IEEE (2010)

Computer Model for Assessment and Visualization of Specific Absorption Rate of Electromagnetic Field, Generated by Smartphone

Magdalena Garvanova[1]([✉]), Ivan Garvanov[1], and Daniela Borissova[1,2]

[1] University of Library Studies and Information Technologies, Sofia, Bulgaria
{m.garvanova,i.garvanov}@unibit.bg, dborissova@iit.bas.bg
[2] Institute of Information and Communication Technologies, Bulgarian Academy of Sciences, Sofia, Bulgaria

Abstract. The widespread and prolonged use of smartphones in recent years has led to the exposure of the human body to signals in the radio frequency range. It raises many questions about the impact of these technologies on humans. The effect of radiation is assessed with the dosimetric parameter Specific Absorption Rate – SAR. To evaluate and visualize SAR in the depths of the human head, this article has created and verified a computer model using COMSOL Multiphysics software. The model takes into account the specific characteristics of the human head and the parameters of a working smartphone and has great opportunities for visualization of absorption processes. It is also suitable for studying the effects of radio waves on humans. With its help it is possible to assess and visualize the thermal effect in depth of the human head caused by the use of a smartphone.

Keywords: Smartphone · Computer model · Specific absorption rate · Electromagnetic field · Thermal effect

1 Introduction

Smart technologies consist of a large number of sensors that generate heterogeneous data and are processed and analyzed for human needs. Thanks to them, the way of life in the home (smart home), in the enterprises (smart industry) and in the city as a whole (smart city) is facilitated and improved. Communication between the many sensors is mostly wireless, which multiplies the level of the electromagnetic field (EMF) in smart homes and smart cities. In order to improve the quality of life in smart cities, it is necessary to take preventive measures regarding the impact of electromagnetic fields on people. One of the most powerful sources of such radiation are smartphones and routers in homes. Smartphones are devices that are used more and more often for a long time, both for work and entertainment. In recent years, smartphones have been owned by younger children, who spend much of the day with them. There is a lot of research on the impact of smart technology on humans. Various psychological and physical effects have been identified,

© Springer Nature Switzerland AG 2022
B. Shishkov (Ed.): BMSD 2022, LNBIP 453, pp. 299–307, 2022.
https://doi.org/10.1007/978-3-031-11510-3_21

but the problem is not yet fully resolved. Studying the impact of electromagnetic fields generated by smartphones on humans is proving to be quite a difficult task. In most cases, it is possible to determine or measure surface effects on the human body, and inside the human body it is not clear what the magnitude of the effects is. In order to study this effect in depth, it is possible to use computer models.

Computer modeling is a powerful tool for studying complex processes in practice that are difficult or impossible to study with conventional methods. The development of a computer model to study the process of absorbing electromagnetic energy emitted by a smartphone and the subsequent thermal effect in the depths of the human head is crucial in analyzing the effects caused by prolonged use of wireless communication devices. The effect of radiation can be assessed by the dosimetric parameter Specific Absorption Rate – SAR. Simulating and visualizing the effect of absorbing electromagnetic radiation from a smartphone and the subsequent thermal effect in the human head will facilitate the study and analysis of these processes [1]. The accumulation of knowledge in this direction will lead in the future to the design and creation of technologically safe devices with less risk to human health.

In [2] the SAR and thermal effect of a human head of a child when using a mobile phone with a computer model created with the help of CST Microwave Studio software package was studied. According to [3], the most significant effect caused by high-frequency radio waves is the heating of the tissues of the human head. In [4, 5] the question of the influence of electromagnetic fields generated by a mobile phone on the EEG signals of the human head is analyzed. All these effects are difficult to explain without studying and visualizing the process of absorption of the electromagnetic field. The conditions of a person after a long conversation with a smartphone, such as headache, dizziness, distraction, etc. obtained from studies in [6] are also difficult to explain without visualization and study of the depth of penetration of electromagnetic waves in the human head.

The creation of a computer model to visualize the process of absorption of the electromagnetic field in the human head allows to study and scientifically explain the various physical effects caused by prolonged use of a smartphone by a person. This model can be easily reconfigured and studied by both adults and younger individuals. By changing the parameters of the smartphone, it is possible to study the different modes of operation of the smartphone as well as different generations of smartphones operating in different frequency ranges.

The computer model for SAR visualization of the electromagnetic field generated by a smart phone in-depth of the human head discussed in this article was created similarly to the model in [7, 8]. The computer model takes into account the characteristics of electromagnetic fields, environmental parameters such as the specific heat capacity of tissues, cooling of blood circulation and ambient temperature, as well as thermophysi-ological processes of the human body. This model has been verified and corrected with data obtained from a thermal imaging camera. After comparing the results of the model with those of a thermal imaging camera, a visualization of the SAR and the thermal effect in-depth of the human head is made for the specific studied individual. Thanks to the model, in-depth research will be conducted in the future and the effects of long-term smartphone use by adults and adolescents will be analyzed. It should be noted that not all biological effects necessarily lead to negative effects on human biophysical conditions, but the computer model will help to study and analyze all of them. The conceptual framework of the current study is presented in Fig. 1.

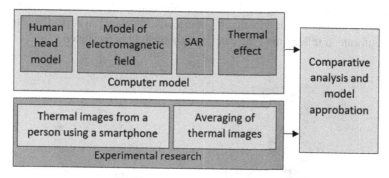

Fig. 1. Stages of the study

The remaining of the paper is organized as follows: Sect. 2 focuses on the creation of a computer model of SAR and thermal effects in-depth of the human head obtained by a smartphone, while Sect. 3 describes the visualization of SAR and thermal effects. Section 4 provides model verification and setup. Finally, we conclude the paper in Sect. 5.

2 Computer Model of SAR and Thermal Effects In-Depth of the Human Head

In [1] a computer model is used, which aims to determine the impact of EMF on adults and young organisms, examining the process of absorption of electromagnetic energy and giving recommendations for the use of GSM devices. In [7] and [8] are proposed computer models implemented with the program COMSOL Multiphisics, as in [8] the process of influence of Wi-Fi is modeled, and in [7] – the influence of GSM on humans. The models provide an analytical view on the processes of EMF absorption in the depth of the human head, as well as visualize the thermal effect of this process. Computer models allow research to be performed on both young and older people and to test different EMF frequency ranges and powers. The possibilities for visualization are great and are preferable to conducting real experiments. The model used in this article is implemented with the program COMSOL Multiphisics similar to [7, 8], and the results obtained were tested using a series of real experiments and the use of a thermal camera to determine the thermal effect. The approbation of the model is possible only in the 2D surface of the head, and in depth it is to be tested by measuring and processing EEG signals.

It consists of a human head model including layers of different thickness, skin, skull and brain tissue models. The characteristics of the human head and the parameters of the biological tissues used in the model are as close as possible to the real ones. The design and geometry of the human head is imported into the COMSOL Multiphysics software from a file named sar_in_human_head.mphbin, which is provided by IEEE,

IEC and CENELEC from their standard specification for SAR measurements. The source of electromagnetic radiation is a model of a smartphone with specific technical characteristics that is added manually on one side of the head at a certain distance from it near the ear. To obtain more realistic SAR results when operating the antenna in infinite free space, it is necessary to close the model of the human head and the antenna of the smartphone in a spherical air domain using Perfectly Matched Layer (PML) (Fig. 2). In this way, unwanted reflection of the electromagnetic field is prevented.

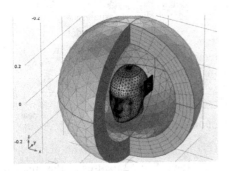
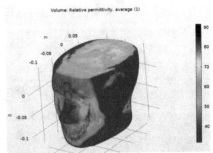

Fig. 2. Model of the environment around the human head

Fig. 3. Average relative permittivity of a human head

Using the radio frequency (RF) module of the COMSOL Multiphysic, the local SAR values on the human head model are calculated when it is close to a working smartphone. The direct connection between SAR and the warming of the tissues of the human head allows the computer model to calculate and visualize the thermal effects caused by the use of a smartphone. The advantage of the model is its ability to visualize the processes of penetration and absorption of electromagnetic energy from the tissues of the head in-depth. The electromagnetic parameters of the biological tissues of the human head are modelled using an interpolation function that applies the characteristics of a particular tissue inside the human head. The output data for this function is directly taken from a system file that is created using multiple magnetic resonance images of human head sections. The sar_in_human_head_interp.txt system file can also be used to visualize the dielectric permittivity and perfusion inside the head (Fig. 3).

The distribution of the strength of the electric field E is obtained by solving the equation [9]:

$$\nabla \times \frac{1}{\mu_r} \nabla \times E - k_0^2 \varepsilon_r E = 0 \tag{1}$$

where μ_r is the relative permeability, k_0 is a wave vector and ε_r is the permittivity of the tissues.

The depth of penetration of the electric field into the biological tissue of the human head depends on the frequency of electromagnetic waves and is determined by the formula:

$$\delta = \frac{1}{\omega}\left(\frac{\varepsilon_r \mu_r}{2}\left(\sqrt{1 + \frac{\sigma_{eff}^2}{\omega^2 \sigma_r^2}} - 1\right)\right)^{-1/2} \quad (2)$$

As already mentioned, SAR is a characteristic that describes the absorption of the power of the electromagnetic field that propagates in different types of tissues [10]. Local SAR is defined as the loss of power dP_1, absorbed in an infinitesimally small mass dm, and can be described by the following equation:

$$SAR = \frac{dP_1}{dm} = \frac{\sigma_{eff} E_{rms}^2}{\rho} = \frac{J_{rms}^2}{\rho \sigma_{eff}} \quad (3)$$

where E_{rms} and J_{rms} are the root mean square values of the electric field strength and the density of electricity, respectively σ_{eff} is the effective conductivity of human brain tissue and ρ is the tissue density. As it is known, the energy from the electromagnetic fields in the radio range is absorbed into the tissue of the human body and transformed into heat. This leads to another definition of SAR, namely:

$$SAR = c_p \frac{\Delta T}{\Delta t} \quad (4)$$

where c_p is the specific heat capacity of the tissue and ΔT is the change in temperature over a period of time Δt.

A distinction between the instantaneous SAR and the permissible SAR should be made, where an average value is measured for a given mass of tissue and a specified period of time.

The increase of the temperature can be estimated by the equation [10]:

$$\Delta T = \frac{SAR\tau}{c_p}\left(1 - e^{-t/\tau}\right) \quad (5)$$

where τ is the thermal time constant. The created computer model examines the interaction of heat transfer between tissues due to the presence of two heat sources. It does not take into account the influence of vascular geometry on heat transfer.

3 Visualization of SAR and Thermal Effects In-Depth of the Human Head

The simulation of a computer model created in the environment of COMSOL Multiphysics and setup to a concrete individual allows to assess the SAR and thermal effect of each tissue in-depth of the human head. The local SAR value in the human head when testing the model is shown in Fig. 4. The source of electromagnetic radiation is a model of a mobile phone that is manually added. In the considered model, the location of the device is chosen to be on the left side of the head in order to facilitate the comparison of the obtained results with thermal images from experimental studies. The mobile device is modeled at a distance of 1 cm from the head and operates at a frequency of 900 MHz. When talking to a smartphone, the human head is irradiated by an electromagnetic field that penetrates the head and releases some of its energy to the tissues or is absorbed into the head tissue. Electromagnetic energy affects the particles in the tissue due to the electrical and magnetic components of the electromagnetic field. SAR values are higher in the surface layers of the human head.

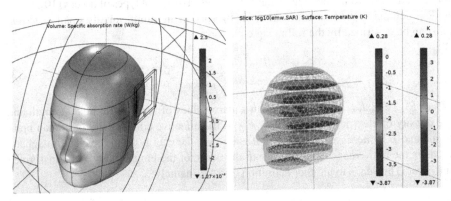

Fig. 4. Human head SAR model

The created computer model calculates only the local value of the SAR parameter. The maximum value of the local SAR is always higher than the maximum value of the average SAR value. The propagation of electromagnetic waves in biological tissues takes the form of absorbed energy. Most of the absorbed energy is converted into heat, which leads to an increase in temperature in biological tissues. The thermal effect, obtained from electromagnetic radiation of a mobile phone, is most pronounced on the surface of the head skin (most often the area of a person's ear) [2]. The increase in temperature depends on the physiological properties of the tissues (blood perfusion) and can be calculated using a biothermal equation that takes into account heat loss due to blood circulation in the human body. The thermal effect in the depth of the head is shown in Fig. 5.

4   Model Verification and Setup

A series of experiments were performed to adjust the model and bring its results closer to real experimental data obtained with a thermal camera. The results of the thermal images in the testing of an individual were averaged and a thermal image was obtained on the surface of the head of the person who participated in the experiment. By changing the parameters of the model, a result was obtained for the thermal effect on the surface of the head, which is very close to the real one. The model set up in this way is convenient for visualizing the effects obtained from the irradiation of the head of the tested individual.

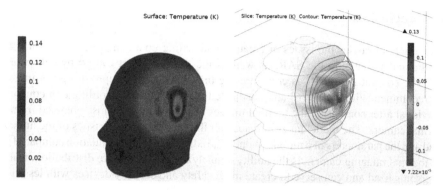

Fig. 5. Thermal effect in-depth of the head

The participant in the experiment declares in writing his/her consent to conduct the study, as well as that he/she is physically healthy. The experimental part includes 36 experiments regarding person, talking on a smartphone for 20 min. The position of the phone is on the left side of the head. At the end of the talks, images were provided with the FLIR P640 thermal camera to establish the thermal effect of EMF absorption. The obtained thermal images from the surface of the speaker are averaged and compared with the result of the model (Fig. 6).

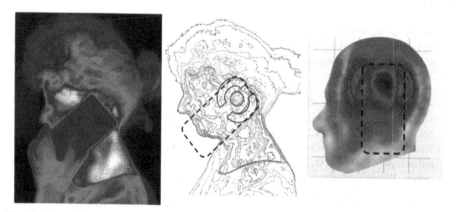

Fig. 6. Thermal image from the experiment (left), averaged thermal effect obtained by the thermal camera (center) and the computer model (right)

This result is close to the result of the model at 86%, which with great reliability verifies and confirms the proper functioning of the model. The comparison of the results of the experiment and the model was obtained in the areas marked with a red line. The analysis was performed on the surface of the head, but it can be considered that the model is adequate to the real experimental situation, where warming is found on the left side of the head, where the position of the mobile device is. The figures show that the thermal effect on the human head depends on the position of the smartphone.

5 Conclusions

This article discusses the issues of creating and setting up a computer model for estimating and visualizing the SAR, as well as the thermal effect caused by cell phone use. The computer model was created using the COMSOL Multiphysics according to the recommendations of [5, 6] and is adjusted and configured according to a concrete individual after comparing the thermal images of the model and those obtained from a thermal camera. The model takes into account the specific characteristics of the human head and the parameters of a mobile phone. The advantage of the simulation compared to the thermal imaging camera is the ability to analyze the temperature distribution inside a person's head and can serve to create more safety and security devices with less risk to human health.

Our future research efforts are oriented towards creating a comprehensive model for studying the risk factors of excessive use of smart technologies among children and adults.

Acknowledgement. This work is supported by the Bulgarian National Science Fund, project title "Synthesis of a dynamic model for assessing the psychological and physical impacts of excessive use of smart technologies", KP-06-N 32/4/07.12.2019.

References

1. Stanković, V., Jovanović, D., Krstić, D., Cvetković, N.: Electric field distribution and SAR in human head from mobile phones. In: 9th International Symposium on Advanced Topics in Electrical Engineering (ATEE), pp. 392–397 (2015). https://doi.org/10.1109/ATEE.2015.7133835
2. Stanković, V., Jovanović, D., Krstić, D., Cvetković, N., Marković, V.: Thermal effects on human head from mobile phones. In: 12th International Conference on Telecommunication in Modern Satellite, Cable and Broadcasting Services (TELSIKS), pp. 205–208 (2015). https://doi.org/10.1109/TELSKS.2015.7357770
3. Wyde, M.E., et al.: Effect of cell phone radiofrequency radiation on body temperature in rodents: pilot studies of the National Toxicology Program's reverberation chamber exposure system. Bioelectromagnetics **39**, 190–199 (2018). https://doi.org/10.1002/bem.22116
4. Garvanova, M., et al.: Effects of mobile phone electromagnetic fields on human brain activity. In: ACM 10th International Conference on Telecommunications and Remote Sensing (ICTRS'21), 15–16 Nov 2021, Virtual Conference, Bulgaria, pp. 31–36 (2021). https://doi.org/10.1145/3495535.3495541
5. Garvanova, M., Garvanov, I., Borissova, D.: The influence of electromagnetic fields on human brain. In: 21st International Symposium on Electrical Apparatus & Technologies (SIELA), Bourgas, Bulgaria, pp. 111–114 (2020). https://doi.org/10.1109/SIELA49118.2020.9167099
6. Garvanova, M., Shishkov, B., Vladimirov, S.: Mobile devices – effect on human health. In: Proceedings of the Seventh International Conference on Telecommunications and Remote Sensing – ICTRS'18, 8–9 Oct 2018, Barcelona, Spain, pp. 101–104 (2018). https://doi.org/10.1145/3278161.3278176
7. Griesmer, F.: Specific Absorption Rate (SAR) in the human brain (2013). https://www.comsol.com/blogs/specific-absorption-rate-sar-human-brain/

8. Patel, D.: Measuring the SAR of a human head next to a wi-fi antenna (2020). https://www.comsol.com/blogs/measuring-the-sar-of-a-human-head-next-to-a-wi-fi-antenna/

9. Halla, P.: Specific Absorption Rate Design of 3rd Generation Handsets. Master Thesis in Helsinki University of Technology, Finland (2008)

10. Bhat, M.A., Kumar, V.: Calculation of SAR and measurement of temperature change of human head due to the mobile phone waves at frequencies 900 MHz and 1800 MHz. Adv. Phy. Theor. Appl. **16**, 54–63 (2013)

Author Index

Printed in the United States
by Baker & Taylor Publisher Services